Classical Hollywood Narrative

CLASSICAL

HOLLYWOOD

NARRATIVE

The Paradigm Wars

★ ★ ★ *Edited by Jane Gaines*

Duke University Press   Durham and London 1992

© 1992 Duke University Press
All rights reserved
Printed in the United States of America
on acid-free paper ∞
Library of Congress Cataloging-in-Publication Data
appear on the last printed page of this book.
The text of this book was originally printed
without the chapters by Richard Dienst, Christine Gledhill,
Chris Straayer, and John O. Thompson and without
the index, as volume 88, number 2 of the
South Atlantic Quarterly.

Contents

Introduction: The Family Melodrama

of Classical Narrative Cinema

Jane M. Gaines

★ ★ ★ ★ ★ ★ The authors in this volume all circle dubiously around the basic paradigm that has dominated film studies since the 1970s: classical Hollywood narrative cinema. That is, the protagonist-driven story film, valued for the way it achieves closure by neatly resolving all of the enigmas it raises as well as for the way it creates this perfect symmetry by means of ingenious aesthetic economies. This cinema's supreme achievement is that by using these narrative and imagistic economies it is able to convince viewers that it is one and the same with the physical world—thus its famous "realistic effect." What is more, classical narrative is said to be a form so powerful that its aesthetic devices are able to reinforce gender positions in society.

What I am describing is really two kinds of paradigm at once—a cinematic one as well as a critical one. This doubling up is not surprising since it is the genius of criticism to will its own position into being so effectively that the discourse of the object of analysis fits the discourse of the method of analysis like a glove. And I am yielding to this illusion by which the object is made to order by the criticism in my double use of the term "paradigm." At this time in history, scholars in the field enjoy a kind of love-hate relationship with the classical paradigm, a structure that has two problematic methodological legs: "formalism" and "patriarchy." Much is at stake since the formalist model of classical narrative cinema is the cornerstone of David Bordwell and Kristin Thompson's *Film Art: An Introduction*, the best-selling film textbook in the United States, now in its third edition.[1] Although this paradigm was first introduced into the field through the British journal *Screen* in the 1970s, it has been refined as well as institutionalized in the United States primarily through the work of Bordwell. David Bordwell, then, is a kind of "structuring absence" as well as the absent structuralist in this collection, the antagonist for Rick Altman and Bill Nichols and the contemporary protagonist for Norman Holland, who champions Bordwell's turn to cognitive theory, which to many scholars offers a new paradigm for the field.

The other methodological leg of the paradigm—the approach that understands classical Hollywood film as patriarchal form—has been the mainstay of feminist film theory. Just as much is at stake here, given that Laura Mulvey's seminal essay "Visual Pleasure and Narrative Cinema" is so widely known, having been reprinted in English at least eight times since it first appeared in 1975.[2] Although the two methodological legs (formalism and patriarchy) do not necessarily approve of one another, they mingle in our teaching and have cemented a film studies foundation against which new paradigms (such as the televisual) must define themselves.

Relying on current gay and lesbian film theory, Chris Straayer produces one such rival approach by replacing the sexualized female form of classical narrative cinema with the She-man from recent experimental video. Straayer nullifies the mechanisms of compulsory heterosexuality in classical cinema with counterexamples from the subcultural underside of the dominant culture. Since the She-man is "envied" rather than feared or repressed, the process of fetishization which produced Mulvey's "phallic woman" (Mae West, Marlene Dietrich) is, according to Straayer, effectively voided.

In the past fifteen years, significantly different strategies for unseating one paradigm and replacing it with another have been deployed within film studies. While gay and lesbian criticism from the late 1980s has been perceived as using a frontal assault on reigning theories, in contrast the post-structuralist challenge that predates it insinuated itself in criticism as an erosion of the ground of existing positions. Janet Staiger, reading the French film *The Return of Martin Guerre* as a parable of the threat of new theory to traditional humanist criticism (and especially its notion of the real), suggests how post-structuralist methodologies undermine earlier approaches. Staiger sees *Martin Guerre*, a text heavily invested in the discourse of historical representation, as an allegory of the French critical stance summed up by Barthes, Kristeva, Derrida, and Foucault. The classical realist text is always lying anyway, its aesthetic a trick aesthetic whose signs only cross-reference one another, like Martin and Martin 2 who are locked into a pattern of deadly deferral to one another. But while the truth-claims of aesthetic realism have been discredited, critics of popular culture have not abandoned their interest in the last remaining real—what we might call the political real. Perhaps, as Fredric Jameson suggests in "Nostalgia for the Present," we can only know the "deeper realities" we would want to know (that is, the story of global imperialism) through the allegorical tellings of popular film and television. The last resort of the political real is leftist criticism.

This is thus a collection of and about warring discourses, some tilting at the windmill of classical Hollywood cinema, others taking off for other fields of contention. The scholars represented might be grouped in relation to the classical paradigm as "having already contributed significantly to it," "having contributed to the skepticism about it," "never having contributed to it and therefore not needing to rethink it," "wanting to attack it directly," and "wanting to shift the emphasis in the field"—to television/video, to cognitive theory, to reception context, to legal theory, and to melodrama. These authors circumvent the established paradigm as though to say "What would film studies be like if. . . ."

In the lead essay, "Dickens, Griffith, and Film Theory Today," Rick Altman formulates the "what if" as melodrama's "if only." That is, "If only film history had not forgotten its roots in theatrical melodrama. . . ."[3] Altman's account of film history and theory makes us think of other "what ifs": What if D. W. Griffith had admitted that he was drawing on popular theater instead of insisting that he was filming Charles Dickens's novels a page at a time? What if Sergei Eisenstein had not made the connection between Griffith and Dickens in the 1944 essay troped in Altman's title? What if Gerald Mast and Marshal Cohen (editors of the basic *Film Theory and Criticism*, now in its fourth edition) had edited the 1944 essay in such a way that Eisenstein's own observation about the importance of melodrama to early cinema had been retained?[4]

Altman's article suggests another "what if": What if we were to read the history of cinema itself as Freud's family melodrama? As a tale of birth and growth to maturity, casting early cinema as an orphaned foundling whose parentage was concealed from it? In this narrative, the proper parent, the "father" of cinema, is the novel, characterized as something like the petit bourgeois merchant out of Flaubert: tight, mean, exacting, ruddy-faced—the small-time patriarch. The villain of the piece is Russian Formalism—an icy-cold, immobile, fur-coated czar, the "dominant" that organizes cinema. For Bill Nichols, the problem with formalism is the way it stands apart from and above history, self-sufficient and aloof. But, says Altman, it is the very absolutism of the formalist "dominant" that explains the counterforces that it can't contain. What the dominant leaves unaccounted for—spectacle, episode, coincidence (the "riffraff" of the text)—will inevitably return as "resentment, resistance, and revolution." What formalism finds superfluous to its economy is "outlaw" to it.

As it turns out, melodrama, "outlaw" to the dominant, is none other than cinema's other parent, that low-moraled theatrical form, banished and disclaimed by motion picture pioneer D. W. Griffith. As Miriam Hansen sees Griffith, however, he struggles with his tendency to see a likeness to the cheap and tawdry mother in the new art; hence, for him, cinema is a "prostitute," secretly loved while publicly reviled.

But Christine Gledhill offers another version of the legacy of classical cinema, confirming the family resemblances to realism and melodrama, but introducing a scenario of colonial immigration and European banishment for the first time in this volume. She asks another "what if" question, a paternity question still, about the way two national cinemas betray family resemblances to melodrama or realism. It is a complicated history, beginning in the second half of the nineteenth century in the theater, with a trial separation of melodrama from realism such that the two became exclusive rather than inclusive as they had historically been. The family tree of cinema split into British and American branches as the two cinemas became increasingly differentiated along high and low lines, with the low corresponding in Britain with class and in the United States with gender. Her account suggests that British cinema produced a weakened line from the 1920s, after divorcing itself from melodrama, while American film, in contrast, "naturalized" melodrama in classical narrative as psychological realism. If we follow this account, the paternity question becomes less a matter of the repression of melodrama than a question of perceiving melodrama and realism as recessive or dominant traits in the genetic makeup of classical Hollywood narrative.

Still, this account doesn't resolve the confusion over the "gender" of cinema: in Griffith's version, cinema may be female; in contemporary theory, cinema emerges as the male child who must have experienced its own mirror phase in the 1970s, the period when melodrama (now the castrated mother) was most violently repressed in the writing of classical narrative as patriarch. Film theory in the 1970s also gave patriarchal cinema a procreative function—it spawned patriarchs like itself, thousands of male spectators who were pathologically prone to looking.

The "many-sidedness" of Freud's family romance allows us to see this spectator as both villain and victim. The Peeping Tom spectator later becomes the hapless female victim tortured in the vise of the subject-positioning instrument operated by the patriarchal narrative machine-text.[5] And it is this brutality that new accounts of viewing have finally ameliorated. Thus, the reception theory that Jane Feuer critiques here was recruited in the mid-1980s as a means of empowering the limp spectator who was then able to stand up to the text, even reading "against" it. More recently, cognitivism has given us a kinder, gentler account of film functioning, as Bordwell and others have explained it. Science (empirical evidence of how people process images) promises a way out of the fictional structures of the family melodrama. Is cognitivism not, then, the doctor who records the clinical data, the data that only much later become the family melodrama—demonstrating how (between 1909 and 1989) scientific theory could become literary theory?[6]

Looking back to this scientific report, Freud's 1909 "Der Familien-roman der Neurotiker" (the tale told by the neurotic), we are able to continue where Altman leaves off. The family romance gives us the revenge against the parents wrought on brothers and sisters who were made bastards in order to explain the low-culture promiscuity of the mother (melodrama). And why shouldn't this explain television—with its family resemblance to narrative realist cinema but its physical features and formal qualities in constant dispute? If melodrama is the mother of the bastard television (evident in the structure of soap operas like *Dynasty*), who or what is the father?[7]

And here the story stops because we have come to the socially dysfunctional 1950s, where, at Jameson's suggestion, we must read the period of television's birth through *The Twilight Zone*. The latter set of essays in this collection seem to be ruled by the new moon of the postmodernism paradigm, which might be described as the methodology made to explain cultural aberration and aesthetic dysfunction. Under the influence of the postmodern paradigm, image and reality are said to have "swapped places" (as with Jacqueline Onassis's "image," which claims an identity of her own in court); readers are no longer separate from texts, but indistinguishable from them (as with Jane Feuer's *Dynasty* fans); and television no longer pretends to be separate from capital but is unapologetically one and the same as capital (as Richard Dienst affirms in his article in this collection).[8]

John O. Thompson's essay stands far back from the critical tendency to lump television with postmodernism in such a way that the idiosyncrasies of the one define the idiosyncrasies of the other, the down side of criticism willing its object into being. Thompson's approach to critically taming television suggests that over history what happens is that forms merely find new technologies to inhabit. The "Dialogues of the Dead" that go back to the ancients resuscitate themselves in the format of the television talk show. Rather than viewers as inseparable from the text, this gives us the program itself as separated from its viewers as the living are separated from the dead.

And yet it is not as though new technologies move into old forms like beach crabs taking up life in discarded shells. Rather, as critics we produce these new forms with critical metaphors such as the "Dialogues of the Dead." So to return to my original question about the doubleness of the term "paradigm," the criticism and its object: it is clear that, as much as anything, the paradigm wars (however tame and bloodless), are over the territory of the most elusive and impossible of critical objects—broadcast television. The stakes are high since as critics we produce its discourse in our discourse about it.

Notes

1 David Bordwell and Kristin Thompson, *Film Art: An Introduction* (New York, 1990). Also of indisputable significance in the field is David Bordwell, Janet Staiger, and Kristin Thompson, *The Classical Hollywood Cinema: Film Style and Mode of Production to 1960* (New York, 1985), and David Bordwell, *Narration in the Fiction Film* (Madison, 1985).

2 Laura Mulvey, "Visual Pleasure and Narrative Cinema," *Screen* 16 (1975): 6–18, reprinted in *Women and Cinema*, ed. Karyn Kay and Gerald Peary (New York, 1977); *Popular Television and Film*, ed. Tony Bennett, Susan Boyd-Bowman, Colin Mercer, and Janet Wollacott (London, 1981); *Art after the New Modernism: Rethinking Representation*, ed. Brian Wallis (New York, 1984); *Film Theory and Criticism*, ed. Gerald Mast and Marshall Cohen (New York, 1992); *Movies and Methods II*, ed. Bill Nichols (Berkeley, 1985); *Feminism and Film Theory*, ed. Constance Penley (London, 1988); Laura Mulvey, *Visual and other Pleasures* (New York, 1989); and *Issues in Feminist Film Criticism*, ed. Patricia Erens (Bloomington, 1990).

3 The same point was made by Christine Gledhill in "Dialogue," *Cinema Journal* 25.4 (1986): 44–48. The first attempt in recent years to put melodrama back into film theory and history was Thomas Elsaesser's "Tales of Sound and Fury: Observations on the Family Melodrama," *Monogram* 4 (1972): 2–15; Michael Walker also argued that melodrama was the key "generic root" of American cinema in "Melodrama and the American Cinema," *Movie* 29/30 (1982): 2. See also Christine Gledhill, "The Melodramatic Field: An Investigation," in *Home Is Where the Heart Is: Studies in Melodrama and the Woman's Film*, ed. Christine Gledhill (London, 1987).

4 Mast and Cohen, eds., *Film Theory and Criticism*, 370–80; Sergei Eisenstein, "Dickens, Griffith, and the Film Today," in *Film Form*, ed. Jay Leyda (New York, 1949).

5 For an extremely comprehensive history of the "female spectator" as concept in

feminist film theory, see *Camera Obscura* (May–September 1989), the "Spectatrix" issue.

6   The positions in the debates are spelled out in David Bordwell, "A Case for Cognitivism," *Iris* 5.2 (1989): 11–40; Dudley Andrew, "Cognitivism: Quests and Questionings," *Iris* 5.2 (1989): 1–10; and the continuance of the exchange in *Iris* 6.2 (1990): 107–16.

7   Some of the basic articles on the relationship between television soap opera and melodrama are Tania Modleski, "The Search for Tomorrow in Today's Soap Operas"; and Robert C. Allen, "A Reader-Oriented Poetics of the Soap Opera," both reprinted in *Imitations of Life: A Reader on Film and Television Melodrama*, ed. Marcia Landy (Detroit, 1991). And see Jane Feuer, "Melodrama, Serial Form and Television Today," *Screen* 25 (1984): 4–16.

8   See Richard Dienst, *Still Life in Real Time: Theory after Television* (Duke University Press, forthcoming). Jean Baudrillard describes the postmodern condition as "the dissolution of TV into life, the dissolution of life into TV" in "The Precession of Simulacra," *Art and Text* (Spring 1983): 34.

Dickens, Griffith, and Film

Theory Today

Rick Altman

★ ★ ★ ★ ★ ★ Thus Sergei Eisenstein opens his classic essay on "Dickens, Griffith, and the Film Today":

> "The kettle began it. . . ."
> Thus Dickens opens his *Cricket on the Hearth*.
> "The kettle began it. . . ."
> What could be further from films! Trains, cowboys, chases.
> . . . And *The Cricket on the Hearth*? "The kettle began it!" But,
> strange as it may seem, movies also were boiling in that kettle.
> From here, from Dickens, from the Victorian novel, stem the
> first shoots of American film esthetic, forever linked with the
> name of David Wark Griffith.[1]

Item: *The Cricket on the Hearth*. Charles Dickens, 1845. Theatrical adaptations: Albert Smith, 1845, in three parts; Edward Stirling, 1845, in two acts; W. T. Townsend, early 1846, in three chirps (!); Ben Webster, early 1846, four versions (straight play, pantomime, burlesque, and extravaganza); Dion Boucicault, 1862, three acts entitled *Dot, A Fairy Tale of Home*; the Pinkerton translation, in 1900, of Goldmark's German three-act opera; H. Jackson, 1906, a burlesque called *What Women Will Do*; N. Lambelet, 1906, a drama; W. T. Shore, 1908, an adaptation simply named *Dot*. Griffith is known to have based his version on the Albert Smith adaptation.[2]

Eisenstein again, later in the same essay:

> When Griffith proposed to his employers the novelty of a parallel "cut-back" for his first version of *Enoch Arden* (*After Many Years*, 1908), this is the discussion that took place, as recorded by Linda Arvidson Griffith in her reminiscences of Biograph days:
>
>> When Mr. Griffith suggested a scene showing Annie Lee waiting for her husband's return to be followed by a scene of Enoch cast away on a desert island, it was altogether too distracting. "How can you tell a story jumping about like that? The people won't know what it's about."
>>
>> "Well," said Mr. Griffith, "doesn't Dickens write that way?"
>>
>> "Yes, but that's Dickens; that's novel writing; that's different."
>>
>> "Oh, not so much, these are picture stories; not so different."
>
> But, to speak quite frankly, all astonishment on this subject and the apparent unexpectedness of such statements can be ascribed only to our—ignorance of Dickens.[3]

Item: *Enoch Arden*. Alfred Lord Tennyson, 1864. First theatrical adaptation: Arthur Mathison, 1869, Booth's Theatre, New York. Felix A. Vincent's manuscript promptbook indicates a pictorial, episodic construction with crosscutting between simultaneous lines of action. In the third act, as Annie Lee waits for Enoch to return, she opens the Bible, asking, "Enoch, where art thou?" Choosing a random passage to guide her, she reads, "Under a palm tree." Suddenly the flats are drawn and Annie disappears, revealing a firelit tropical vision scene, with Enoch sitting under a palm tree. The fourth act then follows Enoch, while the fifth cuts back to Annie. Subsequent stage adaptation: Newton Beers, 1889, expanded to seven acts and thirty episodes. "A complete denial," according to A. Nicholas Vardac, "of the manner of the well-made play." Act 5: "The ghostly walls of England, a line of gruesome, shadowy cliffs, rising abruptly from the sea. . . . Afterward comes the return of Annie to her cottage, where she invokes heaven to give her some token of Enoch's fate. . . . [T]he wondrous vision of the Isle of Palms is disclosed; the humble cottage disappears, and a transformation unfolds itself to the audience. Opening with the tropical night, scene follows scene, light gradually growing, until a glorious burst of sunlight reveals Enoch under a palm tree, upon which beams the blazing light of day."[4]

Few articles in the history of cinema theory have had the lasting impact of Eisenstein's treatise on "Dickens, Griffith, and the Film Today." Though the Soviet filmmaker and theoretician was hardly the first to connect American cinema to the nineteenth-century novel, his essay now serves as the locus classicus of an important strain of criticism stressing direct ties between film and the novel.[5] Eisenstein clearly knew that the ties were not as direct as he made them seem. Indeed, there are passages later in the essay that fully recognize the importance of theatrical texts in setting the pattern for cinema. Still, what is consistently remembered from Eisenstein's juxtaposition of the British novelist and the American filmmaker is a clear statement of influence: Griffith learned important aspects of his craft by paying close attention to the technique of Dickens. What Eisenstein claimed in a limited context, others have raised to the level of general pronouncement: a fundamental continuity connects the narrative technique of the nineteenth-century realist novel and the dominant style of Hollywood cinema.

By and large, critics have ignored the influence of theatrical adaptations. Eisenstein provides information on the stage source of Griffith's *Cricket on the Hearth*, yet he never attributes any importance to the existence of a theatrical intermediary. Many other critics follow precisely the same logic; they identify the dramatic version from which the film author directly borrowed, but assume that little is to be gained by comparing the film to an ephemeral and undistinguished stage adaptation.[6] More often, critics blithely postulate a direct connection between a film and the novel from which it is ostensibly drawn, when even minimal research clearly identifies a dramatic adaptation as an important direct source for the film. This approach is especially visible in the numerous checklists that cite well-known novels and the films apparently made from them, or well-known films and the novels that seemingly serve as their models.[7]

It is easy enough to demonstrate the debt that early cinema owes to theatrical adaptations. Robert M. Henderson identifies many of Griffith's Biograph films as coming from novelistic originals, as do Richard Schickel, Elaine Mancini, and most other critics.[8] *Ramona* (1910), for example, is said to derive from Helen Hunt Jackson's celebrated novel of the same name, but what of Virginia Calhoun's successful 1905 stage adaptation, in which Griffith himself had played the part of Alessandro?[9] Two of Griffith's Biograph films, *Pippa Passes* (1909) and *The Wanderer* (1913) are regularly traced to Browning's narrative poem, "Pippa Passes," yet this poem was regularly produced in a stage version. On 13 November 1906, for example, the *New York Times* singled out Henry B. Walthall for "a word of mention for intelligent acting" in an otherwise long and gloomy production of "Pippa Passes" at the Majestic. This is the same Henry B. Walthall who came to Biograph just two months before Griffith's version of *Pippa Passes* and who starred in *The Wanderer*. Cinema histories generally identify the Apocrypha as the source for Griffith's *Judith of Bethulia*.[10] Yet Blanche Sweet notes that a copy of Thomas Bailey Aldrich's 1904 theatrical adaptation (a play well known to Griffith through Nance O'Neil's production) was present on the set during filming.[11]

Griffith is not alone in his dependence on stage versions of well-known novels. In 1917, a "tie-in" edition of Frank Norris's novel *The Pit* reinforced spectators' impressions that the film was directly adapted from the novel. Yet the film's director, William A. Brady, had produced Channing Pollock's 1904 dramatic adaptation of Norris's novel, while the star of the film, Wilton Lackaye, played the role of Jadwin, as he had done on stage in 1904.[12] Newspaper advertisements in 1932 proudly announced "Ernest Hemingway's A FAREWELL TO ARMS, A Paramount Picture adapted from the novel of the same name," yet Paramount hired Lawrence Stallings to write the script, based on his 1930 stage production. Stallings may have been paid just as much as Hemingway for the rights to his adaptation, but the resulting film has nonetheless always been presented as a direct adaptation of the Hemingway novel.[13]

The last half of the nineteenth century and the first quarter of the twentieth were so fertile in theatrical adaptations that it is not safe to bet against the existence of an adaptation of any novel, however unlikely. In fact, at one point in his famous essay on "Theater and Cinema" André Bazin assumes with a great deal of assurance that no theatrical adaptation has ever been made out of *Madame Bovary* or *The Brothers Karamazov*.[14] Bazin's assurance piqued my curiosity.

Item: *Madame Bovary*. Gustave Flaubert, 1857. Theatrical adaptation: William Busnach, 1906. *The Brothers Karamazov*. Fyodor Dostoyevski, 1879–80. Theatrical adaptation: anonymously published in volume 2 of the *Moscow Art Theatre Series of Russian Plays* (1923).[15]

Take any list of silent films apparently derived from novels, submit it to a few hours of research in a serious library, and you will have little trouble discovering that a very high proportion of the novels were turned into extremely popular stage shows in the years preceding the film. Yet, systematically, it is the novel that gets the attention, the novel that is mentioned in the ad, the novel that draws the screen credit. For by the turn of the century novels were clearly a drawing card, cinema's tenuous connection to culture.[16] There is, then, a community of interest between early filmmakers and today's critics: both prefer to stress the printed word and its cultural status rather than the ephemeral popular spectacle. To critique the ideological investment apparent in preference for the novel is not, however, my purpose here.

Frankly, what difference does it make whether Vitagraph's 1911 version of *The Tale of Two Cities* derives directly from Dickens's novel or from one of the dozen or so dramatic adaptations that had held the stage continually for the half-century since the novel's publication? Not simply to contribute yet another footnote to film history, but to question a certain tendency of today's cinema theory—that is what interests me. To put it bluntly, just what has Eisenstein's insistence on connecting Griffith to Dickens rather than to theatrical adaptations cost today's film theory?[17] What difference does it make to our theoretical practice that generations of film producers and scholars have repressed film's debt to popular melodrama in favor of the more durable, more culturally acceptable novel or well-made play? Or, to formulate the question in a more provocative and productive way, of what current tendencies and stresses within film theory is the neglect of cinema's debt to melodramatic stage adaptations symptomatic?

How classical was classical narrative? Eisenstein's essay on "Dickens, Griffith, and the Film Today," written during the war and published in English in 1949, inaugurated a long period of careful attention to filmic adaptations of well-known novels. Under the structuralist influence of the late 1960s, however, and especially after the publication of Roland Barthes's *S/Z* in 1970, a new approach to novel/film relationships prevailed. Abandoning the specific analyses by which earlier critics had attempted to establish localized novelistic contributions to the cinema, the new theorists sought instead to discover a broad set of traits shared by the realist novel and the dominant mode of commercial cinema. Already in 1953, Barthes's *Le degré zéro de l'écriture* had set up Balzac as the official representative of a mythically pure "straight" narration.[18] In the same period, André Bazin publicly recognized in Hollywood cinema all the maturity of a classical art.[19] With *S/Z* the term "classical" was finally fully stripped of its traditional historical reference to seventeenth-century French literature and associated with a specific type of narration exemplified by Balzac. "Classical," says Barthes at the outset of *S/Z*, "is the term we use to designate the readerly text." Throughout the early 1970s the importance of Barthes's terminology was reinforced by a series of paired terms that appeared to parallel his classical/modernist opposition. Barthes himself contributed the readerly/writerly (*lisible/ scriptible*) distinction, as well as the related opposition between pleasure and bliss (*plaisir/jouissance*). Structuralist critics of film and literature alike repeatedly referred to Benveniste's distinction between story and discourse (*histoire/discours*).[20] Film theorists often opposed Hollywood cinema to alternative cinema or countercinema.[21]

Conceived from the start as part of a binary opposition, the notion of classical narrative necessarily involved concentration on a narrow range of targeted features, with a consequent leveling of all but certain key differences among texts. With the Balzacian model as a guide, theorists of the past two decades have built a coherent but limited model of classical narrative. With few exceptions they have stressed omniscient narration, linear presentation, character-centered causality, and psychological motivation. In addition, film theorists have pointed out the importance of invisible editing, verisimilitude of space, and various devices designed to assure continuity.

At the heart of every evocation of classical narrative lies a textbook assumption about the meaning of the term "classical." For Bazin the term implies maturity, ripeness, harmony, perfect balance, and ideal form. For Barthes it refers to a text whose integrity and order provide assurance and comfort for the reader.[22] In David Bordwell's use, "classical" means harmony, unity, tradition, rule-governed craftsmanship, standardization, and control.[23] All three critics, it seems quite clear, ultimately owe their definition of the classical in large part to the neoclassical French literary theorists of the seventeenth century. Borrowing from Boileau and his contemporaries not only a general sense of harmony and order, but also numerous specific tenets (the central importance of the unity of action, concentration on human psychology, preference for mimetic forms), critics have found in a broadly shared notion of classicism a ready-made theory. But is that theory built strongly enough to carry the weight of the novel and cinema as well?

Was classicism classical? The century of Corneille and Racine apparently provides an important model for the concept of classical narrative. According to the familiar account, French writers of the second quarter of the seventeenth century, under the tutelage of Malherbe and the Académie Française, and with the guidance of Aristotelian principles, subordinated their creative genius to a series of rules for proper literary production, resulting in works of a more ordered and pleasurable nature. During the latter half of the century, these rational rules came to be second nature to a growing group of writers, including Molière, Racine, Boileau, La Fontaine, La Rochefoucauld, La Fayette, and La Bruyère, all gathered around the Sun King, Louis XIV.[24] The good taste of these writers permitted them to reflect through the harmony of their writings the social stability of the era as well as the overall unity of the court and its regal master.

Today this traditional view of French classicism no longer counts many supporters. Inspired by the methods of the Annales School, historians have increasingly challenged the assumptions of social unity that once appeared to undergird classical doctrine. Little by little, literary scholars have revised their model of classical unity. Before World War II, Thierry Maulnier provided perhaps the strongest challenge to the traditional static conception of classicism. Where other critics stress the delicacy and order of Racine's language, Maulnier points instead to the strong opposition between the refined dignity of Racine's language and the savage emotions that it often expresses. Maulnier reveals Racine's tendency to stretch a civilized, finely crafted surface over the chaotic energy of a smoldering volcano.[25]

Maulnier's reading echoes the intriguing formula of French novelist André Gide: "A classical work is strong and beautiful only through its ability to tame its own romanticism."[26] Whereas dictionary definitions always define classicism as opposed to romanticism, Gide recognizes that the classic always *includes* the romantic. Classicism for Gide is thus not a stable style but a constant effort to corral, tame, and harness the chaotic forces that give classicism its particular power. "The more rebellious the thing mastered," says Gide, "the more beautiful the work."[27] Gide invites us to read the order of classicism as the result of tension. For him, the renowned balance characteristic of classical works is not the permanently secure balance of a symmetrical drawing, but the unstable equilibrium of a ballet dancer on point, straining her muscles to the utmost in order to appear motionless and calm.

Following the tension-based model proposed by Gide, postwar criticism has systematically reconsidered French classical authors and the classicism that they constitute. The first to undergo massive re-evaluation was Racine. During the years when an apparently unproblematic notion of "classical" narrative was being elaborated, the very foundations of the term were being undermined from multiple directions. Lucien Goldmann's Marxist reading of Racine dwells on the turmoil and impossible quandaries built into the tragic genre.

Charles Mauron's psychoanalytic approach reveals Racine's personal obsessions operating beneath and through the surface activities of his characters. Philip Butler was the first of many to discover Racine's predilection for baroque traits, however well he might control them in his writing. Roland Barthes gave a strong impetus to this new reading of classical texts by applying the insights of Freud's late works to Racine.[28] Over the last quarter century, this reevaluation of the orderliness and harmony of classicism has continued without abatement.

For our purposes, a simple lesson is to be learned here. The understanding of literary structure that grounds familiar notions of classicism is by no means a current one. Recent critics have not claimed that earlier researchers were wrong to stress the rule-governed craftsmanship, the standardization, the control, or the harmony of those texts thought of as classical. They have instead insisted on a more complex, more dynamic, multilevel understanding of the style and texts in question.

How classical is the classical novel? Discussions of narrative continuity from novel to film commonly privilege two novelists, Charles Dickens and Honoré de Balzac, Dickens because his are the novels that have most often been adapted into film (with or without theatrical intermediaries), and Balzac because he is regularly taken as the locus classicus of the type of omniscient narration adopted by Hollywood. Apparently representing the source—or at least a historically important example—of Hollywood's approach to narrative, Dickens and Balzac need to be carefully analyzed if we are to understand the role they play in our understanding of classical narrative. This is of course not the place for full-scale analysis of two such prolific authors. A rapid survey of some basic concerns may nevertheless be helpful.

The works of Charles Dickens play an intriguing role in arguments about the relationship between the novel and cinema. Of all highly respected nineteenth-century novelists, the most closely allied to popular sensibility and the melodrama is surely Charles Dickens. Among novelists his is an ambiguous name, for it invokes not only the respect for realism due a Stendhal, an Eliot, or a Hardy, but also the more popular infatuation with less respected and apparently more ephemeral writers of episodic fiction like Eugène Sue and Alexandre Dumas. In short, Dickens sits astride two opposed nineteenth-century conceptions of novel writing: one has become, through the influence of such figures as Flaubert and James, a central tradition of our high culture; the other has had difficulty surviving. Much popular fiction of the last century is as hard to locate today as the popular melodramas of the same period. Dickens retains his importance because he is a pivotal figure—accepted by scholars of the novel, yet shot through with the themes and structures of the popular serial.

Because of Dickens's connection of these two apparently separate traditions, attempts to base a model of narrative development on Dickens must be taken as fundamentally suspect. Typically, Dickens is invoked by film theorists because of his use of episodic structures, his tendency toward overstated, oversimplified emotions, and his contributions to the technique of crosscutting. In other words, he is mentioned because of his connections with popular melodrama. Yet the conclusions drawn from his presence in an argument are rapidly applied to the classical novel, to that aspect of Dickens least associated with the examples actually adduced. Because of this ambiguity, Dickens has served a spuriously pivotal function in discussions about the relationship between the cinema and the novel.

The similar position held by Balzac in French literature and narrative theory reveals more clearly the stakes of the argument. Typed by Barthes in the 1950s as the perfect "classic" in opposition to which the "modern" might be better defined, Balzac continued to serve this rhetorical function for French structuralist critics and their American followers. It was during this period that the notion of "Hollywood classical narrative" took on the status of received idea. Not just "Hollywood narrative," but "classical narrative," for the whole point was to establish important continuities between cinematic practice and the traditions of the nineteenth-century novel.

During the 1970s, however, Balzac scholarship underwent a minor revolution. While popularizing the notion of classical narrative, Barthes's *S/Z* provided a reading of *Sarrasine* that revealed the potential modernity of the Balzacian text. Many other critics, in reaction to the typing of Balzac as a "straight" or "transparent" narrator, went out of their way to demonstrate the eminently discursive nature of Balzac's narration. Within the classic novelist the seeds of modernity could be seen sprouting.

At the same time, Balzac's debt to the Gothic novel, the serial romance, and popular melodrama was being recalled by Peter Brooks in his influential treatise, *The Melodramatic Imagination.* "Melodrama," affirms Brooks, "is hence part of the semiotic precondition of the novel for Balzac—part of what allows the 'Balzacian novel' to come into being. We can best understand this novel when we perceive that its fictional representations repose on a necessary theatrical substratum—necessary, because a certain type of meaning could not be generated without it."[29] Until recently, only the popular serial novelists of the nineteenth century seemed directly indebted to the melodramatic stage. We now more easily see that not only Sue and Dumas depend on melodrama for their inspiration and style, but Balzac, Hugo, Dostoyevski, Zola, and James as well.

The role of melodrama in an apparently classical narrative will be clarified by the example of one of Balzac's most durably popular novels, *Le père Goriot.* According to the now familiar definition, classical narrative induces the reader to follow a linear chain of psychologically based causes leading from an initial question or problem to a final solution. From this standpoint, *Le père Goriot* is the most classic of novels, for it assures continuity, linearity, and psychological causality by focusing the narrative on the social and moral growth of young Eugène de Rastignac. Following the protagonist almost exclusively from beginning to end, the narrator invites us to pay primary attention to Rastignac and to his twin roles of detective and student of life. With Rastignac we discover the activities, nefarious and charitable, of his fellow boarders at the Pension Vauquer; with Rastignac we also learn about the social mores and moral dilemmas that attend life in the modern world.

Viewed in this manner, *Le père Goriot* stands as the very model of the classical novel. From the picaresque episodes of a *Lazarillo de Tormes* to the historical novels of Mérimée or Scott, from the Bildungsroman of a Marivaux or a Goethe to the nascent modernism of Flaubert, from the *roman d'analyse* of a Madame de La Fayette to the point-of-view experiments of a Henry James, the pattern remains the same. Continuity is assured by consistent following of a single character along with whom we discover the surrounding world. In contrast to the melodrama's characteristic dual-focus concentration on two separate centers of interest, I have called this type of narration "single-focus."[30] While the protagonist's body continues to serve the familiar adventure functions assigned to it by romance, the protagonist's mind here takes on a newly expanded role. Opinions and attitudes usurp the position once reserved for decisions and actions. Sleuthing replaces dueling as the key to success.

Note that this pattern systematically requires a dual vision of the world. Watching the protagonist watch the world, we simultaneously view the protagonist and the world. The protagonist of the single-focus novel provides only one possible interpretation of the world. Though it is commonly called into being by the protagonist's vision or ratiocination, the world retains its independent existence and thus its mystery and fascination. In Le père Goriot, the independence of the world around Rastignac is demonstrated by the rhetorical effect of his two neighbors: Vautrin, the Mephisthophelean ex-convict whose get-rich-quick schemes simultaneously horrify and intrigue his young charge Eugène, and Goriot, the realist Lear, the spaghetti-making saint who would pair Rastignac with one of his money-hungry daughters.

Though Balzac carefully assured the continuity and rationality of his novel by sticking to Rastignac and his vision, his readers were not fooled. They immediately recognized that Rastignac is not alone at the center of the novel. In fact, the stage play made from the novel returns Vautrin and Goriot to the directly and melodramatically opposed positions that they have retained in the popular memory of the novel.[31]

It is important to note just how differently Rastignac is treated as a character from Goriot and Vautrin. While Rastignac is the consummate classical novel character, tying scene to scene through his well-developed psychology, ever-changing throughout the course of the novel, Goriot and Vautrin seem drawn from another world, held in ritual bondage to their roles like the blocking characters in New Comedy or, more to the point, like the antagonists of melodrama.

Though Balzac psychologizes them schematically, they appear to be beyond psychology; they call instead for a mythic definition. They represent two static models of paternity, as Balzac termed them, one for Good and the other for Evil.

Balzac's novels stage a "double-tiered drama," according to Peter Brooks, "where what is represented on the public social stage is only a figuration of what lies behind, in the domain of true power and significance."[32] The domain of true power and significance in *Le père Goriot* is clearly that occupied by the timeless divinities of charity and theft, of senseless Good and intriguing Evil. In order to understand what is going on in *Goriot* we cannot remain at the levels of the character and plot that assure the novel's classical nature. We must instead view the novel as the chance passing of a historical, time-bound, psychologized character through the latest incarnation of the eternal realm of stereotypes and changeless values. Balzac's novel is not a melodrama, it is a classical novel, yet embedded melodrama is essential to its meaning, as generations of readers attest by all but forgetting Rastignac while vividly recalling Goriot and Vautrin. In order to make sense of *Le père Goriot*, we need to pay close attention to the unpsychologized stable monuments constituted by Goriot and Vautrin as well as to the young man whose itinerary is responsible for the text's unfolding.

The classical novel, I would suggest, works this way as a matter of course. Though the protagonist's trajectory may be what holds the novel together, assuring its "classical" nature, the novel's internal dialectic is completed by the presence of an unpsychologized, dual-focus tradition that the protagonist continually confronts. Quixote wants to be Amadís, the Consalve of Madame de La Fayette's *Zaïde* is living in a world of Alexandrian romances, Robinson Crusoe sets out in search of an adventure romance life, Emma Bovary would recreate the world according to the version promulgated by the popular press, while Hollywood's psychologized characters live with a supporting cast drawn from Griffith. I do not mean here simply to repeat the claims of René Girard, who taught us about the role of literary and historical figures in the triangular mediation of desire.[33] The point is not simply that the conduct of novelistic protagonists is mediated by previous literary or mythic figures, but that the novel as an overtly single-focus form has a strong capacity for absorbing and displaying—in the background, as it were—the stable values and unpsychologized characters of previous dual-focus traditions.

We have learned from Bakhtin the importance of considering the novel not as a fixed form but as a process. In developing his notions of "novelization," "heteroglossia," and "hybridization," however, Bakhtin would appear to have given too little attention to the relationship among the various strains together present in a single work.[34] While this is hardly the place to expound at length on possible modifications of Bakhtin's intriguing theories, it seems clear that an understanding of the novel requires not only a model that makes room for the presence of multiple genres and modes, but also a theory of the relationship among those diverse components: We must understand the "classical" version of the novel, from *Quixote* to Proust, in terms of the relationship between the classical single-focus surface, where values are degraded and decisions are partial, and the embedded dual-focus realm of permanence and power.

In short, the classical novel is classical *and more*. Without understanding the "more" we have little chance of avoiding systematic impoverishment of the classical novel. As the example of *Le père Goriot* suggests, it is possible for a novel to display all the characteristics of classical narrative and yet not to operate through them alone. If we are to develop a model of classical narrative that is not only descriptive but also systematic, we must look past current accounts.

Was the nineteenth century theater well-made? The split between "classical novels" and "popular serials" in nineteenth-century fiction is mirrored and heightened by an even more evident split in nineteenth-century theater. On the one side stands the so-called "well-made play," championed by Sarcey, Sardou, Scribe, and other students of theater history. Corresponding fairly closely to the efforts of an Austen or a Flaubert, the well-made play held out for Aristotelian principles, with particular emphasis on the importance of unity of action, in an era when the popular stage was consistently held by melodramas built according to principles of crosscutting and episodic construction like those borrowed by Griffith from the stage versions of *The Cricket on the Hearth, Enoch Arden, Ramona, Judith of Bethulia*, and *The Clansman*.

Two basic principles regarding the relationship of the novel to the nineteenth- and early twentieth-century popular stage deserve mention here. First, dramatists tended to choose their material from existing texts whose melodramatic proclivities were quite obvious. Thus Balzac, Dumas, Dickens, Hugo, and Zola remain their subjects of choice. Second, whatever the source of material, the stage adaptation tends to imprint the popular theater's own stamp on the original. I have already mentioned that Balzac's *Le père Goriot*, which so carefully concentrates not directly on the mythic figures of Vautrin and Goriot but on the young sleuth who uncovers their stories, was rapidly made into a melodrama featuring the very characters shunned by the novel's classical single-focus technique. Any of Zola's novels could easily have provided the subject for a well-made play. *L'assommoir*, for example, might well have been given a stage version respecting Aristotelian principles, with Gervaise serving as *fil conducteur*. Instead, *L'assommoir* was turned into a sensationalistic melodrama, with emphasis on Coupeau and his delirium tremens.[35] The opposition between well-made play and popular melodrama thus heightens the difference between two prose fiction traditions, each stressing separate and opposed aspects of the available narrative material.

What makes it possible to move back and forth with such ease between single- and dual-focus versions of the same story, between classical and melodramatic versions of the same tale? The case of *L'assommoir* is instructive. Anyone who has read Zola's famous *Ebauche*, his working notes for the novel, is struck by their judgmental and sensationalistic character. The *Ebauche* begins with the notes taken by Zola during his long period of research on the living conditions of the Parisian lower classes. Especially influential in Zola's thinking at this early point in his preparation was Denis Poulot's *Le sublime ou le travailleur comme il est en 1870 et ce qu'il peut être*, from which Zola borrowed many details and secondary characters for the completed novel. More to the point here, however, is the categorization of workers established by Poulot and borrowed by Zola. Constantly contrasted to the *sublime* or bad worker is *l'ouvrier vrai*, whom Zola's notes describe in these terms:

> The true worker, three hundred days of work a year, no debts, savings at home or in the bank, loves his wife and children and takes them out regularly; teaches his children, buys books, owns a clock or a watch; never drinks and doesn't work on Sunday; offers an arm to his wife (the *sublime* never does). Stays at the same job, works hard and fast, looks after himself, stays clean, and thinks clearly.[36]

When Zola reached the point of composing his novel, he retained Poulot's judgmental division, styling Lantier as the archetypal bad worker and Coupeau as his good counterpart, until Coupeau too falls prey to Lantier's bad influence and is replaced as archetypal good worker by the mythically pure Goujet. As in *Le père Goriot*, however, *L'assommoir* is held together not by the melodramatic opposition of good worker to bad, but by the rise and fall of a character as yet unmarked as good or evil. Gervaise serves as our introduction to the world of the Parisian worker in order that the continuity, linearity, and psychological causality of classical narrative might be respected. As Zola advanced in his writing, however, he was constantly tempted to bring the melodramatic possibilities of his plot back to the foreground. According to his first sketch for the novel's ending, for example, Lantier was to take on Goujet in an apocalyptic battle. Gervaise would find Lantier in bed with Virginie and break a bottle of sulfuric acid over their naked bodies. Lantier, maddened by pain, would then drag Gervaise by her hair into the courtyard in front of her industrious but selfish in-laws. At that point Goujet would appear and engage Lantier in a formidable duel, lit by the setting sun.[37] That this scene never appears in the novel is a mark, one is tempted to say, of Zola's good taste; in any case, it clearly indicates that Zola's commitment to a classical mode of narration precluded overt construction of a novel along melodramatic lines. Yet Zola does not entirely suppress his melodramatic material. While it does not serve as an organizing principle, it remains constantly present, ever available as part of Gervaise's and the reader's experience. And available as well to the many stage adapters of Zola's novels. Indeed, melodramatic adaptations of nineteenth-century novels are so prevalent because the novels themselves contain a melodramatic substratum ready to erupt through its classical covering. Like Balzac, Dickens, Hugo, Dostoyevski, and James, Zola consistently turns melodramatic material into classical narrative by drawing a psychological veil over it, by taking the static elements of the melodramatic spectacle and stretching them out in linear fashion like so many links in a chain.

It is not, however, the melodramatic adaptations of novels that have been stressed by critics. Peter Brooks, whose *Melodramatic Imagination* is directly interested in the relationship between the nineteenth-century novel and melodrama, always deals with Pixerécourt and original melodramas rather than with the melodramatic adaptations drawn from novels. This is hardly surprising, however, given the near impossibility of locating texts for these popular plays. Even clear references to adaptations are hard to find; often the existence of a stage version of a popular novel must be inferred from a chance comment or discovered by careful reading of the contemporary press. Certainly, the unsure copyright status of all but authorized adaptations, along with the low critical esteem accorded them, contributes to the invisibility of the adaptation as cultural phenomenon.[38]

Most accounts of Hollywood classical narrative jump directly from nineteenth-century novels to the cinema. Only David Bordwell and Kristin Thompson have remained systematically attentive to the nineteenth-century stage as a contributing element to classical Hollywood cinema. While Bordwell stresses the influence of the well-made play in stamping out coincidence as a central form of causality, Thompson invokes the well-made play as a major source for thorough motivation and the resulting continuity of action. Thompson is especially clear in setting up a progression stretching from the novel through original well-made plays and the increasingly popular short story form to Hollywood classical narrative.[39] Like other students of cinema, however, Bordwell and Thompson pay little attention to the possible contribution of melodramatic material to the classical paradigm. This repression of popular theater has the effect of denying Hollywood cinema its fundamental connection to popular traditions and to their characteristic forms of spectacle and narrative. By eschewing the more popular serial forms and theatrical adaptations, critics abandon the opportunity to understand what is going on beneath and within the classical aspects of Hollywood narrative.

Where does this leave film theory today? I cannot fully develop here a theory of Hollywood classical narrative's popular unconscious—a theory, in short, of its dual-focus foundations. But I can suggest a few of the important concerns that a focus on popular narrative and theatrical adaptations might bring back to our notion of Hollywood classical narrative, along with the major theoretical problems implied by the symptomatic shunning of Hollywood's consistently melodramatic underpinnings. The important point is not that critics should literally pay more attention to stage intermediaries (though they probably should); by and large such stage intermediaries become rare after the early 1930s. At stake is not just a blueprint for research but an understanding of the theoretical concerns underlying the notion of classical narrative. The absence of attention to stage intermediaries is not itself the problem; it is a symptom of the real problem.

To be sure, Hollywood classical narrative is not overtly episodic. In keeping with the familiar Aristotelian strictures of the well-made play, Hollywood cinema is goal-driven, its hermeneutic moves through character-based causality toward a logical conclusion. At the same time, however—and the simultaneity of the two processes is what I want to stress here—Hollywood perpetuates the menu-driven concerns of popular theater. Spectacle is needed, as are variety and strong emotions. How can these be obtained in a form that precludes overt episodicity? With no difficulty. Decide which spectacles are needed, then make it seem that they are there for internally motivated reasons.

To be sure, Hollywood classical narrative disguises its dualisms. Unlike the Dickens of *Oliver Twist*, the Eugène Sue of *Les mystères de Paris*, and the Dion Boucicault of *Arrah-na-Pogue*, Hollywood prefers to embed its oppositions, to hide them during all but the most crucial scenes. Yet the narrative operates as it does in order to work these dualisms to the surface. Hollywood's typical linear progression, character-based causality, and continuity editing style serve as mise-en-scène of a fundamentally dualistic relationship whose presence is a precondition for Hollywood cinema, as it is for the novels of Balzac, Dickens, and Zola. The ability to foreground dualisms is, of course, the very stock-in-trade of popular theater. Constantly preferring the metaphoric to the metonymic, in Jakobson's sense of the terms, popular forms of entertainment typically operate according to familiar dual-focus patterns. Hollywood may smooth out the bumps of melodramatic theater, but no amount of smoothing can entirely dissimulate the bulge.

To be sure, Hollywood classical narrative ties its realism and its causality to character psychology. Without the possibility of development, the Hollywood character would be diminished indeed. Yet how many of Hollywood's greatest stars borrow from the nineteenth-century stage their virtual identification with a particular type of role? And how many Hollywood actors are consistently cast according to their tendency to fit into a preexisting category rather than their ability to adapt to a new one? By and large, Hollywood's character categories were set by the popular stage of the last century; the activities of individual characters must appear free in order for the film's inner motivation to operate properly, yet from the outside we easily see just how ritually bound these activities are.

For historical reasons, the notion of classical narrative has evolved in such a way as to privilege Dickens the classical novelist while repressing Dickens the source of popular melodramas. Classical narrative has thus evolved into a term designating a particular *style* more or less continuous from Balzac to Bogdanovich. Symptomatically separated from the ephemeral spectacles of the popular stage, the notion of classical narrative has never been allowed to grow into a dynamic, multilevel *system* in which coexisting contradictory forces must regularly clash. What we have is a complex description of Hollywood's most successful modes of secondary elaboration. What we need is a new look at the other Dickens, a recognition of Hollywood's debt to popular drama, and an opportunity to discover the primary operations of Hollywood's narrative work. Before we can proceed, however, we need to scrutinize some of the basic operations on which the very notion of classical narrative is founded.

"In Hollywood cinema, a specific sort of narrative causality operates as the dominant, making temporal and spatial systems vehicles for it," affirms David Bordwell at the outset of his arguments regarding Hollywood classical narrative.[40] The formalist notion of the dominant is clearly central to Bordwell's influential description of classical narrative. "The dominant," says Roman Jakobson in a 1935 article, "may be defined as the focusing component of a work of art: it rules, determines, and transforms the remaining components. It is the dominant which guarantees the integrity of the structure."[41] For Jurij Tynjanov, the dominant consists of "a group of elements in the foreground."[42] Historically, the notion of the dominant appears to have served the primary purpose of allowing the formalists to justify theoretically the notion of aesthetic text. A poetic text, asserts Jakobson, "is defined as a verbal message whose aesthetic function is its dominant. . . . The definition of the aesthetic function as the dominant of a poetic work permits us to determine the hierarchy of diverse linguistic functions within the poetic work."[43]

The need for a concept like that of the dominant is easily understandable. If a text contains numerous components, comprehension of the text derives only partially from description of those components; some statement of the relationship among components is also required. It is thus appropriate to pay particularly close attention to the metaphors used by the formalists to develop the notion of the dominant. For Tynjanov, dominant elements are foregrounded elements; for Jakobson, the dominant rules and focuses, it is at the summit of a hierarchy. The relationship between the dominant and the dominated is thus imaged as static and absolute. This is not surprising when we recall that the concept originally served to reinforce the formalists' notion of the aesthetic text, a purpose for which a nuanced notion of dominance was hardly necessary. It is certainly to Bordwell's credit that his version of the dominant remains more dynamic in nature, theoretically at least, "with the subordinated factors constantly pulling against the sway of the dominant."[44]

A forgotten episode in the history of classical narrative criticism will help us to understand what is at stake here. Near the beginning of his study on Balzac's *Sarrasine*, Roland Barthes represents his analysis graphically, imaging the different strains of the text as instrumental parts in a musical score. Borrowing the familiar technique popularized by Lévi-Strauss, Barthes clearly models the text as an infinite set of complex interactions. "The classic text is thus truly tabular (and not linear), but its tabularity is vectorized."[45] In classical narrative, Barthes implies, there is no single component capable of dominating a text from beginning to end in the same fashion. Even the notion of linearity, so important to descriptions of classical narrative, must be seen not simply as linearity, but as vectorized tabularity, as constantly retaining the sense of the relationship between the line and the other points on the matrix within which that line momentarily appears.

Yet the notion of linearity as vectorized tabularity was not adopted by students of classical narrative. Instead, they typically follow the far more simple notion of linearity derived from an earlier article in which Barthes images narrative not in a tabular fashion but as a chain of causally connected nuclei.[46] The disappearance of vectorized tabularity as a critical notion, in favor of the less complex concept of linearity, serves as a cautionary tale. Barthes proves to be his own competition, the cause for simplification of what could have been one of his most important contributions. I fear that the same simplification dogs Bordwell's theoretical devotion to a dynamic definition of the dominant.

The notion of dominance, as it is used today, recalls the impoverishment involved in the slippage from vectorized tabularity to simple linearity. First conceived at the level of the whole text, now commonly used at the level of an entire narrative tradition, the concept of the dominant has become through use a rather coarse tool, a global designator that does little to foster a dynamic understanding either of inter- or intratextual relationships. Whenever Bordwell is confronted with features that do not neatly fit into his description of the continuous linear causality of classical Hollywood narrative—as in the case of melodramatic attributes like spectacle, episodic presentation, or dependence on coincidence—he explains the anomaly by reference to generic conventions which operate "as limited plays within the classical compositional dominant."[47] Neither generic conventions nor the excessive practice of individual texts are ever seen as acting in any kind of structured tension within the dominant, but only as contesting the dominant from without.

The same thing holds true with Bordwell's overall approach to spectatorship. Treating the spectator's responsibilities and possibilities primarily in terms of the gap-filling activity described by Meir Sternberg, Bordwell (rightly, I believe) insists on the classical Hollywood film's attempt to lead the spectator through a carefully planned trajectory that reduces the viewer's ability to recognize other possible trajectories.[48] This gap-filling activity reduces the viewer's freedom, but does not destroy it altogether. Are there never secondary strategies of gap-filling, leading the spectator into a structured tension between the primary classical stance and an important (if not dominant) secondary position? The appropriate model is surely the schema-processing that Bordwell so cogently evokes, and not the either/or duck-rabbit model that seems to inform the notion of dominance employed by most theorists of classical narrative.

Either/or models tend to cut off any possible nuancing of our understanding of classical narrative. Kristin Thompson claims that "the causal chain with an interweaving of lines of action won out easily over parallelism as the basis for the classical film."[49] One may well agree that the causal chain is important in classical narrative, but the competitive metaphor employed here ("won out") implies a single winner, alone on the podium, never interacting with the other competitors. What if texts were complex enough to permit the same words or images to generate multiple structures, to embed parallelism within the causal chain?

The term "dominant," it is worth recalling, derives from a Latin and French present participle. It thus refers not to a state but to an active process. When students of social process speak of a dominant class, they are referring to a momentary situation within an ongoing *rapport de forces*. Dominance, in this sense, implies more than just primacy. It also implies pressure within a closed system. This pressure in turn produces a counterpressure that may eventually surface as resentment, resistance, or revolution. This counterpressure must not be thought of as separate and secondary but as part and parcel of the very process of dominating. In a similar way, genetics identifies certain traits as dominant and points out their ability to mask recessive traits. In this context, dominance suggests primacy, to be sure, but it also implies a capacity for dissimulating the presence and potential of the nondominant. Only through recognition of a systematic relationship between dominant and recessive tendencies can actual traits be predicted. So the notion of dominance must be used as a tool promoting structured understanding of the text, not as a label that keeps us from opening the text. Before suggesting how this might be possible, I need to consider two further theoretical assumptions regularly made by even the most adept students of classical narrative.

As it has been used by Bordwell and Thompson, the notion of dominance has become primarily a rationale for preferring one solution to another or for sorting texts into categories, according to their dominant. Bordwell devotes approximately half of his study, *Narration in the Fiction Film*, to analysis of four separable categories of narration, defined by their differing dominants: classical narrative cinema, international art cinema, historical-materialist cinema, and parametric cinema. The category of parametric cinema is heavily dependent on the importance of paradigmatic relationships, which Bordwell relegates to the level of stylistic analysis in classical Hollywood narrative.[50] This use of the dominant as principle of categorization appears to me extremely useful, quite in line with the original formalist reasons for promulgating the concept. The notion of dominance permits us to recognize clear differences between texts dominated, for example, by syntagmatic relationships and those dominated by paradigmatic relationships. What concerns me here, however, is the attention that will be given to the syntagmatic relationships in the paradigm-dominated form, and vice versa. What place, or rather what activity, will be ascribed to the dominated characteristic?

In this regard, one of the footnotes to Bordwell's treatment of

Hollywood classical narration is particularly indicative. His initial discussion of Hollywood narration asserts that "causality is the prime unifying principle. Analogies between characters, settings, and situations are certainly present, but at the denotative level any parallelism is subordinated to the movement of cause and effect."[51] There appears to be little reason for disagreement with this claim, since it leaves an opening for treating problems of parallelism and analogy at the connotative level. Bordwell's footnote, however, dismisses "the need to consider the importance of character parallels as 'paradigmatic' relations in the classic text." Admitting that "analogies and contrasts of situation or character occur in classical films," he nevertheless claims that "these relations are typically dependent upon logically prior causal relations."[52]

We recognize in the notion of logical priority the familiar linear arrangement of classical narrative. Prior events, given as causing subsequent events, are typically treated as classical narrative's first causes. In the classical film, as Bordwell asserts, "the conclusion acknowledges itself as a result of the beginning."[53] One can hardly contest this statement—the conclusions of Hollywood films clearly grow out of and respond to the activities that take place at the start. Nevertheless, another perspective on this all too obvious assertion may be needed. Apropos of endings, Bordwell points out that "of one hundred randomly sampled Hollywood films, over sixty ended with a display of the united romantic couple—the cliché ending, often with a 'clinch'—and many more could be said to end happily."[54] Bordwell does not similarly assess the beginnings, but it is safe to assume that, outside of formal similarities, the beginnings of Hollywood films have no such common content. What are we to make of a mode of filmmaking that systematically assures the same basic ending?

We must conclude, I suggest, that these films do not start at the beginning but at the end. That is, their beginnings are retrofitted to a preexisting ending, to which the beginnings must appear to lead. The end is made to *appear* as a function of the beginning in order better to disguise the fact that the beginning is actually a function of the end. This contention corresponds precisely to the various pressures that beset Hollywood screenwriters during the classical period: generic conventions, production code requirements, studio notions of audience preference, and so forth. The very similarity of Hollywood endings suggests that classical narrative reasons backward, from the preordained desired ending to a beginning that will appear to produce that ending according to accepted notions of psychological causality.

What then of the notion of logical priority? I take it that Bordwell means by logical priority that one system is dominant over another, that causal logic outweighs imbedded paradigmatic relations. As we see in the case of the typical Hollywood happy ending, however, the direction of causality as perceived by the spectator is exactly the reverse of the direction of causality required by the text's creation. To invoke logical priority, as Bordwell does, is to assume that logic runs in only one direction, that dominant systems are univocal. What we need instead is a theory that, without relinquishing the hierarchical virtues of the notion of the dominant, recognizes multiple modes of logic and establishes a method of dynamically describing the relationship among those modes—a system, in short, of *dia*logical priority.

It is hardly surprising that a dominance-oriented account of classical narrative structure should have led to a notion of textual excess. Restricting notions of structure to a single model, the concept of dominance necessarily leaves aspects of the work unaccounted for. Over the past decade, increasing attention has thus been concentrated on the notion of "excess," defined by Thompson as "those aspects of the work that are not contained by its unifying forces."[55] The more a static notion of dominance leads us to concentrate on a specific definition of textual unity, the more elements there are that fall outside the bounds of that unity. "Motivation is the primary tool by which the work makes its own devices seem reasonable," suggests Thompson. "At the point where motivation fails, excess begins."[56] Excess, as Thompson defines it, complements the dominant. The dominant organizes the text; that which remains unorganized is perceived as excessive. Totality minus dominant equals excess.

As tempting as this formulation may seem, it conceals a potential impoverishment of critical discourse. The availability of the notion of excess provides the critic with a convenient *rien ne va plus* that immediately cuts off analysis, thus reinforcing the apparent authority of the dominant. In totalitarian regimes, dominance has long been perpetuated by the leader's right to declare certain individuals *de trop*. The dominant party is strengthened by its ability to brand other parties as unpatriotic and thus excessive. The right to identify excess carries enormous power, always in favor of the dominant. To name the excess is thus just another way of naming the dominant. Totality minus excess equals dominant.

Defined in this manner, excess becomes no more than the outlaw by which the law reaffirms itself. Yet in an advanced society the telling moments rarely involve the simple opposition of the lawful to the lawless. Far more penetrating are those instances when the dominant legal system confronts laws of another order. The case has followed its course through the legal system, but the killer still has not been executed. They all know the law, but they refuse to leave the Greensboro lunchroom. The law prescribes a course of action, a well-motivated narrative, but other "laws" break away from the prescribed pattern.

In spite of the presence of an acknowledged dominant—call it the law of the land or the principle of narrative causality—we repeatedly find multiple logics at work. Moments of excess, from the point of view of one logic, systematically serve as the shifter that permits us to recognize the concurrent operation of another logic. Sit-in, shooting, strike, revolution—these are the gaps in the legal scenario that remind us of the counterpressure created by dominance and that reveal the alternative principles according to which the disenfranchised operate. Unmotivated events, rhythmic montage, highlighted parallelism, overlong spectacles—these are the excesses in the classical narrative system that alert us to the existence of a competing logic, a second voice.

Hollywood's excesses, like those of the novel, systematically point toward the embedded melodramatic mode that subtends classical narrative from *Clarissa* to *Casablanca*. If systems can be defined and categorized by their dominant, as the formalists believed, then they can be further understood through the nature and coherence of their excesses. However strong the dominant voice, excess bears witness to the existence of another language, another logic. Unless we recognize the possibility that excess—defined as such because of its refusal to adhere to a system—may itself be organized as a system, then we will hear only the official language and forever miss the text's dialect, and dialectic.

We have seen how Balzac's *Le père Goriot* and Zola's *L'assommoir* embed in their classical linearity elements of melodrama as part of the semiotic precondition for the novels' operation. How might we have imaged these texts from the point of view of dominance and logical priority? On the one hand, we would have no hesitation in recognizing within them the familiar components of classical narrative, with Rastignac and Gervaise providing the continuity and character-based motivation typical of classical narrative linearity. On the other hand, we cannot neglect the popular memory of these novels, in which certain characters and scenes loom large: the diabolical Vautrin, the saintly Goriot, Coupeau's delirium tremens, the contrast between the good worker Goujet and the troublemaker Lantier. Which should dominate in our model of these novels?

The Freudian concept of overdetermination keeps us from having to answer that question with the single response that the formalist notion of dominance would seem to require. In dealing with the work of dreams, Freud recognizes that individual elements of the dream-content can be determined in multiple ways. To read an element according to one explanatory system alone would infallibly impoverish our understanding of the dream. Yet, as Freud points out, one of the aspects of the dream work exists primarily to induce us to read the dream-content in a single, simplified manner. Whereas individual elements of the dream-content may be overdetermined through the primary processes of displacement, condensation, and symbolization, the process of secondary elaboration, providing connective material among the various parts of the dream, offers yet another possible reading. Indeed, the material added during the process of secondary elaboration may well appear primary to the interpreter, since it is the connective tissue of secondary elaboration that appears to hold the entire dream together.

Freud's familiar description of the dream work provides a strikingly fruitful model for understanding classical narrative. Whereas

Bordwell describes linear narrative causality as classical narrative's dominant, I would suggest that we consider it instead as the secondary elaboration of classical narrative's text work.[57] It is, of course, useful to have an accurate description of classical narrative's strategies for secondary elaboration, but even a description as careful as that provided by Bordwell, Staiger, and Thompson remains just a description until it can be placed within a broader system such as the one described by the Freudian model.

Borrowing Freudian models is a dangerous enterprise, one that deserves a generous dose of precaution. In particular, we rapidly recognize the danger of adopting the hierarchical aspects of Freud's primary/secondary terminology. Returning us to the potential traps of dominance and logical priority, the Freudian model invites us to disenfranchise one aspect of the text in favor of another. While some genres may stress the paradigmatic more than others (the musical, for example, foregrounds paradigmatic concerns more than *film noir*), little is to be gained from simply reversing the order of dominance advanced by previous critics of classical narrative. Our goal must instead be to devise a new model in which the text's paradigmatic foundations and its syntagmatic facade would appear as interrelated and integral parts of the same edifice.

Recognizing the importance of visual models, in 1925 Freud represented the play between primary and secondary processes through the "mystic writing-pad" metaphor. What is written on the cover sheet remains embedded in the slate beneath even after the cover sheet has been lifted and the message rendered invisible. Only one message at a time is visible on the cover sheet, but the hidden slate is an ever-growing palimpsest, with all previous messages simultaneously present.[58]

For our purposes the plot metaphor—in all its meanings—is more appropriate. Before there can be a plot, the stakes must be set out. Once plotted, the space is open to investment. As schemes lead to intrigues and intrigues to plots, a purely spatial realm takes on a temporal dimension. Space, we might say, is thus narrativized. Virgin land become civilization, space transmuted into time, plot/parcel making way for plot/story. The text work necessarily involves—and conflates —both types of plotting. The linear intrigue makes no sense without the spatial gesture of setting out stakes; the stakes themselves take on reality only when they become part of a temporal investment. History cannot be written without plotting the deeds recording each land transaction, nor can it be conceived without the map identifying each plot transferred. We might be tempted to see one plot as primary in a temporal sense, as preceding the other, as a precondition for the other, yet this would assume that the culture sets the stakes permanently. On the contrary, the stakes themselves are constantly being modified. Space and time are bound together as equals.[59] The Freudian model, then, may serve as an indication of the important role that embedded material plays in an apparently linear and perfectly readable configuration. I will not follow Freud, however, in assigning secondary status to the process of displaying a complex set of paradigms in a syntagmatically satisfying sequence.

What about film theory tomorrow? What might this approach to classical narrative mean for cinematic analysis? It certainly does not mean that the notion of classical narrative is somehow untenable. Quite to the contrary, recognition of the "secondary elaboration" status of familiar classical narrative descriptions opens the notion of classical narrative to a new and more dynamic career. Far from spelling the closing of the classical narrative frontier, *The Classical Hollywood Cinema* provides us for the first time with a coherent description not only of Hollywood's secondary elaboration but also of the systems that helped develop and support it. What remains is for us to understand more fully how classical linearity fits within the overall vectorized tabularity evoked by Barthes.

One aspect of this move must necessarily involve a rediscovery of the paradigmatic analysis championed by Lévi-Strauss. Where Bordwell and Thompson follow the lead of Propp, Tomachevski, Jakobson, and other formalists primarily attentive to syntagmatic concerns, Lévi-Strauss and his American followers remain staunchly attentive to paradigmatic connections. An adequate theory of the interrelationship between the syntagmatic and the paradigmatic in classical narrative would combine these two approaches, relinquishing none of the specificity of either while recognizing the constant tension between the two that is characteristic not only of Hollywood cinema but of Western narrative as a whole since the Middle Ages.

Increased attention to the paradigmatic dimension of textual functioning will of necessity also lead to renewed interest in the dual-focus narrative tradition underlying single-focus narrative production. From martyrs' lives to melodrama, from the oral epic to the nineteenth-century serial novel, from the Alexandrian romance to preclassic silent cinema, dual-focus narrative establishes the stakes for the personal and cultural itineraries of single-focus texts.

With the return of the paradigmatic will come a new sensitivity to the techniques typically associated with texts that overtly stress the paradigmatic dimension. Historians of Hollywood classical narrative have consistently insisted on the importance of match-cutting, by which they usually mean match-on-action cutting.[60] Close attention to paradigmatic concerns, however, rapidly leads to the recognition that only metonymic matches are included within the traditional definition of match-cutting. Yet the metaphoric match is an essential part of Hollywood's stock-in-trade.

In a similar fashion, attention to Hollywood endings has largely been restricted to the hermeneutic code: the ending constitutes a solution to a problem established near the beginning. This single-focus approach systematically foregrounds concerns that we might recognize as predicate transformations, for the operative variables of the hermeneutic code are the changing predicates. The typical Hollywood ending involves more than just predicate transformation, however. The defeat of a foe, the displacement of a rival, the discomfiting of a foil are all likely to set up an opposition between the fate of one character and the fate of another, thus establishing a paradigmatic relationship between the two characters and a relation of subject substitution. While it can rarely be perceived directly from the viewpoint of the text's classical linearity, subject substitution provides an important complement to the more familiar predicate transformation.

For years the classical text was seen as opposed to the modernism of the Brechtian, the reflexive, and the dialogic. Then, in the wake of Barthes's S/Z, study after study attempted to champion this or that novel or style of filmmaking by demonstrating its relative modernity.

Perhaps we have now reached the point where we can acknowledge the shortsightedness of both enterprises. If so many apparently classical texts in fact have modernist leanings, then maybe the classical text is not as unitary as was once thought. It operates as a dialogic text precisely because its single-focus linearity presupposes an embedded dual-focus context. With one foot in history and the other still in myth, the classical narrative text must always speak with two voices, each using its own logic.

Take the case of the quintessential Hollywood film, Warner's 1942 *Casablanca*. The film's linear narrative stretches from Rick and Ilsa's idyll in Paris, through their reunion in Casablanca, to Rick's final heroic decision to send Ilsa off with her husband, while he and the French Captain Renault walk off into the distance toward a career in the Resistance. Like *Le père Goriot*, however, *Casablanca* does not owe its longevity to this familiar linear story. If *Casablanca* continues to enjoy success, it is not so much because of the ability of Bogie and Bergman to express the changing state of their emotions (in fact, in this film they are better at hiding emotions than expressing them), but because of the stakes for which they are playing. The secret of this film lies in its apocalyptic intensity. With the stereotypically sinister German Major Strasser and the archetypally pure Resistance hero Victor Laszlo embodying the values of Good and Evil, as represented by the Nazis and their victims, the atmosphere of *Casablanca* provides a melodramatic backdrop for the personal actions that capture our more immediate attention.

While character psychology appears to advance the film through a chain of cause-and-effect relationships, the major moments are either coincidental or only minimally motivated. What brings Ilsa to the very café run by the man she jilted in Paris? (Little more than coincidence.) How does Rick gain possession of the visas apparently needed to liberate Ilsa and her husband? (Through the minimally motivated activities of the Peter Lorre character Ugarte, who is killed off as soon as this function has been fulfilled.) What motivates Rick's decision to send Ilsa off to freedom with her husband? (The overall melodramatic setup much more than any clearly developed line of psychological reasoning.) How do Ilsa and her husband actually escape from Casablanca? (Not through the use of the much-touted visas, which turn out to be nothing more than a plot-unifying MacGuffin, but by an armed confrontation between the Nazi commander and his liberty-loving American opponent.) What leads Captain Renault, ever the self-serving neutral womanizer, to break his bottle of Vichy water and march off toward a life of bravery and moral rectitude? (Congenital hatred of the Hun? Embodiment of audience desires? No explanation is offered except to recognize that Renault is making the right decision within the film's melodramatic framework, even if the decision is not clearly motivated by the film's psychological progression.)

Nearly every character, every glance, serves to heighten the air of impending doom—or freedom. With the exception of *Casablanca*'s profiteers (and even profiteering has long been recognized as a common symptom of apocalyptic intensity), every character is directly defined by the conflict between national allegiance and personal dependence. An aroused soldier, a sad woman, an expectant old man— all embody the hope and freedom represented by the United States in opposition to the cruelty and imprisonment threatened by the Nazis. Even the paradigms of money, clothing, and linguistic accent contribute to this opposition. Indeed, this effect has been heightened by the fact that one of the film's descriptive terms—concentration camp —has since taken on such strong connotations of inhuman cruelty.

We should not conclude, though, that the entire power of the film's melodrama is spent on the local and the historical. By its very nature, melodrama carries eternal mythic qualities, like those that make Major Strasser embody not just Nazism but Evil itself, and those that make Bogie and Bergman an archetypal couple. The film's theme song further reinforces this sense that we are witnessing more than just an episode in the life of some guy named Rick.

> Moonlight and love songs, never out of date
> Hearts full of passion, jealousy, and hate
> Woman loves man and man must have his mate
> That no one can deny.
>
> It's still the same old story
> A fight for love and glory
> A case of do or die
> The world will always welcome lovers
> As time goes by.

Whenever the film moves toward psychology and time, it is wrenched back toward myth and eternity. Neither is dominant. It is the very conflict between the two that leads to the bittersweet conclusion.

Why does *Casablanca* continue to enchant audiences around the world? Because of its linear narrative causality? Yes, without a doubt. The film's suspense and expectation are carefully used to focus our attention on the future. As we dutifully fill all the plot's little gaps we settle comfortably into the spectator position allotted to us. Because of the film's melodramatic underpinnings? Yes again. *Casablanca* is a film about human allegiance to things of eternal beauty and value. The one pushes us toward a temporal solution, the union of Bogie and Bergman, the beautiful couple, while the other pulls us toward the eternal apotheosis of Good. That the melodramatic reasoning holds sway in the end does not mean that we should accept mythic causality as the film's dominant, overwhelming classical narrative causality. Instead, we should retain from this analysis the importance of reading the text—even at this schematic level—as an amalgam of deformed, embedded melodramatic material and carefully elaborated narrative classicism. To the personal identification that pushes us forward along a suspenseful linear hermeneutic corresponds a process of cultural identification that keeps us ever-mindful of a broader set of oppositions compared to which the problems of three people don't amount to a hill of beans.

Written according to familiar notions of dominance and logical priority, the traditional linear history of classical narrative reads like the legendary double-play combination: novel to well-made play to film. Borrowing its conception of narrative organization from the apparent linearity of the texts that constitute it, this kind of history has little room for gaps and excesses, for cloverleafs and dead ends.

A dialogical textual practice, however, calls for a dialogical approach to history as well—a heterogeneous history. For decades historians have labored to devise a linear history of the rise of the novel. Recognizing the novel as a different entity from romance, scholars have systematically combed late Renaissance society and literature in search of the conditions and practices that led to establishment of a new mode of literary production. The problem with this search for something new as the key to the rise of the novel is that it systematically precludes an understanding of the role of the old in the development of the new. For Bakhtin the newness of the novel lies precisely in its ability to swallow the old, to ingest and combine any number of discourses previously thought unmixable. Looked at from this point of view, the novel clearly requires a history that charts not only the new but also the old, along with the revised standards and methods of combining the old with the new.

A heterogeneous history of the novel would devote increased attention to those dual-focus strains, like the Alexandrian romance and the *roman feuilleton*, that never achieve cultural recognition. The history of the novel would thus presuppose understanding of the development of melodrama and the comic strip, of dime novels and serialized stories. More important still, such a history would dwell on the development of methods for integrating these dual-focus traditions into the novel: baldly, as in Sue; classically, as in Balzac; mentally, as in James. Instead of the linear history of a single form, the history of the novel would be recognized as the dialectical account of a matrix of dialogisms.

The history of classical Hollywood cinema would also undergo a vast upheaval. Genres would be recognized as cohering not only through their surface classical characteristics, but through their differing embedded melodramatic traditions as well. For not all melodrama is alike. Religious, social, and nationalistic strains provide textual foundations of a different nature. Just as these differences must have their history, so must the various methods and degrees of recognizing the text's dual-focus foundations. In some soils an underground stream will seep to the surface, in others it forms a spring, in others it erupts. Cinema history must become a geology, charting the soils, the strata, and the seams that permit the text's second voice to be heard.

Individual devices must no longer be seen as unitary, but as changing meaning as the textual dialogue proceeds. Bordwell points to the deadline as an important classical narrative element.[61] Yet the deadline is one of those moments when time-bound single-focus linear concerns and the spatial conflicts of dual-focus narrative most clearly combine to produce multiple determinations of individual events.

What is the history of the deadline? Are the conflictual deadlines of Griffith just like the psychologically conceived deadlines of the fifties? The history of the deadline depends in large part on the interplay between the differing types of determination at work in every Hollywood deadline. Where overdetermination is at work, the only priority must be dialogical—if we are to respect, that is, the meaning of those famous last words of the Eisenstein essay that formed my point of departure: "a unity of the whole screen image."

Notes

1. Sergei Eisenstein, "Dickens, Griffith, and the Film Today," in *Film Form*, ed. Jay Leyda (New York, 1949), 195.
2. From F. Dubrez Fawcett, *Dickens the Dramatist: On Stage, Screen and Radio* (London, 1952), 244–45.
3. Eisenstein, "Film Today," 200–201.
4. From A. Nicholas Vardac, *Stage to Screen: Theatrical Method from Garrick to Griffith* (Cambridge, Mass., 1949), 70–72.
5. See, for example, George Bluestone, *Novels into Film* (Berkeley, 1968); Marie-Claire Ropars-Wuilleumier, *De la littérature au cinéma: Genèse d'une écriture* (Paris, 1970); and Keith Cohen, *Film and Fiction: The Dynamics of Exchange* (New Haven, 1979).
6. For examples of this strategy, see Noel Carroll, "Becky Sharp Takes Over," and Janice Welsch, "The Horrific and the Tragic [on Mamoulian's *Dr. Jekyll and Mr. Hyde*]," in *The English Novel and the Movies*, ed. Michael Klein and Gillian Parker (New York, 1981), 108, 165.
7. Among the most complete (outside of the absence of theatrical intermediaries) are Klein and Parker, eds., *The English Novel and the Movies*, and *The Classic American Novel and the Movies*, ed. Gerald Peary and Roger Shatzkin (New York, 1977).
8. See Robert M. Henderson, *D. W. Griffith: The Years at Biograph* (New York, 1970); Richard Schickel, *D. W. Griffith: An American Life* (New York, 1985); Elaine Mancini, "D. W. Griffith et les romanciers de son temps: Le commentaire social," in *David Wark Griffith: Colloque international*, ed. Jean Mottet (Paris, 1984), 195–208; and Cooper C. Graham, Steven Higgins, Elaine Mancini, and Joao Luiz Vieira, *D. W. Griffith and the Biograph Company* (Metuchen, N.J., 1985).
9. Henderson, *Years at Biograph*, 27, 101, 240. Henderson's willingness to conflate novelistic and theatrical versions is exemplified by the following sentence: "The next to last film of the first California season was an ambitious adaptation of Helen Hunt Jackson's *Ramona*, the same story in which Griffith had appeared as an actor" (101). The use of the term *story* to bridge the gap (and erase the differences) between novel and play is a characteristic move.

10   See, for example, David A. Cook, *A History of Narrative Film* (New York, 1981), 73.

11   Henderson, *Years at Biograph*, 152. Schickel, *An American Life*, claims that Griffith's film was directly based on the Aldrich play (190–93). The complexity of determining exact sources for Griffith's feature films is perhaps best revealed in Sarah Kozloff's analysis of novel, serialization, play, novelization, and film sources for *Way Down East*, in "*Way Down East* and *Tess of the D'Urbervilles*," *Literature/Film Quarterly* 13.1 (1985): 35–41.

12   Warren French, *Frank Norris* (New York, 1962), 32.

13   For a complete treatment of the practical and theoretical problems involved in reading *A Farewell to Arms* as an adaptation of Hemingway's novel, see Robert Arnold, Nicholas Peter Humy, and Ana M. Lopez, "Rereading Adaptation: *A Farewell to Arms*," *IRIS* 1.1 (1983): 101–14. For other examples, see A. Nicholas Vardac, *Stage to Screen*, especially 59ff., 63–64, 69ff., 76, 79, 83, and 220ff.; and John L. Fell, *Film and the Narrative Tradition* (Norman, 1974), especially 17, 21, 24, 30 (though chap. 4 of Fell's book, on the novel, is disappointing in its failure to recognize the potential importance of theatrical adaptations of novels with what Fell terms "filmlike pre-dispositions" [54]).

14   "Strictly speaking," says Bazin, "one could make a play out of *Madame Bovary* or *The Brothers Karamazov*." While recognizing the possibility of such an adaptation, Bazin has clearly chosen what he believes are extreme examples, unlikely ever to have spawned theatrical versions (André Bazin, *What is cinema?* trans. Hugh Gray [Berkeley, 1967], 83).

15   *The Brothers Karamazov*, in *Moscow Art Theatre Series of Russian Plays*, ed. Oliver M. Sayler (New York, 1923).

16   Early editions of *Variety* and *Moving Picture World* regularly insist on a film's novelistic paternity, recognizing a recent theatrical adaptation as a second parent only when the film borrows its title from the dramatic version rather than from the original novel (e.g., the United Artists 1926 release of Herbert Wilcox's *The Only Way*, adapted from Sir John Martin Harvey's 1899 stage version of Dickens's *Tale of Two Cities*). There is good reason for cinema to avoid mentioning its debt to the stage, especially through the teens, for the popular theater remained cinema's strongest competitor through the war years.

17   Eisenstein is perfectly aware that Griffith's debt is more often to stage productions than to Dickens's novels ("Film Today," 199, 224, 230), yet his use of the metonymy "Dickens" to refer to "theatrical versions of Dickens" has led nearly all of his readers to forget the theatrical connection and to privilege the novelistic influence.

18   Roland Barthes, *Le degré zéro de l'écriture* (Paris, 1953), especially 29ff., 49ff., where Barthes mirrors Eisenstein's identification of Dickens and Griffith with bourgeois society.

19   Bazin, *What is Cinema?* 29. This essay is made up of separate texts written in 1950, 1952, and 1955.

20   Roland Barthes, *S/Z* (Paris, 1970), 10, and *Le plaisir du texte* (Paris, 1973); see also Emile Benveniste, *Eléments de linguistique générale* (Paris, 1966), 237–50.

21 See, for example, Peter Wollen, "Godard and Counter-Cinema: *Vent d'Est*," *After-image* 4 (Autumn 1972): 7–16. Wollen's article is built on yet another series of specific oppositions: narrative transitivity vs. narrative intransitivity, identification vs. estrangement, transparency vs. foregrounding, single diegesis vs. multiple diegesis, closure vs. aperture, pleasure vs. displeasure, and fiction vs. reality.

22 Bazin, *What is Cinema?* 29; Barthes, *Plaisir du texte*, 20–21, 25–26.

23 David Bordwell, Janet Staiger, and Kristin Thompson, *The Classical Hollywood Cinema: Film Style and Mode of Production to 1960* (New York, 1985), 3–6.

24 For a traditional historical account of the growth of classicism, see René Bray, *La formation de la doctrine classique en France* (Paris, 1927). A more recent view of the evolution of classical theater may be found in Jacques Schérer, *La dramaturgie classique en France* (Paris, 1966). The best statement of received notions regarding classicism is Henri Peyre, *Qu'est-ce que le classicisme?* (Paris, 1965).

25 See Thierry Maulnier, *Racine* (Paris, 1936), and *Lecture de Phèdre* (Paris, 1943).

26 André Gide, "Billets à Angèle," in *French Classicism: A Critical Miscellany*, ed. Jules Brody (Englewood Cliffs, 1966), 65.

27 André Gide, quoted in Peyre, *Qu'est-ce que le classicisme?* 144.

28 Lucien Goldmann, *Le Dieu caché* (Paris, 1956); Charles Mauron, *L'inconscient dans l'oeuvre et la vie de Racine* (Aix-en-Provence, 1957); Philip Butler, *Classicisme et baroque dans l'oeuvre de Racine* (Paris, 1959); and Roland Barthes, *Sur Racine* (Paris, 1963).

29 Peter Brooks, *The Melodramatic Imagination: Balzac, Henry James, Melodrama, and the Mode of Excess* (New Haven, 1976), 148–49. Thomas Elsaesser also stresses the melodramatic nature of popular nineteenth-century novels in "Tales of Sound and Fury: Observations on the Family Melodrama," in *Film Genre Reader*, ed. Barry Keith Grant (Austin, 1986), 284–85. Christine Gledhill has recently made still broader claims regarding the role of melodrama as the repressed of bourgeois modes of representation in "Dialogue," *Cinema Journal* 25.4 (1986): 44–48.

30 On single- and dual-focus narration see my "Medieval Narrative vs. Popular Assumptions: Revising Inadequate Typology," *Diacritics* 4 (1974): 12–19; "Two Types of Opposition and the Structure of Latin Saints' Lives," *Medievalia et Humanistica*, n.s., 6 (1975): 1–11; "Interpreting Romanesque Narrative: Conques and the Roland," *Olifant* 5 (October 1977): 4–28; *The American Film Musical* (Bloomington, 1987), especially chap. 2. A long book currently in preparation, tentatively entitled *A Theory of Narrative*, will treat this approach to narrative in greater detail.

31 On the play adapted from Balzac's novel, see Pierre Barbéris, *Le père Goriot* (Paris, 1972). It is interesting to note that Balzac's contemporaries accused him of plagiarizing for his novel another melodrama, Etienne's *Les deux gendres*; see Pierre Citron, preface to *Le père Goriot* (Paris, 1966), 13.

32 Brooks, *Melodramatic Imagination*, 121.

33 René Girard, *Deceit, Desire, and the Novel*, trans. Yvonne Freccero (Baltimore, 1965).

34 M. M. Bakhtin, *The Dialogic Imagination: Four Essays*, ed. Michael Holquist,

trans. Caryl Emerson and Michael Holquist (Austin, 1981). See especially the essays entitled "Epic and Novel" and "Discourse in the Novel."

35 It is an adaptation of *L'assommoir* that causes the father's reform in Griffith's 1909 film, *The Drunkard's Reformation*.

36 Emile Zola, *Ebauche* for *L'assommoir*, original in the Bibliothèque Nationale, Nouvelles Acquisitions Françaises 10.271, fol. 142. Reprinted in Emile Zola, *Oeuvres complètes*, ed. Maurice Le Blond (Paris, 1928), vol. 8.

37 Zola, *Oeuvres complètes*, 8: 473.

38 See Christopher Prendergast, *Balzac: Fiction and Melodrama* (London, 1978), for another example of careful work on Balzac's debt to melodrama that nevertheless sidesteps the question of melodramatic adaptations from novels. The most careful scholarship on the relationship between novels and theatrical adaptations is in Martin Meisel, *Realizations: Narrative, Pictorial, and Theatrical Arts in Nineteenth-Century England* (Princeton, 1983), especially 247–82.

39 Bordwell, Staiger, and Thompson, *Classical Hollywood Cinema*, 13ff., 168–71.

40 Ibid., 12. On the notion of the dominant, see also Kristin Thompson, *Eisenstein's Ivan the Terrible: A Neoformalist Analysis* (Princeton, 1981), 34, 63–67.

41 Roman Jakobson, "The Dominant," in *Readings in Russian Poetics: Formalist and Structuralist Views*, ed. Ladislav Matejka and Kristyna Pomorska, trans. Herbert Eagle (Cambridge, Mass., 1971), 82. Though Jakobson's 1935 essay lecture is often cited as the source of the notion of the dominant, the concept was of course already widely accepted in formalist circles during the 1920s. Sergei Eisenstein also uses the term repeatedly in the 1920s essays included in Leyda, ed., *Film Form*.

42 Jurij Tynjanov, "On Literary Evolution," in Matejka and Pomorska, eds., *Readings in Russian Poetics*, 72.

43 Jakobson, "The Dominant," 84.

44 Bordwell, Staiger, and Thompson, *Classical Hollywood Cinema*, 12.

45 Barthes, *S/Z*, 36–37.

46 Roland Barthes, "Introduction à l'analyse structurale des récits," *Communications* 8 (1966): 1–27; see also Roland Barthes, *Image, Music, Text*, trans. Stephen Heath (New York, 1977), 79–124.

47 Bordwell, Staiger, and Thompson, *Classical Hollywood Cinema*, 72; see also 21 and 71.

48 Ibid., 8, 38–39.

49 Ibid., 177.

50 David Bordwell, *Narration in the Fiction Film* (Madison, 1985), 276ff.

51 Ibid., 157.

52 Ibid., 349. In this footnote, Bordwell is referring to my article, "The American Film Musical: Paradigmatic Structure and Mediatory Function," *Wide Angle* 2.2 (1978): 10–17.

53 Bordwell, Staiger, and Thompson, *Classical Hollywood Cinema*, 36. Bordwell is here paraphrasing Raymond Bellour, "To Analyze, to Segment," *Quarterly Review of Film Studies* (August 1976): 331.

54 Bordwell, *Narration in the Fiction Film*, 159.

55 Thompson, *Eisenstein's Ivan the Terrible*, 287. On the notion of excess, see also Stephen Heath, "Film and System: Terms of Analysis," *Screen* 16 (Spring 1975): 7–77. Barthes is commonly taken to be referring to the same concept in "The Third Meaning," in *Image, Music, Text*, 52–68. In fact, however, Barthes is dealing with a type of meaning that is inaccessible to systematic analysis, while the very definition of excess for Thompson and Heath depends on the notion of system.

56 Thompson, *Eisenstein's Ivan the Terrible*, 294.

57 In using the term "text work," based on the Freudian model, I follow Thierry Kuntzel, in "Le travail du film," *Communications* 19 (1972): 25–39, and "Le travail du film, 2," *Communications* 23 (1975): 136–89. As a rule, Kuntzel is far more interested in displacement, condensation, and figuration than in secondary elaboration, but see 161–62 of the second article.

58 On Freud's 1925 essay, "A Note Upon the 'Mystic Writing-Pad,'" see Thierry Kuntzel, "A Note Upon the Filmic Apparatus," *Quarterly Review of Film Studies* 1 (August 1976): 266–71.

59 On the necessity for equal treatment of paradigmatic and syntagmatic concerns in classical narrative, see my "Classical Narrative Revisited: *Grand Illusion*," *Purdue Film Studies Annual* 1 (1976): 87–98. When first delivered at the Purdue Film Conference, this paper provided David Bordwell and me our first opportunity to spar over a topic that has often brought us together in friendly disagreement over the years.

60 See, for example, Noël Burch, *Theory of Film Practice* (New York, 1973), especially chap. 1; and Bordwell, Staiger, and Thompson, *Classical Hollywood Cinema*, 46, 69, 231, 278, 305.

61 Bordwell, *Narration in the Fiction Film*, 159ff., and Bordwell, Staiger, and Thompson, *Classical Hollywood Cinema*, 44ff.

Form Wars: The Political Unconscious

of Formalist Theory

Bill Nichols

★ ★ ★ ★ ★ ★ Narrative's not the thing it used to be. More than standing as one form of artistic expression to be worried over by those
attending to the nature of art, narrative has become a central preoccupation in its own right, pushing matters of art and levels of culture to the side. What is a narrative? From that structuralist question
issued an agenda distinct from ones that emerge from questions about
artistic expression, literary creation, or the relationship of art and
society. An object distinct from literary questions of aesthetic value
came into being. And for a while it appeared that this object might
become the raw material of a science. From Northrop Frye's *Anatomy
of Criticism* to the Christian Metz of *Language and Cinema*, the stage
was set for the science, or poetics, of narrative.

This was always, however, a science with a difference. The object
was not an aspect of nature, as in the natural sciences, nor of directly
manifested human behavior, as in the social sciences, but a verbal,
written or semiotic structure, a representation distinguishable from

other semiotic structures less on the basis of aesthetic values than of discursive features. How does narrative differ from other discursive structures that might be called, collectively, non-narrative? What social functions does narrative play that other structures do not? And what qualities do representations possess that narrative inflects in systematic ways?

These questions take science into unfamiliar terrain, and other issues compound the difficulty. The study of the individual work, even when filtered through scientisms like "textual system," invites an attention to specificity that belies the general principles upon which a science need rest. (In fact, many of the structural and post-structural theories that raised a scientific banner seem in retrospect quite formulaic and reductive.) Matters of ideology, central to so much discussion of narrative systems from Roland Barthes's *Mythologies* to Fredric Jameson's *The Political Unconscious*, also confound any notion of an objective narrative structure readily detached from its historical, social context. But perhaps most forcefully of all, psychoanalysis and feminism knocked the idea of a narrative science for a large, political loop. Narrative, once it was linked irrevocably to Oedipus, lost its innocence. Stories place us within their webs of meaning in ways inseparable from questions of the politics of gender. They do so in ways that are intimately related to narrative structure and the psychic processes by which we engage with a story, and that extend far beyond matters of content. These are issues that call for qualification, critique, rereading, rewriting, and contestation more than for taxonomies, anatomies, and dispassionate science. And in the pursuit of these issues the original impetus and yearning for a science or poetics of narrative has been largely turned aside, ignored, or rejected.

A capsule summary of what several writers have said about narrative suggests some of the ways in which questions of ideology and gender have provided the political ground against which the figure of narrative comes into view:

HAYDEN WHITE: [Historiographic] narrative masks its status as discourse to imply that historical reality has the appearance of narrative and, with it, an inherent moral order. Narratives address issues of order, desire, and law, authority and its legitimation or subversion.

"The historical narrative . . . reveals to us a world that is putatively 'finished,' done with, over, and yet not dissolved, not falling apart. In this world, reality wears the mask of a meaning, the completeness and fullness of which we can only *imagine*. . . . The demand for closure in the historical story is a demand, I suggest, for moral meaning, a demand that sequences of real events be assessed as to their significance as elements of a *moral* drama."

COLIN MACCABE: [Realist, Hollywood] narrative cannot represent contradiction because there is a hierarchy in which the final level [of authorial omniscience] functions to embody truth or certainty. Such narrative is inadequate to a radical politics of any kind because the form recuperates any type of radical content, placing it within the grip of Truth. It is the form itself that must be rejected. Moments of subversion must give way to strategies of subversion.

RAYMOND BELLOUR: [Classic, Hollywood] narrative form embodies the oedipal trajectory (masculine maturation through "tests" of ability and through the discovery of a suitable mate—a trajectory usually subsumed under the categories of sex and violence in popular criticism). Narrative is the enactment of desire. Narrative posits woman as different in order to reassure men that they are the same as those other men who produce the narrative, define its moral order, and shape the destiny of characters accordingly.

LAURA MULVEY: [Hollywood, dominant] narrative constructs men's pleasure at women's expense. Men identify with active male characters and adopt either sadistic or fetishistic/voyeuristic relations to women characters. These narratives take an ambivalent view of women because the view given is from within the imaginary where women do not have the phallus and symbolize its loss or lack and are therefore a threat as well as an attraction. Male pleasure at the expense of women must be rejected and a new aesthetics created.

ROLAND BARTHES: [Classic, readerly] narrative is the result of weaving five major codes together to give the sense of the real even though this is entirely a textual effect. These codes can be dissected into their smallest units (units which the analyst constructs) to show how they achieve the effect of a lifelike narrative dependent on the naturalizing agency of the sentence. Narratives work "on the page" to lift the reader "off the page." Psychological character attributes like volition, pensiveness, and the sense of an unsaid wealth of mystery and complexity are all the result of specific textual strategies that give the effect of a world without its substance and a logic without its proofs.

FREDRIC JAMESON: [Classic, novelistic] narrative must always be historically located on three levels: in terms of (1) the experiential embodiment of social contradictions, constituting a felt reality that, in fact, may never have had so strong and compelling a presence prior to its embodiment; (2) the textual and often dialogical manifestation and working out of central aspects of class conflict and discourse such as *ressentiment* in nineteenth-century novels; and (3) the history and ideology of form where the novel at any given moment carries within it traces of sign systems from distinct modes of production (patriarchal or oedipal modes, for example, as well as capitalist ones). Poised between ideology and utopia, narratives require a double hermeneutic that is in turn both suspicious and revelatory, teasing out the links between history, the unconscious of hegemony and ideology on the one hand and history, the political unconscious and utopia on the other.

DAVID BORDWELL: "We can, in short, study narrative as a *process*, the activity of selecting, arranging, and rendering story material in order to achieve specific time-bound effects on a perceiver. I shall call this process *narration*, and it is the central concern of this book. . . . I argue that filmic narration involves two principal formal systems, syuzhet [plot] and style, which cue the spectator to frame hypotheses and draw inferences. [The spectator] is a hypothetical entity executing the operations relevant to constructing a story out of the film's representations. . . . [Metaphors like the "position" or "place" of the subject] lead us to conceive of the perceiver as backed into a corner by conventions of perspective, editing, narrative point of view, and psychic unity. A film, I suggest, does not 'position' anybody. A film cues the spectator to execute a definable variety of *operations*."

This last summation, culled from the first twenty-nine pages of Bordwell's *Narration in the Fiction Film*, sounds a different note.[1] The quest for scientific knowledge, with all its ostensible brackets of the social, ideological, and political, is with us once again, now in the form of a continuation of the work of the Russian formalists and the resurrection of the project of a narrative poetics.

Like the champions of this project in the 1970s, who promoted their cause in *Screen* and elsewhere, Bordwell is intolerant of impressionistic criticism, thematic readings that lack a solid formal basis, and analyses that neglect underlying structures and processes in favor of meaning or explication. But Bordwell is also intolerant of theories that try to cram filmic narration into the confined categories of linguistics (especially the *histoire/discours* distinction). He does not choose to base his poetics on the terra infirma of structuralist linguistics but instead turns to formalism and cognitive theory. With this move, Bordwell overcomes one of the major limitations of the earlier quest for a science of narrative—the disregard of the viewer in favor of textual structures—although not the far greater one of disregard for the *subjectivity* of the viewer as historical being.

The achievement, though, is not trivial. Whereas the earlier science of semiotics painted itself into a corner full of arid taxonomies that floated in an ahistorical ether, Bordwell points the way to a science, or poetics, centered on how a viewer might process narrational information. In other words, he demonstrates what a true science of narration might be by defining an object of study both suitable to a science and yet not totally devoid of intersubjective relations. He also demonstrates the limitations that continue to plague any poetics of narrative: the price we pay for the science we get is quite a steep one.

Why formalism? Why a poetics? I suggest some answers to these questions in another article that concentrates on the ways in which politically motivated criticism, broadly conceived, has, in recent years, become lumped into the monolithic category of "ideological criticism" the better to dismiss it as single-minded and insensitive.[2] My assertion there, and here, is that this monolith is an imaginary construct that could only be posited from an antithetical position since it flattens significant differences. The converse point seems far more apt: that "ideological criticism" readily fractures into a plurality of approaches (gay, lesbian, black, third world, feminist, psychoanalytic, Marxist, sociological, poststructuralist, and so on) which are often inimicable in specific ways and share a fairly diffuse affinity. What ideological criticisms in fact lack is a master code or narrative, a fixed agenda (such as Marxism is wont to provide) that would unify them. Unity itself has fallen into question and a politics of affinity replaces it. This very diversity—a turning away from "master narratives" and masters, from grand theory and the self-legitimated, authorizing agency at its center—necesssarily welcomes the pluralism that terms like "ideological criticism" belie. The value of this designation lies less in its descriptive accuracy than in its rhetorical agency: it helps make room for a presumably open-ended, nonmonolithic, nonideological theory and criticism that will restore those qualities of nuance and detail, complexity and contingency, that ideological preoccupations neglect.

Neo-formalism is one such alternative to "ideological criticism" and its most active proselytizer is David Bordwell.[3] This approach values the strict delimitation of the object of study, rigorous attentiveness to textual specificity, and an emphasis on pattern or order as a form of organization in contradistinction to thematic meaning or ideological effect. Neo-formalism may not simply contest the meanings that a feminism, say, might find, but contest the very grounds on which meaning rests. Thus in a debate with the editor of *Enclitic*, Bordwell compares a Lacanian analysis of the look, specifically the glance of a character in a fiction film and how this constructs a voyeuristic dynamics, with his own approach to the look and the construction of narrative space: ". . . the analysis of the articulation of space in a sequence seems to me no less semantic in revealing how a denotative space is (or is not) constructed—this construction yielding meanings and effects."[4] *Which* meanings and effects, however, becomes an issue deferred, perhaps interminably.

At best, the formal analysis of denotative dimensions of film narrative may offer the solid, scientific base upon which more ideological criticisms can rest. In the "conclusion" to *Narration in the Fiction Film*, Bordwell admits that his work does not answer questions of sexuality and fantasy, nor cultural, economic, and ideological questions, but it may set out the terrain upon which such matters can be analyzed more clearly. "Studies of ideology in cinema can usefully recognize that through schemata a society's ideological constructs are taken up by its members; and that narrational modes are central mediations between ideology and its manifestations in artworks." He ends his point with an injunction: "If ideological analysis is to avoid vacuous overgeneralization, it must reckon in the concrete ways that narrational processes function in filmic representation."[5] But can a neo-formalism provide the scientific knowledge that might become the ground for ideological analysis? Factual knowledge seems less at issue than the concepts and categories used to generate facts. As Bordwell himself argues, in a prolix rebuttal to an equally prolix critique of "the Wisconsin project" (works by Bordwell, Kristin Thompson, and Janet Staiger) in *Screen* magazine, ". . . the materialist researcher should hold that the theorist's conceptual frame of reference at least filters what concepts and data are selected and perhaps even governs what concepts and data are recognizable."[6]

Whether Bordwell himself subscribes to this position is left unclear, but Fredric Jameson offers no such uncertainty. In his dramatic critique and use of the work of Greimas, Jameson argues that Marxism subsumes other interpretive modes and retains some of their findings through a "radical historicizing of their mental operations." Jameson goes on to say that Greimas's semiotic rectangle can not only be a tool of Marxist analysis but that by analyzing the tool itself, it can be shown to map "the limits of a specific ideological consciousness and [mark] the conceptual points beyond which that consciousness cannot go, and between which it is condemned to oscillate."[7]

Bordwell's analysis of narrational process has many strengths, not least among them its supple blend of theory, criticism, and, to a more limited extent, history. In fact, much of the instructiveness of his work lies in the close readings he provides of diverse films, precisely those parts of the book most quickly set aside in reviews, where his theory of cognitive processing is more easily summarized and debated. These readings are all the more distinctive for not focusing on moments of subversion or crisis, on gaps or fissures, on the hidden apparatus that achieves "suture," continuity, or closure, and for not making broad claims on the basis of cursory and selective reference to texts of dubious representativeness. Bordwell's readings tend to focus on what often seem the most pedestrian moments of sometimes pedestrian films as well as the seemingly unremarkable moments of extraordinary ones. His discussion of a dinner scene from *Miss Lulu Bett*, for example, identifies how narration constructs a scenographic space of volume, consistency, and axes of action relative to the camera to orient us in relation to characters and their conduct. His discussion of time in *The Spider's Strategem* demonstrates how the film embeds inconsistent cues about temporal relationships and subjectivity (the alignment of the camera with the character's point of view) in very concrete and minute ways in order to render space and time fundamentally ambiguous.[8] The readings exemplify processes at work in classical and art-cinema narration, but do so by showing how such processes are embedded in the most local levels of the text where cognitive activity is continuously at play.

These critical readings lend his theoretical account considerable weight by insisting that the theory accounts for films in their entirety rather than, as much poststructural criticism has, suggesting that the bulk of a film is devoted to a repetitive process of containing excess, positioning the viewer, and assuring ideological effects—processes that leave little to specify or puzzle at a local level unless crisis is in the air. These poststructural accounts seek out telling moments when ruptures or reflexivity appear, flaws or barings of the device occur, in order to expose the overall ideological operation.

A prime example of this more sporadic reading strategy is Stephen Heath's "Narrative Space," an essay that gives excellent articulation to the poststructural critique of narrative but that also allows a general theory to govern narrative process so consistently that the routine operations of a text become unproblematic. In this context specific scenes and instances are cited that expose what is usually lost from view. An example is Heath's astute selection of a single moment in Hitchcock's *Suspicion*—when a detective becomes inexplicably and improperly distracted by a portrait—as a moment of risk. The detective's roving eye threatens to derail the narrative. It momentarily threatens to expose the constant process of containment that holds the narrative on track and prevents its slippage toward "somewhere else again, another scene, another story, another space."[9]

Bordwell's attempt to account for every moment as part of a continuous process, never inactive and never mechanical, holds great appeal in a time of symptomatic readings. He never fails to attend to the entire body of the text rather than rush to identify symptoms. This is quite vividly demonstrated in his reading of what he somewhat oddly calls the "parametric" mode of narration: films that give priority to style rather than plot (or syuzhet). He dwells on works of stylistic sparseness, such as those by Dreyer and Bresson where there is a great temptation to seize on the few laconic moments that seem to bear the full weight of the emotional and thematic import, or on the specific, recurring strategies that seem to support the work's characteristic themes. Bordwell takes issue with both of these approaches and shows no small measure of disdain for (unidentified) thematic critics who squeeze meaning from works not designed to yield it: "The sense of an order whose finest grain we can glimpse but not grasp helps produce the connotative effects of which thematic criticism records the trace. These effects arise from a formal manipulation that is, in a strong sense, *nonsignifying*—closer to music than to the novel."[10] Bordwell likens parametric, sparse styles to serial music and, through a close analysis of passages of *Pickpocket* and other films, shows how minute variations in stylistic parameters like shot/reverse-shot or camera tracking movements generate a sense of order and aesthetic pleasure that may also be mistaken for ineffable or religious meaning.

In large measure, Bordwell argues that the effects of narrative process present us with a coherence which bears meaning because it is organized to do so; it is therefore possible to describe this process and its coherence without attending to the meanings that derive from it. Further, to attend to meanings without first establishing a narrative poetics typically results in positing anthropomorphisms (like the "ideal spectator," "implied author," and omniscient or "invisible observer") where none exist or where they exist as secondary consequences, not initiating agencies. He argues that narration may mimic everyday encounters between senders and receivers of messages and cue us to posit a narrator or authorial presence but that this is not at all necessary. When it does occur, Bordwell argues, "we must recall that this narrator is the product of specific, organizational principles, historical factors, and viewers' mental sets. . . . [T]his sort of narrator does not create the narration; the narration, appealing to historical norms of viewing, creates the narrator." [11]

Narration may therefore be read as emanating from an anthropomorphic source, but this is a procedural effect much like the impression that a computer playing chess is "intelligent," and thus human. Bordwell prefers to focus on the process itself, not its effects or meanings. He also prefers to eschew any phenomenological impulse to ponder the trace of an intersubjective address that such locutions as "implied author" invoke. For him, narrational process involves continuous, active engagement by the viewer instead of the passive "positioning" described by poststructural theory. Though active, it requires primarily problem-solving intelligence rather than socially grounded evaluative or interpretive skill.

Cognitive activity begins with our predisposition to sort sensory information into patterns that lead to inferences about the world that then guide subsequent information processing. Bordwell calls the patterns that emerge "schemata." Once schemata form, comprehension precedes by top-down and bottom-up processes of inference-making and hypothesis-formation. We make assumptions and hold to expectations, subjecting the process to constant review and revision. Knowledge becomes a model we use to answer questions about the world. The model we form in relation to fictional worlds is the fabula: "the imaginary construct we create, progressively and retroactively, was termed by Formalists the *fabula*," or story. "The fabula is thus a pattern which perceivers of narrative create through assumptions and inferences." [12] The fabula is an expanded version of those end-of-film recountings by crime investigators of what-really-happened-and-why-it-was-important that take place in certain detective films.

Interestingly, this definition aligns the fabula with those artificial intelligence models of knowledge where problem-solving occurs without reference to human subjectivity. A mental model is some kind of machinery or set of operants that "[provide] us with a simple explanation of what we mean by knowledge: *Jack's knowledge about A is simply whichever mental models, processes, or agencies Jack's other agencies can use to answer questions about A.*" [13] The process of fabula-formation demonstrates our knowledge of narrative at the level of comprehension. Narrative poetics studies this process in a scientific spirit, in the sense that, according to Benjamin Hrushovski, the term science "delimits conveniently the purposes of such a systematic field of knowledge, which has as its primary aim the understanding of a field of reality and the construction of theoretical models for that purpose, and is clearly distinct from subjective, impressionistic or didactic criticism." [14]

Narrative comprehension becomes an exact science. The viewer, the "hypothetical entity," executes operations based on inferences and assumptions to generate the fabula from the syuzhet, which provides cues as to the order, frequency, and duration of events. The viewer performs tasks that can be readily scored against a master answer key since messy questions of connotation and interpretation have been deferred. This allows a poetics or science of narrative to identify its object as narrational process, something which yields repeatable and verifiable results (the fabula). Impressionism and subjectivity are avoided; objectivity and scientific knowledge prevail.

Yet the process of comprehension must contend with the nonmaterial presence of the fabula. In fiction, the fabula is our creation, the story we construct from the material cues given to us by the plot and style. What's more, the narrational process has a variety of tactics available to organize its presentation of fabula information: it can convey different degrees of knowledgeableness about important data from highly restricted—limited to a single character's knowledge— to completely unrestricted. It can signal different degrees of "subjectivity" or alignment with the thoughts and perceptions of characters. Narratives vary in their degree of self-consciousness: from a strong sense of narrative overtness, where the viewer is made aware that "a tale is being presented for a perceiver," to the invisibility usually attributed to "classic" or readerly narrative. A narrative may also exhibit varying degrees of communicativeness: what the narrative's degree of knowledge entitles it to know may or may not be relayed to the viewer in a direct and timely fashion. Information may be suppressed only to be revealed later, as in many detective films, or suppressed never to be revealed, as in many "art-cinema" films where ambiguity becomes a prized effect. Finally, there is tone, that array of "judgmental factors," in Bordwell's scheme, that suggests the attitude of the narrative toward its own characters, or viewers, a quality that receives minimal attention in the remainder of the study.[15]

Bordwell's model is one of "hollow forms," operational processes devoid of any necessary meaning, that then cluster themselves to establish norms (or paradigms). These norms arise in history but, accepting the license offered by Hrushovski's description of a historical poetics, Bordwell proposes to study them synchronically, as stable systems existing in history, persisting across time, but relatively independent of the messinesses of historical determinations. (Bordwell calls his approach "diachronic" as opposed to a synchronic taxonomy of procedural schemata. I prefer to see his approach as the distillation of a synchronic system from its historical surrounding.) Extrinsic norms are the most pertinent historically: "the canonized style, the mainstream practice—and deviations from that." Historical study, for Bordwell, is the effort to determine how extrinsic norms combine into patterns less variable than genre and more fundamental than schools, movements, and "entire national cinemas."[16] History is the realm from which the synchronic order of a mode of narration can be extracted by the scholar who then describes the formal order of the object he has defined. Showing that a mode of narration actually existed, out of all the possible modes of narration that might have existed, confers the title "historical" on Bordwell's enterprise. Questions of how the rest of existence, or history, receives representation, how history impinges on, or how narration invokes the viewer's subjectivity or compels paradox and contradiction in relation to a given mode, lie outside Bordwell's restricted conception of historical placement.

Two of Bordwell's modes—classical and art-cinema—are quite extensive in historical scope, but the other two—Soviet historical-materialist and "parametric" narration—are surprisingly limited in their historical occurrence. How these modes impinge on one another, and, in particular, to what extent the dominant, classical mode of narration conditions or inflects the historical form of the other modes, which can be seen as revolts against it, remains unexamined. Each mode occupies a separate piece of historical turf. Each mode simply invites the viewer to take a different tack. Classical narration asks the viewer to "construe the syuzhet and the stylistic system in a single way: construct a denotative, univocal, integral fabula." The "art-cinema" mode of narration charges the viewer with the task, "Interpret this film, and interpret it so as to maximize ambiguity." The "historical-materialist" mode of narration, exemplified by the Soviet cinema of the twenties, asks the viewer to regard the syuzhet as a rhetorical argument of conceptual simplicity accompanied by stylistic complexity; "this is done by calling on procedural schemata that urge: when in doubt, construct a fabula event as perceptually forceful and politically significant." [17]

Bordwell's concept of history and historical placement then leads him to argue that the spirit of historical-materialist narration lives on in an interrogative cinema deriving from Brecht and posing more open-ended questions of political efficacy for a contemporary scene where "no fixed doctrine serves as a point of departure." [18] Although this demonstrates a certain measure of historical endurance for the mode, within Bordwell's self-imposed confines of the feature fiction film (mainly before 1970), it overlooks at least two more intriguing questions: the degree to which historical-materialist narration exists in ideological tension with the classical mode that has co-opted it as "Hollywood montage" (those succinct summaries of duration or process in which conflict disappears in favor of evocation), and the extent to which historical-materialist narration informed a great deal of documentary filmmaking practice only to reemerge in yet another sanitized narrational mode as the television commercial.

Ads repeatedly display the characteristics Bordwell attributes to historical-materialist narration: argument by example, forceful perceptual engagement, and significant political effect, albeit a politics measured in terms of consumption and an innoculation against any more direct political involvement. What Bordwell says of Soviet cinema applies uncannily well to advertisements: ". . . the fabula world stands for a set of abstract propositions whose validity the film at once presupposes and reasserts. The film's argument works by appeal to example; the narrative cause and effect demonstrate the necessity [for a given proposition]. . . . Narrative causality is construed as supraindividual . . . [C]haracters thus get defined chiefly through their class position, job, social actions, and political views. . . . [T]hey become prototypes of whole classes, milieux, or historical epochs."[19]

None of these parallels and transformations receive consideration, however, leaving the "history" of this mode strangely pristine, as if a relatively obscure interrogative cinema had quietly gone its own way alongside the other modes and the cinema had remained thematically, formally, and institutionally immune to television and commerce. He disregards the massive struggle to channel meaning and control effect that the broad social history of montage, rhetoric, style, and historical-materialist narration might examine. By letting each mode exist in its own temporal cocoon, Bordwell avoids the urgent questions of how "revolts" against reigning norms arise, contend, undergo repression or distortion, and do so in relation to formal properties as well as thematic issues. Instead, his approach tends to dramatize how formal systems take on a life of their own, drawing on historical referents to vitalize their own dynamic, but remaining impressively immune to any materialist history.

Bordwell's priorities lie with the formal system that a poetics provides for study. This leads him to pose a relation between history and form that is diametrically opposite that of an ideological or Marxist analysis, even though he tells us elsewhere that "narrational modes are central mediations between ideology and its manifestations in artworks." In summarizing the achievements of Resnais's *La guerre est finie*, for example, Bordwell describes how "political material" comes to be "appropriated and transformed by formal conventions: . . . By focusing on the individual psyche and maintaining a shifting narrational game with the spectator, *La guerre est finie* transmutes political material into a unique treatment of the conventions of a particular narrational mode."[20] Might we not also say that the film transmutes a particular narrational mode into a unique treatment of political material? Or that formal conventions become appropriated and transformed by the force of political material? These inversions are the basis for Jameson's argument for a political subtext: "The literary or aesthetic act . . . cannot simply allow 'reality' to persevere inertly in its own being. . . . [T]he literary work or cultural object, *as though for the first time*, brings into being that very situation to which it is also, at one and the same time, a reaction."[21] In Jameson's dialectical view, the "reality" of the political material does not truly precede its textual realization: the text gives us our most vivid apprehension of a historical world whose significance eludes us until caught within the webs of textual form. Such a perspective, however, cannot be simply appended to Bordwell's scheme; it requires opening up the formalist circle to which poetics attends.

But history for Bordwell is merely the temporal ground against which the full range of formal options associated with a mode of narration congregate into more restricted, specific paradigms. These specific norms persist across time, with variations on the basic paradigm continually occurring (new stories, or fabula, in classic narration; new *auteurs*, or personal styles, in art-cinema; a tradition of interrogative cinema for historical-materialist film and so on). Throughout Bordwell's text, history exists as a relatively inert ground for the dynamics of cognitive, narrational process. Why a given mode might appear at a specific moment, or how that mode's characteristics, its extrinsic norms, might bear the trace of historical-material determinations over time, remains outside the bounds of the study. Bordwell's view seems to be that he has laid out the streets and waterlines for his theoretical subdevelopment; all that others need to do is hook them up to the historical/ideological power grid of their choice.

An aura of quaintness presides over Bordwell's project. His references are almost entirely to a cinema that has never seen or heard of television, to a sample of texts that takes into account nothing of Latin American, Asian, African, Australian, or Canadian production, to a perspective in which the last twenty years or so of production are of only passing importance, and to a vision of history so severely restricted to the cinema that the massive, formal similarities and social parallels between film and other arts go almost entirely unnoticed.[22] Bordwell cheerfully deflects criticisms of these gaps by reminding critics that he has stated his goals openly and has frankly admitted to what he is not doing as well as to what he is.[23] In true formalist spirit, seeking answers to questions provides its own justification and the nature or use-value of the questions, or answers, the purposes and intentions that might surround them, can be comfortably bracketed in the service of science and the avoidance of subjectivity.

This quaintness gains in magnification when it is compared to the feminist critique of narrative. Bordwell's adroit demolition of mimetic and diegetic theories of narration centers on the work of writers like Münsterberg, Arnheim, Kuleshov, Bazin, and Eisenstein for mimetic theory and, for diegetic theory, Barthes, Metz, Bellour, Heath, and MacCabe, who is credited with "the most influential instance of a structuralist approach to filmic narration," astonishing news to the film studies community, I suspect. Conveniently, it seems, there have not been any women nor any feminist theories based on mimetic and diegetic assumptions that need to be cleared away as well, no "vague and atomistic analogies among representational systems" lodged within the feminist perspective, no privileging of certain (film) techniques at the expense of others, nor any efforts lacking in the broad and supple principles Bordwell wishes to introduce.[24]

Feminist film theory, which I would argue has been the most influential form of narrative critique in the past two decades, can be ignored presumably because its structuralist underpinning has been knocked away or because Bordwell has provided a more satisfactory foundation on which it can readily rebuild. Feminist theory is an intriguing "gap" or omission in a text that often goes to some pains to announce what it is excluding from consideration. By making mimetic and diegetic theory into "bad" science performed by other males, Bordwell presents himself as a friendly helper to the befuddled among us who are still casting about for a scientific way to make sense of the narrational process. Feminism, with its own distinctly subjective agenda, simply doesn't enter into the picture. Bordwell proposes a poetics, or science, that comfortably excludes feminist theory and regards the viewer as a sexless, genderless, classless, stateless "hypothetical entity." He also biases viewer activity to favor information processing over parallel acts of engagment (empathy, identification, scopophilia, etc.) and interpretation. These are significant clues to the cost of a narrative science.

His choice of categories and of hierarchies among them determines his results in numerous ways, as does his attempt to found an "objective" level of syuzhet presentation, distinguishable from "subjective" and rhetorical levels. Objectivity, or the denotative level of narrative, which Bordwell identifies as the direct presentation of the fabula when it is not relayed through a character's subjectivity and when the narrational process does not call particular attention to itself, serves as the cornerstone of the syuzhet/fabula relationship. Every film contains a mix of "objective diegetic reality, characters' mental states, and inserted narrational commentary," and by first knowing what is objective or denotative, the viewer can then go on to determine what is subjective or argumentative.[25]

Objectivity is central to the project of describing the fabula as singular and empirically accessible, and constructing the fabula is the viewer's primary task. Even this fundamental tenet, though, is open to question. The case for the centrality of fabula construction is made most strongly for classical cinema, at the level of narrative comprehension, but its centrality becomes increasingly dubious as we take up art-cinema, historical-materialist, and parametric modes of narration where unraveling a "story" becomes less and less essential. For the viewer's task with historical-materialist cinema—to construct a "fabula *event* as perceptually forceful and politically significant" —requires closer attention to the locus of represented events, the syuzhet, than to the "never materially present," "imaginary," "verbal synopsis" that we construct.[26] The force and significance of events derive from their material, stylistic embodiment in the syuzhet, not our reconstitution of them into something more summary-like.

And if the all-absorbing task of fabula construction is much less absorbing than Bordwell claims (such that the comprehension of style and syuzhet relations comes to the fore, for instance), then objectivity may be less clearly decidable than Bordwell wishes. An early casuality of Bordwell's clean-cut objective/subjective/narrational commentary declension is the link proposed by Barthes and others among connotation, myth, and ideology. (Barthes's later rejection of denotation's claim to ontological status—"denotation is not the first meaning, but pretends to be so; under this illusion, it is ultimately no more than the *last* of the connotations . . . the superior myth by which the text pretends to return to the nature of language, to language as nature"—receives no consideration at all.)[27] Bordwell regards all third-person representation as the objective denotation of a fictional space. Connotation or subjective representation becomes confined to a character's subjectivity, as evidenced by devices like point of view shots, rather than linked to a culture's ideology. If this relay of an objective diegetic world or of character subjectivity is interrupted, this must then be the work of the narrative calling attention to itself, rhetorically signaling its awareness of its own viewer.

Bordwell invokes style (unusual camera angles or movements, odd editing patterns, disjunctive sounds) as the narrative's mechanism for calling attention to itself. This schema very neatly isolates the narrational process from reference to anything beyond itself: subjectivity and commentary fold back into the narrational process rather than inflect the fabula world with meaning or significance such that the narrative becomes about something other than itself. For a narrative to be "about" something beyond itself would require a theory of comprehension that includes rather than brackets interpretation; it would require an understanding of the fabula as the construction of an imaginary world rather than as the computer-like deciphering of a story's intelligibility. It would throw into doubt whether a clear-cut, objective fabula world exists apart from the stylistic inflections that inform it, not only in order to call attention to the narrational process, but even more to establish the nature of the imaginary world the narrational process constructs.

The difference can be illustrated by Bordwell's analysis of melodrama. He characterizes melodrama as a highly communicative narration, with few "focused" gaps (specific pieces of missing information), unrestricted range (not tied to what characters know), a strong primacy effect (where what happens at the outset colors everything that follows), an effect that prompts minimal curiosity about the past, and a strong feeling of suspense about the future. Melodrama also cues us to expect an emphasis on how characters will react to new revelations and depends on retardation (delaying the introduction of important fabula information in the syuzhet) and coincidence to intensify our engagement.

It is somewhat difficult to recognize this as the same object that has occupied a great deal of feminist attention. The central place of female characters and subjectivity, the relation of this subjectivity to sexist ideology, the importance of beginnings not in terms of a non-explanatory tautology ("primacy effect") but in terms of narrative structure and psychoanalytic theory (disturbance and closure, condensation and displacement),[28] the debates on the function of style in relation to a return of repressed, character-based symptoms where oddities of style are not commentary but a crucial dimension to the imaginary world itself, the representation of male power and female desire, and the political effect of melodrama on viewers, especially women—none of this is anywhere to be seen in Bordwell's analysis. Were his "hypothetical entity" (that information-processing unit also known as a viewer who produces intelligibility from syuzhet/style systems) to become a human subject—embodied, gendered, and situated in history, the moves from comprehension to interpretation, from information to meaning, from imaginary fabulas to imaginary worlds would immediately take on enough urgency to break through Bordwell's perpetual oscillation between the encapsulated, formal poles of syuzhet signifiers and fabula signifieds.

Science craves objectivity—a somewhat unscientific way of speaking of its procedures and protocols. The extent of this craving can be seen in Bordwell's dry, matter-of-fact treatment of retardation, the ways in which a narrative's beginning initiates a journey which the middle of the narrative must delay and retard, not once but frequently, through a range of techniques. For Bordwell, this is just another process, requiring procedural schemata to cope with it. Bordwell describes how a melodrama will use gaps in the relay of information to retard the narrative and cue the viewer in the formation of hypotheses: "The syuzhet also manipulates interest through unfocused temporal gaps. The melodrama's syuzhet will inform us of initiation of a chain of action and then skip over some time or move to another line of action; we will then wonder what happened in the interval. . . . In general, the practice of parallel plotting retards the revelation of fabula information, compelling us to suspend questions about the progress of one line of action while another occupies our attention."[29]

Compare this to Roland Barthes's treatment of the hermeneutic code and the management of enigmas. Barthes brushes aside immediately any sense of an objective, information-based process.[30] Enigmas conform to a strategy for the organization of desire and meaning. Enigmas sustain a paradoxically static dynamics, prolonging the original uncertainty in the face of the narrative's ineluctable march forward. This hermeneutic code distinguishes narrative from exposition by giving truth a structural, nonobjective definition: truth "is what is *at the end* of expectation," what comes last, with the closure of narrative teleology. Retardation is not merely an aspect of a formal process but part of a code inflected by the historical world in which it functions: "the hermeneutic narrative, in which truth predicates an incomplete subject, based on expectations and desire for its imminent closure, is dated, linked to the kerygmatic civilization of meaning and truth, appeal and fulfillment."[31] Retardation, by this account, is never only formal, never strictly or simply a matter of cues and hypotheses, information and comprehension, but instead part of a socially symbolic act *always* laden with meaning.

But Bordwell assumes that objectivity is self-evident. If we do not enter a character's subjectivity, if the narration does not offer commentary, and if style does not depart unexpectedly from norms we have begun to apply, then we are left with the denotative relation between syuzhet and fabula. The only fly in the ointment is "denotative." Virtually all cybernetic theory and semiotics allow for some slippage between signifier and signified, between signal and information, between information and meaning. Bordwell does not want slippage but certainty. The notion of a "ground" that provides a context for a sign and renders some attributes of it more pertinent than others, not only adds the complicating likelihood that different viewers will construct different fabula en route to different interpretations and meanings, but also suggests that empty or "hollow" forms are not entirely so free-floating. They remain anchored to a ground—the term is Charles Peirce's—through the purposefulness of communication and perception.[32]

Bordwell locates himself off any such ground. Fabula construction and narrative comprehension are processes of model building, of constituting a model of narration that we can use to answer questions about narration (to paraphrase Marvin Minsky). This is a project in which the simulation or model becomes the real or, better, displaces the real as a ground in favor of an implosion of meaning into "hollow forms." (Mental models bear uncanny resemblance to those industrial models which Baudrillard identifies as "third-order simulacra," from which new forms arise by means of the modulation of difference more than from copying or serial reproduction.[33]

For humans, information processing is linked to purpose on more than one level and more than locally. Aspects of a sign, or of the syuzhet, are brought into pertinence, foregrounded, purposefully. The qualities made pertinent by the ground, by the context marked out by the constraints of a discursive formation and the history of the subject, have to do with rhetoric, ideology, contradiction, and struggle. In science and in culture, the interpretant and its ground (the signifier and its context, the syuzhet and style) do not anchor denotative truths so much as existential meanings. An excellent example of this point occurs in Teresa de Lauretis's *Alice Doesn't* when de Lauretis examines Virginia Woolf's account of her realization of her status as a woman in terms of how the ground, in this case a ground of sexist ideology, foregrounds one possible interpretation of a passing male's comment so that cognitive activity, interpretation, meaning, and history all coalesce into what de Lauretis aptly calls "experience." Experience becomes the ground on which *nachträglichkeit* operates, that second order process of learning to learn that confounds any simple or linear concept of cognition and knowledge.

Bordwell's concept of empty or "hollow forms" deserves some attention of its own. This hollowness is necessitated by the absence of meaning and interpretation, by the restriction of subjectivity to the optical point of view of characters, by the isolation of gaps, retardation, and suspense from a hermeneutics à la Barthes, or a psychodynamics à la Laura Mulvey's case for sexist pathologies, or Gay Studlar's case for a masochistic aesthetic.[34] The viewer does not engage with the text subjectively in Bordwell's model, but cognitively, as an information processor, a level of engagement, that if it can be isolated at all, can only be turned into an end in itself by slicing through its densely reticulated associations. What this implies is that empty or hollow forms are only so while they are being constituted for the first time, while hypotheses and inferences are being made that lead to the emergence of form, or pattern, from noise. But once

constituted these forms are also, simultaneously, grounded. They become part of our experience, or history, and to the extent that they
are materialized in texts or social practices, they become part of our
collective history as well. The context in which they arise informs
them. The meanings they have accrued, whether in the course of a
single film or across a large expanse of social history, accompany
them. We do not first process and comprehend texts; we are simultaneously moved and subjectively engaged by them. We do not simply
recognize a sign, form, or syuzhet pattern and automatically process
a narrative in a particular way. Instead, according to Peirce's system,
we attach overlapping interpretants to a given sign so that it is no
longer and never again empty. These interpretants, which allow us
to establish purposeful, affective relations to the world, narrative or
real, are:

1. The emotional interpretant that associates connotative richness,
feelings, and affect with a sign.

2. The "energetic" or active interpretant that generates physical or
intellectual effort; generally this would be the kind of cognitive processing discussed by Bordwell as well as physical actions and those
purposive responses from which narrative normally excuses us.

3. The "logical" interpretant whereby the subject's tendencies toward action or comprehension become modified as a result of the
experience of applying these emotional and active interpretants to
particular tasks or situations. This may also be called the existential
interpretant since it places us in an enduring but alterable relation to
a sign or set of signs. This interpretant engenders habit and the potential for a change of habit (or "schemata"). Action or comprehension,
then, occurs not only in relation to immediate contingency but also
in relation to sets of expectations and assumptions, predispositions,
tendencies, and habits. Such activity does not "fall from the sky";
it is concretely, materially grounded in the referential, ideological
nature of communication and discourse.[35]

This activity is of a different order and kind from that proposed
by Bordwell, who limits himself to the cognitive processing of empty
narrative forms. Though he refrains from a direct critique of alternative approaches, such as psychoanalysis, he goes on to add, ". . . I
see no reason to claim for the unconscious any activities which can

be explained on other grounds." And within this formal separatism, it is cognitive activity that Bordwell sets out to rescue and explain: explain in terms of a constructivist psychology and rescue because in his view ideological criticism has deprived the viewer of his or her activity. The vocabulary of positioning and constituting subjects, of ideological effect and the work of the apparatus, of *histoire* and *discours* all serve to deprive the subject of initiative. Cognitive processing becomes a way to restore activity to the subject: "The spectator performs cognitive operations which are no less active for being habitual and familiar."[36]

Habit, though, is not simply pre- or unconscious repetition. It is, precisely through being unconscious, where cognition and ideology meet, where existential interpretants join us to social webs of signification, where, in another vocabulary, qualification takes place.[37] I am not aware of any poststructural theory that claims the viewer or reader is inert, passive, and inactive at the level of cognitive processing. On the contrary, this level is taken for granted (too cavalierly no doubt) in order to argue that the viewer's activity still leaves him or her positioned or placed within a larger ideological structure that remains unquestioned, that persists through habit, that constitutes a ground upon which subjectivities form. Most poststructural analysis stresses moments of risk and strategies of containment that are always jeopardized by the return of what these strategies sought to repress, deny, or displace. Even if the process of containment were mostly successful, the potential for action remains (at least through poststructural criticism itself). The viewer's passivity, or more properly, his or her constitution within subjectivities like the masculinist scopophilia analyzed by Laura Mulvey, remains at risk; the potential for active contestation is always there.

Contestation has the ring of socially significant action, of existential interpretants recast against a ground of raised consciousness. That is, poststructuralism has never rejected the level of cognitive activity "redeemed" by Bordwell; instead, it has associated that activity with the social ends it served. The postmodern "positioned" viewer does not cease to function mentally; cognition, however, serves to sustain a limited range of subjectivity. Schemata do not treat empty forms but highly loaded ones. Priority goes to determining the existential, unconscious anchors that hold mental processing to certain paths more than others, not to the denial of such activity in its entirety. By showing in detail how the viewer is cognitively active during the storytelling process, Bordwell gives us a more complete picture of narrative, but since such activity was never denied by other theorists, only contextualized, he can hardly be said to have rescued the viewer from theories that deprived us of a set of mental activities, despite his frequent claims to the contrary.[38]

Given his linear, one-dimensional model, Bordwell must neglect the subjective and socially constrained processes of interpretation. Likewise, he gives little attention to retroactive reading (and none to the central formalist tenet of *ostranie*). His analysis suggests that all viewers form the same fabula after one viewing where the recall and revision of previous syuzhet or stylistic material during the course of the narrative plays a secondary role. The greater the degree of retroactive reading and repunctuating according to logical type (classes and classes of classes, commentary and metacommentary, etc.), the greater the degree to which the fabula is subject to variation and dispute. It becomes increasingly less "in" the narrative process, waiting for us to reconstitute it, and more in the act of reading itself, subject, therefore, to all the personal, historical, and ideological inflections that reading is heir to. What's more, retroactive reading and the effect of *ostranie* are themselves of a different logical type. Whether in the course of viewing a film for the first time or during a process of critical analysis, retrospection is dialectical. It is part and parcel of our cognitive activity but of a different order from the mere reception of data or the comprehension of information; retrospection places information in the context of other information.

Retroactive reading (Freud's *nachträglichkeit*) involves comprehending "the diversity of contexts to put the information in (learning how to learn)."[39] Part of this contextual diversity would surely be the way in which the fabula constitutes a world, populated by values and bearing significance, rather than simply being a plot made intelligible. But to propose a dialectical cognitive process also opens out onto worlds and readings where loaded forms are placed into diverse contexts not by "hypothetical entities" programmed for narrative comprehension, but by gendered, historically situated subjects who may not only read but simultaneously reread, not only view but review, not only comprehend but also, and at the same time, resist, challenge, qualify, and contend, who view works not only in accord with a comprehension program but also negotiate, revise, or resist that very process.

This alternative would require unbinding style and rhetoric from the constraints Bordwell places on them. Style might do more than "simply [name] the film's systematic use of cinematic devices." Rhetoric might be more than "argument" where "the fabula world stands for a set of abstract propositions whose validity the film at once presupposes and reasserts." [10] Style might become a qualitative dimension that guides us in the effort to differentiate levels, assess tone, assign value, and establish identificatory or subjective relations simultaneously with cognitive ones. Since style doesn't create or determine the syuzhet's unfolding, it is secondary to Bordwell, but if it creates and determines the *world* of the narrative, it becomes a primary means of establishing a domain and the nature of its plausibility. Rhetoric might become an omnipresent element of persuasion, linked inevitably to address, intentionality, and meaning, as it is in Soviet cinema and in advertising but as it also is in classical and art-cinema. It would involve not only moments of obvious argument or assertion but the more diffuse, omnipresent process of persuading us of the moral or ideological pertinence of the world we encounter.

Logic has its limits and narrative constantly exceeds them. Narrative depends on paradox and contradiction to activate cognitive processes, if we choose to call them that, which require exercises in logical typing and the "Aha!" discovery of new contexts, new interpretive grounds for making sense of things. Taxonomies of syuzhet/fabula temporal relations that discuss the four possible combinations of simultaneity and successiveness between the two (successive syuzhet occurrences representing simultaneous fabula occurrences, for example), which Bordwell discusses in detail, involve nothing dialectical. Such categories are valuable to an analytic logic only; they provide no assistance in the task of explaining insight, discovery, or reinterpretation. His questions circle around the task of constructing the fabula: where does this occurrence fit in the story, is this commentary or description, how are space and time configured, what schemata will render this narrative comprehensible? Bordwell readily concedes that other questions can be asked, but the question of whether the ones he poses exist in such isolation from human subjectivity, desire, and power haunts the entire project.

So though formally correct, Bordwell may be wrong in a more fundamental sense. Localized knowledge has its value and logic is one of its most indispensable tools. Global knowledge—to which concepts like *nachträglichkeit, aufhebung, ostranie*, insight, paradox, discovery, intuition, synthesis, and totalization apply—also has its value and logic, and those reasoning procedures that rely on clear-cut rules to reach verifiable conclusions can be one of its most treacherous allies. How are we to regard the individual who takes up a delimited challenge resourcefully and produces results, perhaps brilliantly, if those results run contrary to some more global need? Within a local frame, the individual deserves acknowledgment and reward; within a global frame, such a response may be extremely dubious.

We must set aside the temptation to create a false, binary polarization by ignoring logical types and elevating the local to the status of the global so that achievement within a restricted or specified domain becomes the sole criterion with "larger questions" ruled irrelevant or a challenge only to the user, not the producer of the result. A more appropriate criterion involves recognizing that the pursuit of local knowledge has its virtues: it is quicker and allows for many, simultaneous but discrete forms of inquiry; it excuses errors or failure that follow from accepting the established rules governing that particular domain without introducing complicating issues of larger effect or competing claims. In this context, assessment of use-value might come more appropriately from asking how that dimension of ourselves whose task it is to learn *how* to learn (how to learn which strategies and assumptions serve us best in given circumstances) may benefit from the methods, tactics, and results we employ.

By this criterion, the use-value of Bordwell's effort must be said to be sharply limited, particularly in its lack of a human dimension from which we may learn. *Narration in the Fiction Film* could be regarded as a prolegomenon to the production of a computer program or expert system designed to construct the fabula from a given syuzhet and style. But the work allows for no history, no subjectivity. Bordwell conceives of history as the dimension in which specifiable modes of narration coalesce rather than as the ground (in Peirce's sense) of human experience. And he conceives of subjectivity as optical alignment with a character's point of view rather than as the fulcrum point of power and desire, those determinative structures which "pursue aims in indifference to perceptual reality, creating the imagised, eroticised concept of the world that forms the perception of the subject and makes a mockery of empirical objectivity."[41]

Bordwell's is a poetics that, at a local level, succeeds according to his own criteria: it is comprehensive, discriminates effectively, possesses coherence, matches the domain of data, and is fecund. At a more global level these claims become doubtful: this is a poetics that excludes more cinema and modes of visual representation than it includes, that neglects differences that make a difference, that achieves coherence by excluding history and subjectivity, that treats narrative as data or information for genderless, classless, stateless "processors," and whose fecundity is that of any system that has the wherewithal to perpetuate itself. As such it is of value wherever narrative is processed by "hypothetical" entities or "organisms"—better called, perhaps, cyborgs. For gendered, historically situated subjects whose very being is at stake within the arena of history, Bordwell's poetics must seem a terribly diminishing thing.

Notes

1 David Bordwell, *Narration in the Fiction Film* (Madison, 1985).
2 Bill Nichols, "Ideological and Marxist Criticism: Towards a Metahermeneutics," *Studies in the Literary Imagination* 19.1 (1986): 83–107.
3 Of primary concern here is Bordwell's *Narration in the Fiction Film*. Also exemplary of a neo-formalist approach and of a proselytizing posture is David Bordwell and Kristin Thompson, *Film Art: An Introduction* (New York, 1985), which is one of the most widely used introductory texts in the country. Other neo-formalist works include David Bordwell, Kristin Thompson, and Janet Staiger, *The Classical Hollywood Cinema: Film Style and Mode of Production to 1960* (New York, 1985); Kristin Thompson, *Eisenstein's Ivan the Terrible: A Neoformalist Analysis* (Princeton, 1981); and Edward Brannigan, *Point of View in the Cinema: A Theory of Narration and Subjectivity in Classical Film* (Berlin, 1984). In a somewhat more

empirically centered vein is Barry Salt, *Film Style and Technology: History and Analysis* (London, 1983). One of the few books applying cognitive psychology (and generative linguistics) to filmic narration prior to Bordwell's is John M. Carroll, *Toward a Structural Psychology of Cinema* (The Hague, 1980).

4 David Bordwell, "Textual Analysis Revisited," *Enclitic* 7.1 (1983): 93.

5 Bordwell, *Narration*, 335–36.

6 David Bordwell, "Adventures in the Highlands of Theory," *Screen* 29.1 (1988): 84 (a reply to Barry King's two-part critique, "The Classical Hollywood Cinema," *Screen* 27.6 [1986]: 74–88, and "The Story Continues . . . ," *Screen* 28.3 [1987]: 56–82).

7 Fredric Jameson, *The Political Unconscious: Narrative as a Socially Symbolic Act* (Ithaca, 1981), 47.

8 Bordwell, *Narration*, 169–77, 88–98.

9 Stephen Heath, "Narrative Space," in *Questions of Cinema* (Bloomington, 1981), 24.

10 Bordwell, *Narration*, 306.

11 Ibid., 62.

12 Ibid., 49.

13 Marvin Minsky, *The Society of Mind* (New York, 1985), 303.

14 Benjamin Hrushovski, "Poetics, Criticism, Science," *PTL: Poetics and Theory of Literature* 1 (January 1976): vi.

15 Bordwell, *Narration*, 58, 61.

16 Ibid., 150.

17 Ibid., 165, 212, 243.

18 Ibid., 272.

19 Ibid., 243, 235.

20 Ibid., 335, 228.

21 Jameson, *Political Unconscious*, 81–82; emphasis mine.

22 See, for example, Michael Schudsen, *Advertising, the Uneasy Persuasion: Its Dubious Impact on American Society* (New York, 1984), especially "Advertising as Capitalist Realism," 209–33.

23 Bordwell, "Adventures in the Highlands," 82–84.

24 Bordwell, *Narration*, 18, 26.

25 Ibid., 162.

26 Ibid., 243, 49; emphasis mine.

27 Roland Barthes, *S/Z*, trans. Richard Miller (New York, 1974), 9.

28 In *Steps to an Ecology of Mind* (New York, 1972), Gregory Bateson speaks of the use of such principles in science under the rubric of the "dormative effect," the "explanation" originally given to the question of why certain derivatives of the poppy plant produced a depressive reaction in humans: something that cannot be explained is identified by the result it produces so that the naming of this result gives the appearance of having explained the cause. What has actually happened is that a pseudo-explanation has arisen to mark the limits of knowledge within a

given theory or of the theory itself. Bateson sees this procedure as indicative of the muddle in the social sciences generally: "The state of mind or habit which goes from data to dormative hypothesis and back to data is self-reinforcing. [It leads to] a mass of quasi-theoretical speculation unconnected to any core of fundamental knowledge" (xx).

29   Bordwell, *Narration*, 71.

30   Barthes, *S/Z*, 75–77.

31   Bordwell, *Narration*, 76.

32   Charles Peirce, *Collected Papers*, ed. Charles Hartshorne and Paul Weiss (Cambridge, Mass., 1931–58), 1: 291–98.

33   Jean Baudrillard, *Simulations*, trans. Paul Foss et al. (New York, 1983). Bordwell's disavowal of any such postmodern regress in favor of certainty and science is ironically underlined by the strange, apparently nonsignifying juxtaposition of two essays on the general topic of "cybernetics, ownership, ontology," in *Screen* 29.1 (1988): 4–46 (John Frow, "Repetition and Limitation: Computer Software and Copyright Law," and Bill Nichols, "The Work of Culture in the Age of Cybernetic Systems") and a lengthy debate among Janet Staiger, Kristin Thompson, David Bordwell, and their reviewer, Barry King (Barry King, "A Reply to Bordwell, Staiger and Thompson," *Screen* 29.1 [1988]: 98–118; see also King, "Classical Hollywood Cinema" and "The Story Continues . . .").

34   Laura Mulvey, "Visual Pleasure and Narrative Cinema," and Gay Studlar, "Masochism and the Perverse Pleasures of the Cinema," in *Movies and Methods*, ed. Bill Nichols, 2 vols. (Berkeley, 1985).

35   Peirce, *Collected Papers*, 5: 326–27.

36   Bordwell, *Narration*, 30, 164.

37   See Göran Therborn, *The Ideology of Power and the Power of Ideology* (London, 1980), for a full discussion of qualification as an alternative concept to Althusser's subject subjected to a subject. Qualification carries the double meaning of becoming qualified for social tasks and also of becoming capable of challenging or qualifying these tasks and their accompanying subjectivities.

38   Bordwell, *Narration*, xiii, 29, 47, 53, 164.

39   Anthony Wilden, *The Rules Are No Game* (New York, 1987), 249. Wilden argues that all "Aha!" style experience "marks a new level of organization or patterning that produces a reinterpretation of the past, a rereading, in a new context, of the logical typing and other relationships of past events, and thus a re-evaluation of the future" (250).

40   Bordwell, *Narration*, 50, 235.

41   Mulvey, "Visual Pleasure," in Nichols, ed., *Movies and Methods*, 2: 308.

Film Response from Eye to I:

The Kuleshov Experiment

Norman N. Holland

★ ★ ★ ★ ★ ★ In 1929 the Russian director and theorist, V. I. Pudovkin, described an experiment that has since passed into the mythology of film as "the Kuleshov effect." I say the "mythology" of
film because it is not clear exactly what happened in the experiment.
Indeed it's not clear that the experiment ever took place at all. Nevertheless, people have written as though some experiment had in fact
taken place, and, as so often, that is enough to constitute "research"
in the humanities. "The 'Kuleshov effect,'" notes Dana Polan, "becomes the film theorist's equivalent of a palimpsest, an ink-blot test
out of which one can read almost any aesthetic position."[1] In that
carefree spirit, I propose to reread the experiment in the light of later
thinking about response to films. Pudovkin described the experiment
this way:

> Kuleshov ["a young painter and theoretician of the film"] and
> I made an interesting experiment. We took from some film or
> other several close-ups of the well-known Russian actor Mos-
> jukhin. We chose close-ups which were static and which did

not express any feeling at all—quiet close-ups. We joined these
close-ups, which were all similar, with other bits of film in three
different combinations. In the first combination the close-up of
Mosjukhin was immediately followed by a shot of a plate of soup
standing on a table. It was obvious and certain that Mosjukhin
was looking at this soup. In the second combination the face of
Mosjukhin was joined to shots showing a coffin in which lay a
dead woman. In the third the close-up was followed by a shot
of a little girl playing with a funny toy bear. When we showed
the three combinations to an audience which had not been let
into the secret the result was terrific. The public raved about the
acting of the artist. They pointed out the heavy pensiveness of
his mood over the forgotten soup, were touched and moved by
the deep sorrow with which he looked on the dead woman, and
admired the light, happy smile with which he surveyed the girl
at play. But we knew that in all three cases the face was exactly
the same.[2]

In an interview published when he was sixty-eight, Kuleshov recalled that they had kept their experimentally edited films around for
years, looking at them repeatedly, until they were destroyed during
World War II. He remembered the experiment somewhat differently
from Pudovkin, mixing it up with a second experiment involving the
actor's intention. The film was never shown to a theater audience,
he said. Only the experimenters looked at it. (If that were true, of
course, it would be the same as the experiment's never having taken
place at all, since the whole thing depends on an audience "which had
not been let into the secret.") Kuleshov also remembered the shot of
the dead woman differently, as a half-naked woman lying seductively
on a sofa, but perhaps that is the memory of a sixty-eight-year-old
man thinking of half-naked women.[3]

Pudovkin said the experiment showed the dominant role of the
director's editing: "It is only by an able and inspired combination
of pieces of the shot film that the strongest impression can be effected in the audience." Often in his theory, he speaks of effecting an
impression and in general of "effects": "Quick short pieces rouse excitement, while long pieces have a soothing effect." Pudovkin posits
a stimulus-response psychology to explain how film works.

Contrast to Kuleshov's cuts a more modern, more sophisticated example of montage, the time-flow segment in Mike Nichols's *The Graduate* (1967). Nichols's editing plays off Benjamin's trysts with Mrs. Robinson against his summer by the swimming pool at home. Benjamin walks through a door at home—and into the hotel room where he meets Mrs. Robinson. He gets out of bed with Mrs. Robinson, and he is in the living room at home. In the living room at home, sipping a beer, he is lying on the bed in the hotel room as Mrs. Robinson walks back and forth in front of him, getting dressed. He dives into the pool, pulls himself up onto a rubber float, and finds himself on top of Mrs. Robinson.

Consider, too, a more complex way of assessing response than Kuleshov's and Pudovkin's counting of heads. Take into account free associations to that segment of film. When I watch that sequence, the thought occurs to me that rolling over onto Mrs. Robinson has become routine. She has become as empty as a rubber raft. Perhaps she is full of hot air. When he opens the door, I think of the doors and windows that occur throughout this film all the way to the climax which takes the form of barring the doors to the church. From doors, I go to transitions. They occur throughout the film, from the moving sidewalk in the airport at the opening of the film to his frantic driving to and from Berkeley to the bus in which the lovers escape at the end. For me *The Graduate* is a film about transitions, notably Benjamin as a young man in transition from university to career, from sex to love, from his parents' program to his own.

Pudovkin treated the Kuleshov effect as stimulus-response, and many later writers on film share his explanation of an audience's response to film. I read, for example, in Arthur Knight's history of the movies that Kuleshov demonstrated that "It is not merely the image alone, but the juxtaposition of images that creates the emotional tone of a sequence."[4] Gerald Mast's history says that Kuleshov proved the "power" of editing "to control the film's structure, meaning, and effect."[5] David Cook's textbook of film history says that the purpose of Kuleshov's experiments was "to discover the general laws by which film communicates meaning to an audience—to discover, that is, the way in which film *signifies*."[6] "Signifies" is an important word, to which I shall return. Polan describes still other interpretations: "What the experiment demonstrates . . . is not that audiences find their own situation in film but that film can create its own situation, turn itself into an independent and advanced force."[7] In all of these readings, the critics treat the experiment as showing the power of film to cause a certain response.

Kuleshov described the experiment differently, although, like Pudovkin, he proclaimed the predominance of editing. More than Pudovkin, however, Kuleshov acknowledges the role of the viewer. He makes clear that it is the viewer's *perception* of the edited strip that gives the film its apparent power to associate disparate images.[8] "With correct montage, even if one takes the performance of an actor directed at something quite different, it will still reach the viewer in the way intended by the editor, because the viewer himself will complete the sequence and see that which is suggested to him by montage."[9] He recognized the psychological function of the viewer, and that seems to me crucial. In general, as Vance Kepley, Jr., summarizes him, "Kuleshov developed a thoroughly utilitarian conception of cinema, film's utilitarian value being measured in its social impact, in its effect on spectators." That is the reason he drew on such unlikely and pragmatic sources as John Dewey and the efficiency expert Frederick Taylor.[10]

In 1963 Jean Mitry rethought Pudovkin's and Kuleshov's experiment. Like Kuleshov, he concluded that the shots did not in and of themselves mean. It was their *juxtaposition* that created a "logic of implication." Then, according to Mitry, the spectator has to recognize and draw from himself feelings and images that fit, for example, the juxtaposition of Mosjukhin and the half-naked woman. As Mitry sensibly points out, "The child who knows nothing yet of sexual desire cannot get the meaning of the connection 'Mosjukhin–woman lying on sofa.'"[11]

Mitry visualized the psychological process in two stages. The juxtaposition of shots implies a "logic" between them in the spectator's mind, but the spectator then has to project the appropriate feelings and associations from his own memory of a similar experience into both the individual shots and the sequence of shots. The spectator is passive so far as the connection between the shots is concerned—

that functions as stimulus-response. The spectator is active in interpreting the human meaning of the shots—that functions by spectator projection. Edward Branigan has suggested, justly it seems to me, that Mitry's use of spectator psychology could be considerably more precise.[12]

In 1971 Christian Metz criticized both Pudovkin's interpretation and Mitry's from the point of view of audience psychology. Drawing on the Hungarian theorist Béla Balázs's *Der Geist des Films* (1930), Metz stated that "when two images were juxtaposed purely by chance, the viewer would discover a 'connection.' That, and nothing else, is what Kuleshov's experiments demonstrated." Images, says Metz, are linked together internally through the inevitable induction of a current of signification (that word again). The filmmaker's hand is "forced by the viewer, or rather, by a certain structure of the human mind, that obdurate diachronist."[13] Where Mitry said the viewer received the connection from the editing and then projected into it, Metz has the viewer making the connection, even from shots randomly put together. In 1971 Metz wrote—he would say it differently now—that a psychological process is involved in which a viewer who has gotten the message thereby develops the code by which he got it. People make the connections between the images and then remember and use the way they made them. In other words, Metz carries the viewer's activity one step further.

To explain montage, Pudovkin and the film historians drop human psychology out of cinematic response. Mitry and Metz say that we ought to put it back in. Hooray! I could not agree more, but, alas, that is not the direction film theory after them has taken. Probably, vis-à-vis Kuleshov's experiment, the most important concept—and it is only a concept, there is no empirical evidence for it as far as I know—is "suture." It is a term that grows out of theory rather than observation, as the Gabbards lucidly explain:

> Suture is usually understood in terms of a medical metaphor implying that cinematic gaps created by cutting or editing are "sewed" shut to include the viewer, who identifies himself with some aspect of the "gaze" created by the camera. . . . Instead of asking "Who is watching this?" and "Who is ordering these

images?" the viewer accepts what he is seeing as natural, even when the camera's gaze shifts most abruptly from one character or scene to another. Suture works because of the cinematic code which makes each shot appear as the object of the gaze of whoever appears in the shot that follows, the most commonly cited example being the "shot/reverse shot" formulation in which each of two characters is viewed alternately over the other's shoulder. We do not ask "Who is watching?" because each shot answers the question for the previous shot. The Israeli theoretician Daniel Dayan calls this "the tutor-code of classical cinema": "Unable to see the workings of the code, the spectator is at its mercy. His imaginary is sealed into the film."[14]

So far as movies are concerned, it was Jean-Pierre Oudart who brought the Lacanian idea of "suture" into film theory,[15] but most critics adopt the version given by the Israeli critic, Daniel Dayan, as in the passage above. That, David Bordwell points out, may not be exactly what Oudart had in mind.

Bordwell offers a clear and full explication.[16] (Oudart is Lacanianly obscure; that is why I rely on explicators.) According to Bordwell, Oudart does not confine the suture (as Dayan does) to the shot/reverse shot technique. There is a suture whenever the camera angles show the same portion of space at least twice, once on-screen and once as an offscreen presence, for example, as a space behind the camera or beyond the edge of the frame. The suture operates by creating gaps (these offscreen spaces) and then filling them by showing the imaginary space in another shot, usually the next.

What, if anything, does the spectator do? The first shot, by framing a visible space, triggers an act of imagination. The spectator imagines the space outside the frame. Then the second shot channels the spectator's imagination by showing what is in that imaginary space. First, the spectator recognizes an object on-screen (say, a bowl of soup). The spectator then realizes it is in a cinematic space of indefinite boundary—there are things, for example, behind the camera. In discovering the frame, the spectator realizes that the image has been framed (by somebody) to have some effect. The spectator realizes that the object is a "signifier" (like a word spoken) from the somebody who framed it, some absent creator. The suture, however, contains this discovery by finding the missing space in the second shot (for example, by showing Mosjukhin's face looking down at something). By finding in this second shot a previously offscreen zone, the film closes off the spectator's larger imagining of an offscreen narrator. The spectator can simply unify the image around a semantic meaning, a "signifying sum," something the film "says," namely, that the man is looking at a bowl of soup. In effect, the film, by framing and by editing, enables the spectator to tune in to someone "narrating" it, but the narrator is then hidden in the activity of the film. The film seems to tell itself.

Apparently, in this model, the spectator of a conventional fiction film simply imagines, over and over again, every time there is a new shot: narrator? no—gaze of next shot; narrator? no, gaze of next shot; narrator? no, gaze of next shot. Edward Branigan has called this kind of theory an "error theory," contrasting it usefully with a "hypothesis theory."[17] Hypothesis theory emphasizes the role of the perceiver and examines the procedures by which the spectator makes sense of the text (as I shall shortly do). An error theory makes the viewer a passive receiver of stimuli. In error theory, it is the "gaze" of the camera that tells the story, and both the teller and the hearer-spectator are identified with it—sewn into it—to form a single unity: invisible narrator, the camera "gaze," passive spectator. Whether we take Oudart or Dayan-Oudart, then, *It is the film that acts.* It is the film that triggers or channels spectators who passively do what the film tells them to do.

So much for the psychology broached by Metz or Mitry. The work of such theorists of the suture as Stephen Heath, Colin MacCabe, or many another in the '70s and '80s turned away from the actual activities of spectators (as in the Kuleshov experiment). Instead they posited "the" spectator arrived at by theory, and "the" spectator was reduced to little more than an eye—all the activity was the film's. Even such praiseworthy attempts as Teresa de Lauretis's to loosen up this unitary "spectator" to allow for gender differences run into baffling rigidity. The model allows her only two possibilities: identification with the gaze; identification with the image.[18]

Theory's reduction of the spectator to a "pure act of perception," a mere eye, pleases critics, because critics can then posit responses to film by looking simply at film—easier, faster, and more fun than trying to see how people actually respond. The critic's own response becomes the standard for the rest of us. Alternatively, the critic sees better than we poor "spectators" can, locked as we are into sutures or identifications.

Unfortunately for critics, there is no empirical evidence for this reduction of the spectator—it seems to rest wholly on the gospel according to Lacan. In fact, suture theory runs contrary to the last two decades' work in the actual psychology of perception and cognition. That is the point at which David Bordwell's powerful 1985 book, *Narration in the Fiction Film*, cuts in. Bordwell criticizes "mimetic" and "diegetic" film theories on several grounds. They lack empirical backing. They multiply entities unnecessarily (for example, creating a "narrator" who is then absorbed back into the film). They privilege "camera work (and at a pinch, editing) over other film techniques," although all "materials of cinema function narrationally—not only the camera but speech, gesture, written language, music, color optical processes, lighting, costume, even offscreen space and offscreen sound." [19]

Bordwell most strongly criticizes such theories, however, for making the spectator passive. Why is that wrong? Bordwell points to the contemporary "constructivist" psychology of perception. Actual experiments on actual people show that when we perceive anything (not just movies), we do so by trying out a series of hypotheses against what our senses make available. "Every fiction film . . . asks us to tune our sensory capacities to certain informational wavelengths and then translate given data into a story."

> The film proffers cues upon which the spectator works by applying those knowledge clusters called schemata. Guided by schemata, the spectator makes assumptions and inferences and casts hypotheses about story events. These assumptions, inferences, and hypotheses are checked against material presented to the perceiver.

Contrary to Oudart, the viewer checks the shot against what he or she expected to see and adjusts hypotheses accordingly. By using conventional schemata to produce and test hypotheses about a string of shots, the viewer often knows each shot's salient spatial information *before* it appears.[20]

In the same vein, Branigan, who worked with Bordwell, argues that viewers have a "competence" (in Chomsky's sense) to apply hypotheses so as to imagine the space described by a film, its meaning, the states of minds of its characters, and the rest.[21] Bordwell, by his term "schemata" (as well as by his footnotes), shows that he and Branigan draw on such modern psychologists of perception and cognition as Robert Abelson, Donald Bobrow, Marvin Minsky, Ulric Neisser, Donald Norman, David Rumelhart, Roger Schank, and many others engaged in, as Howard Gardner titled his introduction to the field, "the mind's new science."

These psychologists' ideas converge around a single principle. We perceive by imposing schemata on the sensory information available to us. Terminologies may differ—"schemata," "frames," "definitions," "scripts," or "plans"—but the idea is the same. We are not passive tape recorders, simply recording what the world imposes on us. We are constantly trying out hypotheses on what we sense. Indeed, we sense *by* trying out hypotheses. We process and reprocess the raw data from our senses by posing hypotheses. We thereby impose structure and produce structured knowledge from mere sense data. We process outside-in *and* inside-out, bottom-up *and* top-down. That is, we act toward sensory information to make it come in to us, and we impose high-level hypotheses on low-level data to synthesize and make sense of it.[22] By contrast, conventional theories of film response, like the "suture," Bordwell writes, use "terms like the 'position' or the 'place' of the subject. Such metaphors lead us to conceive of the perceiver as backed into a corner by conventions of perspective, editing, narrative point of view, and psychic unity. A film . . . does not 'position' anybody. A film cues the spectator to execute a definable variety of *operations*."[23]

The spectator "operates" on the film by applying hypotheses to it. Where, then, do these hypotheses come from? Conventional theory suggests the film creates them in "the" spectator. Bordwell suggests a more obvious source. "Children learn to follow ordinary films by learning schemata and norms, by discovering what notions of causality, time, and space are permitted within the dominant mode and are appropriate to the cues supplied. People come to appreciate a range of films by acquiring schemata and by sensing what is normative within given modes." Edward Branigan says we learn a Chomskyan competence: "A film spectator, through exposure to a small number of films, knows how to understand a potentially infinite number of new films. . . . This ability to understand—however it is acquired—is evidence of the prior knowledge, or competence, of a spectator."[24]

By allowing for the more and less skills of actual spectators, Bordwell (and constructivist psychologists generally) admit a social function for teaching and criticism. Just seeing movies may not be enough. By contrast, conventional film theory has society or the genre of the film "constructing" its spectator, as Dudley Andrew suggests: "The viewer can be expected to inhabit the film in just a certain way because of the fact of preconstructed subjectivity. 'Construction' refers to the specific place eventually assigned to the viewer in any given filmed narrative."[25] Even while learning, the spectator is passive.

From a position much like Bordwell's, Henry Jenkins suggests another probable explanation.[26] We have learned, over the years, what sorts of schemata will work with this or that film. Genre, for example, tips us off. I perceive a man in a trench coat differently in a James Bond movie than in a Monty Python. I watch a classical Hollywood western or gangster film differently than I do an Eisenstein or Costa-Gavras, even though they all have good guys and bad guys. Further, Jenkins points out, ads, publicity, and all kinds of "interviews, previews, and reviews" cue us to apply certain schemata, to watch for Jack Nicholson's leer or Hitchcock's cameo appearance.

Different directors answer to different hypotheses. To read films by Bresson or Godard, you need to apply different hypotheses than for films by de Sica or Bergman. Bordwell persuasively distinguishes four different groups of hypotheses for four large classes of films. In effect, then, we could read Bordwell's whole book as defining genres by the schemata we now bring or should bring to four large classes of films.

Alternatively, we could say that the schemata that work with this or that film define its genre.

This is not to say that the schemata are carved in stone. Some films, writes Bordwell, "undermine our conviction in our acquired schemata, open us up to improbable hypotheses, and cheat us of satisfying inferences. But no matter how much a film arouses our expectations only to frustrate them, or creates implausible alternatives that turn out to be valid, it still assumes that the spectator will initially act upon those assumptions which we use to construct a coherent everyday world." Indeed, "Only when cues become inconsistent does the spectator start to notice narrational interventions," that is, the narrator presupposed by the suture and other conventional theories.[27]

Any inventive film will test and change our customary schemata. Whether the film is trite or challenging, however, Bordwell equates response to the spectator's applying certain learned hypotheses to the film and having them satisfied or defeated. We can make sense of the conventional notion that a film "preconstructs the subjectivity" of its viewer by translating it: a film (or its publicity, or society in general) cues a spectator to bring certain schemata into play. These are part of the spectator's subjectivity—if you use that term. I try not to. I would say they are part of the spectator's I. They are the way an I relates to movies and the rest of its world.

Bordwell takes us well beyond the conventional explanations of the "Kuleshov effect," but I would take us even further. Granted that we can distinguish *types* of hypotheses we bring to different *types* of movies, I would like to add a personal element. In the same way, I would like to urge the mere eye and gaze of conventional film theory toward the I-that-includes-an-eye of psychoanalytic psychology. To do so, we can combine today's work in the psychology of perception, which Bordwell uses, with the theory of individuality that one can get from psychoanalysis. That brings me to my recent book *The I*.[28]

Very briefly, for the all-too-large number of you, my readers, who have not had the incomparable benefit of *The I*, I visualize the mind as a personal identity governing a hierarchy of feedbacks. "Identity" I can best read as a theme with variations played upon that theme.

One can use other ways, but theme-and-variations works best for me. However one reads it, though, identity is a construct, an essay by the person formulating the identity.

Identity, we now know, may also be a psychic structure. The human brain, like the brain of all higher mammals, goes through a process of growing and ungrowing neurons and synapses (the gaps between neurons where thought takes place). In the first few years of our life we sprout synapses at an astonishing rate. The six-year-old child has a brain that is as big as an adult's and uses twice as much energy (as those of us who have parented six-year-olds had suspected). From the age of eleven on, however, only the fittest of these neurons and synapses survive. That is, only if we use them do neurons and synapses get the neurochemicals they need. Furthermore, that has been true *from birth*. Only the neurons and synapses that we used got the necessary chemicals to survive. Hence, the patterns of relationship that we established from earliest infancy to adolescence became inscribed in the very structure of our brains. That inscribed structure is, it seems to me, the physiological basis for psychoanalytical and Jesuitical sayings about the importance of early childhood. That inscribed structure is what we call identity.[29]

Nevertheless, even if it is "in" our brains, identity is necessarily imperfect, elusive, decentered, because identity is always somebody's representation of an identity, and the somebody can only do that through the somebody's identity. Identity, in other words, is one identity's reading of the psychic structure underlying another's identity. Even if I try to read my own identity, I do so by splitting myself. The part of me that (consciously and unconsciously) interprets identity is not quite the same as the part that (consciously and unconsciously) created that identity.

So identity is a representation, but it is also an agency and a consequence. In contemporary cognitive science, a person (an identity) perceives or knows the world by bringing to bear on it tests (or hypotheses or guesses or schemata). Is this ice solid enough to skate on? Does that eight-sided red sign mean "STOP!"? Does this set of free associations have a theme? Does the causality in this movie make sense? You pose a hypothesis, and you get back an answer that may or may not meet your standards for satisfying that hypothesis. If unsatisfied, you will try a new hypothesis. If satisfied, you will subside. Yes, that eight-sided red sign is at the entrance to another road: it fits the ideas I have about stop signs, and I can go on to think about something else. Or, No, that eight-sided red sign is on a billboard— so what does it mean?

One can think of each such test as Bordwell's posing "schemata" to a movie, but this movie is the world. We experience our world by testing it. If our tests make sense—that is, if we feel coherence or satisfaction—we accept what we are testing. If our tests give us unsatisfactory (or incoherent or painful) feelings, we defend against it. We have to try some other line of inquiry or deal otherwise with the stimulus. Because we perceive through this testing, our identities experience the world, so to speak, on their own terms. Ulric Neisser writes (incidentally clarifying Metz's description of a viewer's learn-ing the code by which he has already got the message) that "[s]che-mata develop with experience. . . . Only through perceptual learning do we become able to perceive progressively more subtle aspects of the environment. The schemata that exist at any given moment are the product of a particular history as well as of the ongoing cycle it-self."[30] Because identity relates to the world through feedback loops, identity both acts and is a consequence of its own acts. Each I has— is—a unique history of such acts. Hence perceptions, Neisser points out, are personal: "Every person's possibilities for perceiving and act-ing are entirely unique, because no one else occupies exactly his position in the world or has had exactly his history."[31] Moreover, be-cause we read an I through its actions, we cannot separate the I from the way it uniquely tests and acts on the world. To think of iden-tity at all, I have to think of it "always already" governing a unique repertoire of feedback loops.

That repertoire forms a hierarchy, in which "higher" loops govern "lower" loops by setting the standard to which the feedback directs itself. Higher levels decide for lower levels what will feel satisfying or unsatisfying. That is, my notion of what makes sense in a movie requires that when it shows an eight-sided red sign, it means "STOP!" If that familiar lower-level loop does not work, I have to try a more complex reading of the red octagon before I can get about the larger business of reading the scene it is in. Within such a hierarchy, we

can draw useful distinctions between lower and higher loops, between, for example, physical or physiological loops (like testing thin
ice) and cultural loops (like reading stop signs). The former read the
"hard" facts in the mind's relation to the world, the latter the changeable relations. Similarly, we can draw distinctions between personal
perceptions and cultural ones. Branigan, in his otherwise excellent
formulation of a "hypothesis" theory of film response, seems to lose
this distinction. Like many critics of both film and literature, he
sets up an opposition between cultural convention and individual
response.[32] In film response, though, "individual" and "cultural" are
neither opposites nor a dichotomy. *Three* kinds of hypotheses—individual, cultural, and physiological—are nested in a hierarchy.

We can divide the lower-level feedback processes that identity uses
into two types or levels. The lower consists of the body's hard-wired
circuits, the physical systems of eye or ear or nose by which we make
brightnesses and tones and edges and tastes in our minds. When Dr.
Johnson kicked the stone, he was using a lower-level, physiological
loop. The higher group of feedback processes embodies more complex
hypotheses that we have internalized from our culture. The higher
loops use the lower ones, interpreting their simpler data by what we
have learned from our culture. We convert curves into the letter a. We
edit a clustering of tones into the sound of "aha!" or we understand
a jumble of tastes and smells as "soup." We understand the black and
white and grey reflections from the screen as a man's face. Henry
Jenkins formulates such a hierarchy for film: interpretive schemata
for a genre *use* perceptual schemata for an image or a cut.[33]

To model the Kuleshov experiment more fully than Jenkins does,
we can further subdivide individual, cultural, and physical. There
are two kinds of tests among the higher loops we have internalized
from our culture. We can distinguish them by the shibboleth, "No
member of this culture would normally say the rule was otherwise."
For example, one cannot "normally," in our culture, read an eight-
sided red sign at an intersection as other than a stop sign, a certain
mix of stars and stripes as other than an American flag, or a concave
piece of porcelain with some meaty liquid in it as other than a bowl
of soup. "In a department store, you are given goods in exchange
for money or a debt." No member of our culture would normally

believe that department stores give their wares away. No member of our culture would normally hear the sound "r-eh-d" as a form of the verb "to go." In reading, no member of our culture would normally read "r" other than as r, as g, for example, or n. No member of our culture could normally think that the sentence "The house is red" is saying that red has houseness. On the other hand, lots of members of this culture might normally read "seal" otherwise than as a furry creature that flaps flippers and barks—if they were lawyers, for example, or in the bottlecap business. A lawyer might try out a legal seal for "seal," a bottler a cork disk. In other words, "could be otherwise" hypotheses come from the interpretive community to which you belong (as Stanley Fish has long pointed out).

So with hearing words. Lots of normal members of American culture, on hearing "He's r-eh-d," might try as a first meaning, neither a color nor the past participle of "read," but a political epithet. Indeed, the meanings we supply to words make one of the best examples of these higher-level cultural hypotheses. We differ about the meanings of words, no matter how fervently theorists call them signifiers.

I prefer the terms "codes" and "canons" to divide rules according to this "otherwise" shibboleth. "Codes" cannot, if you are a normal member of the culture, be otherwise. "Canons" can, depending on which interpretive community you belong to within a given culture. You can read as a lawyer or a bottler, a deconstructionist or a Lacanian, a reader response critic or a theorist of "suture." These are canons. Even if we cannot get loose from "a" or "4," you and I can, at this higher level of "could be otherwise," differ. In particular, we can differ as to what theme runs through a set of free associations, indeed as to whether it is right to talk of themes at all. We hold these canons as a function of belief, perhaps, or efficiency. That is, we may use ideas of human perfection or conservative reluctance, strategies of theme or of deconstruction, because they have worked for us in the past. Canons can readily be "otherwise." That is, we can easily change these ideological feedback loops. Only with great difficulty, however, perhaps not at all, can we change our sense of alphabet or subject-verb.

The distinction I am drawing is analogous to that proposed by the Canadian psychologist Zenon Pylyshyn (and somewhat like one of the "modularities" of mind proposed by the philosopher Jerry A. Fodor).[34] Pylyshyn distinguishes between those mental capacities that are routinely affected by an individual's symbolic processes, including wishes, beliefs, or values. These are "cognitively penetrable": they change with what we know or believe. Other capacities are automatic, encapsulated, "cognitively impenetrable" by an individual's particular values. Only these impenetrable capacities can be thought of as "hard-wired" or "inscribed" on the individual's brain. By contrast, penetrable capacities are like software, programmable and subject to change. "Codes" in my sense are "cognitively impenetrable." Codes include things like rules for interpreting shapes as letters or numbers; the fixed rules of syntax, arithmetic, or algebra; or firmly established cultural codes like "Red means stop, green means go." About canons, however, it is usual (and desirable) for people to disagree. Canons express politics or values or beliefs, a person's "philosophy" in the loose sense, a mental "set."

Mary Crawford and Roger Chaffin point out that some reading strategies result from differences in background, others from differences in viewpoint. Background-canons reflect heritage, education, and experiences. Viewpoint-canons would relate to opinions and beliefs and would be easier to change than background-canons. Particularly important aspects of personality would give rise to both kinds of canons: for example, one's psychological sense of oneself as female or male.[35] In this vein, we should also notice that the distinction between code and canon overlaps the psychoanalytic distinction between what is conscious and what is unconscious. We will be aware of our canons and some of our codes, but all canons and codes will have unconscious roots.

Because we cannot perceive without using them, canons and codes (both conscious and unconscious) determine our perceptions. On the other hand, it is we who *use* codes and canons to serve our conscious and unconscious wishes. This cognitive-psychoanalytic model does not force a choice between a response to a film determined by codes, canons, culture, or the film itself and a response that an autonomous individual chooses. Rather an individual *uses* codes and canons. They both limit us and enable us, as a carpenter is both enabled and limited by his saw. He can cut boards with it but not hammer a nail. We are dealing with a spectrum. Large "otherwise" hypotheses (beliefs, ideology) do not limit us as strictly as smaller "otherwise" hypotheses (like the meanings of words or images) do. And none of these "otherwise" hypotheses that we get from our culture constrain us as absolutely as do "codes" (the "not otherwise" cultural feedback loops like shapes of letters and numbers) or "not otherwise" physical and physiological constraints.

To make the most of the Kuleshov experiment, we can state this model of an I in its most general form. A personal identity sets the standards for canons ("otherwise" cultural feedback loops) which in turn set the standards for codes ("not otherwise" cultural feedback loops) which in turn set the standards for "not otherwise" physical and physiological feedback loops. A personal identity governs these three levels, consciously and unconsciously using them to serve that I's idea of pleasure and to defeat that I's idea of pain. The I, however, is decentered, some necessarily other I's way of phrasing an individuality.

The Kuleshov experiment cut precisely between canon and code, between the "otherwise" and the "not otherwise" kinds of cultural loops. Reading the expression on the actor Mosjukhin's face was evidently like supplying the meaning for "seal" or "red." It could be otherwise. The audience could read the same image on the screen as heavy pensiveness or deep sorrow or a light, happy smile. So when Mitry writes about projection, we can translate: he means trying out a hypothesis and getting feedback. The hypotheses about Mosjukhin's expressions are canons, since a given image accepts a variety of interpretations.

In reading the montage, however, in interpreting the juxtaposition of Mosjukhin's face with a bowl of soup or a playing child, everybody responded the same way. "It was obvious and certain that Mosjukhin was looking at this soup." Evidently, no person in the Kuleshov interpretive community would normally see two shots, one after the other, as unrelated. They were using a "not otherwise" code, but one for interpreting the juxtaposition of shots rather than the image of a face or a bowl of soup. Although Pudovkin naturally felt no need to mention them, we are also seeing a number of other lower-level "not otherwise" loops at work in the Kuleshov experiment. Some were cultural. The spectators all saw the soup as soup and Mosjukhin as a man. They all treated the blacks and whites and greys on the screen as representations of reality. They all saw filmic "syntax" in action. Other low-level, "not otherwise" loops were physiological. The audience all saw sixteen frames a second as motion. They all were able to discern whites, blacks, greys, and the edges of the images. In short, the Kuleshov experiment proved three things. In relating two shots, we use a code. In reading a single shot, when we identify a facial expression, we use a canon, but when we identify an object we use a code.

Pudovkin did not report any individual responses, but you can see personal systems and values at work in the responses to Just Jaeckin's soft-porn film *The Story of O* that I reported and analyzed.[36] My interpretation of the sequence in *The Graduate* illustrates the same phenomenon: my individual reading uses readings that everybody shares. That is, everybody sees the door as a door, Benjamin as a young man, and Mrs. Robinson as an older woman. I think everybody in our culture must also interpret Nichols's cuts from the pool to the hotel room as showing two aspects of Benjamin's life. We all interpret Nichols's images and cuts through feedbacks from very basic "not otherwise" codes by which we learned early in life to see film. Different people, however, will interpret differently the putting of Benjamin on top of, first, the raft, second, Mrs. Robinson. Not everybody will think of Mrs. Robinson as full of hot air. That interpretation might be otherwise. It reveals a canon at work. Then, when I read from Nichols's jump cuts to a whole film about transitions, I am showing my unfashionable beliefs in pattern and wholeness. You might read the film from a feminist or a psychoanalytic perspective. Someone else might deconstruct it or treat it as an act of production. Each of us would use Nichols's cuts in the service of our high-level canons in different ways. Each of us would be using *codes* so as to work out our various *canons*.

When I unpack my reading of Nichols's cuts, I can see what I did in terms of a general model of film response. I used three kinds of hypotheses. The base is the physical film—no one denies that, although

I am often accused of it—and the audience applies different levels of feedback to perceive it. Vis-à-vis the physical film, I worked a purely physical recognition of colors and speeds and sequences. Vis-à-vis the images and cutting, I used two kinds of cultural hypotheses: canons that could be otherwise and codes that could not. If the whole audience gets similar results, they are using a low-level feedback, either a physical-physiological loop or a "not otherwise" cultural code. We all see twenty-four frames a second as motion. We all see Mrs. Robinson as Mrs. Robinson and the rubber raft as a rubber raft. But when different people get different results, that is the sign of a "could be otherwise" canon. We may well differ as to whether the cuts represent Benjamin's sexual fantasies, his guilt, or his boredom.

As in suture theory, some might claim that the previous shots of Benjamin and Mrs. Robinson in the hotel room dictate the significance of the later images and cuts by the pool. Some might say, "The context determines the meaning," but that phrasing collapses a subtler process. We try out a meaning, and we get good or bad feedback from the context. It is not the context per se that causes the audience's response. Rather, "context" changes the feedback the audience gets from its hypotheses. "That expression on Mosjukhin's face means something, but what? Ah. The other shot shows a bowl of soup. He has forgotten his soup. What would make a man forget his soup? Heavy pensiveness. Yes, his face does look as though he is thinking hard." All this, of course, very fast, quite unconscious, and almost automatic.

That automaticity is why, if we consider the process by introspection alone, it *feels* as though we are being physically controlled by the film. These lower-level feedbacks happen willy-nilly, without our being aware of them. We cannot do otherwise. Everybody gets the same results. We feel as though we are being caused, simply responding in some Pavlovian or Skinnerian way to a stimulus without any action on our part.

But we aren't. Even at the very lowest levels of perception, we are applying hypotheses to what the world supplies us. In school, if your experience was like mine, you were told that the eye is like a camera. Light passes through the lens and falls on the retina, where it stimulates nerves that send images to the brain along what amounts to a one-way street. That picture, according to modern perceptual psychology, is false. The eye has to scan the world, and if the movements of the eyeball are canceled out, we see nothing. We see colors, not because a certain frequency of light falls on the retina, but because we process the blue-green and the red peaks in retinal sensitivity into a certain sensation. We use the same kinds of feedbacks at the lowest, physiological level that we do at the highest interpretive level.

This model of response spans our individual interpretations of a film, the ideological consensus of an interpretive community, the grammar and syntax by which we read films, and even the physiology by which we sense its simplest elements. We can link everything from eye to I in a hierarchy of feedbacks governed by a personal identity. By doing so, I think we can enrich even such already powerful models of film response as Bordwell's.

Nevertheless, much of contemporary theory and criticism is altogether psychology-less. I think that is because many contemporary theorists proceed by simple introspection. They apply to higher-level processes the control they feel with lower-level processes. Lower-level processes *feel* as though they are determined in some behaviorist way. Then, if I believe ideologically that people are determined by their culture, I will be tempted to attribute to high-level interpretations the same kind of determinism that apparently causes me to see Mosjukhin as longing for the soup. Modern perceptual psychology, however, shows this supposed control is the other way round. I can sense myself applying feedback as I try out my complicated hypotheses on a film, but not when I see an image as a bowl of soup or a child playing. Nevertheless the same kind of feedback is operating unconsciously, automatically, and rapidly in my small perceptions of an image or even the seeing of sixteen and twenty-four still pictures a second as motion. "Apparent movement," writes Bordwell, "is 'bottom-up' and mandatory. No one can choose *not* to see movement in a film. Yet these effects are still the product of the organism's inferential activity, here at a psychophysical level."[37] The illusion of stimulus-response at lower levels cannot provide a model for high-level processes. Rather, the higher-level processes provide the model for the lower. The feedbacks by which I understand Mrs. Robinson as full of hot air or *The Graduate* as a film about transitions continue the feedbacks by which I see sixteen or twenty-four frames a second as motion or a cut from a bowl of soup to a man's face as different angles on one event.

Probably, however, the psychology-lessness of contemporary theory has a more ideological source: an omnipresent faith in "signifying" or "signified" or "signifier." I realize that Lacan, Derrida, and those who derive their thought from them radically redefine at least some of these terms. What they cling to, however, is the idea of signifying itself. Texts mean or refer or shift or point or force—texts *do* things. Even if much of modern theory redefines the old idea of a signifier signifying a signified, it does not give up the idea of the active text—as in the "suture."

Ultimately, "signifying" comes from Saussure's *Cours de linguistique générale* from the first decade of this century, long before there was a psychology that could deal with our speaking or understanding speech or writing. Saussure knew that and wisely chose to dismiss psychology from his account of the way we understand language. As he tells us at the beginning and end of the book, his aim is to model language in purely linguistic terms, free of psychology, sociology, or anthropology. The verbal stimulus, he says, "imprints" itself on the brain, and he draws pictures of trees and horses to illustrate what is signified, namely ideas in our minds about trees and horses. What he does not illustrate or explain is how a physical thing (*matière phonique*, he calls it) becomes an idea of that thing. He just says it does. Something physical simply becomes something mental. So much for psychology.

According to Saussure, the sign (usually a word in his examples) "associates" signifier and signified. In his fuller, more formal account, the signifier is not a thing in itself, but the difference between itself and other signifiers. It does not matter, however, whether we think of that stimulus as a physical sign or as the difference between physical signs, it is still physical. As my arithmetic teacher used to have to remind us seventh-graders, the difference between one mile and two miles is not one, but one *mile*. The difference between one *matière phonique* and another *matière phonique* is still *matière phonique*. In Saussure's model, a signifier's difference from other signifiers simply imprints a difference from other ideas in the hearer's mind, and this is where Saussure thinks he eludes psychology. He has only swept it under the rug, though, hiding the psychological process in "imprints." Saussure's "signifying," far from being something the theorist of film or literature can take for granted, rests on a highly questionable but unexamined set of *psychological* premises. Saussure formalized language as a sheet of signifying differences mapped onto a sheet of signified differences. Whatever its *linguistic* credibility (and that is very limited in 1989), this idea of signifying entails a radically behaviorist, stimulus-response psychology of perception.[38]

Because the juxtaposition of Mrs. Robinson and the raft will admit a variety of responses, a stimulus-response, text-active explanation of response to the film (like "signifying" or "suture") fails. We can call the individual shots the stimulus (or signifier) as the "suture" theorists do, or we can call the sequence of shots the stimulus (or signifier) as do Pudovkin and Mitry. Either way, we then have to say, as Pudovkin seems to, that the stimulus was the combination of shots but not the content of either one, as though "red" were a stimulus, but not r, not e, and not d. Kuleshov and Metz take a different tack. The stimulus changes according to what the audience brings to it— but that is a clumsy way to think about it. Why not simply say, as Bordwell, Branigan, Jenkins, and Holland do, that we are seeing a feedback process?

Stimulus-response psychology is not strong enough to explain your or my response either to a film or to a novel, and Saussurean linguistics suffers from the same weakness. As Mark Turner notes, the extension of Saussure's signifier-signifying-signified model from phonemes to words is "wrong on a grand scale."[39] And it has elicited wrong film and literary theory on a grand scale. Hundreds of film and literary theorists write as if the linguistic revolution of 1957 hadn't happened yet.

Chomskyan (antibehaviorist) linguistics provides a far more powerful account of language than Saussure does and one that can be extended to visual perception as well, and hence to film. Just as Chomsky proved in 1959 that a behaviorist account of language fails, so Fodor and Pylyshyn proved in 1981 that even a sophisticated quasi-behaviorist stimulus-response account of "direct" perception fails. Interestingly, they refer to an experiment in which hearers used cough-sounds to stand for various phonemes in just the way Kuleshov's audience used the image of Mosjukhin's face to stand for various emotions.[40]

A Chomskyan "grammar of film" would predict the pattern of audiences' judging that such-and-such a film maneuver is well formed—as Kuleshov's audiences accepted his juxtaposition of Mosjukhin's face and a bowl of soup. Thus John M. Carroll, working out a transformational-generative grammar of film, draws a distinction between a "model" of filmic language in which some usages are acceptable ("filmic") and others not, and the "aesthetic" (or "cinematic") use of such a model in which a Pudovkin or a Nichols will violate grammar, as a poet would, for personal artistic purposes.[41] Carroll, I take it, is drawing a distinction parallel to mine between "not otherwise" code and "otherwise" canon.

Such a grammar would be a purely formal description of a language, as an algebraic equation describes a child on a swing. A post-Chomskyan thinker like Lakoff would go even further. One cannot separate competence in language from knowledge of the world. No purely formal account of language can succeed. When we speak of the audience's "competence," we edge even a purely formal description toward the psychological, as, for example, Metz did when he spoke of the role of "a certain structure of the human mind, that obdurate diachronist." This "psychologization" is the tactic that Bordwell, Branigan, and Jenkins usefully apply. Even Metz surmised, however, that the audience has a film grammar "in mind" somehow, although how is a question not answered easily or yet.

A feedback model is admittedly an oversimplification, but it does at least allow us to account for the actual variability of response to a given filmic image and for the complicated way in which audiences edit and rewrite the stimulus in front of them, as in the Kuleshov effect. It allows us to imagine roughly how a film audience might have a grammar "in mind." The feedback model is consistent with Chomskyan and post-Chomskyan theories of grammar and competence, but I am asking for further distinctions. That is, even Chomsky's immensely useful term "competence" does not distinguish between "otherwise" and "not otherwise" feedback circuits, although a Chomskyan grammar distinguishes between optional and mandatory transformations. It seems to me that we need, in thinking about how we test and so perceive the "out there," to draw that distinction. We need to distinguish codes from canons, in order to model our understanding of films (or, I should think, sentences). "The language of film" is fourfold: a personal idiolect (from identity): a dialect (canons from internalized culture); a language (codes from internalized culture); and linguistic universals (the bodily level of language).

I am resting my model on psycholinguistics and cognitive psychology, drawing distinctions that have little to do with psychoanalysis's "conscious" and "unconscious." Even so, this model has a profound connection to psychoanalysis. It fits what Freud said in *The Interpretation of Dreams* about calculations, speeches, and, in general, intellectual activity in dreams.[42] Freud points out that the dream work uses any methods within its reach, such as sounding a word, spelling it, arithmetic, or drawing on far-fetched associations and allusions. The dreaming mind *uses* arithmetic, phonics, grammar, association, quotation, and symbolism, to fulfill the higher-level wish of the dreamer.

Interestingly, Freud draws something like the distinction I have been making between voluntary canons and "not otherwise" codes. In dreaming, he says, we do not actually do calculations or form sentences. We only remember them. We do, however, associate, allude, work out the sounds and spellings of words, know the sequence of numbers, and, of course, we remember. To put that another way, there are some processes that we cannot vary, like the sounding of a word or the configuration of a flag, and those are available to the dreamer. Other processes, such as doing arithmetic or inventing a sentence, we have to vary by some higher-level thinking, and that we cannot do while dreaming. The various puns, rebuses, jokes, and puzzles in dreams simply show lower-level processes—codes—used to fulfill unconscious wishes in dreams rather than to solve real-world problems in waking thought. In my terms, he is saying we can use codes (but not canons) to make the images of a dream.

Perhaps I am trying to work out too close a correspondence between Freud's explanation of the puns in dreams and my extension of his model of dreaming into the response to film. One thing, however, seems to me quite clear. Both Freud and I describe a self or an identity that *uses* lower-level processes of syntax or arithmetic or phonics. We are both talking about a generalized model of perception as well as invention (as in dreams), the two being, for most psychologists these days, kinds of construction. If so, then we are saying that interpreters of films (and of dreams and identities) are always engaging their selves, their identities, decentered, deconstructed, and systematically elusive though those identities may be. The processes of interpretation may be as automatic as those of arithmetic or grammar or phonetics, but there is always a self applying them. Sometimes the responder will feel as though he or she is being controlled, merely responding to a stimulus. In fact, though, response is always a feedback process, even if it "could not be otherwise." By contrast, the idea that films (or texts) signify puts the film in the active role, just as the stimulus-response model does.

The Kuleshov audience may quite automatically have identified a bowl of soup or supplied a connection between two shots, but their automatic loops served personal feedbacks. Each self applied those automatic processes in the interests of that self. To use the automatic process to model the personal one is like doing psychoanalysis without acknowledging transference and countertransference. It is to try and do criticism, be it of fiction or film, without acknowledging the way critics recreate the text. It is to resort to the older model (like that of the not-so-new New Critics) of an "objective" world "out there" independent of the fluctuating, "subjective" world in here that knows that outer world. We need instead, in the language of cognitive linguistics, an "experientialist" account.[43]

What Kuleshov demonstrated—and now *I* am using the experiment as my ink-blot (and to confirm something I argued in 1976)— is that we have been moving, in this century, into a new paradigm.[44] Not all at once, of course. We encounter some very popular ways of thinking that rest on that older subjective-objective paradigm: formalist or structuralist criticism; stimulus-response psychology; the sender-message-receiver model for communication; signifier-signified and Lacanian and Derridean theories that rely on "signifying." In this final quarter of the century, however, I think it an essential intellectual exercise, every time one encounters one of these modes of thought, to ask: How would this idea change if we used a different model of the I, the I testing the world through a hierarchy of hypotheses? Seen that way, the Kuleshov experiment shows precisely the difference between an eye and an I.

Notes

1 Dana Polan, "The 'Kuleshov Effect' Effect," *Iris* 4.1 (1986): 98.
2 Vsevelod I. Pudovkin, *Film Technique and Film Acting: The Cinema Writings of V. I. Pudovkin*, trans. Ivor Montague (London, 1929), 140.
3 Steven P. Hill, "Kuleshov—Prophet without Honor?" *Film Culture* 44 (Spring 1967): 8.
4 Arthur Knight, *The Liveliest Art: A Panoramic History of the Movies* (New York, 1957), 71.
5 Gerald Mast, *A Short History of the Movies* (Indianapolis, 1981), 154.
6 David A. Cook, *A History of Narrative Film* (New York, 1981), 139.
7 Polan, " 'Kuleshov Effect' Effect," 104.
8 Ron Levaco, "Kuleshov," *Sight and Sound* 40 (Spring 1971): 86; Cook, *History*, 140.
9 Lev Kuleshov, *Kuleshov on Film*, ed. and trans. Ronald Levaco (Berkeley, 1974), 53–54.
10 Vance Kepley, Jr., "The Kuleshov Workshop," *Iris* 4.1 (1986): 6.
11 Jean Mitry, *Esthétique et psychologie du cinéma* (Paris, 1965), 1: 283.
12 Edward Branigan, *Point of View in the Cinema: A Theory of Narration and Subjectivity in Classical Film* (Berlin, 1984), 212–15.
13 Christian Metz, *Film Language: A Semiotics of the Cinema*, trans. Michael Taylor (New York, 1974), 47.
14 Krin Gabbard and Glen O. Gabbard, *Psychiatry and the Cinema* (Chicago, 1987), 332, citing Daniel Dayan, "The Tutor-Code of Classical Cinema," *Film Quarterly* 28 (1974): 30.
15 Jean-Pierre Oudart, "La suture, I and II," *Cahiers du cinéma* 211, 212 (April and May, 1969); "Un discours en defaut," *Cahiers du cinéma* 232 (October 1971); "Cinema and Suture," *Screen* 18.4 (1978): 35–47; with S. Dancy, "Travail, lecture, jouissance," *Cahiers du cinéma* 222 (July 1970).
16 David Bordwell, *Narration in the Fiction Film* (Madison, 1985), 110–13.
17 Branigan, *Point of View*, 55.
18 Teresa de Lauretis, *Alice Doesn't: Feminism, Semiotics, Cinema* (Bloomington, 1984), 143–44.
19 Bordwell, *Narration*, 20.

20   Ibid., 46–47, 100, 112.

21   Branigan, *Point of View*, 18, 157–58, 175, 179.

22   David E. Rumelhart and Andrew Ortony, "The Representation of Knowledge in Memory," in *Schooling and the Acquisition of Knowledge*, ed. Richard C. Anderson, Rand J. Spiro, and William E. Montague (Hillsdale, N.J., 1977), 99–100.

23   Bordwell, *Narration*, 29.

24   Ibid., 154–55; Branigan, *Point of View*, 17–18.

25   Dudley Andrew, *Concepts in Film Theory* (New York, 1984), 124.

26   Henry Jenkins III, "The Amazing Push-Me/Pull-You Text: Cognitive Processing, Narrational Play, and the Comic Film," *Wide Angle* 8 (1986): 35–44.

27   Bordwell, *Narration*, 47, 112.

28   Norman N. Holland, *The I* (New Haven, 1985).

29   Deborah M. Barnes, "Brain Architecture: Beyond Genes," *Science*, 11 July 1986, 155–56; Richard M. Restak, *The Infant Mind* (Garden City, N.Y., 1986), 19, 55–57, 68–70, and especially 92; Sandra Blakeslee, "Rapid Changes Seen in Young Brain," *New York Times*, 24 June 1986, sec. 3.

30   Ulric Neisser, *Cognition and Reality: Principles and Implications of Cognitive Psychology* (San Francisco, 1976), 61–62.

31   Ibid., 53.

32   Branigan, *Point of View*, 53.

33   Jenkins, "Amazing Push-Me/Pull-You Text," 37.

34   Zenon W. Pylyshyn, *Computation and Cognition: Toward a Foundation for Cognitive Science* (Cambridge, Mass., 1984); Jerry A. Fodor, *The Modularity of Mind* (Cambridge, Mass., 1983).

35   Mary Crawford and Roger Chaffin, "The Reader's Construction of Meaning: Cognitive Research on Gender and Comprehension," in *Gender and Reading: Essays on Readers, Texts, and Contexts*, ed. Elizabeth A. Flynn and Patrocinio P. Schweickart (Baltimore, 1986), 11–13.

36   Norman N. Holland, "I-ing Film," *Critical Inquiry* 12 (1986): 654–71.

37   Bordwell, *Narration*, 103.

38   Ferdinand de Saussure, *Cours de linguistique générale*, ed. Charles Bally and Albert Sechehaye (Paris, 1955), 29–31, 98–99, 121, 157, and 317.

39   Mark Turner, *Death is the Mother of Beauty: Mind, Metaphor, Criticism* (Chicago, 1987), 6.

40   Jerry A. Fodor and Zenon W. Pylyshyn, "How Direct is Visual Perception?: Some Reflections on Gibson's 'Ecological Approach,'" *Cognition* 9 (1981): 139–96, especially 171–72.

41   John M. Carroll, "A Program for Cinema Theory," *Journal of Aesthetics and Art Criticism* 35 (1977): 337–52; *Toward a Structural Psychology of Cinema* (Berlin, 1980).

42   *The Standard Edition of the Complete Psychological Works of Sigmund Freud*, ed. and trans. James Strachey (London, 1953–74), 5: 405–60.

43   George Lakoff and Mark Johnson, *Metaphors We Live By* (Chicago, 1980), chaps.

25–30; George Lakoff, *Women, Fire, and Dangerous Things: What Categories Reveal about the Mind* (Chicago, 1987); Mark Johnson, *The Body in the Mind: The Bodily Basis of Meaning, Imagination and Reason* (Chicago, 1987).

44 Norman N. Holland, "The New Paradigm: Subjective or Transactive?" *New Literary History* 7 (1976): 335–46.

Securing the Fictional Narrative as

a Tale of the Historical Real:

The Return of Martin Guerre

Janet Staiger

★ ★ ★ ★ ★ ★ In the first sentence of his review of *The Return of Martin Guerre*,[1] Vincent Canby writes: "This is, as they say, a true story."[2] Given contemporary philosophy and historiography's skepticism over using, much less combining, the words "true" and "story," it seems pertinent to consider the ideological and psychoanalytical implications of our narrativization of the historical real and our repetitive compulsion to appropriate, mobilize, dramatize, and yet to fix in that movement the past for the present—"to fix" in a double sense as in "to halt" and "to cure." If narrative is understood as "taking place" and as operating on trajectories of desires, it is also a framing, an aggressive act of holding "in place," and a settling of that desire into its proper space. Additionally, if the narrativization of the past is symptomatic of the subject's search for a mastery and coherence of self and other and self-as-signifying, then, doubly pertinent, are cases of films which for all practical purposes might remain neatly entrenched in fictional narrative but are claimed for the historical real as "authentic," "realistic," a "true story." What is the meaning of saying: "This is, as they say, a true story"?

I am interested in exploring not only Canby's remark but also the American popular critical response to *Martin Guerre*. Specifically, the questions that mobilize my plot are: How was this fictional narrative secured as a tale of the historical real? What intertextual and textual processes and what ideological and psychoanalytical drives promoted the double fixing of a commercially released art film as some kind of "true story"? What has this to do with "who needs narrative"? The answers, I think, are embedded in—or perhaps, really, on the surface of—Canby's sentence.

The American critical response to *The Return of Martin Guerre* was generally positive. Of the nineteen reviews or review-background articles that I sampled, only one would fall into the "thumbs down" category. I shall have more to say about these reviews later, but for now I would like to localize what the American critics laid out as significant features of the film. In particular, a contradiction develops in their descriptions, and it is around and through that contradiction that I would like to explore the methodical neurosis of our compulsion to fix history.

Canby thought *Martin Guerre* was a "social history of an unusually rich sort." He writes that Gerard Depardieu who played one of the Martins looked the way a sixteenth-century peasant should look and that the film was shot in southwest France, near the place where the events represented occurred between 1542 and 1561. Canby also remarks that the cinematographer lit the film in "the tones of amber, olive and umber associated with Brueghel's paintings of 16th-century village life." While pointing backwards to all of this "historical accuracy," Canby at the same time references the present by claiming that the film has an "immediacy." Although set in the past, it speaks to us.

Annette Insdorf suggests that the film "gives new life to a legendary folk tale by insisting on its 'timelessness.' . . . With visual compositions that recall Flemish painting and music that blends medieval sounds with electronic instrumentation, the film conveys the flavor of the Middle Ages as well as the modernity of the tale's implications." Stanley Kauffmann says that for artful historical films—this one included—one is struck with the anachronistic problem of how a camera could be there to photograph the events: the film "enters a world of data communication to which it doesn't belong."

These responses suggest at least one contradiction. The critics speak of the believability and historical accuracy of certain details but also of a timelessness, a universality, something that transcends historical time. So one asks, can this film be both specific in time and place and also universal? How did the film seem to achieve a sense of historical accuracy and also seem to have some universality?

Intertextuality seems a useful notion for explaining this experience. Whether or not we believe that our knowledge of the world is totally mediated by language, few would disagree that once we enter into representations of the real, we are embarked within semiotic activities and, hence, into all sorts of language systems. Our sense of the real becomes mediated by and through specific sociohistorical discourses. In fact, other texts are our sources of suggesting what the real is to us, and every kind of text is in some sense a representation of the real. In English, the word "representation" means to "re-present" something else, but it also has a possibility of meaning "to refer to." That is, in a representation the original is never there but always absent, a representation of, a referring to, some authentic or original real. The semiotic process, then, is a compulsive attempt to point to and to fix the real, a kind of valiant but vain talking cure for the split subject. This proposition about semiotics is well known in our poststructuralist era. Despite this, however, semiotic gestures continue—not the least of which are conference papers and articles about semiotic gestures.

Whole sets of knowledges are accepted as providing us with our notions of the real. These include scientific discourses, popular knowledges, religious beliefs, and the kinds of pointings we produce from paintings, sculptures, novels, and, of course, from films. Let me suggest an instance of how crucial this intertextuality is in merely comprehending a narrative. When we read a story or view a film, no innate comprehension occurs. Even so simple an act as organizing the chronology of events requires the intertextual discourse available from scientific texts about time. Specifically, Western religions and Western science assume that geo-centered time has particular characteristics. It is unidirectional, continuous, regular, and unique. Other ways of thinking about time exist in other cultures, some believing that time is cyclical, returning to an eternal beginning.

This conjunction between Western religious and geo-centered scientific discourses about temporality is a powerful one—these intertextual discourses not only inflect the production of our narrative texts but also their reception. Obviously, because of the potentials of plot manipulation, story events can be put in nonchronological order. In addition, temporal gaps are common for dramatic intensification. It is not uncommon, either, for texts to represent two or more times the same story event—motivated usually as partial or conflicting accounts of that event.

Martin Guerre can be segmented into forty-one plot scenes.[3] Scenes 1 through 4 occur on "one Sunday in August in 1542" in the small village of Artigat when the very youthful Martin Guerre weds, but apparently does not bed, the similarly young Bertrande de Rols, consolidating the properties and wealth of two peasant families. Scene 5 depicts the arrival some eighteen years later of Jean de Coras, a magistrate from the region, who has entered the village to conduct an investigation, to make an account of and to account for the past. He proceeds to take the oral testimony of Bertrande, now an older woman. Scenes 5 through 27 alternate between this moment of the magistrate's lawful and forceful acquisition of a tale of the past and a series of flashbacks motivated by Bertrande's story of the families' history. Represented in visual images, then, are the villagers' ridicule of Martin at Candlemas when no children are produced from the union, as well as Bertrande's humiliation because she remains with Martin; the successful use of exorcism to cure Martin of impotence; the birth of a son but the continuing emotional distance of Martin; Martin's quarrel with his father; Martin's disappearance for eight years, contributing to his parents' death and removing Bertrande from her social position as wife of the major village landowner. Then a man arrives— I shall label him Martin 2—whom, after some hesitation, the villagers and Bertrande accept as the "returned" Martin. This is the first return of Martin Guerre.

The changes in Martin 2 seem positive: he is now the center of the family social life through his storytelling, his ability to read and write, and his acts as a good husband and father. Any questions of his identity are quelled through his apparent knowledge of so many facts of the past public and private life of the villagers. A daughter is born. For some three years or so, all goes well until two vagabonds enter the village and declare that the "real" Martin lost a leg in a war and that Martin 2 is Arnaud from Tiel. Martin 2 requests an accounting from his uncle Pierre of the profits from Martin's lands during his absence. The conversation deteriorates when Martin 2 threatens to turn to the law in order to obtain these assets, and Pierre responds through the authority of the vagabonds' insinuations that Martin 2 is an impostor. The tenor of the village becomes acrimonious as sides are chosen, and Martin's cousins physically attack Martin 2, trying to murder him.

In scene 28 Coras concludes the trial, arguing that no document— oral or written—exists that would prove Martin 2 is not who he says he is, that would split the body of this man from the name of Martin Guerre. Furthermore, Pierre is fined for slandering Martin 2. Scene 29 shows Martin 2 and Bertrande in bed that evening. The following morning, in scene 30, Pierre, Martin's cousin, and the village priest arrive with a document that they claim Bertrande has signed, saying this is not the real Martin. Scenes 31 through 39 constitute the taking and weighing of more testimony in the second trial, with the surprise appearance at just the last moment of a one-legged man—for our purposes Martin 3—who is finally declared the "true" Martin, stripping the appellation from Martin 2 and affixing, halting, and curing the unstable relation between proper name and body. This is the second return of Martin Guerre.

The trial's drama centers on varieties of documents—physical, written, and oral—as well as hypothesized explanations of the individuals' actions, including witchcraft, greed, bribery, and sexual desire, to establish the "facts." In particular, the village priest is represented as supportive of doctrines of witchcraft whereas Coras is impressed, and in some sense awed, by Martin 2's rationality and appeal to logic. Martin 2's defeat finally comes when Coras discovers a contradiction in Martin 2's storytelling. Upon Martin 3's arrival,

Martin 2 denies ever seeing him before, but later Martin 2 explains Martin 3's knowledge of intimate domestic details as due to Martin 3's cribbing the information from conversations with Martin 2. The incoherent discourse about the past sunders the bond of name and body, but the court reattaches the sign to a newly returned Martin Guerre. Scenes 40 and 41, in a classic denouement, cover Coras's final questioning of Bertrande, what she really knew and her interiorized motivations, as well as Martin 2's public execution. A short voice-over postscript informs us that Coras "found this prodigious imposture so awesome that he recorded it for posterity." We learn as well that twelve years later, during the St. Bartholomew's Day massacre, Coras was hung, "a victim of his Protestant convictions."

The digressionary accounting of the "facts" is a good instance of the function of intertextual discourses in mediating comprehension of semiotic systems. In particular, *Martin Guerre* displays some very common characteristics of Western cinematic narratives: the technique of flashbacks not only provides critical expositional information, it also clothes that information in all the glory of the visual rather than the dry oral testimony of Bertrande. Our film experience becomes quite at odds with what it might have been had the events been ordered sequentially. Actually, not only have intertextual discourses on "real time" mediated the filmic experience, so too have discourses on narratives, character psychology, and the cinematic apparatus. Because of knowledges of the way a camera works, the processes of printing, and the potentials of editing, no spectator is surprised when films present events out of order, in fast or slow motion, with gaps, or multiple times. The technological apparatus has permitted the representation of the events that way.

Additionally, Gerard Genette explains that "public opinion" provides a norm against which events in a text are judged for their plausibility: "To understand the behavior of a character (for example), is to be able to refer it back to an approved maxim, and this reference is perceived as a demonstration of cause and effect."[4] In the case of *Martin Guerre*, Coras acts for the reader as a textual interrogator, especially as he seeks to correlate Bertrande's behavior with some accepted rationale, in particular trying to locate it in a discourse about woman's sexual desire. As Genette suggests, this attempt by "public opinion" to *locate* is ideological, or as Roland Barthes might express it, it is the desire for a myth which will "transform history into nature . . . [so that history] is immediately frozen."[5]

Such a fixing, securing, or pinning down of the past as coherent is not attempted for the past's sake but for the sake of the present—such a representation appears to ward off the threatening anxiety of having to recognize the inability of an individual to control and master the self-as-subject. In this way, Coras's standing-in-for-the-reader is not innocent; he functions to propose and affirm contemporary twentieth-century bourgeois and patriarchal ideologies of character motivation, cultural stereotypes, and sexual difference.

So the intertextuality I have in mind is not simply a moment in a text or some relation between two texts, but rather a fundamental and unceasing spectatorial activity, the semiotic action of processing a filmic narrative by repeated referencing and referring to other texts. Intertextuality as understood from a poststructuralist perspective is a constant and irretrievable circulation of textuality, a returning to, a pointing toward, an aggressive attempt to seize other documents —the results of this procedure of referencing other texts are also complicitly and irrevocably circular and ideological. For although the activity of intertextuality is neutral and without cessation, none of the discourses invoked are neutral nor is the real ever fixed, halted, and cured but only referred to, compulsively and repetitiously.[6]

One of my questions has been why *Martin Guerre* managed to secure in its United States critical reception the sense of appearing to be historically specific yet universal. Understanding the processes of intertextuality is useful in beginning to answer that question. In a more substantial way, I return to Canby's sentence, "This is, as they say, a true story," to focus on "as they say" as a gesture provoking intertextuality. The "they" is, no doubt, no specific group of people; "they" are a set of texts in circulation in the social formation that give authenticity to the notion that "this" is "a true story"; "they" are its adjacent texts, including publicity articles, talk show interviews, advertising, and, of course, reviews. "They" are something else as well. For the "they" in Canby's remark is ironically, and with some subterfuge, not only a set of texts. The "they" is also "me"—Vincent Canby —the author of a text which will be read by hundreds of thousands of potential film-going spectators. "This is, as they/I say, a true story."

How does Canby know that "this" film is an instance of "as they say, a true story"? It might seem simple to pin down this "they" to a single text—the pressbook distributed with the film.[7] In fact, Canby's review is not unique. Of the nineteen reviews sampled, fifteen specifically mention that the film was based on past events, two clearly do not, and two were somewhat ambiguous. The two reviews that ignore the "truth" of the story are by Roger Ebert, in which he stresses that *Martin Guerre* is a "perceptive mystery, a charming love story," and by Janet Maslin, who dotes on the congruence between the body of Depardieu and the role of Martin 2. Now if the "they" is circulating and replacing "I," and if "I" replaces "they," from where did the pressbook derive its knowledges? In part from social historian Natalie Zemon Davis who served—we are told in four of the film reviews, in two book reviews, an interview, and the film's credits —as "historical consultant." But also from a number of other texts, ranging through the genres of two novels, a play, an operetta, and the original Jean de Coras's narrative. His story, the film tells us, came from the oral testimony of the participants who recounted the events during the two trials. All we have as "origin" is another text, the oral history and testimony of "eye" witnesses.

Turning back to the present, I would note a second feature of the reviews besides their general claim that *Martin Guerre* recounts a true story. The reviews also emphasize that the film has specific characteristics that make it historically authentic. These include facts about the film's production as well as one other set of texts. Ten of the reviewers consider this film authentic in part because it reminds them of other representations created in the same period. Such a proposition derives from the notion that somehow Brueghel, La Tour, and Flemish paintings should be considered reasonably authentic representations of the people of the sixteenth century because of the adjacent date of their manufacture. Since we do not assume that early Egyptian paintings faithfully mimic real Egyptians, our assumption that Brueghel's or the Flemish paintings might do so must result from our pointing to other texts: discourses on art history. Brueghel is, "as they say," a "representational" painter. Yet our knowledge of this period's visible, physical surface is dependent wholly on paintings and sculptures: we have—as Stanley Kauffmann reminds us—no photographs.

I stress the point of intertextuality so much, particularly for this film, because of the critical attention the reviewers have paid to what might be called surface or physical or visible features: that is, features such as props, sets, costumes, lighting, bodies, and bodily gestures. The *physical* world of the film has been described as authentic and consequently true; its visible world has been pointed to and fixed as specifically historical. What has been used by the film and its contextualizing discourses to authenticate its claim to be a "true story" is, as one reviewer put it, "a surface sheen."

You already may have read my subtext. Even if one could say that the film in some sense really did represent completely the physical or visible world of the 1500s, it would be said within an ideology that what is visible is what is real. The gesture of saying, "this is, as they say, a true story," has been complemented by texts pointing to the authentic as "visible," unmediated, and by knowledges apparent to the perceiving subject's eye and ear—from "eye and ear witnesses": the oral testimonies recorded by Coras of the villagers and Bertrande de Rols.

Thus, on the one hand, this film and its adjacent texts promote spectatorial activity of reference to other "authentic" texts, hoping to secure for a fictional narrative the status of being a tale of the historical real, of fixing it as a coherent representation, and a return of the bonding of the body of the past and its name. This referencing is primarily accomplished through pointers related to texts about the visible or physical world. In fact, the process is duplicating the film's obsession with the returning Martin Guerres—where matching witnesses' accounts of visible bodily features is considered critical empirical evidence in establishing Martin's identity. At the same time, however, and perhaps more significantly, aspects other than visible authenticity can very easily, by something of a parasitic attachment, be dragged along as seemingly part of the real. Not the least of these is the fictional narrative as a distortion through elision, conversion, emphasis, and incompleteness of the real. Although previously written somewhat ironically, I would now say that only Roger Ebert's review resisted this fallacious procedure, refusing as it did to consider *Martin Guerre* as other than "a charming love story." On the other hand, although this film and its readers may aggressively attempt to secure *Martin Guerre* for the historical real through surrounding texts ("this is, as they say"), its "realism" is also pursued through the film's narrative structure and narrational procedures. Although I do not have space to consider all of the textual features operating, two seem particularly significant: the voice-over narrator and the flashbacks.

As indicated above, scenes 1 through 4 represent the major events of Martin and Bertrande's marriage day. More particularly, in the third scene when a marriage broker arrives, the voice-over of a narrator says the following: "You won't regret having taken the time to follow this narrative, for it is neither a tale of adventure nor an extravagant fantasy that you will hear but a true story in all its purity. It all began on one Sunday in August in 1542. . . ." We must add to our list of "they's" this narration as one of those "saying" this is a true story. But the words of this narration are only of minor note in the more subtle operations. Beside the statement's content is its procedure. For one thing, the narration is highly specific. It is not "sometime in the sixteenth century" but Sunday, August 1542. It isn't just any place in France but Artigat. And the voice of this narrator is masculine. It is a voice of some authority, being neither weak nor high-pitched, and it is nondiegetic: this masculine narrator never appears in the story itself. Because the narrator is not a participant, a typical viewer would tend to assume that the narrator has no motivation for lying to us. Not only that, but through "public opinion," patriarchal structures, narrational conventions, and intertextual knowledges, the narrator is positioned as all-knowing. The function of this voice-over, nondiegetic narrator is to get us to believe what it says.

Beginning a film with a voice-over, nondiegetic narrator is a common device, and sometimes this function is served by intertitles. Even so, those intertitles take on a kind of distance from the events which are embedded and presented as diegetic. Because framing information is a "separate" text, at a distance and not part of the enclosed story, it can easily take on an authenticity in comparison to that which it embeds. Yet this voice-over of masculine authority assures (or perhaps reassures) us of the educational value of this true story—doubling and redoubling its claims.

Thus the voice-over narrator acts here in a subtle way as a textual device of compulsively repeating, "this is, as 'I' say, a true story." And, equally subtly, so do the flashbacks. In the fifth scene, Coras, the magistrate, begins an interrogation of Bertrande who recalls—in chronological sequence—the events following her marriage. Alternating between the questioner and filmic visualizations of Bertrande's oral speech, scenes 6 through 26 represent the events leading up to and including the dispute between Martin 2 and Pierre over the truth of Martin 2's identity and of Pierre's greed. Each accuses the other of lying. In some sense, scene 26 is the cause of scene 5: village life has been so destabilized over the issue of property rights that the State, in the form of Coras, must enter the conflict between the two versions of "the true story." The rest of the film, scenes 27 through 41, operates as consequences of scene 5.

I am interested in the fact that much of the film's exposition used later to authenticate Martin 2's claims relies upon a reader matching Bertrande's visions and Martin 2's oral references to the events represented in those visions. Specifically, scenes 6, 8, 10, 11, 13, 15, 16, and 18 through 26 are motivated as visual versions of her oral testimony—from the woman's voice. I would ask, why flashbacks? Why not just have Bertrande testify? Yes, it is pleasurable (from conventional standards and psychoanalytical processes) to "watch" Bertrande's discourse for fifteen or thirty minutes. But more pertinent to my analysis is that the flashbacks, by which we seem to "see" the events, render them some implicit authenticity. The visible is conventionally more believable than the aural. Furthermore, the way the flashbacks are put together tends to elide the fact that this is Bertrande's testimony, one version of the story, perhaps abetted by stereotypes of the sixteenth-century peasant women. Very little overlap of Bertrande's or Coras's voice exists within the space of the images, as the sound track rapidly converts to a diegetically synchronized voice. That is, the image-sound coordination as well as Bertrande's testimony-under-oath seem, if not actually to authenticate the images, at least not to raise the possibility of their being anything but what they seem to be—representations, a fixing of visual space as narrative real. By diminishing the role of Bertrande's voice and by using the ideology of an apparent truth in the visible, the flashbacks operate much as the adjacent texts and the voice-over narrator to say, "this is/was, as they/I say, a true story." Nevertheless, in spite of the activity of intertextuality as well as the textual devices of a voice-over narrator and flashbacks that claim this film is pointing to, referring to, historical authenticity, there remains a contradiction in the critical response, one which, not surprisingly, overthrows this attempt to make coherent the name of "true story" and the body, *The Return of Martin Guerre.*

A period film points toward a particular moment and place, while a film that implies universality references a much wider body of time and space. How can both references exist simultaneously? The answer is, through a very typical strategy. The film implies that what's historical is a physical reality. It is the mise-en-scène, the props, the costumes, and the people that are historical. What is universal is "inside" or "beneath" this—essences of humanity and relations among people. What is really being claimed as universal and hence *real* are the constant social relations and explanations of human beings. Physical particularities, though "true," provide only the surface sheen; they are transitory; they are merely of the moment, and not the "real truth." Thus a sign points to a sign that stands for another sign—the fixing, halting, curing of our desire to reference the real. That final sign is a "myth," a public opinion certified only by social contract and hegemonic ideological discourses.

Martin Guerre can be said to propose two conflicting explanations of the significant "depth" relation, or "essence of humanity," upon which or from which social relations and institutions work and function: medieval Catholicism and bourgeois liberal humanism. Like our two returned Martins, the true identities of these ideologies (and their respective "universality") are at stake. In fact, however, just as the claim of historical authenticity in this film is questionable, so too is the narrative's purported explanation of the causal chain of events.

The story's precipitating event is Martin 2's request for an accounting of assets, which provokes overt violence and the entrance of institutions to resolve the family's differences. Intriguingly, notions of the separation between the private sphere and the public are dissolved in the sequence of these events. The family cannot solve the dispute because it is not separated from the public; its very structure has been set up upon an economic contract—the marriage agreement. The family is an institution based in the economic sphere, incapable of settling its own dispute because it is within the problem. Yet the institution that is called in is not neutral. In fact, in a major displacement of the final voice-over narration, this dispute—the war of the Guerres—is not merely about the truth of one potential patriarchy, but about dominance among institutions. At a transitional time when the Catholic church is losing sectors of its power to insurgent Protestants, and as the liberal state takes authority over the economic base, *Martin Guerre* traces wide disturbances in the discourses of "the truth."

I have said that the final voice-over narration is significantly displaced, putting at the end of the film what is the narrative's teleological origin. In this conclusion which is also a beginning, our authoritative masculine nondiegetic narrator gives us only two small bits of information: he explains how the story managed to be recorded (Coras was so impressed with it), and informs us that in the religious prosecutions twelve years later, Coras was killed: "a victim of his Protestant convictions. But as surely as death awaits all mortals, the spirit lives on forever."

Retrospectively, the opposition between the village priest and Coras reproduces the larger conflict. The narrative represents the priest as believing in witchcraft, demons, and spirits; he argues that Martin 2's actions have been controlled by the devil. Coras seeks other explanations, appealing, as the priest does, to public opinion: it is plausible that people have such good memories, that the past is a text that the subject can reference, and that Martin's logic and reasoning could only come from an innocent. In the denouement, Coras's final interrogation of Bertrande seeks a source or explanation for her testimony, which he finally provides for her through his suggestion that sexual desire is the cause. The Catholic church is thus associated with the irrational past, the judge with future rational humanism—which the narrator claims still exists.

Subtending the film, then, is the proposition that the conflict is over explaining the subject within the social. It is not by chance that it is *Coras*'s record that remains for our history; it is not to the priest's account that we refer for our "true story." The film explicitly sides with Coras's version, his spirit, his rational, humanist version of the subject as a unified speaking self, cohering in mind, body, and speech. Yet Coras falls into the ideological difficulties of empiricism, taking the document to say what it appears to say, to match signs and referents. "This was and is, as they/I say, a true story." Strangely enough, "the true story" contradicts him (and itself and the reader) as the "true Martin" arrives in a deus ex machina climax.

Yet I would agree that, in another sense, this is a true story. For *Martin Guerre* might well be said to represent history as an ideological struggle over power and hegemony whose actors are driven by instincts of desire and death. The film points to the real, or true, in the sense that it represents human beings within the social formation as split subjects. Anxiety about the subject's helplessness within this state of affairs, I would argue, compulsively propels the narrative's repetition, my own repetition as a reader analyzing it, and the drive to order the past.

Having said this, I need to step back once more, turning this film and my argument around one more time. Pierre Macherey has written:

> We understand then what we must seek in texts; not signs of their cohesion and of their autonomy, but the material contradictions which produce them and which are produced there in the form of conflicts. If literature is an objective reflection of reality, it is because literature is determined by the antagonisms which constitute it not as a totality, but as a historical and social material reality. Literature expresses these conflicts and adds to them an imaginary resolution; but these solutions, these com-

promises which are finally the texts, continue to bear the mark of the divisions which give them a real base, a reality, and also an interest.[8]

Although a number of Macherey's remarks are valuable, for my purposes two points stand out as I return to my questions about securing together narratives and the historical real and about who needs narratives and why. For one thing, Macherey assumes a relation between literature and the historical real, but with literature "add[ing] to [the material conflicts] an imaginary resolution." Although I have only implied how I might define a narrative, if I were to note one feature, it would be "resolution," if not outright closure. Macherey's comments also indicate that the major distinction between texts and the real is not objective coherence or autonomy in either case, but imaginary coherence or autonomy for the textual—imaginary in the double sense of not real and pre-oedipal. If I have just said that this film does represent the real, it is because I have employed the process of intertextuality and have claimed the authority of my textual representation of the real (historical materialism and poststructuralism) in so doing. I have narrativized the historical real into a resolution of imaginary coherence in order to compare the propositions of the text before me with the text of the historical real which I believe to be "a true story." This compromise bears its mark in my circulating around and around "this was/is, as they/I say, a true story." I am securing my fictional narrative, this article, as a tale of the historical real as has *Martin Guerre* and its adjacent texts. Not content with allowing the fictional narrative to be the only narrative, the critics, the film, the voice-over diegetic narrator, and I have narrativized history. And, I would add, so has Macherey.

Macherey's remarks about imaginary resolutions, however, contain a gesture directed in a second way. Any text will bear the traces of its own compulsion to point to an imaginary coherence since its compromises "continue to bear the mark of the divisions" which produced them. Perhaps here Freud's observations about the compulsion to repeat will now make sense as one of the controlling motifs for this essay. It is in his later work in relation to the famous reformulation and postulation of the death instinct that he uses the concept of repetition compulsion as part of his proof.[9] The death instinct as aggressive, potentially directed outward or inward toward the self, operates in conflict with Eros, but also at times in conjunction. This instinct is functionally critical for cessation of tension, but also, for Freud, for the survival of the species. Freud writes, for instance, that "order is a kind of compulsion to repeat [in which] . . . one is spared hesitation and indecision."[10] In this thesis, sadism and masochism "contain an element distinct from sexuality, in the form of a desire for mastery or subjugation."[11] The death instinct could also be seen in dreams, in the child's fort-da game, and in any compulsive repetition where repetition is a form of discharge which, when carried to extremes (that is, as a compulsion), functions both "to restore a state that is historically primitive and also marked by the total draining of energy, i.e., death." What is repeated and transformed rather than remembered is the repressed material. The neurotic " 'repeats instead of remembering.' "[12] Freud considers masochism older than sadism, but when the instinct is directed aggressively against the external world, sadism may be how we avoid our own self-destruction. In fact, it is the cohesion of an outward aggression and Eros that permits our continued living. This sadism, Freud notes, is "accompanied by an extraordinarily high degree of narcissistic enjoyment, owing to its presenting the ego with a fulfillment of the latter's old wishes for omnipotence."[13]

In so many ways, while *Martin Guerre* displays the trajectories of desire associated with Eros, it also aggressively turns outward and then inward to try to master and order the self's history, to order plot and past, to contain separations of body and name, to restore, finally, a primitive and imaginary narcissistic state in which the subject is presumed whole.

Peter Brooks applies the notion of compulsive repetition to the text of *Great Expectations* and expands it to include both narrative structure and the reader's relation to the narrative. For Brooks, "repetition is a symbolic enactment referring back to unconscious determinants, progressive in that it belongs to the forward thrust of desire . . . but regressive in its points of reference."[14] The climax or resolution of a narrative becomes the "scene that decisively re-enacts both a return of the repressed and a return to the primal moment of childhood [that was forgotten]."[15] It is an attempt to master the past—which is ultimately the "return to the quiescence of the inorganic, of the nontextual," of death.[16] Hence Brooks argues that "*Great Expectations* is exemplary in demonstrating both the need for plot and its status as deviance, both the need for narration and the necessity to be cured from it": a desire to plot "the meaning of life" but, in its nonavailability, the condemnation to "repetition, rereading."[17]

If Macherey and Brooks are correct, the resolution of a narrative should still bear the marks of its primary divisions, pointing back to the forgotten past, if not necessarily reproducing it. The opposition that is animating *Martin Guerre* is marked not only in the text, but also in the critical discourse in and surrounding the film. Is the real surface or essence? How is it knowable? Here, another aspect of Freud's work is of use: his revised understanding of anxiety in relation to the crises of the individual, whereby anxiety becomes a cause (not an effect). If the individual forecasts the possibilities of a dangerous situation, anxiety can be used as a signal mechanism which the subject hopes will prevent the future difficulty. In terms of the psychic functions of narrative, telling stories may be pleasurable as they serve the aggressive instinct; they may also be acting as signals when the individual constructs an idea that the future holds the danger of the helplessness associated with loss of coherency of self. If narratives are about the past, they are also about the present and the future.

In Alfred Hitchcock's film *Stagefright*, the plot is structured around a flashback, but in the resolution of the film, we discover that the flashback was a lie told by one of the protagonists who turns out to be the sought-after-murderer. In *Martin Guerre*, I do not believe that the audience questions the testimony of Bertrande as it is presented. Yet the final encounter between Coras and Bertrande requires a reevaluation of this presumption. The conversation leaves a strong sense that Bertrande lied throughout the trials and either suspected or knew all along that Martin 2 was not her husband. Significant to this interpretation is the telling absence of any scenes in which Martin 2 and Bertrande discuss the events through which they are living.

If it is possible that Bertrande lied, then it is highly probable that all of her testimony and all of the flashbacks are colored, subjective, and incomplete. More broadly put, it is reasonable to conclude that the visible (as physical surface and as photograph) refers inadequately or not at all to the reality of the subject's discursive interiorized social utterances which motivate his or her actions and discourse in human relations; that the visible, through cinematic narrative, can point only subjectively and distortingly toward the real. Phrased in another way, all there is is surface, text, representation rather than recollection, return, and reconstitution.

Besides the subjective flashbacks and the omission of events is the implication of the climax, the imaginary resolution. Note that Martin 2 maintains his credibility by his knowledge and use of small details about the past—that is, surface features. In particular, for instance, he references Bertrande's accounts of events to authenticate his identity. Similarly, the film tries to gain its credibility. Using props, sets, costumes, and lighting to give the appearance of authenticity, of telling through these visible features that its representation of the past is the truth, it uses small details of the visible just as Martin 2 does in his attempt to secure his narrative fiction as a tale of the historical real. "This is/was, as they/I say, a true story."

But it turns out that Martin 2 lied as well, that according to all standards of judgment of the institutions, he was merely a simulacrum of Martin Guerre. If he lied, contradicting what he said he saw and said, then, as in the case of Bertrande, the truth of the story's fiction is suspect. And surface reality, the visible reality of cinema, may lie too: the potential for lying is something endemic to representations as semiotic systems. A cinema that relies on the visible or that requires intertextuality for its credibility is always involved in representations, and how can cinema not do this? Representations, while possibly referring to a historical real, will always be imaginary references and resolutions, "compromises," as Macherey says.

And once discourse can lie, can point elsewhere, and once the speaking subject can be elsewhere, then Western rational humanism meets its crisis. Is it by accident that a text so grounded in the visual real should also conclude itself by referring to the death of Coras-as-believer-in-narrative-as-historical-document? Yet an imaginary resolution of coherence of name and body, torn asunder by the subjective subject and potential liar, symptomatically concludes in the return of the oral testimony of an omniscient nonbodied masculine narrator, compulsively and repetitiously "fixing" history. The narrative ends, doubly self-destructively, in the death of not only Martin 2 but also of Coras, the liberal humanist who hoped to account for the past and who stood in for us, the viewers, who try unsuccessfully to know the truth through two trials, an ex post facto interrogation of Bertrande, and a final written history. It ends with the death of visible surface as document, in a cessation of desire to master the past as reproducible for the present, to retrieve narcissistically the self-as-signifying and unified. As a text built upon intertextual circulations, its origins continue to refer to, to point to, but not to recollect and remember as it asserts that Coras's essence lives on. Again, the repetitions symptomatic in the duplicating returns of Martin Guerre stake out this film's neurosis as did the other vain attempts to fix by representing the text via intertextuality as historical real.

If I were to ask, then, "who needs narrative?", Freud would, I think, say, "everyone." The drive to narrativize the past and to secure the fictional tale as pointing to that historical real is understandable as a repetitious desire to fix, to halt and cure. It is the death instinct aligned with Eros, a signal anxiety of our time. In some sense, then, I can end only with a small final amending of Vincent Canby's sentence: "This is/was, as they/I say, maybe kind of a true story." That's the imaginary resolution that I desire for the end of this time through the narrative.

Notes

This essay is a revision of a lecture presented at the "Film: Who Needs Narrative?" Conference at the City University Graduate Center, New York, New York, 24 April 1987. I would like to thank those participants for their comments. In particular, I thank Ann Kaplan and assure her that I do believe in history even if knowing it is somewhat complicated. Additionally, I thank Vincent Rocchio whose thoughts about anxiety were very stimulating to me at just the right time.

1   Daniel Vigne (director), *Le Retour de Martin Guerre*. French release in May 1982; United States release through European International Distribution in June 1983.

2   Vincent Canby, "Film: 'Martin Guerre,'" *New York Times*, 10 June 1983, sec. 3,

p. 5. Two review/background articles and seventeen reviews composed the sampling for this study. The review/background articles are: Michael Blowen, " 'Martin Guerre' director Vigne surprised at film's U.S. success," *Boston Globe/Independent Press* reprinted in Chicago *Sun-Times*, 21 August 1983, 4; and Annette Insdorf, "A Medieval Tale Is Relived on Film," *New York Times*, 5 June 1983, sec. 2, pp. 1, 19. Besides Canby's, the reviews are: David Ansen, "Great Pretender?" *Newsweek*, 27 June 1983, 80; Lewis Archibald, "The Return of Martin Guerre," *The Aquarian*, 25 May 1983, 4; Edward Benson, "*Le Retour de Martin Guerre*," *Film Quarterly* 38 (Fall 1984): 34–37; Michael Blowen, " 'Martin Guerre' is one of year's best," *Boston Globe*, 24 June 1983, 30; David Denby, "The Return of Martin Guerre," *New York/Cue*, 23 May 1983, 91; Roger Ebert, " 'Martin Guerre' is perceptive mystery, charming love story," Chicago *Sun-Times*, 18 August 1983, 74; Michael Feingold, "Peasant Under Glass," *Village Voice*, 14 June 1983, 54; Stanley Kauffmann, "The Historical Present," *New Republic*, 2 May 1983, 24–25; "Len," "Le Retour de Martin Guerre," *Variety*, 9 June 1982, 16; Ernest Leogrande, "A Moving, sensitive 'Martin Guerre,' " New York *Daily News*, 10 June 1983, Friday sec., 5; Mark Levinson, "The Return of Martin Guerre," *Cineaste* 13 (1984): 47–49; Janet Maslin, "When Role and Actor Are Perfectly Matched," *New York Times*, 21 August 1983, sec. 2, p. 17; Marcia Pally, "The Return of Martin Guerre," *New York Native*, 9–22 May 1983, 49; David Sterritt, "Disappointing French films," *Christian Science Monitor*, 26 May 1983, 16; Judy Stone, " 'Martin Guerre'—Bed and Bored," *San Francisco Chronicle*, 1 July 1983, 64; Archer Winsten, " 'Guerre' crackles with French suspense," *New York Post*, 10 June 1983, 43. It should be pointed out that this is not an unbiased sample, relying as it does on the indexing and clipping services of the New York Public Library and the Lincoln Center Performing Arts Research Center. It does, however, have the advantage of covering many of the sources of United States tastemaking.

3   By "plot" I mean the events as represented in the text; by "story" I refer to the chronology that we mentally produce through textual and intertextual semiosis and which has existence only as an ex post facto generalization.

4   Gerard Genette, cited in Nancy K. Miller, "Emphasis Added: Plots and Plausibilities in Women's Fictions," in *The New Feminist Criticism: Essays on Women, Literature, and Theory*, ed. Elaine Showalter (New York, 1985), 340.

5   Roland Barthes, *Mythologies*, trans. Annette Lavers (New York, 1972), 129.

6   It is "neutral" in so far as it occurs in multiple modes of production and thus should not be characterized as a symptom of bourgeois capitalism or patriarchy.

7   See Benson, "*Le Retour*," 34.

8   Pierre Macherey, "The Problem of Reflection," *Sub-stance* 15 (1976): 18.

9   Sigmund Freud, *New Introductory Lectures on Psychoanalysis*, ed. and trans. James Strachey (New York, 1965), 102–8; Sigmund Freud, *Civilization and Its Discontents*, ed. and trans. James Strachey (New York, 1961); *Abstracts of the Standard Edition of the Complete Psychological Works of Sigmund Freud*, ed. Carrie Lee Rothgeb (New York, 1973), 329–30, 368–75, 454–55; and Richard Wollheim, *Sigmund Freud* (New York, 1971), 201–13.

10 Freud, *Civilization and Its Discontents*, 40.
11 Wollheim, *Sigmund Freud*, 207.
12 Freud cited in Wollheim, *Sigmund Freud*, 150.
13 Freud, *Civilization and Its Discontents*, 68.
14 Peter Brooks, *Reading for the Plot: Design and Intention in Narrative* (New York, 1985), 124.
15 Ibid., 127.
16 Ibid., 139.
17 Ibid., 140.

Between Melodrama and Realism:

Anthony Asquith's Underground

and King Vidor's The Crowd

Christine Gledhill

★ ★ ★ ★ ★ ★ *The Classical Hollywood Cinema* by David Bordwell,
Janet Staiger, and Kristin Thompson is currently the most comprehensive account of the formation of mainstream cinema. Contributions by Bordwell and Thompson based on the analysis of three hundred films, principles of filmic construction advocated in the trade
and critical press, and how-to books written for aspiring scenario
writers posit the classic Hollywood text in terms of "a system of narrative logic based on causal relations between story events."[1] While
acknowledging the influence of Hollywood's "nonclassical" sources
such as romantic music and melodrama, Bordwell and Thompson
argue that these are subordinated to the needs of narrative logic:
verisimilitude, causality, psychological realism, linearity, compositional unity—all of which are opposed to melodrama and aim in
particular to eliminate episodic structure and the role of chance and
coincidence. The empirical data used to support this argument are
persuasive but limited by their pursuit of a "specificity" necessary

to the establishment of a new subject—a specificity which cannot take into account the ways that a nineteenth-century melodramatic vision accommodates the changing canons of realism and shifting mores of the turn of the century in which an emerging fictional cinema was caught up. Despite their acknowledgment of nineteenth-century sources, a pared-down construction of melodrama persists in Bordwell and Thompson's concern with cinema's separation from surrounding art forms.

Film theory's conception of melodrama is enlarging through contact with recent histories of nineteenth-century popular arts.[2] Such contact changes the questions that can be asked of cinema's formative history and present state, producing a different configuration of the data and a different perspective on the relation of realism and melodrama. From this encounter with the popular theater of another era, it is possible to highlight procedures and strategies that bring into focus unperceived procedures in contemporary culture. Studies such as Peter Brooks's *The Melodramatic Imagination* seek to derive a working concept of the melodramatic not as a descriptive rendering of specific manifestations of nineteenth-century melodrama, but as a distillation of features that become visible because of particular contemporary cultural and aesthetic concerns.

Rick Altman in this volume offers such a rereading, arguing that the model of dominance implied in Bordwell and Thompson's account of the classic Hollywood text "represses" the influence of popular melodramatic theater, which can be acknowledged only as a kind of rule-breaking excess (the principal way in which melodrama has been discussed in film criticism). Citing recent French revision of the concept of classicism and drawing from Bakhtin, Altman opposes the antithetical construction of classicism and melodrama, arguing on the contrary for the necessity of melodrama/romanticism to the classical.

Despite its attraction, this account does not altogether avoid the mutually exclusive opposition it seeks to redress. Melodrama in Altman's analysis moves from an association with "popular" theater, to its function as a "repressed" voice within classicism, to a role in representing the oppressed in the "sit-in, shooting, strike and revolution." At the same time, however, melodrama is disengaged formally from the world of history, change, and realism in an identification with myth and ritual—"the eternal realm of stereotypes and change-less values." Balzac's melodramatic characters are "beyond psychology." Thus Altman argues that embedded within classic narrative cinema the archetypal paradigms of melodrama produce a tension, an "excess," which also constitutes the truly memorable and affective dimension of Hollywood films. In this account, however, as in Bordwell and Thompson's, melodrama remains an archaic form, the difference being that Altman, rather than suggesting the subordination or elimination of elements incompatible with the demands of classic narrative, sees the persistence of melodrama as a constant source of provocation and resistance. What is missing from this account is the specific experience of the world offered by melodrama. My contention is that Americanization and Hollywood in particular facilitated the modernization of melodrama in a transformation that depended on its relationship *with* realism rather than its antithesis to it. Melodrama in, for example, *Coma*, *Witness*, or *The Color Purple*, is neither an inert nineteenth-century residue, nor an excess indicating a Freudian subtext. It's part of the overt narrative structure, characterization, and mise-en-scène.

If melodrama and realism are not to be theorized as antagonists, new terms for their relationship have to be sought, and a different conception of the mainstream film text developed. Recent attempts to derive the "melodramatic" from the variety of forms in which it appeared in the nineteenth century suggest that melodrama emerged as an aesthetic apprehension of reality that could manage the enormous social changes accompanying the secularization and industrialization of the Western world.[3] As a form developed by newly emerging industries of mass entertainment, melodrama was engaged in constructing a version of the "popular" through which a range of audiences could be served. At this level it had to produce recognition for audiences from different classes and social groupings within an overall imaginative framework that could orchestrate the social and psychic contradictions of the new social order.

In Peter Brooks's account, melodrama offers documents from nineteenth-century experience recast in terms of the moral imagination. What demanded representation was the presence of moral forces which would give significance to a secular world in the double sense of having meaning and mattering. Melodrama produced a highly formalized but flexible repertoire of images and dramatic structures through which the melodramatic imagination could process and interpret the events, images, and conditions of lived experience in clarifying and emotionally satisfying dramatic and moral terms. But this function could not be fulfilled without recognizable reference to the world of the audience, made credible according to standards set by increasingly sophisticated technologies for realistic representation.

Martin Meisel's work on the nineteenth-century "realization"—literally the theatrical materialization of popular narrative paintings, but by extension applicable to a range of interactions between painting, poetry, illustration, fiction, and the stage—provides an illuminating model of the relationship between the imaginary and the real. Meisel describes practices that promised repeated renewal of access to the creations of the imagination, in which the realistic dimensions of a medium different from that in which the work first appeared promised to extend—and commercially exploit—the life of characters or situations that resonated for their audiences with a symbolic charge.[4] The theater as, in Meisel's terms, a "living art," focused this drive. The popular theater gave life not only to paintings, but to novels, news events, historical research, and social documents, through the movements, speech, and actions of living bodies in dramatic reenactments, giving substance to a reality increasingly experienced in terms of mass-produced representations rather than at firsthand. With hindsight it appears that the concept of "realization" implicitly acknowledges the role of the image in the construction of the real, extending the concept of material reality to include social discourses and imagery.

In this sense "realization" suggests perhaps a concept of realism far more compatible with current notions of cultural process than that developed on the basis of the nineteenth-century novel and which has dominated film studies in terms of the "classic realist text." The real is a site of contest, of change and redefinition. Realism names a goal, a polemic, a set of continually changing strategies, rather than a fixed aesthetic. What counts as realism is always open to contestation. In a media-aware age, debates over realism and representation participate in the social and cultural construction of reality.

Melodrama as a theatrical practice quite consciously worked in such reimaging of a reality already constructed, processed in discourses, images, symbolic creations. Melodrama lived off translation, adaptation, piracy, transformation. An "original" melodrama scarcely exists, any particular title appearing in a range of versions none of which could be said to be "authentic." The narrative strategies of melodrama replicate this shifting process of representation in plots that turn on the overheard conversation, the spied-on encounter, the reading of a fortuitously acquired document, and so dramatize the construction, misconstruction, and restoration of realities through the socially given images, discourses, practices by which characters live out their lives. Indeed Brooks suggests that recognition and misrecognition are key devices of the melodramatic plot—devices which have a particular heuristic value for contemporary film theory's concern with representation and identity.

Victorian morality appears to have offered a dynamic schema for such dramatization. In the second half of the nineteenth century, however, the images and structures of Victorian melodrama were increasingly challenged by different groups of writers, critics, and audiences because for a variety of reasons they no longer commanded recognition. The struggle for a new kind of realism in the "new drama" from the 1880s into the early 1900s—which first emerged in Britain and America around attempts to stage Ibsen, Chekhov, and Shaw—constituted a struggle to open up new territories for representation, changing social mores, and therefore new methods of writing, performing, and staging. Moreover, these were the struggles of a different group of writers—literati rather than entertainers—on behalf of a different audience—the intelligentsia rather than a popular middle-class or working-class audience. The second half of the nineteenth century sees, then, an increasing separation of the terms of realism and melodrama so that they could no longer imply or include each other. Arguably once a way of constructing a version of the popular which could embrace different classes, melodrama now served culturally to divide them.

The terms of this disengagement are suggested in two collections of nineteenth-century critical writing: George Rowell's *Victorian Dra-*

matic Criticism, and Montrose Moses and John Mason Brown's *The American Theatre as Seen by Its Critics*.[5] The pieces of journalistic and critical writing collected in these anthologies are interesting for the particular currency they give to the terms realism and melodrama, heralding a transition from one set of usages to another. If as Wylie Sypher and others suggest the melodramatic constitutes an epistemological outlook as well as an aesthetic practice, it is possible for specific practices to be rejected while certain values remain transformed in a more "modern" guise.[6] Thus separation at the level of terminology may conceal a refinement and elision of melodramatic practice within the changing practices of realism or naturalism. In this case the name is rejected while the practice is disguised.

This process can be seen at work in G. H. Lewes's praise of the performance of Charles Mathews and Madame Vestris in *A Day of Reckoning*:

> Vestris and Charles Mathews were *natural*—nothing more, nothing less. They were a lady and gentleman such as we meet in drawing-rooms, graceful, quiet, well-bred, perfectly dressed, perfectly oblivious of the footlights. He is a polished villain—a D'Orsay without conscience, and without any of the scowlings, stampings, or intonations of the approved stage villain. There are scoundrels in high life—but they are perfectly well-bred. . . . In every detail of his dress, in every gesture, and in every look, I recognized an artist representing Nature.[7]

Lewes here redefines melodramatic practices so that they can process representations recognizable to middle-class consumers of "art." Paradoxically, this classbound restraint which came to characterize English theatrical practice is read as an indicator of underlying passion authenticated by virtue of its repression. Reviewing John Martin Harvey's adaptation of *A Tale of Two Cities*, *The Only Way*, J. T. Grein singles out for praise the cast's "suppressed" mode of performance as heightening the dramatic climax:

> Later again when the last hour had sounded, and Carton forfeited his life to save her whom he loved, Mr. Harvey made a great impression, but now it was by his composure, by the sobriety of his words and the suppression of his emotions.[8]

Restraint for the critic William Archer combines adulthood, virility, and intellect, as opposed to the "lollipops and candy" served up to the mass audience and the sensational and feminizing emotion of melodrama: "[D]on't you feel that if art is not virile it is childish and that virile art alone is really worth living for?"[9] Archer praises *A Woman of No Importance* as the "most virile and intelligent . . . piece of dramatic writing of our day." However, things break down with the heroine:

> Why does Mr. Wilde make her such a terribly emphatic person-age? Do ladies in her (certainly undesirable) position brood so incessantly upon their misfortune? . . . Well then, what is all this melodrama about? . . . The young man's crude sense of the need for some immediate and heroic action is admirably conceived, and entirely right; but how much better, how much truer, how much newer, would the scene be if the mother met his Quixo-tism with sad, half-smiling dignity and wisdom, instead of with passionate outcries of unreasoning horror![10]

In striving to win the theater back from the "popular audience" for a middle-class intelligentsia, Archer rewrites the terms of melo-dramatic realism, repressing expressiveness now seen as feminizing, while rationalizing a covert male melodrama masquerading as the new realism. The class nature of the new aesthetic is clear in Lewes's essay, where control appears in representational techniques which reproduce class authority. Mrs. Arbuthnot fails *A Woman of No Im-portance* not only because of her direct expressiveness, but because she breaks the codes which should be observed by a "lady."

The American criticism gathered by Montrose Moses and John Mason Brown display a similar demand for literary quality and hos-tility to melodramatic practices. Edgar Allan Poe, using Mrs. Mowat's *Fashion* to attack contemporary drama in general, complains that it has "not one particle of any nature beyond greenroom nature about it."[11] His demand is for new principles of dramatic action "drawn from the fountain of a Nature that can never grow old." Verisimilitude is not a matter of observing social decorum—the "natural" drawing-room proprieties of G. H. Lewes—but of truth to the heart of man: "[N]atural art [is] . . . based in the natural laws of man's heart and understanding."[12]

Class values, which infiltrate English critical debates on realist representation and melodrama, are here displaced by an overriding concern with gender. Steele MacKaye's *Paul Kauvar: Or, Anarchy*— a melodrama of repeated coincidence, sudden reversals, and substituted identities—is praised by Nym Crinkle despite its "inconsistencies, incidental pathos, and . . . melodramatic use of human motives" as "the protest of a vigorous masculine talent against . . . aesthetic inanity."[13] The difference between this protest on behalf of virility and Archer's demand for virile art is that Crinkle objects not to expressive performance as such but to the objects and situations to which feeling is attached. His review is littered with such phrases as "primrose path in dramaturgy," "lawn-tennis actors," "manicure a sentiment," "embroider . . . napkins." Masculinity must be protected not against emotion but against a feminine collusion in class affectation. "In our ladylike condition," declares Crinkle, "masculinity ought to be prized."[14]

The oppositions that displace class in American melodrama pivot on gender: the country, which as source of natural morality opposes the city, is close to the wilderness and masculine values; the civilization which seeks to tame the wilderness threatens not only the corrupting influence of society but a debilitating femininity. In the appeal to nature, it is literally Man's heart that is at stake and the masculinization of art is conceived in terms of an energizing, violent expressiveness rather than as the civilized restraint and social refinement praised by Lewes and Archer.

The importance of the heart as the source of truth suggests the distinctive direction taken by American realism at the turn of the century, which lay behind not only America's warm reception of Stanislavski and the Moscow Art Theatre but its difficulty with Ibsen and the sociological naturalism of European New Drama. The influence of the former can be seen in Stark Young's panegyric "letter to Duse": "You force into everything the soul of its reality. . . . You are an actor, but first you are yourself."[15] Stark Young's analysis of Eleanore Duse's performance style defines a realism uninterested in the impact of environment or society on character. Moreover, it anticipates the Method in its reinvention of the language of gesture in order to convey inner life:

Madame your realism does not accept the surface of things and does not accept your own body but forces these towards a more intricate and luminous expression of the life hidden within. Your realism begins with the pressure of life from within you.[16]

These examples of British and American criticism, which set in opposition or negotiate the categories of melodrama and realism, represent part of the cultural context in which cinema emerged. In the new drama and the naturalist novel, the changing practices and debates around realism charted new territories for representation that were more adequate to changing economic and social relations, to a newly emerging middle class, and to vanguard theatrical audiences. Such discourses were popularized by newspaper critics and handbooks for dramatists, and constituted a pressure on an emerging film fiction struggling to achieve a place among the established arts in order to gain the cultural prestige that would attract higher-paying middle-class audiences. Nevertheless Hollywood, in building a mass entertainment medium, was inevitably driven to attempt a reconstruction of the "popular" as a cultural space in which a wide range of social groups and nationalities could meet, something to which theatrical melodrama had already a century earlier proved amenable. The continuing ideological value of the "heart" in American realism meant that in its Americanization melodrama was well placed to meet new demands for realism and contemporaneity and to shed its Victorian accoutrements. Melodramatic purposes were translated into technical and aesthetic procedures that could both gain the imprimateur of "realism" and at the same time deliver melodramatic experience.

Three areas of classic Hollywood practice might be reconceptualized in order to grasp how so-called "classic realism" harbors melodramatic potential within shared conventions of verisimilitude: *narrative logic, personalization,* and *mise-en-scène*. These broad categories are amenable to dual inflections: narrative logic can yield up cause or consequence; personalization, character or personification; while mise-en-scène may juggle visual and verbal registers.

In classic realist narration everything that happens must be clearly motivated by a plausible cause. This chain of cause and effect produces narrative as a linear sequence of logically motivated events. Melodrama is accused of contrivance and a reliance on devices such as coincidence in order to make its plots arrive at a satisfying denouement. In melodramatic plotting, the evidence, says J. L. Styan, is "rigged," either to prove a pre-given moral point, or to produce a desired outcome.[17]

The emphasis on causes in the realist work arises from a focus on change: causes once understood can lead to a change of attitude or of behavior, thus producing the prized character development that guarantees psychological realism and the resolution of narrative problems. Nora, once she understands that the emotional dynamic of marriage lies in the property relations men hold in women, walks out of the doll's house. This "effect" is dramatic as a confirmation of the causes which the play has laid bare. *The Salt of the Earth* concludes the winning of a strike with the reunion of husband and wife in recognition of the sexual dimension to labor relations which the film's realist project demonstrates. Nineteenth-century melodrama works with a different emphasis. It focuses on consequences that outrun the causes in their catastrophic effects and dramatic power. The lesson of melodrama is not the tracing of causes but an engineered climax in which unanticipated and overdetermined responses erupt. What to the realist looks like contrivance and rigged evidence is for the melodramatist the orchestration of dramatic roles and theatrical signs in order to produce a total signifying configuration. Rather than a set of linear chain reactions, melodramatic narrative functions through the deployment of coincidences, repetitions, fatal intersections, and missed opportunities which function in corkscrew fashion, spiraling around a neuralgic center that finally explodes, enabling unexpected underlying forces to emerge. In this way the consequence of past actions opens up far more than is contained in the initial cause.

Personalization, in Bordwell's argument, is linked to narrative causality: "character-centred—i.e. personal or psychological causality— [is the] armature of the classical story."[18] Bordwell goes on to argue that if impersonal causality does occur (a natural disaster, coincidence, or chance), it is subordinated to psychological causality. Historical causality is always located in a psychologically defined individual. This reflects the general association of realism with the rise of bourgeois fiction in its focus on the individual in whom the social is displaced. Melodrama shares this drive to personalize economic, social, or political forces. However, just as the balance between cause and effect is rendered differently in melodrama, so is the relation of social and personal. Whereas realist characters can be referred to a complex of social, economic, or hereditary factors to which they react or by which they are determined, melodramatic characters are themselves the embodiment of such forces internalized as attributes of personality and moral behavior. Landlord, uncle, guardian, orphaned niece, press-gang, hangman, bailiff, procuress, beggar represent not simply roles to be referred out to social structures but moral personifications or identities. Contrasted to the psychological motives of character, personification suggests a more emblematic representation of abstract qualities. Melodramatic morality, in contrast, rests in personal feelings and behavior, not allegorical values. This introjection of the social as personal and moral is rendered not as interior psychology but re-projected in external signs registered both in the person—bodily gesture, dress, etc.—and in environment and setting. Whereas the gloom of the Norwegian fjords produces the depressed, inturned characters of Ibsen's plays, the entrance of the melodramatic villain stimulates a darkening of the skies and the outbreak of storms. Rather than subordinating coincidence and chance, such figures may well serve them.

The personalization of melodrama leads to an anthropomorphic use of setting, lighting, and other theatrical devices, and to a rhetorical, hyperbolic use of language, music, and sound effects, in which speech becomes gestural and kinetic rather than intellectual and analytic. Characters become agents of causality through the externalization of personality in action. Bordwell quotes Bazin to rationalize such externalization as "the commonsense supposition that a necessary and unambiguous causal relationship exists between feelings and their outward manifestations."[19]

Peter Brooks argues that just such a belief based in eighteenth-century theories of language underlies the actor's handbooks that produced the gestural formulae of melodramatic performance. In his account of melodrama, gesture and mise-en-scène reveal what verbal language conceals or cannot express. Clearly, however, this principle courts the possibility that feelings may, as in melodrama, exceed the expressive capacity of their "outward manifestations."

In support of his argument for the general subordination of gesture, mise-en-scène, and spectacle to narrative causality, Bordwell quotes a twenties' scenario manual on the distinction between impersonal movement and human action:

> [F]or instance, one might write: "The whirring blades of the electric fan caused the window curtains to flutter. The man seated at the massive desk finished his momentous letter, sealed it, and hastened out to post it." The whirring fan and the fluttering curtain give motion only—the man's writing the letter and taking it out to the post provides the action.

It is of action that photoplays are wrought.[20] What the literary scenario writer fails to recognize is the potential of whirring fan blades and fluttering curtains, not to mention the massive desk, to express the momentousness of the letter writing. It is through such devices that writing a letter ceases to be simply the product of a psychological cause but hints at a play of overdetermining forces within which individual lives are caught. Such elements of mise-en-scène do not interfere with the causal chain but link the behavior of human beings into a broader system of significance, making them important, exciting, melodramatic.

Against such theatricalization, the new drama distinguished itself in its search for colloquial speech rhythms, intimate performance style, and responses motivated by human psychology—a contraction and concentration of expressive means that focus on the techniques for producing the rounded and complex character. This led, in Styan's terms, to the displacement of visual signs for verbal subtleties.[21] In the new drama, dialogue expresses character indirectly, creating a subtext of silences, irrelevancies, indirections, half revelations. Direct address to the audience is proscribed.

In contrast, melodrama, as Brooks suggests, aims to say everything—forcing the unspeakable into expression—by orchestrating the theater's full range of visual and aural expressive means to produce concrete, unmistakable signs. Melodramatic plotting organizes their production, not through natural or causal logic, but through an aesthetic or emotional logic. The audience is addressed as witness to a staging: to climaxes of plot, to moments of definitive gesture or vocal delivery, to the virtuoso technical production of hyperrealistic effects which authenticate the emotional and moral claims of melodrama.

These distinctions, however, are not mutually exclusive. An effect may be treated as the result which explains the cause; it may also be exacerbated as an overdetermined consequence for which a cause serves simply as pretext. A text may balance finely between the two poles, justifying melodramatic overdetermination by reference to familiar causes. Characters, psychologically motivated according to contemporary social mores, may be driven by circumstances of the plot to undergo consequences of a catastrophic intensity not explainable in terms of causal logic. An endowment of personality characteristics and psychic history psychologizes characters who under pressure of plot produce the monopathic personifications, states of mind, and moral conditions of melodrama. Indeed the popularization of psychoanalytic ideas provides new and up to date criteria for defining the moral status of characters. Similarly, visual and verbal signs may belong to a register coded for verisimilitude while the orchestration of the totality of expressive means may draw such signs into a rhetoric invested with a melodramatic symbolic charge. Thus the perpetuation and adaptation of melodramatic perspectives turns on a rapprochement between the moral personifications and projected psychic states of melodrama with the motivated responses and reactions of psychologically realist characters.

In his landmark essay on British cinema, "Amnesia and Schizophrenia," Charles Barr argues that "all cinema . . . is founded on a dialectic between documentary and fantasy, objective and subjective; but the British versions of the dialectic are distinctive ones."[22] I want now to take up this proposition in an examination of the process of melodrama's modernization—its adaptation to changing conditions of realism and the rapprochement struck between realist charac-

Anthony Asquith, *Underground*. Photo © British Film Institute. Reproduced by permission.

ter and melodramatic desire in two different cultures as represented in King Vidor's *The Crowd* (United States) and Anthony Asquith's *Underground* (Great Britain), both made in 1928.

Both films in their titles and opening sequences declare an explicit intention to tell stories of ordinary people set in contemporary times. And both films deploy elements of melodramatic structure, characterization, and expression. In each case the narrative involves the formation of a desiring couple which is threatened by the anarchy of individual wants and repressive social forces represented by villainous figures; and in both films value is vested in the heroine for whom hero and villian(s) compete. Each film produces a spiral narrative trajectory that continually turns back literally or metaphorically to earlier positions or events through a set of ironic echoes, refrains, allusions, and images. And both films resort to expressionist camera techniques and lighting in order to generate melodramatic intensity and meaning while also signaling artistic seriousness. Finally, both films fall into the category of domestic melodrama, although the English film incorporates into this ingredients from the crime melodrama.

If modernizing melodrama is an issue for these films, the first question is what kind of reality they construct and how they authenticate their fictional worlds. Since this is part of the establishing procedures of narrative opening, the early sequences of *Underground* and *The Crowd* offer clues to national specificity. Their respective titles, opening shots, and intertitles develop distinct images of a social world and the place in it of the individual protagonist.

The opening title of the English film is materialized in a shot of a London Transport sign, "Underground," thus identifying its fictional world in relation to a real location. Place is emphasized in succeeding shots—for example, a documentary shot from the cab of a train as it enters a station, identified as Warren Street. This documentary look at location continues even in the more expressionist reaches of the film: Nell's walk on the Embankment; a down-and-out pavement artist caught casually by the camera; the views of Regent Street from the top of an open-air London bus; the familiar chimneys and slag heaps of Battersea Power Station at the film's climax. In contrast, *The Crowd* opens with an aerial shot of crowds celebrating the

Declaration of Independence, interrupted by a title giving not a place but a precise date, July 4, 1900. Historical time, not geographical place, establishes reality here. Devices such as the collapsing calendar, intertitle dates, and references to seasonal change emphasize the role of time in *The Crowd*.

Place and time organize each film's fictional world differently, contributing nationally distinct ideological perspectives. *Underground*'s opening intertitle explains:

> The Metropolis of the British Empire with its teeming multitudes of "all sorts and conditions of men" contributes its share of light and shade, romance and tragedy and all those things that go to make up what we call life. So in the "Underground" is set our story of ordinary workaday people whose names are just Nell, Bill, Kate and Bert.

"Conditions" here refers obliquely to predetermined social positions linking character to social location. The American film cuts from public celebration of historical occasion to an unlocated domestic scene and the following intertitle: "But what was a little thing like the Declaration of Independence compared to the great event happening in the Sims household?" A doctor delivers a baby boy to his anxiously waiting father (we scarcely glimpse the mother hidden under sheets in the background): "Here's a little man the world's going to hear from." Rather than a social mosaic based in geography, reality is constructed as an individual trajectory into a future which promises change and progress. Each set of intertitles shares a concern with differences as an element of verisimilitude, but where *Underground* is concerned with social difference, personal individuality is the focus of *The Crowd*. However, since both films have to work within a bourgeois democratic outlook, the figuration of social and individual difference leads to considerable ideological tension which melodrama will be called on to dramatize.

The explanatory intertitles of *Underground* shift from Empire—the self-evident incarnation of different conditions of men predicated on geography and race—to London as the central, heterogeneous metropolis of Empire, then to the underground as a site of social and narrative interaction. At the same time, the title seeks to unite the audience in a common recognition of "those things that go to make up what *we* call life," inviting identification with "*our* story of ordinary, workaday people whose names are just Nell, Bill, Bert and Kate." "Workaday" and the condescending choice of monosyllabic names shift from race to class as a major source of social difference while denying its divisions in the presumed unity of "we." Nevertheless, class background constitutes an essential ingredient of characterization in English fiction. Hence the importance of location as a means of identifying and at the same time separating "all sorts and conditions of men." The haberdashery counter of a West End department store where Nell works under the watchful eye of the patrician floor manager, the cheap lodging house where Kate struggles alone as a humble dressmaker in a single bed-sitting-room, the East End pub where Bert embroils Bill in a fight, the powerhouse at Battersea Power Station where blue-collar Bert works, contribute a range of subtle social differentiations—class, trade, profession, gender, status—to the moral dynamic of the characters' interactions.

As *Underground*'s train pulls into Warren Street, a range of recognizable English social types get off and onto the train. Inside the train a soldier and a sailor both stand up for a young woman, while Bert in cloth cap quickly slips into the vacated seat, laughing over his cigarette as they protest. The underground and other locales, such as the department store or London pub, represent public places where the paths of socially divided protagonists may plausibly cross and conflict. Class embodied in characters distinguished by their environmental location becomes a key to dramatic conflict.

A different narrative pattern is initiated in *The Crowd*, where a specific date links national historical occasion with an individual birth rather than a social fabric. Here the explanatory intertitles shift from the birth of a nation, to a typical American family, to the baby in whom history is to be realized. The crowd of the title represents a nation celebrating severance from the British Empire and a political identity vested in notions of equality, the rights of the individual, and democracy in opposition to difference based on class. The mirroring of political severance in the delivery of the baby identifies nation with individual. The nation's story will be vested in the individual trajectory of this "little man" from whom the world is to hear. Accordingly, the realism of *The Crowd* is founded in biography. Rather than events structured by locations, the narrative relates the stages in a life: loss of the parent, starting work, courtship, first quarrel, parenthood, loss of a child, unemployment, and so on. Unlike the underground system in the English film, the crowd in the American film explicitly obliterates social detail. Public locations in *The Crowd* are important not as the source of social identity but for what they contribute to personal biography: the fairground supports the rituals of courtship; the train provides generational comedy around the sleeper car honeymoon nights; Niagara Falls, a location for sexual consumation; rented rooms a sign of financial restrictions and the irritations of early married life; and so on.

If documentary locations in *Underground* serve social realism and the drama of social interaction, biographical time in *The Crowd* serves psychological realism. The vital intersection here is not between social classes but between past and future. The opening titles suggest the different ideological terrain on which American realism operates. In place of a hegemonic "we" speaking for "all types and conditions of men," a touch of humor negotiates a transition from state to individual: from America to the Sims household to baby Johnny, a sign of the future heralded by his father's promise: "I'll give him every opportunity." Whereas in *Underground* action must be instigated within a static, class-stratified society, *The Crowd*, suggesting no boundary to social mobility, promises a trajectory in which Johnny focuses the hopes of his father and the founding fathers. A later intertitle tells us of "Johnny Sim's achievements, piano playing, choir singing like Lincoln and Washington." However, the opening intertitle's touch of irony—"what was a little thing like the Declaration of Independence"—forewarns of the hubris awaiting the overreaching ambition and overidentification of the father-son bond. The production of difference, then, is a source of ideological tension for both films. For *Underground* the problem is how both to animate and contain the divisions of the English class system; for *The Crowd*, the problem is how to assert difference between generations and within a society contradictorily committed to individualism and an egalitarian legacy.

If the ideological problem of realism is how to contain difference, the reverse is the case in melodrama, for ideological contradiction provides a source of opposition which is central to the articulation of melodramatic identity, desire, and conflict. Melodrama does not negotiate but rather polarizes difference, opening up the contradictions it may be a text's ideological project to conceal. Desire in melodrama is treated less as psychological cause than as source of action and identity. What characters want and how they set about getting it determines who they are. At the same time desire—its objects and its prohibitions—is cast within a moral framework. Melodramatic characters espouse identities in polarized confrontations which set out moral stakes in relation to which human action takes on significance. It is in the shaping of desire and identity—in the objects to which desire can attach, the channels through which it can run, the blocks that impede it, the outlets it can force—that the sociopolitical and personal intersect. In order to transform melodrama, *Underground* and *The Crowd* must reinvest desire and its prohibitions in the social surfaces, psychological explanations, and contemporary mores which authenticate their respective worlds. Their different conditions of verisimilitude and the different cultural histories they draw on produce different moral stakes, different organizations of desire and conflict. In *Underground* "romance and tragedy" ensue from the intersection of social types, while in *The Crowd* we wait to see the triumph of individuation.

National distinctions affect not only how *Underground* and *The Crowd* use and transform melodrama, but the kind of problem melodrama represents for each film. The villain as source of transgressive desire is the dynamic heart of melodrama, focusing the social and psychic contradictions of his or her society. Villainy, then, represents a key site of modernization. Nineteenth-century European melodrama had found in class difference a fruitful source of polar opposition, in which evil was projected into a degenerate, sometimes fascinating but generally ruthless aristocracy, or into the parisitic agents of rising capitalist entrepreneurs. Following World War I, however, such oppositions had to be refound in the imagined societies of a hegemonic bourgeois democracy. The shift from class to other types of opposition was already taking place in American theatrical melodrama. In British culture, however, although class difference might be softened, it could not be eliminated from works claiming verisimilitude.

A second issue concerns the villain himself, traditionally a projection of moral evil externalized through a mode of behavior and style of performance, dress, makeup, and verbal rhetoric too emphatic for modern sensibilities attuned to the nuanced underplaying associated with the new realism. Moreover, increasing concern with psychological character, the growing emancipation of women and the liberalization of sexual discussion complicates the opposition of villain and heroine. Traditionally the aristocratic or capitalist villain comes from outside the community, family, or couple whom he threatens. Changing social mores, however, mean that the heroine cannot unproblematically function as "representation of virtue" in opposition to an alien villain. Increasingly, modernization takes melodramatic opposition into the heart of the couple which tends to become itself the subject rather than a mechanism of melodramatic conflict.

Each film moves from establishing its verisimilitude into melodramatization. In the English film, the proximity enforced by underground travel between characters normally separated by class and social convention initially offers comic vignettes of social interactions which play on the codes of public travel governing the private space of standing passengers or of newspaper readers, eye contact between the sexes and so on. When Nell joins the train at another stop and sits next to Bert, such games serve the narrative connection of characters: Bert impudently adjusts his tie in her makeup mirror; she retaliates by tossing his cap to a group of boy scouts. In these exchanges of looks and gestures between Bert, Nell, and a Salvation Army woman, signs of social, gender, and sexual difference are channeled into oppositions for melodrama. Nell is marked as heroine in her conventional feminine attractiveness, her air of middle-class propriety, and independent spirit. Bert's flirtation combines the male wolf with an indifference to social decorum, which under the repressed eye of the Salvation Army woman evokes the threat of working-class masculinity to "nice" girls. Class antagonism is organized into sexual conflict. However, rather than the degenerate aristocrat (now consigned to women's historical romances), the threat is projected into the sexuality of the working-class male, who dares cross class boundaries. If class in post–World War I democracy cannot be named as an element in "our" story, nevertheless in the following three sequences it serves both to block and channel desire.

In the next episode Bill, a station foreman, stands at the foot of an escalator, polishing its brass, when a close-up focuses his observation of Nell pursued by Bert. Bill is distinguished from Bert by his good looks, authoritative stance, and clear idealistic gaze (from eyes that can only be piercing blue). Nell may be a shop girl and Bill a London Transport employee but their physical characteristics, dress codes, and social behavior define a middle-class type of asexual attractiveness which makes them the film's destined match. Bill comes to Nell's rescue, tripping Bert up, dusting him down with a mock flick of the collar and delaying his ascent up from the escalator. From this fateful encounter forces are put into play that will create a melodrama out of an entanglement of sexual and class relations. In the scrap Nell has dropped her glove: Bill finds it and starts up the escalator as Nell, realizing her loss, starts down. As their eyes meet, they are carried past each other in opposite directions: romantic bonding is simultaneously instigated and thwarted; the escalator is charged with melodramatic potential, as it separates the paths of destined lovers at the moment of their first exchange. This visual metaphor spells out the unforeseen consequence of Bill's overbearing rebuff to Bert with its suggestion of sexual competition harboring class antagonism.

We find Bert as an incongruous customer in a West End department store, where he tries on a range of cloth caps brought into frame, but held out in arm's length close-ups, by a figure who is finally revealed to be a highly superior salesman, under the sign: "Look at Your Hat—Everyone Else Does." In the social world constructed by *Underground*, consumer goods, carrying class markers, demarcate consumers from one another. Bert spies Nell on the haberdashery counter, where his working-class bravado and sexual banter finally bring a smile to her face. Eventually, under the authoritative stare of the paternalistic floor manager, he is shamed into buying a boutonniere and driven from the store.

Bert's class-driven sexuality both animates and threatens to disrupt the social fabric of *Underground*. Sexual behavior becomes the key to the film's polarization of its protagonists: and it is in sexual behavior that class infiltrates the film's moral stakes. Following the still-playful interruption of the department store sequence, the film's tone darkens as camera and lighting intensify their expressionism in a definitive melodramatization of heterosexual encounter. Meeting Bill on her way home, Nell agrees to postpone retrieval of her glove until a Saturday date with Bill. The handshake that accompanies this agreement is intercut between shots of a shadow thrown by kissing lovers hidden on the emergency exit stairs which loom in expressionist distortion over the pair. As Nell innocently walks away and Bill leans dreamily against the tunnel wall, a pan suddenly brings Bert into the picture, staring menacingly at Bill, low-angle lighting emphasizing a lusting and vengeful twitch to his eye. Thus sexual passion is linked to a class threat. The shift from documentary to expressionist mise-en-scène augurs a fate yet to work itself out. The spiral plot will several episodes later return to the hidden corner where the lovers kiss but now it is Bert's shadow that looms over Bill, as he waits for Nell to appear before giving Kate the signal to make a false accusation of sexual assault. The shadow of an embracing couple, turning location into metaphor, prefigures the existence and threat of a hidden place, underground, harboring entangled and dangerous desires.

In contrast to this shadow play of passion, Bill and Nell are marked as hero and heroine through their restrained social decorum and asexual romance, in which a lost glove, a chaste handshake, and delayed gratification provide both erotic charge and class authority, linking sexual repression to power. Rather than making illicit embraces in the corners of the underground system, Bill and Nell travel on an open-top London bus en route to a picnic in the country. Twice Bill morally and physically thwarts and humiliates Bert, opening up a channel of revenge through which socially transgressive sex and class desires produce working-class sexuality as a threat.

This sex/class dynamic is completed by Kate, who is introduced following the formation of Bert's lustful designs on Nell. An overworked seamstress, toiling in her lodging-house room, and anxiously waiting to tell Bert of her pregnancy, Kate occupies the place of the fallen woman and social victim—"helpless and unfriended"—of Victorian melodrama. But in twentieth-century culture she is victim

King Vidor, *The Crowd*. Photo © British Film Institute. Reproduced by permission.

neither of aristocrat nor agent of capitalism but of one of her own class. Whereas Bert is thwarted by class barriers from achieving his desire, Kate is disadvantaged by both class and gender, unable by the social and economic weakness of her position to make her desires known. Rejected by Bert, she becomes his tool in the plot against Bill; betrayed, she is subject to an upsurge of emotional need and sexual demand which will lead to the destruction of both. The world of stratified but stable difference constructed through social location is threatened by the sexual desires of the two characters defined as working-class in a circular passage of blocked desire, in which Bert both desires Nell who desires and is desired by Bill, and is himself desired by Kate.

In *The Crowd* a verisimilitude based on individual biography rather than a social constellation encourages an investment in psychological rather than social realism. Oppositions organized by social location are displaced by generational oppositions of history and biography: America versus Europe, son versus father, and individual versus society. Nevertheless, the ideology that enables the Sims household to stand for the nation is as contradictory as *Underground*'s construction of a "we" to embrace "all sorts and conditions of men." The equation of democratic opportunity with individual ambition threatens the egalitarian ideal and, conversely, egalitarian ideology represses both the acknowledgment of real inequality and the process of individuation.

The Crowd's biographical form demands to know who its hero can become. After Johnny's birth and a brief montage of childhood achievements, a collapsing calendar indicates the passing of time, coming to rest in 1912. Johnny is sitting with friends on a fence outside his home, imagining the future. There are no obvious markers to indicate social difference, despite the presence of a black child. Johnny's identity can be articulated only negatively, in the overreaching namelessness of his ambition, which ironizes melodramatic demand: "My Dad says I'm going to be something big one day." However, this and later scenes from Johnny's life suggest no particular distinction. He is an ordinary, unexciting character who, unlike Bert or Bill in *Underworld*, is not driven by a particular moral force, but makes melodramatic claims on meaning realizable only in fantasy. Johnny is effectively a hero without an agenda.

Since social difference is specifically excluded from the world of *The Crowd*, Johnny's problem is precisely where to locate that difference which will open up a path to his desire and so enable him to attain an identity. His situation foreshadows the problem of masculine identity in 1950s family melodrama described by Geoffrey Nowell Smith as the social and familial problem of how to be oneself yet at home—different but like. Unlike Bill, for whom unequivocal signs —a glove, roses, London transport uniform, an enemy—represent desire, Johnny has no name for his desire beyond the desire to be different, to stand out from the crowd. In this respect difference represents a double need: for opposition against which he can individuate and for a goal into which he can project himself—needs which it has been the traditional role of melodramatic fiction to supply.

In terms of the goal-oriented drive of biographical narrative, however, Johnny represents a vacuum. The collapsing calendar brings Johnny at 21 to New York, "one of seven million," an intertitle ironically comments, "who think New York is dependent on them." Johnny now works as a clerk by day and studies by night. We are not told what he studies, but a close-up at work reveals him perusing a newspaper ad, "Genius Wanted," and the next episode finds him easily persuaded to skip night class for a double blind date in a fairground. From here he embarks on the next stage in a young man's life: marriage and fatherhood. Five years on and two children later he has achieved an eight dollar raise and little else, but still dreams of the day "his ship will come home." The task of the melodrama, then, is to force the identity and meaning of Johnny's life into being within the unpromising parameters established by the film's verisimilitude.

The process of melodramatization in *The Crowd* starts with the death of Johnny's father, which propels Johnny into his future. Sitting on the fence with his twelve-year-old friends, Johnny is an undistinguished member of a group. A cut from the intertitle repeating his father's promise that he will be "something big one day" to a close-up of Johnny's eyes raised to the skies singles him out, at the same time inserting a melodramatic signal into the sequence of childish question and answer. This gesture is a multivalent sign, floating meanings that range from masculine ambition, feminizing hope, and approaching fate. The collapsing calendar, visibly foretelling the erosion of time, suggests a perspective from a future already past—the perspective of the adult who knows the blows which the future stacks up against youthful ambition; while the unmarked presence of the black child hints at the contradictions of an individualistic ideology committed to egalitarian democracy. These ironies are gathered into the suspense created by the close-up which excludes the outer field of vision. The cut to the oppositional field resolves the field of the meaning to one signifier, Fate, as a horse-drawn ambulance pulls into view and stops outside Johnny's door. Johnny is singled out from his peer group—and from the crowd of the title that materializes around his door—not through achievement but through misfortune.

Although the hero, he is also a victim, marked out for pathos rather than grandeur.

Fate which decrees the death of his father (we are offered no cause) shifts the tone from the comic irony of the opening prologue to melodrama—like *Underground*, exploiting expressionist camera angles and lighting to emphasize the momentous consequence of this event. Johnny is thrust out of childhood, his separation from a crowd of gawkers in the doorway depicted as a process of symbolic rebirthing as he slowly climbs the stairs toward his mother. Narratively and visually the scene institutes the strong forward trajectory characteristic of Hollywood fiction. Emotionally it is organized to emphasize loss, severance of bonds, reorientation to a painful new state, with a strong undertow to the past. Johnny's authority as hero is qualified not only by the ironic voice of intertitles and camera, but by the generational (rather than geographic) structure, which entraps him between the weight of the past and an unspecified future, and the emphatic invocation of Fate, which points to the working of antagonistic forces beyond the individual's control. Despite the lack of obvious villainy or antagonists, these elements provide a framework of melodramatic pathos in which Johnny is produced as hero/victim for an audience both better informed than he as to what is at stake and therefore distanced yet moved by his dilemma and therefore involved.

In realist terms, a biographical trajectory involves the progressive development of individual character. Melodrama, however, is concerned not with psychological growth but the personality as a source of moral identity and motivation. In the absence of clear antagonists, the biographical drive of the narrative is propelled by Johnny's search for difference, which in 1928 must take place within the corporate workplace or in heterosexual encounter. Thus the crowd of the title reveals its metaphoric reach. If the underground is where repressed antagonisms erupt, the crowd represents the undifferentiated mass of modern, urban society which threatens the individual with incorporation. This threat to individual aspiration is externalized in expressionist shots of a vertiginous office block through one window of which the camera moves to pick out the anonymity of Johnny's numbered place—no. 137—in a sea of identical desks; or again in the massive and overpowering architecture of the office block's entrance hall, across which workers scurry as soon as the clock allows them to leave. Johnny's reflection in the washroom mirror as passing coworkers belabor him with repetitions of the same monotonous joke, witnesses the persistence of individualistic desire: "You birds have been working here so long you all talk alike." Polarization in *The Crowd* divides individual from society. Metaphorically, perhaps, the crowd represents the desacralized, secular world against which, in Brooks's argument, melodrama is pitted in a demand for significance. Johnny's often-repeated contempt for the crowd and assertion of his own unique but undefined ambitions enact this demand. The achievement of difference is itself the narrative stake.

Abandoning night classes for a blind date introduces heterosexuality as a potential source of differentiation. Boastfully maligning the fairground crowd as "boobs in the same rut," he declares to Mary, "you're different," and is soon married. Marriage, however, does not make Johnny different from the crowd. His proposal is stimulated by a shop window poster linking the marital couple to domestic interiors—"You furnish the girl, we'll furnish the home." On the honeymoon train, magazine advertisements stimulate a vision of domestic prosperity when the promised ship comes home. At Niagara Falls Mary playfully imitates pinup poses. Such images propel and shape the expression of their desires within the sexual economy of capitalism. Consumerism, rather than reinforcing social stratification as in *Underground*, here incorporates the individual into society. The social spaces of *The Crowd* consist less of class-defined locations than sites of leisure and consumerism—Luna Park, Niagara Falls, shop windows, the theater—which promise identities while at the same time incorporating them.

Niagara Falls is also important, however, in recalling nature as a source of authentic selfhood capable of resisting a culture infiltrated by corporate meaning. It is Mary's response to nature—an identification of woman and nature as she holds out her arms to the waterfall, her face flooded with light—that rouses Johnny's passion. He looks at her looking at nature, undergoing deep emotion; she glances back at him; the exchange of looks exchanges emotions and Johnny, after the comic embarrassments of the honeymoon train and suggestiveness of magazine advertisements, makes his first passionate kiss. Thus the woman functions as the source of authentic feeling, the goal of American realism. Through association with Niagara Falls, moreover, the woman is safely sexualized—sex is constructed as a moral good, rather than as in *Underground*, a destructive passion. Through Mary, Johnny gains access to the world he is otherwise detached from. The importance of nature as a touchstone that authenticates feeling and legitimates sexuality is further emphasized in references to the seasons in the progress of the couple, which oppose natural rhythms to the mechanistic routines of workplace. In April Mary averts their near-separation with news of her pregnancy, revitalizing Johnny's thwarted and fading desire. This recourse to nature further differentiates *The Crowd* from the urbanized, socialized world of *Underground*. Significantly, while Nell and Bill conduct their first date on a country picnic, the association of Nell with nature is an identification with chastity and charity (Nell shares their picnic with a hungry child). Here the romantic couple enact repression rather than release.

It is in the central episodes which enact the marital ups and downs of the young couple on a low income, in a threadbare apartment, trying to raise a family and harassed by inlaws, that the film moves most strongly toward psychological realism, highlighting the process of melodrama's incorporation into modern fiction. Although Mary is constructed as the central value of the film, reflecting the Victorian "true woman" in her patient attempts to understand her husband's troubles, in other respects her story turns on the contradictions of gender relations within the family which are rendered with the sympathetic detail of women's domestic fiction: Johnny's flicking of an ill-placed cupboard door as an attention-seeking device and provocation; the differential expectations arising from a gendered division of labor (for Mary a seaside picnic simply transfers the kitchen to a more inconvenient place as the coffee pot overturns and a jumping child shakes sand all over the cake); and use of pointed dialogue titles, in which Johnny's dreaming frustrates Mary's concern with everyday practicalities, while his fantasies are worn down by office and domestic routine. These exchanges focus on microcosmic patterns of daily domestic life in which the larger forces of corporate capitalism and the patriarchal psyche root themselves to produce the overdetermined consequences of melodrama.

These melodramatizing forces are personified not only in the figure of the crowd and expressionist architecture, but in the small group of secondary characters which include Mary's aging mother and her lugubrious brothers. Having lost his own family, Johnny inherits in his inlaws a Victorian configuration through which a repressive force from the past threatens the newly formed couple. In particular the two bowler-hatted brothers are cast and performed as traditional heavies, the personified agents of corporate society and patriarchal authority, who harrass Johnny for his failure to win a raise and later to keep a job, and threaten to take Mary from him.

Within the marital fiction, then, Johnny provokes a melodrama in which his persistent nameless desire not only confronts the undifferentiated crowd of corporate society but threatens to disrupt the domestic sphere. On their first Christmas Eve, Johnny gives up trying to fix the toilet door to strum on the banjo the popular song, "It's heavenly inside our flat but outside it is 'ell"; by April he will reverse this sentiment, declaring after their first major row, "Marriage is not a word, it's a sentence." If, within the context of domestic realism, Johnny emerges as a petty patriarch—bossy and pompous about his wife's domestic failings onto which he displaces his own frustrations—he, and as a result she, become victims of the melodrama. The brothers demand Johnny fulfill his father's hopes—make something of himself—while at the same time they represent desire as conformity to the bourgeois image. Johnny's desire, however, remains locked in fantasy and in so far as this detaches him from others and therefore from reality, it is an immoral condition. Melodrama is necessary to direct his fantasy into a moral goal through which he will be able to find an identity. As a result, Johnny becomes the site of an externalized struggle between the repressive forces of patriarchal conformity represented by the brothers and the personal commitment demanded by Mary representing the feminine sphere. A new moral order requires a new kind of family and the domestication of the male.

Overlaying the forward trajectory of the biographical narrative, a series of repeated images, echoes, and phrases continually spiral back to earlier moments, distort its linear progress, functioning as a kind of fateful undertow which drags it back to an original dilemma. At the same time, the persistent reiteration by Johnny of phrases echoing the ambitions of his father and his own vague promises for the future— "opportunity," "the ship," "something big"—function with increasing irony when set against the visual and narrative context (Johnny told to face the right way in the office lift, wiping babies' bottoms on the beach), which suggests the pathos of a desire that outruns social possibility and cannot be externalized. The most telling image in this series is that of the clown. During the blind date with Mary, Johnny comments vehemently on a fairground clown who functions as a billboard carrier: "Poor sap, I bet his father thought he'd be president," forgetting his own father's expressed ambitions for him. And yet for the audience the irony is clear: clowning is Johnny's only talent, whether strumming a banjo, getting drunk on Christmas Eve, juggling on the beach, or thinking up advertising slogans. The image of the clown will return twice more with potent effect each time.

While the biographical narrative emphasizes a forward trajectory propelled by psychological cause and effect, the melodramatization of causes—their overdetermination—is achieved through patterns of coincidence and dramatic reversal which evoke the behind-scenes working of Fate, representing forces outside the individual's control. The ritualized climaxes which mark stages in a life—birth, father's death, honeymoon, marriage, birth of a son, death of the daughter— are frequently rendered as repetitions of earlier events or dramatic reversals. Birth occurs twice literally and once metaphorically; we have two honeymoon declarations—"You are the most beautiful girl in the world"; two successes with an advertising slogan; and twice Johnny becomes special through the extreme of death and personal grief.

If the biographical drive of *The Crowd* is melodramatized through the ironic undertow of retrogressive allusion, intertitles, repetitive images and phrases, the social structure of *Underground* uses montage editing to ironize narrative progression through juxtapositioning social locations and identities. Rather than causal factors, thematic or visual rhymes provide the means of cutting between locations. A close-up of a mirror bringing Kate into view as she nervously decorates herself on Bert's arrival at his lodgings fades out and up into a second mirror shot in which Bert's reflection appears as he enters his room below, preening himself and sniffing the boutonniere in anticipation of flirting with Nell. Kate is soon rebuffed by Bert, her pain expressed in a big close-up of her pleading hands breaking into the frame at the left of the screen. As he departs she is left staring blankly at the flower which is not intended for her after all. A close-up of the carnation is followed by the close-up of a glove in Nell's mother's hand, recalling a more hopeful union in prospect. Kate's lonely lodging is contrasted to the homely exchanges between mother and daughter as Nell mimes for her mother the incident of the lost glove. A concluding close-up on the women's hands, each folded in their laps, Nell's clasping her glove, is followed by a shot of the missing glove dreamily fondled by Bill's hand. Later, a mutually desiring gaze between Nell and Bill, during which she speaks jokingly of Bert's proposal, is broken by a close-up of Bert viciously hurling darts at a board in a local pub. Such transitions emerge from and emphasize not biographical flow but the intersection of linked and opposed social locations and desires.

While such locations document class and gender position, the use of iconographic and written signs and mimed gesture rather than dialogue titles (as in the more biographically driven *The Crowd*) spell out moral identities and conflicts. The window sign, "Kate Moy, Dressmaker," followed by a close-up of the white and deadened face of Kate at her machine invokes the image of the exploited outworker. Checkered tablecloth and a pool of light from a brass lamp speak of humble virtue and, in this social situation, likely victimization. The class polarization between Bert and Bill is enacted in the way each looks at Nell: Bill's unfocused, idealizing, ascetic gaze contrasted to Bert's voracious, sexualized glint; frequent close-ups of Bert's aggressive and mocking laugh cut across Bill's dreaming gaze; Bert's gestures of malevolent energy oppose the contemplative stasis realized in Bill.

As social location gives rise to literal and subjective points of view, plot complications in *Underground* unfold through one character looking at, often unobserved, or spying on another. Bert's determination to get Nell is fired by his observation of her trysting with Bill; Kate secretly watches for Bert's return and anxiously scans his face for signs of his good intentions, misinterpreting the meaning of the rose; Bill's attraction to Nell is signaled by his faraway gaze; Bert's revenge is fired by his "inner eye" as visual flashbacks of Bill hitting into his face during the pub fight are superimposed over a close-up of his threatening looks. Bert spies on Bill and Nell in order to manipulate the false charge of sexual assault before Nell's eyes.

A dramaturgy constructed through a series of desiring, spying, and invasive looks facilitates the melodramatization of a narrative space which at the same time documents social position. Bert's disruptive desires are registered in a gaze that crosses social and sexual boundaries. He thrusts his face into her mirror on the underground; he intrudes into her workspace in the department store; in the street, he casually leans an arm across her, pinning her against a wall to enforce intimacy, and finally grabs her for a kiss; he later uses the geography of underground tunnels to entrap Bill in a false accusation. These familiar gestures shift from comedy to villainy through their increasing intrusiveness, cutting across and threatening to divert the narrative drive to unite Bill and Nell, and through an increasing use of expressionist lighting, particularly in the encounters with Bill, in which shadow and camera angle substitute for more melodramatic performance. At the same time, Bert's construction as a villain is completed in his ultimate willingness to undertake criminal activity in the pursuit of his aims.

This emphasis on looking, spying, overseeing not only melodramatizes spatial narration as the intersection of divided social locations, but juxtaposes subjective versus objective reality. Melodramatic characters both personify and personalize, producing emblematic types that are socially recognizable, morally legible, and emotionally authentic. In nineteenth-century performance this combination was realized in the highly stylized codes derived from eighteenth- and nineteenth-century treatises detailing a gestural language of the emotions which came to be rejected for its conventionality. Cinema, with its capacity to privilege the human face and a seemingly natural language of the eyes and facial muscles, breathed new life into the codes of gesture. *The Crowd* works toward merging this "naturalism" of the camera with psychologically realistic characterization. *Underground*'s personified social and moral types do not merge so easily with the subjectivism of the camera. Thus a disjuncture marks the relation between social type and melodramatic personalization in *Underground*, creating moments when the eruption of overdetermined subjectivity threatens to overwhelm not only the stability of the social world, but the ethical clarity of melodrama. This difference is exemplified in the climaxes of the two films.

While betrayal is a common motif of the melodramatic plot, the exclusive focus in *Underground* on Kate's raw experience of pain magnifies a particular state of mind beyond the bounds either of psychological explanation or moral value. Although the film uses the resources of cinema—and in particular expressionist lighting schemes and camera angles—to exteriorize the subjectivity of characters undergoing extreme emotion, its equal insistence on the camera's documenting function means the world retains an independent, "objective" existence. In *The Crowd*, on the other hand, the camera is totally at the service of the fiction, objectifying moral forces which operate outside as well as through the characters. The office block that reduces its employees to anonymous uniformity expresses a real malignity—a product of the society in which Johnny finds himself and to which he must in the end adjust. In contrast, the distorting angles and shadows of the stairwell in her lodging house are anthropomorphic reflections imposed by Kate's anguished subjectivity which threatens to overwhelm the reality of *Underground*'s fictional world.

This disjuncture is marked in *Underground* in the penultimate episode at Battersea Power Station, when Bill decides to make Bert face his responsibilities by going to his employers with Kate. The episode opens with a documentary establishment of location: the camera pans down from a cloud-filled sky to the silhouettes of the power station's smoking chimneys that tower over Bill, who wraps his coat protectively around the white-faced Kate before leaving her outside while he goes to speak to the managers. A high-angle close-up of Bert down in the basement power room, grinning evilly up into the camera, is intercut with a shot of the warning sign above him, "Danger. High Tension Cable." A cut to Kate waiting under the power station walls links "High Tension" to her nervously shivering figure as she steps back to gaze up at the power station, over which Bert's leering face is superimposed. Following the movement of her gaze, the camera pans vertiginously down the walls, ending on a shot of Kate which is followed by a rare title revealing her thoughts: "I can't wait: I must see Bert *now*!" She starts to run, and as Bill's coat falls from her frail figure, the camera leaves her to pan past the power station walls, swiveling round and up the chimneys, as Kate's intensifying subjectivity displaces the documentary "look" of the camera. A new shot fades up on the coal yards and to Kate's figure on the skyline, struggling over and down a slag heap. Eventually the camera ceases to imitate her movements, but watches as she continues to run across the slag heaps, increasingly dwarfed by the buildings to which she gains entry. What is documented here is no longer social location but the landscape of a mind.

In the engine house Bert is crouching in front of a control cupboard, the nemesis to Kate's unleashed demand, released by the intervening class authority of Bill; a cut on his upward glance brings the taut figure of Kate suddenly into his view, victim confronting villain. Clutching at him and pleading, Kate threatens to tell his employers of her pregnancy. A dissolve to the "Danger" notice above his head signals his next move, as he pushes her against the installation, electrocuting her. The lights in offices and underground go out, as the force of Kate's subjectivity is destroyed and the film moves into its final confrontation.

Originally a social location, the underground is now fully melodramatized, becoming replete with meaning: the underground as underworld in which sexual/class passion is criminalized, harboring an underclass whose energy animates but threatens to destroy the world of the film. After Kate's murder, in a final coda, Bill takes up the pursuit of Bert, chasing him over the power station roof and down into the underground itself, where a final contest—risking a "too late" scenario as Nell arrives among the crowd of onlookers— leads to Bert's defeat as he is finally knocked out on the floor of the lift by which he hoped to escape. The evil engaged by this story is expelled along with the working-class characters and their desires. Kate as victim is destroyed—a victim to her own suicidal demands—and the bourgeois couple reinstalled in a return to the social comedy of the opening. Nell on the train is once more propositioned, but laughingly she points out Bill, now her husband and promoted to train guard. This attempt to return to the beginning, to reinstall the class-differentiated social fabric of the film's verisimilitude and the film's failure to acknowledge or sanctify the death of the victim, Kate, is also perhaps indicative of the fate of melodrama in British cinema, officially rejected from the culture while infiltrating that cinema's leaning toward subjectivism.

The Crowd reaches its melodramatic climax with the plot reversal which occurs when it seems that Johnny's promised ship is about to dock: he wins $500 in an advertising competition. The excited couple rush out to consume, bringing back toys for the children. As they lean from an upper window to call the children in from the street, the little girl in her hurry is knocked down by a lorry and subsequently dies. The brothers arrive, personifications of retribution, guilt, and punishment. As a consequence that exceeds the cause, the death of the child turns the narrative back in an "if only" movement: Mary cradles the absent child and Johnny at work relives the moment of impact in which he is powerless to intervene. These moments of extreme loss, however, differ from Kate's anguish in Underground in that they confront malign forces that have an objective and impersonal existence in the film's fictional world: the office tower, the advertising racket, consumer toys, the coincidental lorry. The couple is threatened by the world of the film, rather than the film being threatened by the overwhelming loss experienced by a character.

The death of the child opens up an antagonism within the marital couple, first expressed in the funeral car as each parent leans away from the other in a world of private grief. From here on, narrative consequences multiply. Reprimanded at work, Johnny quits, and quits four subsequent jobs. Mary, obedient to the practical realities, is reduced to dressmaking in order to support Johnny's illusory fantasies of "something big" coming up. His refusal of a job reluctantly offered by her brothers polarizes husband and wife in a climactic confrontation. Tormented by her husband, Mary is driven in a rhythmic buildup of close-ups and dialogue titles to name his now entirely negative identity ("big bag of wind," "bluffer," "quitter") and finally, after hitting him, to speak the unspeakable: "I'd almost rather see you dead." Johnny leaves, his son running after him. A montage of close-ups of his face and train wheels as he approaches a railway bridge externalizes his emotional state in a sequence inviting comparison with Kate's experience of desertion in *Underground*. However, after he fails to jump, his unremitting sense of failure is turned around by his son, who catching up with him says he wants to be like him. The ironic pathos of the child's desire for the father produces for Johnny a moral clarification—offers him the identity he has been unable to name. In the role of father, Johnny is at last able to become one of the crowd, as he joins a queue at the labor exchange. Now his idiosyncracy—he can juggle—becomes economically useful, and he dons a clown's costume and billboards. Whereas in Kate's suicidal bid for Bert there was nothing in the socially documented world to recall her from immersion in the full intensity of experience, for Johnny the child represents a force for good contesting those powers that would overwhelm him.

Named by his son, Johnny is saved, but almost too late. He arrives home to find he is about to lose Mary to her brothers. In the traditional coda of melodrama in which what is found is almost lost, Johnny asks Mary to have belief in him once more, although acknowledging her justification in leaving. She retrieves her suitcase from the brothers, who disappear, defeated: whereupon Johnny produces tickets for a show, at which the family joins in laughter at the antics of a clown, and admiration of Johnny's advertising slogan printed in the theater program. The camera pulls back from Johnny, Mary, and their son, to show them incorporated into the now-laughing crowd that makes up the theater audience.

Despite its emphasis on pathos rather than suspense, *The Crowd* produces the happy end. After taking its protagonists to the edge several times, the melodrama permits the situation to be retrieved. Johnny's crises are in each case relieved by the intervention of his wife and child, who offer a reformed, supportive rather than authoritarian family unit. The brothers and their mother—representatives of an older, perhaps European family order—disappear, driven away. But the contradictions have not disappeared. Johnny has returned to the place he started out from, replacing his parental family with his own. Having despised the clown, he became the clown, both metaphorically and literally. Now he joins the crowd as spectator, laughing at the clown onstage, image of victim/outsider which he has cast off. Harnessing fantasy, however, involves a degree of loss. The energy and anarchy of the hero is tamed. The image that unites the couple also sets up a ripple of painfully ironic reverberations that point back to the contradictions and pathos which have circled Johnny's passage through life.

Central to the difference between the British and the American cinema's engagement with melodrama are the shared values of nature and the heart as touchstones of authenticity in the Americanization of melodrama and the development of American realism as opposed to the class-bound values that separated melodrama and realism in Britain. This led to an easier assimilation of the melodramatic within a realist ethos in American culture, which could endure long after theatrical melodramatic conventions had been outmoded by the changing criteria of verisimilitude. The fact that the work of David Belasco or William Gillette has been equally discussed as peaks of American melodrama and as heralds of a new realism is perhaps a product of such symbiosis.

Hollywood inherited that transformation, producing a cinema in which the melodramatic and the realistic—the metaphoric and the referential, the psychological and the social—mesh together. The performance of the self as a source of truth in what was to become a distinctively American performance mode—the Method—is a key feature in Hollywood's transformation of nineteenth-century melodrama's methods of performance and personification in twentieth-century star personae, a transformation that reinvents melodramatic character in line with changing social values and conceptions of personality.[13] American cinematic narration and characterization are capable of externalizing in mise-en-scène, star personae, or musical orchestration melodramatic desires emanating from sets of personal traits and motives which satisfy demands for psychological realism. Thus Bordwell and Thompson's account of classic Hollywood can be read in terms which support a modernized melodramatic aesthetic.

British cinema, however, displays a split between public spaces dominated by the class-differentiating codes of British realism and private spaces in which repressed subjectivities produce melodramatic pressures from within the fiction. In the "schizophrenic" model that Charles Barr proposes, the features of "quality" (as opposed to popular) British cinema that are so much complained of—cut-glass accents, mannered entrances and exits, the refusal of English actors to move, class-bound plots and characterization, emotional constraint, documentary authenticity, stylistic neutrality—constitute a set of surface, public restraints which in repressing also call into being undercurrents of fantasy, subjectivism, and melodrama that are the source of British cinema's peculiar power. Barr's revaluation of a film such as *Brief Encounter* as offering not "a documentary surface, but projected psychic states" suggests a cinema descended from a dramaturgy of suppressed emotions and restrained performance admired by George Rowell's critics.[24] In contrast to the expressive integration of melodrama in Hollywood, dynamic disjunction may better characterize the relation between melodrama and realism in British cinema.

Notes

1 David Bordwell, Janet Staiger, and Kristin Thompson, *The Classical Hollywood Cinema: Film Style and Mode of Production to 1960* (New York, 1985), 6.
2 Peter Brooks, *The Melodramatic Imagination* (New Haven, 1976).
3 See Thomas Elsaesser, "Tales of Sound and Fury: Observations on the Family Melodrama," in *Home Is Where the Heart Is: Studies in Melodrama and the Woman's Film*, ed. Christine Gledhill (London, 1987).
4 Martin Meisel, *Realizations: Narrative, Pictorial, and Theatrical Arts in Nineteenth-Century England* (Princeton, 1983).
5 *Victorian Dramatic Criticism*, ed. George Rowell (London, 1971); and *The American Theatre as Seen by Its Critics*, ed. Montrose Moses and John Mason Brown (New York, 1934).
6 Wylie Sypher, "Aesthetic of Revolution: The Marxist Melodrama," in *Tragedy: Vision and Form*, ed. Robert W. Corrigan (New York, 1965).
7 Rowell, ed., *Victorian Dramatic Criticism*, 206.
8 Ibid., 221.
9 Ibid., 232.
10 Ibid., 229–30.
11 Moses and Brown, eds., *American Theatre as Seen by Its Critics*, 61.
12 Ibid.
13 Ibid., 136.
14 Ibid., 137–38.
15 Ibid., 257–58.

16 Ibid., 258–59.
17 J. L. Styan, *Modern Drama in Theory and Practice: Realism and Naturalism* (Cambridge, 1981), 4.
18 Bordwell et al., *Classical Hollywood Cinema*, 13.
19 Ibid., 15.
20 Ibid.
21 Styan, *Modern Drama*, 29.
22 Charles Barr, "Introduction: Amnesia and Schizophrenia," in *All Our Yesterdays: 90 Years of British Cinema*, ed. Charles Barr (London, 1986), 24.
23 Christine Gledhill, "Signs of Melodrama," in *Stardom: Industry of Desire*, ed. Christine Gledhill (London, 1991).
24 Barr, "Amnesia and Schizophrenia," 28.

The Hieroglyph and the Whore:

D. W. Griffith's <u>Intolerance</u>

Miriam Hansen

★ ★ ★ ★ ★ ★ One of the many idiosyncratic aspects of Griffith's *Intolerance* is the shot of the Woman Who Rocks the Cradle—in Vachel Lindsay's words, "the key hieroglyphic" of the film.[1] Freely appropriated from Whitman, this shot opposes a virginal mother-figure (Lillian Gish) rocking a flower-filled, sunlit cradle to the figure of the three Fates in the left background; it thus emblematizes the eternal struggle of love against the forces of intolerance which the film purports to illustrate with its guided tour through history. Used as a copula between four distinct yet perpetually intercut strands of narrative (the Fall of Babylon, the Passion of Jesus Christ, the St. Bartholomew Massacre, a modern American story), the cradle shot not only asserts a thematic unity between diegetically discontinuous segments; it also pretends to an ideal, transparent mode of signification, composed of universally human, familiar, accessible images. However, in its obsessive repetition (twenty-six times in the tinted Museum of Modern Art print)—not to mention the morbid conno-

Cradle shot from D. W. Griffith's *Intolerance*. Photo from Film Stills Archive, Museum of Modern Art, New York. Reproduced by permission.

tations of the Whitmanian subtext—the shot becomes part of the textual crisis it was supposed to contain, a symptom rather than a solution of psychosexual and historical conflicts.[2]

For Lindsay to refer to the cradle shot as a "hieroglyphic" means highest praise in light of the poet's own peculiar essay on film aesthetics, *The Art of the Moving Picture* (1915). Like many of his contemporaries preoccupied with the quest for a national culture, Lindsay discerned a specifically American idiom in the pictographic manifestations of an emerging consumer economy:

> American civilization grows more hieroglyphic every day. The cartoons of Darling, the advertisements in the back of the magazines and on the bill-boards and in the street cars, the acres of photographs in the Sunday newspapers, make us into a hieroglyphic civilization far nearer to Egypt than to England.[4]

No medium expresses this tendency better than film, and Lindsay proceeds to develop his notion of "Photoplay Hieroglyphics" as analogous to Egyptian "picture-writing," an analogy he finds prefigured in Emerson and Poe. Thus he describes the close-up of a spiderweb (spider devouring fly, ants destroying spider) in Griffith's *The Avenging Conscience* (1914) as "the first hint of the Poe hieroglyphic."[4]

It is no coincidence that Lindsay saw in Griffith the foremost representative of this new "American hieroglyphics," to borrow the title of John Irwin's book.[5] Beyond the literary tradition (to which I will return), Griffith participated in the widespread celebration of film as a new "universal language" which accompanied the formation of cinema as an institution.[6] Used by journalists, intellectuals, social workers, clergy, producers, and industrial apologists alike, the metaphor of film as a universal language drew on a variety of discourses (Enlightenment, nineteenth-century positivism, Protestant millennialism, the Esperanto movement, and the growing advertizing industry) and oscillated accordingly between utopian and totalitarian implications. Griffith's invocation of the universal language myth was primarily indebted to the millennialist vernacular. As Lillian Gish reports, he once chastized an actress for calling a film a "flicker":

> He told her never to use that word. She was working in the universal language that had been predicted in the Bible, which was

to make all men brothers because they would understand each other. This could end wars and bring about the millennium.[7]

A few years later, in an interview of 1921, Griffith specifies the biblical precedent: "A picture is the universal symbol, and a *picture that moves* is a universal language. Moving pictures, someone suggests, 'might have saved the situation when the Tower of Babel was built.' "[8]

In the context of the pre-War period, the universal language metaphor was mobilized largely against the threat of censorship. At the same time, it functioned to mask the contradiction of the industry's bid for middle-class respectability and the simultaneous marketing of film as a democratic art benefiting in particular the working class, immigrant, and urban poor; in that sense, it was part of the long-term strategy of submerging all class distinctions in an ostensibly homogeneous mass and consumer culture. While Griffith no doubt contributed to the industry's efforts of legitimation—especially with the success of *The Birth of a Nation* (1915) which established him as the cinema's first "artistic genius" and "master"—he also had legitimation needs and interests of his own which crystallized around the reception of that very film. Conflating the political protests against the white supremacist stance of *Birth* with the moral and educational concerns of the Progressive censorship campaigns, Griffith joined the industry's lobbying against these campaigns by publishing, shortly before the release of *Intolerance*, a pamphlet entitled *The Rise and Fall of Free Speech in America* which locates "the root of all censorship" in the evil of "INTOLERANCE."

With *Intolerance*, Griffith not only resumes and expands claims for film as a medium of art, history, and metaphysics; more important, the film advances a defense of the cinema as such—as an institution that offers the historically unique chance to "repair the ruins of Babel."[9] As I argue in detail elsewhere, this defense turns on the special status of the Babylonian narrative in relation to the narratives set in later periods. In terms of the film's ideological project, the geographic-historical trajectory of the narratives—ancient Babylon, New Testament Judaea, sixteenth-century France, contemporary American democracy—suggests a pacifist version of the doctrine of Manifest Destiny ("westward the course of empire takes its way"): the catastrophic course of history is reversed with the happy ending of the modern period, a victory which simultaneously asserts the ascendancy of the "universal idiom" of the American story film over competing foreign styles and genres. Undermining this teleological construction, however, is a textual excess which distinguishes the Babylonian narrative from the narratives set in the Christian era. The most elaborated among the historical periods, the Babylonian narrative functions as a counterpoint to the modern—with its emphasis on spectacle, artificiality, and display, its deviant inscriptions of gender and sexuality, its vision of an organic society. Revising the biblical account (Judeo-Christian tradition, after all, takes sides with Cyrus, welcoming his victory as an end to the Jews' captivity and to the reign of sin, wealth, and idolatry), Griffith resurrects the Whore of Babylon as a figure of visual fascination and fetishistic ambivalence. Her forbidden splendor is doomed to perish, to be sure; yet it does so by evoking a different textual and sexual economy, one that threatens to collapse carefully constructed parallels and oppositions.[10]

Griffith's utopian investment in the Babylonian dream is not merely an assimilation of the then fashionable neo-paganism (the Greenwich Village bohème, the dance of Ruth St. Denis), but rather draws its force from the allusive presence of another myth, that of the Tower of Babel. The most explicit reference to the Babelistic tradition occurs at the beginning of act 2, when a series of titles informs us that the events portrayed are based on actual sources, "the recently excavated cylinders of Nabonidus and Cyrus." "These cylinders," the next title reads, "describe the greatest treason of all history, by which a civilization of countless ages was destroyed and a universal written language (the cuneiform) was made to become an unknown cypher on the face of the earth." This title draws an implicit line from the disappearance of the last universal written language (dramatically conflated with the Fall of Babylon) to the vision of film as a new universal language. The insertion of the universal language theme at this point suggests a reading of the Babylonian narrative as an allegory of the cinema as Griffith perceived it at the time, at a crucial juncture between prehistory and a virtually limitless future. As is usually pointed out, the attack on reform and reformers in the modern narrative was Griffith's response to liberal intellectuals such as Jane Addams, Frederic Howe, Rabbi Wise, and groups like the

NAACP who had condemned the racist slant of *Birth*. But a similar case can be made for the Babylonian narrative: like the priests of Bel who betray Belshazzar, thus causing the destruction of an ideal civilization, the advocates of censorship not only infringe on the freedom of speech but unwittingly jeopardize the possibility for film to become the new universal language "that had been predicted in the Bible."

More than just an esoteric allegory, the evocation of Babel in Babylon encapsulates Griffith's ambition to authorize a new language of images, a language that would recover a prelapsarian transparency and univocity. Indeed, the very construction of *Intolerance* can be read as an attempt to put the universal language proposition into textual practice, to demonstrate at once the analogy and superiority of film in relation to verbal language. This is most evident in the structural—or protostructuralist—conception of the film, the parallel narration of historical events whose meaning supposedly lies in their relation to each other, a differential system albeit ordained by metaphysical truth. Since such a system does not preexist, as in verbal language, the film has to establish it through and simultaneously with its own textual movement; hence the emphasis on the paradigmatic quality of narrative motifs, constellations, and gestures. Yet the demonstration of paradigmatic patterns also pushes the limits of the linguistic analogy: the excessive use of parallel editing disrupts the syntagmatic flow and thereby violates codes of unobtrusive and linear narration that viewers had already come to expect by 1916. In other words, the programmatic construction of *Intolerance* impedes conventional routes of access and identification and thus no doubt accounts to some extent for the film's legendary (if often exaggerated) commercial failure.

Many of the "problems" of *Intolerance* could in fact be rephrased in terms of the theoretical issues surrounding the dis/analogy of film and verbal language, especially the contradictory notion of film as a visual Esperanto which Christian Metz first analyzed in his influential essay, "The Cinema: Language or Language System."[11] Yet the universal language that *Intolerance* envisions is not a Saussurean, phonetically based language, but a written language—a language of hieroglyphics. This analogy can be traced on at least two distinct levels. On one level, the film's systematic graphicity suggests a reading of *Intolerance* as a "hieroglyphic text," a notion developed by film theorists like Marie-Claire Ropars-Wuilleumier within a framework indebted to Derrida.[12] At the same time, the hieroglyphic analogy seems to inform the film on a more self-conscious level, motivated by Griffith's ambition to affiliate the cinema with a particular tradition of American culture, for which the reference to Whitman can be seen as a shorthand. Regardless of Griffith's intentions, however, the invocation of the hieroglyph inevitably contaminates the film with the ambiguity—if not contradiction—attached to the concept of hieroglyphics over centuries: on the one hand, its reputation as a pictorial language, universally and immediately accessible because of a natural correspondence between sign and referent; on the other, that of a highly enigmatic and esoteric language requiring the labor of deciphering and translation. A monument to the impossibility of a generalized form of iconic representation, *Intolerance* oscillates between both sides of this epistemological contradiction, between the structural claims to iconic self-evidence, transparency, and unity, and the excessive textuality deployed to back up those very claims.

What most strikingly distinguishes *Intolerance* from any other film of the period is its emphasis on graphic activity and heterogeneity. While "art titles" were becoming fashionable around 1916, the intertitles of *Intolerance*, different for each historical narrative, foreground the fact and style of inscription rather than mood or decor.[13] The stone-engraved hieroglyphics of the Babylonian title cards and the Hebrew tablets of the Judaean provide the background for the phonetic script of English intertitles—which means that different systems of graphic notation are made to coexist within one and the same shot. Likewise, the transitions between historically distinct sequences usually (that is, in the first half of the film) feature a whole series of discrete emblems: the cradle shot, the Book of Intolerance, a graphically marked title card and, finally, a narrative image that opens the particular sequence; toward the end of the film, when parallel editing accelerates to alternate even between single shots, stylistic difference still undermines the unifying thrust of narrative movement. In such display of graphic specificity, *Intolerance* preserves a sense of the activity and artifice of inscription which effectively dispels fictions of film as a spontaneous expression or natural presence.

It is in that sense that *Intolerance* bears out Derrida's insistence on the irreducibly composite character of the hieroglyphic sign (consisting of pictographic, ideogrammatic, and phonetic elements) and its constitutive plurality of meanings.[14] One trajectory of possible meanings points in the direction of psychoanalysis, specifically the connection made by Derrida—and, of course, Freud—between hieroglyphic writing and the figurative script of dreams, which both resist immediate perception and understanding, instead requiring the work of decipherment and interpretation.[15] Yet the hieroglyphic analogy also recalls Horkheimer and Adorno's analysis of the ideological mechanisms of mass and consumer culture. Assuming Marx's definition of the commodity as a "social hieroglyph," Horkheimer and Adorno observe a return of hieroglyphic configurations in the industrial manufacturing of archetypes which spell out orders of social identity—ways of being, smiling, and mating. While mass culture's "priestly hieroglyphics" consummates the historical process of reification in the area of mimetic expression, its ideological function lies above all in its masking of reification, in its disguising of script as pure image, as natural, humanized presence. Nonetheless, the scriptural character of mass-cultural images is the very condition of their critical readability: only as figurations of writing may they be deciphered and made to yield historical meaning.[16]

Like the Tower of Babel, the figure of the hieroglyph surfaces in *Intolerance* through a conflation or cannibalization of various layers of tradition. Thus, the "universal written language" whose disappearance the narration joins to the Fall of Babylon is the cuneiform, a system of writing older than—and probably unrelated to—Egyptian hieroglyphics (though it resembles the latter in the structural organization of its code, playing on both ideographic and phonetic registers).[17] The script on the Babylonian title card, however, is not cuneiform, but a design unmistakably imitating hieroglyphics. For one thing, the cuneiform is a much more abstract type of script which, by the time of the historical period dramatized (538 B.C.), had long since lost any pictographic dimension, hence would not have supported the analogy of film as a new universal, ostensibly self-evident language. More important, by substituting hieroglyphs for the Babylonian cuneiform, Griffith could invoke a more recent, specifically American tradition.

In *American Hieroglyphics*, John Irwin traces the symbol of Egyptian hieroglyphics, especially as redefined by Champollion's decipherment of the Rosetta Stone (1822), in the writings of the American Renaissance. Griffith, imbued with this group of writers, in particular Whitman and Poe, could not have ignored their fascination with the hieroglyph, with its impact on both mystical and literary concepts of representation and interpretation. As Irwin points out, this fascination converged with a long-standing popular undercurrent, ranging from the publication of hieroglyphic Bibles (the latest in 1852) to children's books like *Mother Goose in Hieroglyphics* (1849; reprinted at least until the late 1860s). Irwin makes a case for Whitman's conception of *Leaves of Grass* as a hieroglyphic Bible, a format that would link a practice of esoteric writing with the popular tradition.[18] Whitman's self-image as a popular, democratic poet is a highly complex issue—as is that of his purported quest for a language of natural correspondences. Nonetheless one can draw a trajectory, albeit through a sequence of misreadings, from the tradition of popular hieroglyphics through Whitman to Lindsay, self-appointed guardian of Whitman's legacy in Hollywood.

By placing *Intolerance* in the hieroglyphic tradition, Griffith might have hoped to gain access to this particular lineage of American culture, a filiation that would offset the risk he was taking in foregoing the more calculable effects of classical narration. This very risk—the film's deviation from already elaborated and widely accepted classical codes—could indeed be described more precisely in terms of the hieroglyphic ambition than in linguistic terms.[19] It would account not only for the pedagogical stress on repetition and seriality but, above all, for the peculiar organization of space throughout *Intolerance*, including the modern narrative—a persistent frontality (in which the film seems to revert to primitive cinema), a curious fragmentation of the look, a shifting between representational and presentational registers. The hieroglyphic analogy might also explain the unusually high number of diegetically ambiguous and often unclaimed shots, especially emblematic close-ups of faces and objects. Rather than attribute these deviations to a return of theatrical space, the space of *Intolerance* could be characterized more properly as a reading space, a training ground of hieroglyphic signification and interpretation. This reading space exceeds and unmakes the confines of the book, literalized in the Book of Intolerance (title card) whose defeat is dramatized in the happy ending of the modern narrative.

To circle back, once again, to the allegory of Babel in Babylon, the hieroglyphic analogy, with its historical connotations of veiling and deciphering, has particular political implications for Griffith's geneal-ogy of the cinema and its place in American culture. The Fall of Babylon signifies not so much the end of one kind of language and the beginning of another, qualitatively different one, but a catastrophe that occurred within the history of writing (a history encompassing both clay tablets and celluloid), an event that destroyed the public availability of writing. With this construction, *Intolerance* reenacts Bishop Warburton's discovery that the hieroglyphic was not origi-nally a sacral, esoteric script but a popular medium of preserving knowledge and of civil organization (the radical revision of the pre-vailing view which had enabled Champollion's discovery); likewise, the film affirms Warburton's contention that the deflection of hiero-glyphic writing from common usage, its "encryptment," was an event of historical, political significance in that it rendered writing an in-strument of power in the hands of a caste of "intellectuals."[20] What may appear as a historical inconsistency in the Babylonian narrative —the predating of the disappearance of the cuneiform by about six centuries—more likely constitutes an act of interpretation, suggest-ing that any type of writing loses its universal potential when it falls into the hands of an intellectual elite. The Fall of Writing would thus be synonymous with the triumph of linguistic arbitrariness (epito-mized by the Priest of Bel nominating himself as God), which destroys not only a communal medium but, by synecdoche, the utopian unity in all spheres of life which Babylon holds up as a counterimage to the other periods.

As an allegory of an impossible unity and transparency, the Baby-lonian narrative dramatizes, at the same time, the impossibility of historical continuity. Repairing the ruins of Babel requires an apoca-lyptic break, prefigured or, more precisely, precipitated by the catastrophic movement of the entire film; the future lies in the unful-filled promises of prehistory. This metaleptic tendency defines both the genealogy of film within a history of writing and the relation-ship between cinema and literature in the context of that history. Rather than merely assimilate or reject the institution of literature as a whole, Griffith—for personal and ideological reasons of his own —traces a split within the institution of literature between an intel-lectual elite pursuing its own particular, selfish, and arbitrary inter-ests and a marginalized popular tradition, reincarnated in the figure of Whitman.[21] If *Intolerance* can be read as proposing, among other things, to recover a unity of popular and high art, it does so, not by replacing writing with a superior language of visual presence, but rather by retrieving the common roots of both film and literature in the hieroglyphic tradition.

Yet allegory, says Benjamin, also marks "the death of intention," inviting competing and historically specific interpretations. However ingenious the film's programmatic construction may be, by invoking the hieroglyph as both symbol and model of signification, Griffith put *Intolerance* at the mercy of the very rhetoric the film sets out to stabilize and contain. This is especially the case in the film's repre-sentation of women and femininity, its complex response to changes in gender roles and sexuality.

Intolerance could almost be subtitled variations on the theme of femininity in crisis, centering as it does on the fate and fatal power —of unmarried female characters throughout the ages, especially the closer they get to modernity. Indeed, the struggle between love and intolerance is acted out in terms of the opposition between an in-nocent, life-giving maternity (the heroine of the modern story and the Woman Who Rocks the Cradle) and an excessive, perverse, vio-lent, murderous femininity—from the emblematic Parcae in the cra-dle shot through Catherine de Medici to Miss Jenkins and the three Vestal Virgins of Uplift. If innocent femininity is linked, primarily through the cradle image, to hieroglyphics as a language of natu-ral presence, its perverted counterpart is associated, throughout the film, with scenes of phonetic writing, with activities of weaving, spin-ning, and cutting, both metaphorically and literally. Although these figurative acts of authorship are condemned on the fictional level by their destructive results, the fatal women of *Intolerance* wield an enormous power on the level of enunciation: more often than not, they become the subjective focus of the narration, motivating shot changes and authorizing structures of vision. As long as they retain this power, as Medici does in the Huguenot narrative, catastrophe prevails; when the omniscient narrator asserts his authority over their evil eye, as in the raid sequence of the modern narrative, salvation is in sight.

The film stages a battle for narrative authority in sexual terms, but the violence deployed exceeds the textual framework, suggesting a closer look at the historical inscription of femininity and Griffith's position in the cultural marketplace. For the threat of female spinners, weavers, and cutters of yarn would be void if it weren't for new technologies of writing and reproduction which had drawn large numbers of women into the work force and into public visibility—as authors, writers, teachers, journalists, typists, and even film editors. Thus, despite the reassuring insistence that the woman's productive force belongs with the cradle, the sexual economy of *Intolerance* is inextricably bound up with Griffith's anxieties of authorship, his self-image as an artist, his personal investment in the cinema's bid for cultural respectability.

The character of the Friendless One (Miriam Cooper) emerges in a number of ways as the textual counterpoint to the hieroglyph of the Woman Who Rocks the Cradle. This character is not only pivotal to the modern plot—she commits a murder for which the hero is nearly hanged—but also functions as enunciatory focus for much of the second part of the film. Oscillating between perpetrator and victim, the Friendless One is granted a far greater degree of complexity and ambiguity than any other female character in the film. Moreover, she figures as the symptomatic center of a fantasy that complements the Whitmanian scenario implicit in the cradle shot—a rescue fantasy which links the narrative project of *Intolerance* with the familiar scenario of other Griffith films.

If the Friendless One becomes an important (if unpleasurable) relay of identification for the spectator, she also displays an uncanny

The Friendliness One from D. W. Griffith's *Intolerance*. Photo from Film Stills Archive, Museum of Modern Art, New York. Reproduced by permission.

affinity with the obsessional symptoms of the *Intolerance* text. As the modern narrative threatens to take a catastrophic course—the Boy (Robert Harron) has been sentenced to death in her place—the Friendless One is made to enact a vernacular version of the compulsion to repeat, the murderer's "irresistible impulse" (intertitle) to return to the site of the unexpiated crime. It is the repeated assertion of this impulse which eventually leads to her confession, thus enabling, in one and the same move, the rescue of the Boy's body and the salvation of the murderer's soul.

Griffith himself could be said to have followed such an "irresistible impulse"—by casting Miriam Cooper as the Friendless One and coupling her with Walter Long as the Musketeer of the Slums. In *Birth of a Nation*, Long appeared in the role of Gus, the black rapist, while Cooper played the oldest daughter of the Camerons, a melancholy and proud incarnation of Southern womanhood. As Michael Rogin argues with regard to the sexual/racial economy of *Birth*, the castration of the black male (excised from the final print) both displaces and consummates the repression of female sexuality, in a violent effort to restore a defeated patriarchal power.[22] The love/hate relationship between the Musketeer and the Friendless One resumes this constellation—but undoes the displacement. Long, introduced as a collector of fetishistic paraphernalia (such as the pornographic statue in his study), is once again emasculated, this time without the detour of racist projection. And Cooper's transformation from a Southern virgin into an anonymous urban tramp reconstitutes the object of male anxiety: the sexual woman, fantasized as phallic woman (Cooper in a pantsuit, slapping her lover; Cooper with a gun).

Cooper is not merely resexualized; she is modernized—or, rather, the role allows her to shatter the Victorian delicacy that Griffith favored in his actresses as well as his lovers. The Friendless One could almost pass as a contemporary of her literary cousins, Maggie Johnson, Sister Carrie, or Susan Lenox. Cooper's performance actually points beyond the Progressive conception of the character. Anthony Slide, remarking on "the modernity of her beauty and her eyes," calls her a star of the wrong decade: "she belonged more to the era of Clara Bow and Louise Brooks."[23] If not quite the carefree flapper, Cooper's Friendless One comes closest to the image of the

New Woman, the problematic yet undeniably distinct construction of femininity which crystallized significant—and, for men like Griffith, traumatic—changes in women's social, sexual, and economic roles.

Although the Friendless One is not a working woman (she does not support herself by means of wage labor), her fate is motivated by economic exigency, as a result of the strike which leaves her stranded, hungry, and lonesome in the city. She is unmarried, though definitely not a virgin; she is a kept woman, though not exactly a prostitute; she is economically dependent, though not without erotic initiative of her own. In short, despite her name, the character of the Friendless One eludes the rigid dichotomies of middle-class morality such as they persisted in mainstream reformist discourse throughout the Progressive Era.[24] To be sure, moral judgment is still waiting in the wings—it is displaced onto the murder (which is attributed to her neurotic jealousy) or, more precisely, onto her pinning the murder on someone else. Her fate remains unresolved at the end of the film, but there is little doubt that she will rejoin her Victorian predecessors whose redemption was invariably tied to suffering and early death.

The multiple ambiguities surrounding the character of the Friendless One seem to evolve, on the most obvious level, from contradictions in the ideological project of *Intolerance*, in particular its attack on the liberal critics of *Birth*. The peculiar sexual—and sexist —turn of Griffith's polemics against reform, personified by the three Uplifters of the modern period, may have a more specific source in Jane Addams and Lillian Wald, prominent NAACP members who had joined the protest against *Birth*. Addams, founder of Hull House, leading social reformer and suffragist, must have vexed Griffith in a number of ways, not merely on account of her political dissent. Besides possessing the public authority he coveted for himself, she remained unmarried and childless, and (like Wald) had lifelong primary relationships with women. The insinuations of lesbianism in Griffith's caricature of the Vestal Virgins of Uplift, not to mention the imputation of sexual frustration as a motive for reform, are unmistakable hints in Addams's direction.[25]

Addams had also written a major work on prostitution, *A New Conscience and an Ancient Evil* (1912)—a subject which held a strong fascination for Griffith. What is more, in this book, Addams stressed the analogy between the fate of blacks under slavery and the plight of the prostitute—an analogy already present in the label "abolitionist" for the dominant Progressive position on prostitution (defined by the aim to abolish rather than regulate or segregate prostitution), as well as the popular term "white slavery."[26] Thus, by ridiculing this "new abolitionism" in *Intolerance*, a film designed to establish its director as above racial prejudice, Griffith implicitly resumed his denunciation of the struggle against slavery in *Birth*. This ideological continuity is further enforced by the parallel between modern Uplifters and the Priest of Bel who betrays Babylon to Cyrus: with the exotic display of various tribes, the Persian camp is marked as the locus of both racial difference and brute masculinity, forces unleashed by selfish intellectuals to destroy the Babylonian dream—but no Klan to ride to the rescue.

By including prostitution among the social problems ostensibly exacerbated by the Uplifters' meddling, *Intolerance* both acknowledged and opposed the shift in reformist discourse which had made the prostitute the prime target of Progressive moral reform. As Ruth Rosen elaborates in her study, *The Lost Sisterhood*, "what earlier Victorians had discreetly regarded as a 'necessary evil,' turn-of-the-century Americans came to view as the 'Social Evil,' a moral problem and a national menace."[27] While the nineteenth-century preoccupation with "fallen" women had focused on saving the souls of individual prostitutes (as evidenced by the tradition of the "Magdalen" homes), the Progressive crusade aimed at abolishing prostitution through the agency of the state, primarily on the municipal level but on a national scale. As a result, prostitution was driven underground and criminalized.

Intolerance's concern with prostitution largely resumes the Victorian discourse, with a highly specific link to the Magdalen tradition. Yet with its ambiguous analysis of the raid on the brothel, the film also echoes contemporary critics of the Progressive vice campaign, though with a particularly misogynist slant.[28] In the context of the popular media, *Intolerance* no doubt cashed in on the white slavery panic of the pre-War years—as did a whole slew of films before it, most notably *Traffic in Souls* (1913). The public obsession with innocent women being lured into profitable bondage was linked, as historians have pointed out, to other anxieties, precipitated by the pressures of industrialization, urbanization, and immigration. Whether in its concern for the victim, the newly arrived immigrant girl, or in its vilification of the procurers, allegedly all foreigners, the crusade against organized prostitution often assumed a nativist tone, projecting the problem on an ethnic/racial other.[29]

At the same time, ethnic (though not avowedly racial) difference played a significant part in the fascination with commercially available sex—as Griffith's own memoirs, written in 1938–39, illustrate in rather graphic terms. Reminiscing on his first exposure to the Lower East Side in 1899, when he was twenty-four and poor, Griffith reflects upon the inaptness of the term "melting pot"; it was "more like a *boiling pot.*"

> Here were Italians, Greeks, Poles, Jews, Arabs, Egyptians, all hustling for a living. Emotional, tempestuous, harrowing Rivington Street was perpetually a steaming, bubbling pot of varied human flesh. And the Bowery by night! I would not attempt to describe it; that has been done by experts. But I knew every hot spot there. . . . Gaudy women swung in and out of doors of the various bagnios and bistros. . . . The skin of the Bowery women was of every known hue. After the age-old manner of the siren, they chanted in many languages and accents the one hymn to lust.[30]

Following the conventional prohibition against representing ethnic difference, the modern narrative of *Intolerance* does not thematize this source of fascination. The suppressed connotations of ethnic otherness, however, persist on the intertextual level, both in Cooper's dark persona and in the film's mobilization of contemporary discourse on prostitution. Perhaps the film's preoccupation with erotic triangles (both modern and Babylonian) also feeds on these connotations —which would link the troubling figuration of the "other woman" to the cultural repression of the "other" woman.[31]

Another source of fascination—and ambivalence—in the focus on unmarried women must have been the different standards of respectability that governed gender and sexual relations among the urban working class. The simple joys and leisure-time pleasures that *Intolerance* so piously defends against the puritan reformers—dancing, drinks, a Coney Island day—were available to most single working women only at the price of sexual favors, as Griffith himself had discovered, much to his chagrin, when he first came to New York. With the increased commercial organization of leisure activities (dance halls, movie theaters, amusement parks), a whole "subculture of treating" had come into being which allowed the working woman to "have a good time," to enjoy a man's attention and company without being stigmatized as a "fallen woman."[32] *Intolerance* acknowledges this practice repeatedly, not only through the sympathetic portrayal of mill workers looking for a date but also from the perspective of the heroine, the Dear One (Mae Marsh), who is introduced to the art of attracting men by watching a flamboyant young woman on the street.[33] Yet soon enough, her flirtatious urge is channeled, rather violently, into the itinerary prescribed by middle-class morality. The ambivalence attached to working-class sexual culture remains to be acted out, no less violently, by the Friendless One.

The anti-reform, antipuritan agenda of *Intolerance* was bound to confuse the repressive oppositions which Griffith had been asserting so relentlessly in his previous films. These oppositions were anything but stable to begin with: many of the Biograph films in fact register a traumatic breakdown of boundaries—between domestic and public space, between good and evil, between virgin and prostitute—and the work of the narrative usually consists of reaffirming these boundaries. Staged most forcefully through last-minute rescue races, the ideological project crucially relies on parallel narration, on subcodes of crosscutting and accelerated editing. Yet as Rick Altman argues in his reading of *The Lonely Villa* (1909), difference and resemblance easily become sliding terms, particularly in the alternation between male aggressor and paternal rescuer figures. Thus parallel narration itself provides the basis for a radical critique of the conservative oppositions it set out to restore.[34] If crosscutting within one and the same diegesis can trigger such processes, the cross-diegetic use of parallel editing in *Intolerance*, overriding conventions of simultaneity and linearity, would be likely to subvert its own binary constructions all the more thoroughly—and perhaps even more knowingly.

Hence the ambiguities surrounding the character of the Friendless One could also be described as one of the more radical effects of parallel montage. While the narrative construction of the character is circumscribed by the gender economy of the modern narrative—the familiar stereotypes of old maid, virgin mother, and prostitute —these stereotypes are put into question by transdiegetic references between the Friendless One and various female figures in the other narratives. Much of the first third of the film, which is relatively weak in narrative exposition and development, reads like an essay on sexual and gender relations throughout the ages, revolving around the problematic status of the single woman.[35] Certainly, the historical women characters are just as constructed as the modern ones and respond, as projections, to the same crisis as the latter. But by multiplying perspectives on female identity, the parallel narration poses this identity as problematic, as discursively constructed and historically changeable.

The interplay of these perspectives is of a palimpsestic—rather than a structural—order, soliciting the spectator's activity without predetermining it in every detail and direction. Indeed, of all the female characters in *Intolerance*, the Friendless One most thoroughly disturbs the lines of the parallel structure of the film, in the sense of an architectonic, hierarchical construction. She shares certain attributes and positions with individual historical characters, but those characters in turn have little in common with one another. As a neurotic murderer, for instance, she resembles Catherine de Medici, the phallic mother; like the Babylonian Mountain Girl, she is defined as a casualty of the marriage market and by her precarious position in erotic triangles; like Mary Magdalen, she is granted a sexual nature, albeit under the auspices of economic exchange, but like the Woman Taken in Adultery she gets a chance to repent and partake of redemption.[36]

The episode of Mary Magdalen (Olga Grey) who, "bedizened . . . in a luxurious litter," is spurned by the Pharisees in the first Judaean episode, must have been cut after the film's first run. In the reedited versions, the character was conflated with the Woman Taken in Adultery.[37] (The latter episode is the only nonmodern sequence of *Intolerance* included in *The Mother and the Law* [see note 33], as a mental vision on the part of a stern older woman [Kate Bruce] who comforts a "fallen" girl in a Magdalen home.) By invoking the Magdalen tradition, Griffith might have hoped to legitimize the film's interest in prostitution and prostitutes, both Babylonian and modern—a ruse that did not go unnoticed in contemporary reviews.[38] Yet more important, the figure of the penitent Magdalen offers an interpretive parallel for the fate of the Friendless One and thus elucidates the rescue scenario of the modern narrative.

The psychosexual complex that seems pertinent here is that of a particular type of male object choice for which Freud uses the semi-vernacular term *Dirnenliebe*, "love for a prostitute." This precondition for loving—that the woman be like a harlot—and the attendant need of experiencing jealousy are often pursued with such compulsive intensity that the corresponding relationships tend to replace one another frequently and hence to form a long series. In conjunction with this type of object choice, Freud observes a "most startling" tendency: the urge, on the part of the men thus infatuated, to "rescue" the woman they love, to keep her on the path of "virtue." As in other contexts, Freud relates the debasement of the love object to "the mother-complex," meaning an unresolved libidinal attachment to the mother which is reactivated at a later stage, with the boy's initiation to sexual knowledge by hearsay (often involving references to prostitutes), and which survives in its fixation on fantasies formed during puberty.[39]

The "rescue-*motif*" as such has a more archaic history which Freud traces through the child's wish to return the gift of life to the mother. Rescuing his mother, with a slight twist of meaning, "takes on the significance of giving her a child or making a child for her—needless to say, one like himself." By "wishing to have by his mother a son who is like himself," the son, in the rescue fantasy, "is completely identifying himself with his father. All his instincts, those of tenderness, gratitude, lustfulness, defiance and independence, find satisfaction in the single wish *to be his own father*."

We can easily detect both strands of this fantasy in Griffith's favorite narrative paradigm: the last-minute rescue plot of victimized womanhood, rehearsed in so many Biograph films and consummated in *Birth*, a psychic drama of threat, hysteria, and penetration enacted through parallel and accelerated editing. In addition to the element of danger and the affect of anxiety (which Freud links to the very experience of birth), the incestuous subtext of the rescue motif would account not only for the relative weakness of male protagonists in many of these films, but also for the "jealous" interventions of the director-narrator, ostensibly in support of the hero's efforts to save the untouchable object of desire. In the Freudian reading of the rescue fantasy, the identification with a paternal authority which restores itself in the act of rescue would indicate less an achieved oedipal transition than an unresolved erotic fixation on the mother—or, in Griffith's case, more likely his unmarried older sister, Mattie. By projecting repressed incestuous desire onto a social or racial other and preventing the violation in the nick of time, Griffith's rescue scenario permits the narrator to pursue an "essentially . . . chivalrous project" that ennobles both object and subject of the rescue fantasy.[40] To be hyperbolic: every blithe virgin trapped in domestic space is a proleptic version of a prostitute in need of rescue.

Moreover, Griffith's rescue scenario shares with the one described by Freud a compulsive quality, a built-in tendency to repeat. The economic pressure of serial production, especially under the conservative production policy of the Biograph Company, provided an incontestable rationale for the compulsive repetition of rescue plots. At the same time, it allowed Griffith to rehearse and refine a narrative idiom which would grant him public success, which would eventually make him the phantom father of American cinema. With the overwhelming success of *Birth*, the repressive shield that masks repetition as progress, maintained by economic and social pressures, might have temporarily broken down; hence *Intolerance* could be said to spell out the unconscious layers of the chivalrous rescue fantasy.

In the rescue scenario of the modern narrative, the figure of virginal victim and paternal rescuer is inverted, giving way to a constellation of a maternal figure, split into the familiar halves of fallen woman and virgin mother, and an oedipal son in need of rescue, ultimately from his own incestuous desire. According to the logic of the narrative, the (spiritual) rescue of the Friendless One is synonymous with the (physical) rescue of the Boy; indeed, her timely conversion makes her at once an object and an instrument of rescue. The logic of parallel editing further suggests that the gender roles in the rescue scenario are reversible, pointing up—in terms of Freud's transformational rhetoric—an earlier layer of the fantasy. Thus the Babylonian Mountain Girl's race for Belshazzar's life, reciprocating for his having saved her twice before, emphasizes the initiative and active role of the female characters in the modern period. Making women the rescuers rather than helpless victims besieged in a domestic space (with the exception of the Huguenot Brown Eyes), *Intolerance* resurrects the female prototype represented in earlier Griffith films by Blanche Sweet, especially in her performance as the parricidal heroine of *Judith of Bethulia*.[41] This inversion also confirms the hypothesis as to the subject in need of rescue—the oedipally entangled son.

It might be argued that, despite such deviations from the familiar Griffith scenario, the telos of the rescue fantasy in *Intolerance* remains the same—the "restoration of the holiness of the American family."[42] Certainly, this is the message of the last shot of the modern narrative, in which the baby is returned to the reconstituted couple. But the happy ending is undermined not only by its imbrication with the parallel catastrophes in the historical narratives; it appears tacked on in view of a regressive sexual dynamic in the formation of the couple, in particular their exclusion from patterns of scopic desire and the curiously incomplete oedipal itinerary of the Bobby Harron character.

If we consider the first third of the film from the point of view of the Boy, the large segment beginning with his exodus from the city charts the young man's transition from a dark woman of sexual knowledge, the Friendless One, to the haven of domesticity offered by the Dear One. Positing the son—whom he calls "Boy" throughout the film—as oedipally defeated in advance, the director-narrator empowers the dark sexual woman to kill the father, charging the Boy with a guilt that all but destroys him. To compound his helplessness, the last-minute rescue is made to depend upon both women, the virginal mother and the incestuous one whose spell he had been trying to escape all along and who (because she is bound to return in some incarnation) can only be dropped from the narrative. Thus, in terms of the unconscious logic of the rescue fantasy, the figure of the mother is beset with an irreducible and fatal ambivalence—the same ambivalence that unravels the emblem of the cradle and links *Intolerance* with the morbid scenario of Griffith's play, *The Treadmill*.[43]

Like the ugly duckling Earth in this cosmic allegory, the Boy drifts about in the social wilderness at the mercy of the institutionalized violence of American capitalism (represented by the father figures of Jenkins, the "industrial overlord," the Musketeer, the Judge, the Executioner). The wish to be rescued revolves around the figure of the mother who, like Whitman's "fierce old mother," has given him life but not immortality, who has displaced a failing patriarchal lineage with an even greater threat of chaos and loss of identity. Since desire seems fixated in this incestuous bind, all erotic relationships in *Intolerance* are doomed to remain unconsummated: in almost Keatsian stylization, death freezes the Babylonian nuptials and, with more explicitly sadistic violence, reaps the fruit of the impending double marriage in sixteenth-century France.

Critics have associated the obsessional and neurotic configurations of Griffith's films with the problematic image of his father, Jake Griffith, whose ignominious decline and posthumous mythification by his son have been read in light of a more general crisis of patriarchy at the end of the nineteenth century.[44] Apposite as these readings may be, the critical emphasis on the father figure often tends to reproduce the exclusion of the mother—or other primary female figures—in the familial scenarios that were to inspire familiar narratives on screen. Insofar as biographical trajectories are capable of illuminating the psychosexual economy of filmic texts, *Intolerance* urges us to reconsider the female part of Griffith's own rescue fantasy and to add his sisters, especially his favorite sister Mattie, to the ghoulish presences that trouble his films.

If *Birth* attempts to lay to rest the ghost of his dead father, *Intolerance* seems to struggle with the conflicting feelings surrounding his dead sister. Mattie Griffith, about seventeen years older than young David, was "a brilliantly cultured woman," as Griffith told an interviewer at the time he was making *Intolerance*. Not only did she give him and the other children their basic education but, unlike their somewhat distant mother, she was the only person who had emotional access to the father. "Mattie found in her father an intellect that met her requirements and a character that she adored; she never married, and would say, either jokingly or seriously, I was never certain which, but suspect the latter, that she never had found a man equal to her father and that none of less quality would ever satisfy her as a husband." Having just moved the fatherless family to Louisville, she died in 1889, at the age of thirty, by popular standards an "old maid."[45]

Griffith's father died when the son was ten, too early for him to come to terms with the father's violence and defeat, let alone his own resentment of both. Mattie died when Griffith was still an adolescent, and left to him a powerful incestuous fantasy, a model of the father-daughter relations he was later to put on the screen—Austin and Elsie Stoneman, Ben Cameron and the Little Sister in *Birth*; the Dear One and her father in *Intolerance*; and, in a more perverse variant, Lucy and Battling Burrows in *Broken Blossoms*. The case of the "missing mother" in so many Griffith films is thus more likely a case of the dead sister. Whatever Mattie's problem might have been—and the phrasing in the interview suggests that it was at least as much Griffith's as hers—he appropriated her incestuous fantasy as part of his own, doubling the stakes of repression, fixation, and guilt. The films' obsession with father-daughter incest is hence not merely a vague and general defense against that between mother and son, but rather functions as a fantasy within another fantasy, involving a complex triangle of father, son, and older sister.

Considering *Intolerance*'s concern with the fate of the single woman, Mattie's spirit seems to preside over the host of abandoned, unadjusted, excessive women who populate the film, its major source of fascination and anxiety. From that perspective, the vehemence and crudity with which the film exploits the stereotype of the old maid, and its simultaneous nonchalance regarding the figure of the prostitute, can be read as symptoms of one and the same repressed desire, revolving around the dead mother surrogate. What links these two symptoms, however, is not only an economy of incestuous guilt, but also an urban-industrial economy of exchange which clashed with traditional values of femininity and culture—values Griffith associated with the memory of his sister.

Prostitution, after all, provided a metaphor in which the mysteries of sexuality and those of the marketplace converged—the commodity form become flesh and blood.[46] A populist anticapitalist by background and conviction, Griffith was sensitive to the inequities of exchange, especially if it involved an object traditionally defined as a value in itself—like chastity, like art. Even in *Judith of Bethulia*, a film set in biblical antiquity, one gets a sense of the scandal involved in the *quid pro quo*, when Judith, the righteous widow, uses her sexuality to liberate the Jewish town from the Assyrian siege; revising the Apocrypha, Griffith inserts a moment of private agony before she kills Holofernes, explaining that Judith has fallen in love with her victim. The fiction of erotic reciprocity—in sentiment at least—may be intended to soften the blow against masculine pride; yet it also makes clear that her phallic victory, based on an unholy exchange, requires the sacrifice of her own sexuality.[47]

In *Intolerance*, the conjunction of money and femininity becomes thematic early on in the film—in a series of marginal figures like Mary Magdalen, the young woman peddler in the streets of sixteenth-century Paris, and the mill worker who tries to solicit Jenkins as a date. By the code of parallelism, the Pharisee who rejects the favors of Mary Magdalen has to be read as a variant of the puritanical industrialist who displaces the erotic look onto a dime; this may explain why, contrary to the New Testament, the voluptuous courtesan remains uncensored in the Judaean narrative (it may further explain why the whole sequence was eventually cut). The revisionist pleasure notwithstanding, the parallel reanchors the figure of the prostitute in the economy of incestuous desire, repression, and guilt that it so demonstratively tries to escape. For Jenkins's money derives its value not merely from the expropriation of human labor (as suggested, on a secondary, narrative level, by the strike sequence); rather, it is bound up, on the figurative level, with the repression of female sexuality. For it is also the money which finances his sister's and, thus, the Uplifters' charities and which the film's first dialogue title—"If we can only interest Miss Jenkins – with *her money*"—establishes as the missing link between a femininity gone stale and the fatal chain of events in the modern narrative.

The mutual contamination of money and femininity reveals the spinster and the prostitute as two sides of the same coin, both obstacle and challenge to the circulation of desire. Not having balanced their sexuality with the only legitimate equivalent, a child, they turn into a many-headed gorgon of incestuous guilt and economic

194 : Miriam Hansen

threat. In the sinister pact between Jenkins and his sister, money figures as the compensation for the sister's projected sacrifice, her having remained "pure" for her brother's sake. This deadly variant of a sibling relationship, however, presents the flip side of Griffith's own family romance. Mattie's "sacrifice," imagined as the stake of oedipal rivalry, crucially depended on her capacity of earning money—which the father not only failed to accumulate but, to be exact, had lost by drinking and gambling. Yet in *Intolerance* the only women who work, who support themselves by means of paid labor, are prostitutes. The metaphoric debasement of the woman who makes money —and the concomitant investment of money with sexual guilt—inscribes Mattie even more inescapably in the psychosexual quandary elaborated by Freud.

The emphasis on the cash nexus, moreover, suggests yet another level of the rescue fantasy, involving Griffith's relation to both industry and audiences, the construction of his public persona. Griffith's fascination with the prostitute was very much part of his belated encounter with modernity, in its economic, social, and cultural manifestations. Given his still recent initiation to the more advanced capitalist society of the Northeast, the display of female flesh that overwhelmed the young actor on the Bowery came to symbolize— along with the troubling appeal of ethnic diversity—the pervasiveness of the marketplace, whether in Eros or art. The passage from his memoirs quoted above concludes with a rhetorical gesture familiar from his films, a defensive transmuting of traumatic aspects of modernity into a mythologizing and allegorical idiom: "After the age-old manner of the siren, they [the Bowery women] chanted in many languages and accents the one hymn to lust . . . the same against which Ulysses had roped himself to the mast. That was one man who had the right idea. These women sang only to the cash register." The choice of this particular mythological example is no coincidence: the episode of the Sirens in the *Odyssey* marks, in Horkheimer and Adorno's reading, the birth of art in its bourgeois form, as a promise of happiness to be endured only at the price of a social division of labor.[48] Himself without the means to indulge in the Siren's song, Griffith registers the economic mediation of desire—but attributes it, in a provincial and universalizing manner, to the women who happen to be the most striking incarnation of this economy, as if it were an expression of female sexuality.

Yet since the Sirens also sing the dirge of his own family romance, prostitution offered itself as a shorthand of his artistic/erotic impasse. With its more compassionate attitude toward the fallen woman, *Intolerance* suggests an aspect of Griffith's fascination which the philistine reminiscence veils: a secret—if unconscious—affinity with the fate of the prostitute on the part of the artist. As an actor seeking a career on the legitimate stage, Griffith knew how it felt to put oneself, body and soul, on the cultural marketplace, even if his eventual success as a director restored, for a while, the belief that he was still his own entrepreneur. A threshold figure like the nineteenth-century poet/*flaneur* (to invoke Benjamin's characterization of Baudelaire), Griffith entered the newly created marketplace of the cinema, ostensibly surveying it for its artistic possibilities, though already in search of customers. The image of the prostitute, vendor and commodity in one, encapsulated this historical ambiguity. Likewise, as a phenomenon of urban society and mass production, the prostitute came to personify the artist's ambivalence toward the urban masses—whom he embraced as consumers but also blamed for the alienation which linked their fate to his own. In other words, the metaphorical debasement of the woman who works betrays both fear of and desire for the woman who has money to spend—the consumer.[49]

Figures of sexual exchange in *Intolerance* are thus linked to Griffith's ambivalent relationship with a consumer-oriented art, his romance with the muse who had brought him success but not the undivided acclaim of the cultural arbiters. Indeed, the way he conceptualized the discrepancy between his, to put it mildly, anachronistic notion of "art" and the standards of mass-cultural entertainment resembles the neurotic split that characterizes the figurations of femininity in his films. "In Griffith's trenchantly binary world," Dudley Andrew observes, "art was . . . associated with the quiet, the uplifting, the moral, the delicate and (certainly for him) the feminine." The cinema, then, as an art form that thrived on intimate commerce with the urban masses, promising happiness to everyone but faithful to no one, could only be troped as a prostitute.[50]

In return for her having enabled him to resurrect his "father's sword," Griffith felt called upon to redeem the cinematic muse, to secure her a place among—or even above—the traditional, more respectable arts. A chivalrous project of grandiose ambition, it made him enact, for his public persona, a version of the rescue fantasy outlined above. In that scenario, *Intolerance* would figure as a gift to the dead sister, repaying the debt of his emotional life, his education, his cultural values—by "purifying" the very power that had liberated him into creativity. In a mixture of naiveté and hubris, Griffith seems to be testing the "virtue" of the market he himself had conquered so aggressively with *Birth*, risking the capital, in both a literal and a metaphoric sense, he had attached to his name. *Intolerance*'s abstention from classical strategies of viewer absorption and identification —in particular its nonlinear narration and curious fragmentation of the look—might be considered as part of such a test; its reward, in turn, would be a new hieroglyphics that would establish the cinema as the model and centerpiece of an integral American culture. Whatever the rationale, the deviations of *Intolerance* raised the stakes of the rescue project to a self-defeating dimension—not unlike the parallel deployment of danger, anxiety, and catastrophe within the film itself.

Yet the cards were stacked against Griffith; the odds—to use a pervasive visual and structural figure of the film—were precisely three to one against him. The father's sword, transformed into a "flashing vision" with *Birth*, returns in *Intolerance* with a double edge. While asserting itself as a strong narrative voice, a unique artistic signature that makes everything cohere, that mythical sword is also reincarnated in the three hangmen's knives, and is thus, as an image of narration, related to the obsessive cutting that haunts the whole film. Experimenting with a type of editing that he knew to be in excess of emerging continuity conventions, Griffith not only cut himself off from the spectator-consumer of classical cinema; transferring his sexual guilt to the realm of art, he also turned the father's sword against himself and performed something like a metaphorical act of self-castration.

The failure of *Intolerance* would be less glorious, and Griffith's rescue effort a gloomy exercise indeed, if it weren't for another prostitute saved from the philistines—the magnificent Whore of Babylon. If the narratives set in the Christian era represent the nexus of money and femininity as one of impossible desire, repression, and guilt, the Babylonian narrative tries to overcome this economy, by releasing it into a bacchanalia of fetishism. With its surplus of visual pleasure, its flaunting of production values, this Orientalist phantasmagoria recalls a more archaic stage of consumer culture, exemplified by the nineteenth-century tradition of world expositions from Crystal Palace (1851) through Chicago (1893) to San Francisco (1915). As Benjamin observed with regard to that tradition, the phantasmagoric images mobilized to transfigure the industrial marketplace have a double edge, promise and delusion in one.[51] While no doubt functioning within dominant ideology, Griffith's Babylonian pageant is shot through with a utopian pathos which, among other things, prevents it from sliding into camp. The invocation of Babel and the hieroglyphic tradition, the image of an integral civilization and a model welfare state, an aesthetics of abundance and polymorphous eroticism—these aspects of Babylon may suspend it in a mythical irreality, but they also hold up a mirror (admittedly a perverse one) to the deficiencies of contemporary American life. In terms of film history, finally, Babylon encapsulates the concrete utopia of a cinema that would develop, uninhibited by studio accountants and moral arbiters, into a public medium for the organization and communication of experience, just as the film as a whole projects a different, less determined relationship with the spectator than what was becoming the norm. In that sense, the failure of *Intolerance* may have been due, not so much to Griffith's miscognition of the film-spectator relations that evolved with classical cinema, but perhaps to a much nobler infatuation with the public as a collective body, investing confidence in their imagination, curiosity, and interpretive capability.

Notes

1   Vachel Lindsay, "Photoplay Progress," *New Republic*, 17 February 1917, 76. Many critics have seen the cradle shot as one of the reasons for the film's failure, most notably Sergei Eisenstein in his beautiful essay, "Dickens, Griffith, and the Film Today," in *Film Form*, ed. and trans. Jay Leyda (New York, 1949), 240–44.

2   See chap. 9 of my book, *Babel and Babylon: Spectatorship in American Silent Film*, forthcoming, Harvard University Press. The second part of the present essay is taken from chap. 10 of that study and is printed with permission of Harvard University Press.

3   Vachel Lindsay, *The Art of the Moving Picture* (New York, 1970), 21f.

4   Ibid., 152–53; see also chap. 13, "Hieroglyphics."

5   John T. Irwin, *American Hieroglyphics: The Symbol of the Egyptian Hieroglyphics in the American Renaissance* (Baltimore, 1983).

6   See Miriam Hansen, "Universal Language and Democratic Culture: Myths of Origin in Early American Cinema," in *Myth and Enlightenment in American Literature: In Honor of Hans-Joachim Lang*, ed. Dieter Meindl et al. (Erlangen, 1985), 321–51.

7   Lillian Gish, *Dorothy and Lillian Gish* (New York, 1973), 60.

8   D. W. Griffith, "Innovations and Expectations," in *Focus on D. W. Griffith*, ed. Harry M. Geduld (Englewood Cliffs, N.J., 1971), 56.

9   Hans Aarsleff, *From Locke to Saussure: Essays on the Study of Language and Intellectual History* (Minneapolis, 1982), 260; Jacques Derrida, *Difference in Translation*, ed. Joseph F. Graham (Ithaca, 1985), 165–248.

10 Hansen, *Babel and Babylon*, chaps. 6 and 7.

11 Christian Metz, *Film Language: A Semiotics of the Cinema*, trans. Michael Taylor (New York, 1974), 63f.

12 Marie-Claire Ropars-Wuilleumier, "The Graphic in Filmic Writing: *A bout de souffle*, or The Erratic Alphabet," *Enclitic* (Spring 1982): 147–61; and *Le texte divisé* (Paris, 1981).

13 David Bordwell, Janet Staiger, and Kristin Thompson, *The Classical Hollywood Cinema: Film Style and Mode of Production to 1960* (New York, 1985), 187.

14 Jacques Derrida, *Of Grammatology*, trans. Gayatri Chakravorty Spivak (Baltimore, 1976), 74–93; see also his essay, "Scribble (writing-power)," *Yale French Studies* 58 (1979): 117–47.

15 Jacques Derrida, "Freud and the Scene of Writing," in *Writing and Difference*, trans. Alan Bass (Chicago, 1978), 207ff., also 240–42; *The Standard Edition of the Complete Psychological Works of Sigmund Freud*, ed. and trans. James Strachey (London, 1953–74), 4: 277–78, 5: 341, 13: 177.

16 Max Horkheimer and Theodor W. Adorno, "Das Schema der Massenkultur" (1942), draft of the chapter on the Culture Industry in *Dialectic of Enlightenment* (New York, 1972), first published in Theodor W. Adorno, *Gesammelte Schriften* (Frankfurt, 1981), 3: 332–35; Theodor W. Adorno, "Prolog zum Fernsehen," in *Eingriffe* (Frankfurt, 1963), 77–79. Horkheimer and Adorno's insistence on the critical transformation of ideological images into writing is indebted to Benjamin's concept of allegory. For Marx's discussion of the commodity as "social hieroglyph," see *Capital* (New York, 1967), 1: 74f.

17 Derrida, *Of Grammatology*, 89. The cuneiform actually survived into the first century of the Common Era, though only in the hands of the priests.

18 Irwin, *American Hieroglyphics*, pt. 1, 30ff.

19 The repetition—across historical periods—of particular gestures, narrative motifs, and character behavior suggests a process of signification and figuration which does not necessarily presume a closed, differential system. The most striking instance of how *Intolerance* eludes the notion of a "textual system" based on a linguistic model is Christian Metz's misreading of the film as a "primarily univocal," "closed," "simple" film in *Language and Cinema*, trans. Donna Jean Umiker-Sebeok (The Hague, 1974), 77–78, 107–12.

20 See Derrida, "Scribble (writing-power)," 124.

21 A locus classicus of Whitman's significance for the cultural criticism of the pre-War years is Van Wyck Brooks's *America's Coming of Age* (New York, 1915): "But it happens that we have the rudiments of a middle tradition, a tradition which effectively combines theory and action, a tradition which is just as fundamentally American as either flag-waving or money-grabbing, one which is visibly growing but which has already been grossly abused; and this is the tradition which begins with Walt Whitman. The real significance of Walt Whitman is that he, for the first time, gave us the sense of something organic in American life" (112).

22 Michael Rogin, " 'The Sword Became a Flashing Vision': D. W. Griffith's *The Birth of a Nation*," *Representations* 9 (Winter 1985): 174–78.

23 Anthony Slide, *The Griffith Actresses* (New York, 1973), 127. Slide quotes Julian Johnson's marvelous comment on Cooper's performance, *Photoplay Magazine* 10 (December 1916): "All actresses who honestly provide for home and baby by the business of vamping and gunning, would do well to observe Miss Cooper's expressions and gestures. Miss Cooper is police dock—she is blotter transcript. Her face is what you *really* see some nights under the green lamps" (80–81).

24 The term "Friendless Girls" was used primarily by female reformers engaged in projects to rescue young women from prostitution. From the perspective of the prostitute whose networks and livelihood were threatened by Progressive reform, it was just another expression of the condescension and ignorance of their middle-class sisters. Ruth Rosen, *The Lost Sisterhood: Prostitution in America, 1900–1918* (Baltimore, 1982), quotes from the letters of Maimie Pinzer: "The kind of girl—the human jelly fish—that is willing to be classed as 'friendless' I haven't much time for . . ." (66).

25 Addams not only signed the protest against *Birth*, but also condemned the film in an interview to the *Evening Post*, which was reprinted in the New York *Post*, the only paper that refused to carry advertisements for the film (see *Focus on "The Birth of a Nation*," ed. Fred Silva [Englewood Cliffs, N.J., 1971], 67f., 117).

26 On the "abolitionist" position, see Rosen, *Lost Sisterhood*, 9, 12, 17, and 30.

27 Ibid., xi, 18. Rosen's study represents a break with the more traditional view that Progressive reform actually benefited the prostitute by shifting responsibility from individual moral depravity to her commercial exploiters.

28 Emma Goldman, "The Traffic in Women," in *The Traffic in Women and Other Essays on Feminism* (New York, 1970), 19, 30f.; Brand Whitlock, former mayor

of Toledo, "The White Slave," *Forum* 51 (1914): 193–216, quoted in Rosen, *Lost Sisterhood*, 18, 31f. The defense of the prostitute against the Progressive crusade could also draw on a bohemian tradition of romanticizing the prostitute, as, for example, in Hutchins Hapgood, *Types from City Streets* (New York, 1910), 125–41, especially 138ff.

29 Egal Feldman, "Prostitution, the Alien Woman and the Progressive Imagination, 1910–1915," *American Quarterly* 19 (Summer 1967): 192–206; Rosen, *Lost Sisterhood*, chap. 7, "White Slavery: Myth or Reality." For a diverging analysis of "white slavery" as primarily an instance of mass hysteria, see Mark Thomas Connelly, *The Response to Prostitution in the Progressive Era* (Chapel Hill, 1980), chap. 6. With regard to the racial—and racist—aspects of the Progressive attack on prostitution, it might be of interest here that one of the leading crusaders against "Black Tenderloin" was the Reverend Dr. Charles H. Parkhurst of the Presbyterian Church of New York; Parkhurst was also one of the major advocates of film censorship until he was converted to the screen by *The Birth of a Nation*.

30 *The Man Who Invented Hollywood: The Autobiography of D. W. Griffith*, ed. James Hart (Louisville, 1972), 56. On Griffith's fascination with prostitutes see also Richard Schickel, *D. W. Griffith: An American Life* (New York, 1984), 45, 55–58.

31 Erotic triangles involving "another woman" can be found in a number of Griffith's films, such as *The Eternal Mother* (1911), *The Female of the Species* (1912), *Hearts of the World* (1918), and *True-Heart Susie* (1919). The repressed ethnic connotations of the fear—and desire—of the "other" woman were more explicit (though still repressed) in the contemporary figure of the vamp, notably her personification by Theda Bara.

32 Kathy Peiss, "'Charity Girls' and City Pleasures: Historical Notes on Working-Class Sexuality, 1880–1920," in *Powers of Desire*, ed. Ann Snitow, Christine Stansell, and Sharon Thompson (New York, 1983), 74–87; Griffith, *Autobiography*, 56. See also Hapgood, *Types from City Streets*, 125–38.

33 The coquettish aspects of the Mae Marsh character are more developed in *The Mother and the Law*, the film that became the modern narrative of *Intolerance* but was released separately only in 1919.

34 Rick Altman, "*The Lonely Villa* and Griffith's Paradigmatic Style," *Quarterly Review of Film Studies* 6 (Spring 1981): 123–34.

35 The sequences beginning with the exodus of the modern protagonists after the strike (shots 265–574 in Theodore Huff's shot-by-shot analysis of *Intolerance*) could be read as a montage unit in a larger sense, presenting variations on the themes of courtship, marriage, jealousy, adultery, prostitution; at least seven couples are formed—or fail to form—across centuries and classes. These sequences are, briefly: the Boy's first encounter with the Friendless One; both defeated by adversity (the Boy turns to crime; the Friendless One listens to the Musketeer); the Babylonian marriage market (the Mountain Girl exempted by Belshazzar; the effeminate rhapsode pining for her in vain); highly ritualized courtship between Belshazzar and the Princess Beloved; the Boy's second encounter with the Friend-

less One (confrontation with the Musketeer); the Dear One's encounter with the Boy, followed by her father's death; the Marriage in Cana; Brown Eyes courted by Prosper (confrontation with the Mercenary); the end of a Coney Island day (the Dear One's virtuous refusal prompts the Boy to propose); the Woman Taken in Adultery; the Uplifters' report, including the flashback of the raid on a brothel; the Boy's decision to go straight (the Dear One, having domesticated him, gives credit to the statue of the Madonna). See Theodore Huff, *Intolerance: The Film by D. W. Griffith: Shot-by-Shot Analysis* (New York, 1966).

36 The processes of condensation converging in the figure of the Friendless One altogether elude a structuralist attempt to systematize the characters in terms of essential qualities and basic oppositions: this inadequacy is exemplified by Pierre Baudry's chart in "Les aventures de l'Idée (sur '*Intolérance*')," pt. 2, *Cahiers du cinéma* 241 (September–October 1972): 38.

37 George Soule, "After the Play," *New Republic*, 30 September 1916, 225. I am grateful to Peter Williamson for alerting me to this important print variant and showing me the respective slides from the copyright deposit of June 1916. The shot was certainly still part of the print shown in New York that fall, since Soule mentions it in his review. The *Chicago Tribune*, 24 December 1916, prints a still showing Olga Grey as Mary Magdalen, surrounded by slaves carrying her palanquin. In the credits to the reedited version (which omits the sequence), Grey is still listed as the Magdalen, and no credit appears for the Woman Taken in Adultery who is a much more haggard, guilt-ridden figure. On the Magdalen tradition in Victorian discourse on prostitution, see Robert E. Riegel, "Changing American Attitudes Toward Prostitution (1800–1920)," *Journal of the History of Ideas* 29 (July–September 1968): 443f.

38 See the *Philadelphia North American* (30 December 1916), a paper that called for a boycott of *Intolerance* on behalf of the Charity Trust, accusing the film of making the argument "for legalized and legally tolerated houses of prostitution." The reviewer seems particularly outraged about the way the "beautiful story" of the Woman Taken in Adultery is linked "with a police raid on a bevy of frowsy strumpets, the inference being that Christ's way of dealing with the modern social cesspool would be to let it go on unmolested."

39 Freud, *Standard Edition*, 11: 164–75, 178–90. A classic example of an adolescent fantasy rehearsing the split analyzed by Freud and the concomitant turn to a prostitute figure can be found in a short story Griffith wrote in his later years, "It Never Happened" (Griffith Papers, Museum of Modern Art, reel 19).

40 Nick Browne, "Griffith's Family Discourse: Griffith and Freud," *Quarterly Review of Film Studies* 6 (Winter 1981): 79.

41 Rogin elaborates on Sweet's role in *Judith* in a convincing argument as to why Griffith, in *Birth*, replaced her with Gish: "Blanche Sweet, in spite of her name, was neither white nor sweet enough to play Elsie Stoneman" ("'The Sword,'" 159–60, 163–64). On the reversibility of Griffith's rescue scenario even with Gish, see Rogin, *Birth*, 190.

42 Browne, "Griffith's Family Discourse," 79.

43 For Griffith's summary of the *The Treadmill*, with echoes of *Intolerance*, see Ezra Goodman, *The Fifty Year Decline and Fall of Hollywood* (New York, 1957), 11. The surviving drafts of the play (Griffith Papers, Museum of Modern Art) actually differ quite a bit from this summary, offering a rather wild phantasmagoria set, successively, in the Garden of Eden, Ancient Rome, the Middle Ages, and the modern Jazz Age.

44 Rogin, " 'The Sword,' " 173f.; Schickel, *An American Life*, chap. 1. Psychoanalytically inspired readings like Rogin's seize upon Griffith's obsession with his father's sword, first reported and embellished in great detail by Henry Stephen Gordon, "The Story of David Wark Griffith: His Early Years; His Struggles; His Ambitions and Their Achievement," pt. 1, *Photoplay Magazine* 10 (June 1916): 31, 35.

45 Gordon, "David Wark Griffith," 35; Robert M. Henderson, *D. W. Griffith: His Life and Work* (New York, 1972), 23–26 (also on Griffith's mother); Schickel, *An American Life*, 24, 26, 34. Gordon registers that Mattie's choice was unusual for a young woman of her time and background: "Miss Griffith had herself fought for an education, and she in Griffith fashion obtained what she wanted, and gave it again to her slender, sensitive brother" (31). Browne notes Mattie's significance, but then shifts his attention to the father's sword ("Griffith's Family Discourse," 72–73).

46 Walter Benjamin, "Central Park" (1938–39), trans. and intro. Mark Harrington and Lloyd Spencer, *New German Critique* 34 (Winter 1985): 28–58; "Paris – the Capital of the Nineteenth Century," trans. Quintin Hoare, in *Charles Baudelaire: A Lyric Poet in The Era of High Capitalism* (London, 1983), 171; Rosen, *Lost Sisterhood*, chap. 3, "Prostitution: Symbol of an Age."

47 Significantly, Biograph reissued the film in 1917 under the title *Her Condoned Sin*.

48 Horkheimer and Adorno, *Dialectic of Enlightenment*, 32–34, 59–60.

49 Benjamin, "Paris," 170f.; Christine Buci-Glucksmann, "Catastrophic Utopia: The Feminine as Allegory of the Modern," *Representations* 14 (Spring 1986): 224.

50 Dudley Andrew, "BROKEN BLOSSOMS: The Art and the Eros of a Perverse Text," *Quarterly Review of Film Studies* 6 (Winter 1981): 83. The literal and metaphorical association of the cinema with the prostitute is rather more prominent in early German discourse on the cinema; see my essay, "Early Silent Cinema: Whose Public Sphere?" *New German Critique* 29 (Spring/Summer 1983): 174–75.

51 Benjamin, "Paris," 165, 171; and *Das Passagen-Werk*, ed. Rolf Tiedemann (Frankfurt, 1982), sec. G.

The She-Man: Postmodern Bi-Sexed

Performance in Film and Video

Chris Straayer

★ ★ ★ ★ ★ ★ The historic absence of the penis from cinema's view has allowed the male body an independence from anatomical veri-fication according to sex and has situated the male costume simply to reflect a heroic (phallic) narrative purpose.[1] It is his charging about that has identified a male film character as male, yet it is his penis that has invested man with the cultural right to charge about—the signifier in absentia. Richard Dyer and Peter Lehman have writ-ten about the difficulty of maintaining the penis-phallus alliance in the event that the penis is seen on-screen.[2] In actuality, the penis (man's hidden "nature") cannot compare to the phallus (man's cul-tural power). Male sexuality, as a representational system, depends on displacing the penis with the phallus.

In mainstream cinema, the female costume delivers sexual anatomy whereas the male costume abandons it. Sex is "present" in both the masquerade of femininity and the female body, doubly absent for the male. Male sex is (mis)represented by the phallus.

Instead of a body with a penis, the male character's entire body, through its phallic position and action, becomes a giant (substitute) penis—a confusion of standing erect with erection. Although sliding signification is integral to the representation of both female and male sexuality, the first effectively relies more on iconographic and indexical relations and the second on symbolic relations. This "visible difference" in the representation systems of female sex and male sex allows the *potential* for an intense double signification of sexuality in the male cross-dresser—composed of both macho male sexuality via phallic action and the unseen penis, and female sexuality signaled by the masquerade's visible display.

In contrast to the traditional conditions and compromises of transvestism in classical film and television, a phenomenon in contemporary popular culture, which I term the "She-man," exploits cross-dressing's potential for intense double sexual signification.[3] I refer to the appropriation of female coding by a male performer as a straight-forward empowering device, rather than as an emasculating comic ploy. The transgressive figure of the She-man is glaringly bi-sexed rather than obscurely androgynous or merely bisexual. Rather than undergoing a downward gender mobility, he has enlarged himself with feminine gender and female sexuality.

In her book *Mother Camp*, Esther Newton relates the drag queen's reliance on visible contradictions, as opposed to the transvestite's attempt to pass as the other sex.[4] Laying bare his feminine masquerade by baring a hairy chest, the drag queen makes obvious the superficiality and arbitrariness of gender costuming. In John Waters's film *Pink Flamingos*, a "transbreastite" squeezes this contradiction onto the body, disrupting sexual as well as gender signification. The sight of "his" hormonally produced breasts is followed by "his" exposed penis, an incongruity that overflows its own binary opposition. Likewise, the bisexual, transsexual Dr. Frank N. Furter (Tim Curry) of *The Rocky Horror Picture Show* makes lipstick seem macho as he undulates a black garter belt in aggressive, seductive exhibitionism. A nude male dancer in *Pink Flamingos* executes anal acrobatics with phallic nerve and Medusan humor, and Divine puts a steak between her legs to simultaneously parody the rhetoric of women as meat and embody the taboo of menstruation, thus pushing the transgression

Tim Curry in *The Rocky Horror Picture Show*.

of sex boundaries beyond anatomy to physiology.[5] *La ley de deseo* (*Law of Desire*) gives us the "slutty" male-to-female transsexual Tina (played by a woman—Carmen Maura), under a jet of water and cling-ing dress, who harks back to a classical harlot, then later outslugs a policeman like a "real" man. *Shadey*'s Oliver (Anthony Sher), a "woman trapped in a man's body," is stabbed in the testicles with a kitchen knife and responds with a look of *jouissance*. In the era of music television, both Boy George and Michael Jackson make louder *scenes* as Boy-Girls.

As these examples suggest, rather than diminishing his phallic power, or amplifying it via a contrast with weakness, female coding lends additional strength to the She-man. The male body's "staying power" remains unchallenged by feminine dress, makeup, and ges-tures which, in popular media, have become one and the same with

female sexuality. More indexical than symbolic, the feminine costume utilizes conventions of spatial and temporal contiguity to deliver its referent. The determined geometry of Tim Curry's bra and
garters bestows a female anatomy on him, even as the bulge in the
crotch of his body corset indexes his male sex.[6] The power of the
She-man, then, is emphatically sexual.

What is the origin of this "feminine" power? Is not the penis the
dominant signifier which defines woman by her lack thereof? Is not
the penis the dominant sexual signifier, reigning by virtue of a proclaimed anatomical visibility (which nevertheless remains covered)?
Perhaps this powerful invisible visibility is born from an exaggerated persona—the Freudian phallic symbol. The empowered feminine, however, must have a different source.

Writing about the early twentieth-century mannish lesbian (for
example, Radclyffe Hall and her character Stephen in the 1928 novel
The Well of Loneliness) in the context of other second-generation Victorian women who were presumed to be empty of sexuality, Esther
Newton has argued that male clothing served as a means for women
to proclaim their de facto sexuality.

> By "mannish lesbian" . . . I mean a figure who is defined as les-
> bian *because* her behavior or dress (and usually both) manifest
> elements designated as exclusively masculine. From about 1900
> on, this cross-gender figure became the public symbol of the new
> social/sexual category "lesbian." . . . Hall and many other femi-
> nists like her embraced, sometimes with ambivalence, the image
> of the mannish lesbian and the discourse of the sexologists about
> inversion primarily because they desperately wanted to break out
> of the asexual model of romantic friendship. . . .
>
> The bourgeois woman's sexuality proper was confined to its
> reproductive function; the uterus was its organ. But as for lust,
> "the major current in Victorian sexual ideology declared that
> women were passionless and asexual, the passive objects of male
> sexual desire." . . . Sex was seen as phallic, by which I mean
> that, conceptually, sex could only occur in the presence of an
> imperial and imperious penis. . . .

How could the New Woman lay claim to her full sexuality? For bourgeois women, there was no developed female sexual discourse; there were only male discourses—pornographic, literary, and medical—*about* female sexuality. To become avowedly sexual, the New Woman had to enter the male world, either as a heterosexual on male terms (a flapper) or as—or with—a lesbian in male body drag (a butch).[7]

The signification of sexuality was under male control: women declared their own active libidos by means of male clothing codes.

How is it that the contemporary She-man is then sexually empowered by female coding? How did female imagery come to signify sexuality and power? Along with the contributions of sexology, sexual liberation, and the feminist and gay activist movements, feminist artists (rather than She-men performers) must be credited for this empowerment of the "feminine." Whether "on our backs" or "off our backs," female sexual responses and desires are now seen as powerful by men. No longer only feared, female sexuality is envied.

Ironically, cinema's sexualization of woman's image is also partly responsible for making possible a representation of femaleness as sexual power. Following a long history of visual representations that established woman's body as the conventional marker of sexual difference, cinema made this body the carrier of sexuality in both visuals and narrative. Woman's image became the visible site of sexuality that was obtained by the male hero—that is, male sexuality was projected onto, represented by, and obtainable through her body. Although quite different from the Victorian woman who announced her sexuality via the male image, contemporary woman's "sexual" image in classical cinema also has the potential to be seen as an involuted image of sexual power.

But the most forceful paradigms for active female sexuality— which deconstruct involution and assert realignment—are found in contemporary women's performance art where artists expose their bodies for purposes of direct address. Such bodily discourse constructs both a new "speaking subject" position and an aesthetics of female sexual presence. Utilizing classic examples from 1970s body art, two concepts relating to the She-man's origin can be narrativized. In practice, however, the two seem inseparable. The first is the story of the phallic femme which evolves from the feminine masquerade; the second story is that of the Medusan femme which evolves from the female body. These are the two powers that are appropriated by the She-man and merge in his/her signifying formation.

Early in the present feminist era, Lynda Benglis attacked the art world's discrimination against women with a self-portrait published in *Artforum* (December 1974) in which she manually "props" a dildo onto her nude body. In this act of appropriation she effectively identified the phallus as the basic qualification for artistic success and she explicitly collapsed the phallus with the penis—via body/object/ photo collage art.

This inspires a first narrative: in the late 1960s and early 1970s, second-wave feminists (in dress-for-success suits) abandoned "femininity," disrupting feminine signification to steal the phallus, which, soon afterwards, they laterally passed on to self-conscious feminist femmes (in leather miniskirts). Through a process quite the reverse of fetishism, these feminists created the phallic-femme whose phallus was locked into a new feminine mode of signification. Today, sex role stereotypes are up for grabs. The attitude of Tina Turner's *What's Love Got to Do with It?* has reversed the cries of sexual oppression once embodied in Janis Joplin's screeching romantic masochism. And, in her *One Man Show*, Grace Jones, "feeling like a woman, looking like a man," gives a new bodily relevance to Marlene Dietrich's transvestite persona. Women spike their hair to match their heels, apply 1950s pink lipstick to "talk back" to the silence imposed on their mothers, hang crosses from their ears instead of from their necks. Indeed skirts are worn (and torn) self-reflexively; the accoutrements of femininity are used to parody patriarchal culture. In an attempt to reconquer phallic signification, the male performer now assumes postfeminist drag. When he is successful, he becomes the She-man, his phallus marked in the feminine.

In "Film and the Masquerade," Mary Ann Doane describes the feminine masquerade as a distancing device.

> The masquerade, in flaunting femininity, holds it at a distance. Womanliness is a mask which can be worn or removed. The

masquerade's resistance to patriarchal positioning would there-fore lie in its denial of the production of femininity as closeness, as presence-to-itself, as, precisely, imagistic. The transvestite adopts the sexuality of the other—the woman becomes a man in order to attain the necessary distance from the image. Masquer-ade, on the other hand, involves a realignment of femininity, the recovery, or more accurately, simulation, of the missing gap or distance. To masquerade is to manufacture a lack in the form of a certain distance between oneself and one's image. . . .

The very fact that we can speak of a woman "using" her sex or "using" her body for particular gains is highly significant—it is not that a man cannot use his body in this way but that he doesn't have to. The masquerade doubles representation; it is constituted by a hyperbolisation of the accoutrements of femi-ninity.[8]

An excess of femininity, then, enables woman to stand back from her image and read it better. The pertinent question to this discussion is where does woman's "sexuality" reside in this improbable sepa-ration—in the cultural construction of femininity which she now consciously manipulates as a "persona," or in some nature within her but beyond her reading? This question is parallel to the situation of women in relation to language. Can women better speak by parody-ing patriarchal language (Benglis's phallic femme), or by narrating their own sexual bodies (the Medusan femme)?

A second process, which can be postulated to explain the feminine power that the She-man usurps, spans this distance between culture and nature. Vagina envy, as evidenced in some She-men performers, suggests that female sexuality challenges the position of the phallus as the dominant signifier. In her early feminist performance "Interior Scroll" (1975), Carolee Schneeman defended the suitability of per-sonal experience as material for art by reading a "diary" scroll with-drawn from her vagina. Thus she asserted the female body to be a producer of meaning.[9]

Female sexuality is now neither simply the sign of lack, as Laura Mulvey has identified it, inciting castration anxiety and thus necessitating fetishization and narrative punishment, nor a generator of signs within Lévi-Strauss's parameters.[10] Female sexuality is erupting into contemporary culture like a volcano in the suburbs. Hélène Cixous's laughing Medusa, who haughtily displays her sex to men's horrified reactions, provides a paradigm for an empowering bodily address.[11] Furthermore, this "imagined" figure, the Medusan femme, exerts a specifically feminine body-signifying process—a multiplying, questioning, digressing, fragmenting language that corresponds to the indefinable plurality of female sexuality spread over a woman's body, as described by Luce Irigaray.

> So woman does not have a sex organ? She has at least two of them, but they are not identifiable as ones. Indeed she has many more. Her sexuality, always at least double, goes even further: it is *plural*. Is this the way culture is seeking to characterize itself now? . . .
>
> [W]oman has sex organs more or less everywhere. She finds pleasure almost anywhere. Even if we refrain from invoking the hystericization of her entire body, the geography of her pleasure is far more diversified, more multiple in its differences, more complex, more subtle, than is commonly imagined—in an imaginary rather too narrowly focused on sameness. . . .
>
> Thus what [women] desire is precisely nothing, and at the same time everything. Always something more and something else besides that *one*—sexual organ, for example—that you give them, attribute to them. Their desire is often interpreted, and feared, as a sort of insatiable hunger, a voracity that will swallow you whole. Whereas it really involves a different economy more than anything else, one that upsets the linearity of a project, undermines the goal-object of a desire, diffuses the polarization toward a single pleasure, disconcerts fidelity to a single discourse.[12]

Rebelling against the symbolic order, contemporary sexual culture demands a "plural" sight/site that can be seen *and* felt. The phallus, a mere abstraction that hides the organ which might go limp, is a holdover from the Victorian age. Today's Medusan femme expresses her sexuality with her entire body, spreading her legs and stomping her feet to join the postmodern laughter.

In "Form and Female Authorship in Music Video," Lisa Lewis has written about the opportunity afforded to female musicians by the music video form. Not only does their role as singers suggest authorship and assign narrative importance to them, but they are enabled by performance strategies to express gender-specific attitudes or viewpoints. She states:

> Female musicians are actively participating in making the music video form work in their interest, to assert their authority as producers of culture and to air their views on female genderhood. The generic emphasis in music video on using the song as a soundtrack, together with the centrality of the musician's image in the video, formally support the construction of female authorship. . . .
>
> Many female musicians have proved to be quite adept at manipulating elements of visual performance in their video act, thereby utilizing music video as an additional authorship tool. In "What's Love Got To Do With It?," the gestures, eye contact with the camera and with other characters, and the walking style of Tina Turner add up to a powerful and aggressive on-screen presence.[13]

This new visual music format requires specific performance talents from male musicians as well. As Richard Goldstein states in "Tube Rock: How Music Video Is Changing Music," these musicians have to learn to communicate with their bodies.

> Tube rock forces musicians to act. Not that they haven't been acting since Jerry Lee Lewis learned to stomp on a piano and Chuck Berry essayed his first duckwalk; but on MTV, musicians have to emote the way matinee idols once did if they're to establish the kind of contact tube rockers covet—the heightened typology of a classic movie star. What once made a rock performer powerful—the ability to move an arena with broad gesture and

precision timing—has been supplanted by a new strategy: the performer must project in close-up.[14]

Because of their different relations to bodily expression, females and males have adjusted differently to the music video form. While MTV's emphasis on body and presence seems to have provided women performers an avenue for gaining authorship, males have attempted to "master" the facial expression of sensuality as well as the language of exhibitionism, efforts which have themselves recast gender and asked new questions about sexuality. As Simon Frith writes in *Music for Pleasure*:

> The most important effect of gender-bending was to focus the problem of sexuality onto males. In pop, the question became, unusually, what do men want? And as masculinity became a packaging problem, then so did masculine desire. . . . On video, music can be mediated through the body directly.[15]

These three authors are identifying and analyzing the same phenomenon. The music video form has instigated repositionings by/of both female and male performers; it has made direct address and personal display necessary for a star persona. These repositionings often result in ambiguous reversals, such as that evident in two Bananarama videos, *I Can't Help It* and *Love in the First Degree*. In each video, the three female vocalists sing in the first-person, to the camera as well as to a male "you" within the fictional performance space. In each, the male body is exploited as visual object at the same time that the song lyrics admit female dependency. "I can't help it," Bananarama sings as a shirtless male dances. "I'm captivated by your honey. Move your body. I need you. I won't give up." Similarly, as a group of males dance (at times down on their hands and knees) in prison-striped briefs and crop-tops, the "fully dressed" female Bananarama trio sings, "Only you can set me free." As one of these singers shakes a dancer's head and then pushes him away, they continue, "cause I'm guilty of love in the first degree." The bare legs of the men contrast strikingly with the women's covered legs.

This new reversal of subjectivity and exhibitionism between female and male performers incorporates ambiguity that satisfies multiple audience identifications and desires. When the She-man collects all this ambiguity on "his" body, subjectivity and exhibitionism reverberate in a "contradictory" assemblage of gender and sexual codes. In this case, the male performer adopts sexualized female body language to achieve a powerful exhibitionistic subjectivity.

What happens when the male performer (metaphoric possessor of the dominant, if out-of-style, signifier) exercises his prerogative to appropriate the phallic femme's masquerade or the Medusan body? He finds himself a split personality, a schizophrenic sign, a media image combining disbelief and an aesthetic of "his-teric," ricocheting signifiers. This is the She-man, whose sexual power depends not on the ostensibly stable male body but on embraced incongruity. And with this incongruity, he is the site of a "nervous" breakdown, the utter collapse of the most basic binary opposition (male and female) into postmodern irrelevance.

The She-man's performance engulfs and rewrites the conventional heterosexual narrative, suturing the viewer into unending alterations of absence and presence, desire and pleasure. First we see a woman. Where's the man? Then we see a man. Where's the woman? Simultaneously we are given the pleasure of conventional reading and the pleasure of subverting convention. The woman *is* the man. The She-man is the shot-reverse shot. Performance is the nouveau narrative.

A discussion of the She-man in music videos and video art calls for a return to modernist concerns. For two reasons, the video medium is especially suitable for the She-man's scheme. Historically, video art has shown an affinity with performance art, perhaps because of what Rosalind Krauss called the medium's property of narcissism.[16] In addition, as Douglas Davis has pointed out, the experience of viewing the small video monitor contains its own particular physicality that seems appropriate for performance.[17] Instead of identifying with some larger-than-life idealized Lacanian "mirror" image, video viewers experience the medium's McLuhanesque tactility or, in Davis's terms, its subtle existentialism. When they do use it as a mirror, as Krauss suggests, it is not to mistake themselves for ideal images, but to check their makeup. Video's mobile viewers, whether in their living rooms or in dance bars, are likely to feel that they are cruising, not dreaming. Video music actually benefits from the viewing logistics of the medium, engaging viewers in a physical/rhythmic identification. Rather than an empty vessel for empathic identification, the performer is a surrogate dance partner, and often this is reinforced by the genre's mobile aesthetics—the artist's continual movement interacts with and against the editing and camera movement.[18]

In contrast to commercial music video, video art is produced with relatively small budgets by independent artists. Expressing the individual artists' concerns, video artworks may break radically in form and content from mainstream conventions. Often they present ideas and images not included in mass media. In the two examples which follow, traditional sexual iconography is upset by explicitly gay dynamics. Conventional boundaries between the sexes become blurred.

John Greyson's *The Kipling Trilogy: Perils of Pedagogy* (1984, Canada) is a humorous commentary on the relation between desire, fantasy, and status differentials between men. The female's position as object of the erotic gaze is assumed by a young male character who flaunts himself exhibitionistically before his male mentor. Thus the conventional representation of desire—directed at women by men— is adopted for a man-boy interaction. The tape cuts between images of the boy dressing up in a number of costumes and the older man watching; however, in many shots, the boy directs a flirtatious look at the camera/video viewer. By lip-synching the song "To Sir With Love," the boy "appropriates" its woman vocalist's voice. The appropriation is assisted technologically as the song is slowed down to lower the pitch of "her" voice. Although the boy is actually standing upright (in the profilmic arena), unusual camera positioning has determined that his monitored image be horizontal; that is, he is technologically "laid." In three ways, then, video technology has been used to confuse "male" and "female": the boy is situated as object of the camera gaze, he is turned on his side to imply a "reclining" position, and a recorded voice is "converted" from female to male by altering its pitch. In addition to being acted upon, however, the boy actively corroborates in his feminization. Conscious of and adept with the specific powers of his female position, he both accommodates and controls the viewer's desire. With his own self-assured

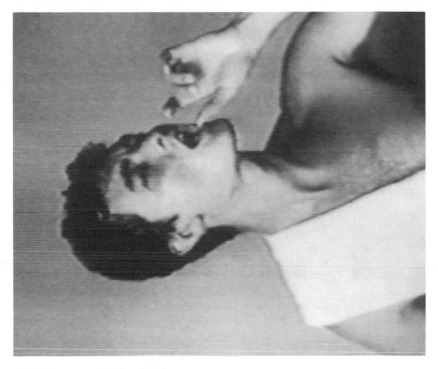

John Greyson, *Perils of Pedagogy*.

seductive look, he fixes the viewer's gaze. As he "sings," he directs the viewer's sexual longings by pointing his finger at his open mouth. Later, lying nude on a floor, he smiles at the camera/viewer and then "gratuitously" turns onto his stomach.

In *Chinese Characters* (1986, Canada), video artist Richard Fung also uses technology to intervene in conventional gender positioning. First he video-keys himself into a pornographic film where he then poses as the lure for a desiring "stud." His presence as both performer and character constructs two different identificatory positions for viewers. In voice-over, he tells us, as the artist, how he learned to make appropriate sounds during sex by listening to women in pornographic films. As a character, he purposefully fondles his nipples. The tape alternates between images of this activity and shots of the conventionally well-endowed porn stud. Camera angles and framing, inherited from the source film, foreground the upper part of Fung's body and the lower part of the stud's body. Hardcore pornography is the only genre that consistently shows the penis, and its convention of featuring large penises can be seen as an attempt to uphold the phallus in the realm of the physical. Twisting this convention, Fung uses performance and technology in this tape to create a She-man whose breasts offer a visual equivalent—as much an alternate as a complement—to the porn star's "cock." Objects of each other's (and our) gazes, both male characters are seductive, desiring subjects.

Because they circulate more in the mainstream (in video clubs and/or on television) and assume a mass (although young) audience, music videos that subvert gender conventions often do so within representations of heterosexuality. Although their gender alterations (especially when accompanied by a camp aesthetics) may connote a gay dynamics or desire, their heterosexual illusion, maintained by heterosexual characters and plots, finally attributes the She-man construction to a wider, popular desire. The She-man can be seen as representing a desire for sexual fluidity (to be both sexes, as well as both genders) rather than simply representing gay desire through an unsuitable but dominant (heterosexual) iconography.

In his music video *When You're a Boy*, David Bowie appears as lead singer as well as (in drag) three backup female singers. As a man he sings, "Nothing stands in your way when you're a boy. . . . Other boys check you out. . . . You get a girl. . . . Boys keep swinging. Boys always work it out." As the female chorus, he echoes himself with, "Boys!" The video ends, not on the handsome Bowie in suit and tie, but with each of the three female singers walking forward on a stage. The first two dramatically remove their wigs and smear their lipstick with the backs of their hands as if attempting to wipe it off. They establish a single Bowie identity beneath the girl group facade; from their duplicated "unmasking" actions we induce that the third female is also Bowie. However, the third backup singer, an older female character who walks forward slowly with a cane, does not "unmask." Instead, she blows a kiss to the camera/audience, thus insuring an open ending to this already ironic declaration about gender and sex.

In *Walk Like a Man*, Divine (who is best known as the transvestite star of several John Waters's films) achieves a most convincing

Divine in *Walk Like a Man*.

gender/sexual transformation—via costume, makeup, gestures, and a look suggestive of Mae West.[19] As Divine stands on a wagon/car singing, swinging, and whipping her imaginary horses, the camera places viewers in the position of the missing horses. Combined with music video's reinforcement of the viewers' physicality, this situates them well for her whipping. The diegetic audience/chorus encourages viewers to "join in the song," yet when we do, we enter into camp S&M theater.

Divine's very corporality—her assertively displayed female (soft and excessive)[20] flesh—along with the accenting of her stomach by the "outline" design of her costume, tend to posit the woman in his/her body. The fact that the costume also covers his male genital anatomy further facilitates the conversion of Divine's image from that of the transvestite to that of the transsexual. Finally, the rapid editing between different subject-camera distances mimics a *fort-da* game, which, combined with her whipping action, suggests Divine as a phallic mother in relation to the audience.[21]

The examples of appropriation in these video works demonstrate a tentative collapse of the phallic femme and the Medusan femme on the She-man's body. Female sexuality originally carried either by the masquerade or by the body abandons these boundaries to slip back and forth between the male performer's body and his masquerade, constantly threatening to engulf and dissolve him. Divine's costume is a masquerade that generates a womb on/in his/her body.

Interestingly, a trace of masculinity is deliberately maintained in these videos, as if this threatened engulfment necessitates the shy penis to peek out. In *Perils of Pedagogy*, the penis of the flirting, feminized boy is once shown and once indicated by a bulge in his undershorts. The eroticization of nipples supplements rather than displaces the "masculinized" anatomy of the "well-endowed" porn star in *Chinese Characters*. Though triply female, Bowie's drag personas ostensibly serve as back-up support for the (currently) real Bowie—the *GQ* male whose pretty looks and fashion stretch gender rather than sex. And, as Divine swings her hips, a cut-in shot briefly focuses on a male masturbatory gesture she enacts with the horses' reins. This copresence of feminine and masculine elements creates the internal distance which establishes the She-man's image as bi-sexed rather than transsexual.

In Dead or Alive's *Save You All My Kisses*, the lead (male) singer appears extremely androgynous but emanates a distinctly feminine sexual energy. This sexuality is both emphasized and checked by an ornate silver codpiece prominently shown during a vertical track up his/her body. Also signaling maleness is the singer's Adam's apple. Coexisting female signals include his/her "dominatrix" whip and long, obviously styled hair. Dressed in black leather jacket and tights, he/she walks, dances, and sings in front of a wire fence while a gang of boys climbs the other side of the fence attempting to get at him/her. The boys' enthusiastic approach displays much ambivalence—they seem both attracted to and angered by him/her. At times their postures and glances seem to signify lust, but at other times they seem to be mocking him/her. While one swings his baseball bat in a way that threatens a fag-bashing, another rips open his T-shirt as if stripping for him/her. A male alter-ego character is also present, also dressed in black leather and resembling his "female" counterpart except that he wears more masculine pants, presents a more masculine posture, and carries a baseball bat. Again it is unclear whether he is attracted to "her" or threatening to attack "her." The contradictory reactions of this diegetic audience confuse straight and gay subjectivities and emphasize the She-man as simultaneously female and male.

It must be emphasized that, although gay audiences may have more to gain from the She-man's radical display of gender *and* sex constructions, the She-man is not a specifically gay figure, nor an effeminate male, nor a hermaphrodite. The She-man, as enacted by both gay and straight performers, is a fully functional figuration signifying both woman and man.

In *The Desire to Desire*, an analysis of 1940s women's films, Mary Ann Doane identifies proper makeup and dress as indicators of a woman's stable narcissism.[22] If that makeup is smeared or that dress torn, the woman is marked with the pathetic condition of impaired narcissism. This is a narcissism marked by too much self-love or brazen love for a man.

Narcissism becomes quite different, however, when two sexes are present in the same body. This condition can signal both heterosexual coupling and bisexuality. When performer Mike Monroe of Hanoi Rocks sweats through his makeup, for instance, a return of the male and a *successful* narcissism is signaled. Doane has argued for seeing a predilection in women for tactility and overidentification, in contrast with the male tendency for voyeurism and fetishism, both of which require distance.[23] Mike Monroe's narcissistically bi-sexed figure makes overidentification a moot point. As sweat seeps through cosmetics, distance abandons difference.

Is there a complementary bi-sexed figure, a reverse of the She-man, built from woman's body and man's masquerade? I think not. Because female sexuality is conventionally imaged and indexed by the female masquerade, and because the male "costume" conventionally serves to mask rather than indicate male (genital) sexuality, there is no mechanism by which a "He-woman" could be produced predominantly via appropriation of masquerade. Even more than the She-man performer's use of gesture to make transvestism corporeal, the "incorporation" of action is essential for a woman performer's successful sex crossing. In order to construct an empowering position and achieve a transgression similar to those of the She-man, women would need to entirely disrupt the "*men act* and *women appear*" sex roles described by John Berger.[24] In short, without also appropriating "male" action (a more difficult accomplishment), women's transvestism fails to achieve the double sexuality of the She-man. Nevertheless, several examples of transgressive transvestism by women suggest possibilities.

Annie Lennox of Eurythmics deliberately recalls/retains the female masquerade when cross-dressing via her bright red lipstick—which, even on young girls, signals *adult* female sexuality. This lipstick sexualizes her image while her *act* of wearing a suit (rather than the mere presence of a suit) pushes it toward a bi-sexed image. Her assertive masculine behavior—speech, gestures, and posture—"invests" the suit with transgressive power. Similarly, when Lily Tomlin impersonates her character Tommy Velour, a working-class, Italian nightclub singer, her sexual come-ons to "girls" in the audience validate and sexualize the hair on "his" chest.

The portrait of Madonna that appeared on the cover of the 1990 issue of *Interview* magazine successfully employs reversal, contradiction, and action to disrupt gender and sex. Wearing dark lipstick, exaggerated eyelashes, fish-net stockings, hot pants, and a polka-dotted blouse with bell-shaped collar and cuffs, Madonna thrusts forward her pelvis, grabs her crotch, and squeezes her thigh muscle in a gesture that young men often use playfully to suggest a gigantic-sized penis. Madonna's "girlish" clowning-around both mocks machismo and usurps the penis. Psycho-sexologists have long referred to penis envy in women and described the clitoris as an underdeveloped penis. Women have been positioned alongside boys, their "lack" diminishing them and disqualifying them for adulthood. Traditionally, when cross-dressing, they achieved boyishness rather than manliness. By plagiarizing a male fantasy, Madonna ironically reassigns and complicates penis envy.

Woman's "counterpart" to the She-man would likely require appropriation of male sexual prerogatives in two areas. First, she needs to trespass the boundaries of sexual segregation relating to pornography and sexual information, erotica, expression of libido, and sexual joking. (Here we might think of Mae West.) Second, she must aggressively expose the untamed sexual imagery of her body. For instance, a woman's unruly mature pubic hair contrasts sharply with the image of female genitals in conventional pornography, where shaving or partially shaving the pubic hair converts a physical characteristic into masquerade and enforces an image of feminine youth.

Instead of a He-woman, this transgressive figure might better be imagined as a "She-butch." In contrast to the She-man's image-actions (actions on images), the She-butch would perform action-images (images containing action). One contemporary figure that might qualify for the status of action-image (a qualification supported by her disturbing, disruptive impression on mainstream culture) is the female bodybuilder. As Laurie Schulze states,

> The female bodybuilder threatens not only current socially constructed definitions of femininity and masculinity, but the system of sexual difference itself. . . . A female body displaying "extreme" muscle mass, separation and definition, yet oiled up, clad in a bikini, marked with conventionally "feminine"-styled hair and carefully applied cosmetics juxtaposes heterogeneous elements in a way that frustrates ideological unity and confounds common sense. . . . Muscle mass, its articulation, and the strength and power the body displays, is clearly an achievement, the product of years of intense, concentrated, deliberate work in the gym, a sign of activity, not passivity.[25]

As might be expected, the arena of avant-garde performance also holds possibilities for the emerging She-butch. Following the taboo-breaking work of performance artists such as Lynda Benglis and Carolee Schneeman, Karen Finley appropriates male prerogatives in her "id-speak" performances. Finley's dirty talk/dirty acts such as "I

Like to Smell the Gas Passed from your Ass," "I'm an Ass Man," and "Don't Hang the Angel" use the language of pornography for radical "feminine" misbehavior.[26]

Another ripe-for-action figure, which I have termed the "nouveau lesbian butch," is the contemporary lesbian who updates the Victorian era's mannish lesbian/female transvestite with a transgressive handling of dildos. Self-consciously appropriating the dominant image of sexual agency, the nouveau lesbian butch attains a shocking difference that is nonetheless compatible with the concept of femininity as construction. Combining visual dominance with bodily audacity, her mocking, dildoed body identifies the penis's cosmetic potential. Simultaneously constructing and deconstructing the male "body," she claims the speaking position in bodily discourse to confess the male facade—a bulge that might just as well be silicone as flesh. Whether such avant-garde/underground transgressions will ever be reflected in mainstream culture will no doubt depend on economic determinants as well as the industry's ability to negotiate as well as package the She-butch's sexual subjectivity in a way that doesn't directly challenge society's prevailing concept of passive/ image/woman.

Evident in popular music culture as well as underground film and experimental video, the She-man is currently the most powerful signifying formation transgressing the male-female sex dichotomy. This figure suggests the collapse of the phallus as the dominant signifier and recognizes a new empowered female sexuality which cannot be reduced to boyishness. Although the She-man is obviously a result of male prerogative, his/her dependency on female sexual imagery for a powerful impact is also evidence of the phallic femme's effectivity and the Medusan femme's signifying power. More importantly, the She-man disrupts the very concept of male-female discontinuity. Through his/her appropriations of femininity and female physicality, the She-man not only achieves a postmodern dismantling of gender and sex differences, but also adopts a *greater* sexuality.

Notes

The core of this article was originally presented at a television and postmodernism seminar at the University of Wisconsin-Milwaukee Center for Twentieth-Century Studies in 1988. Earlier versions occur in my dissertation, *Sexual Subjects: Signification, Viewership, and Pleasure in Film and Video* (Northwestern University, 1989), and in *Screen* 31.3 (1990).

1 Working definitions for sex, gender, and sexuality are in order. Most feminist theorists use the term "sex" to refer to male and female biology and the term "gender" to refer to masculine and feminine attributes which are culturally and historically constructed. The term "sexuality" refers to sexual desire and behavior which also is understood to be socially constituted. See Gayle Rubin, "The Traffic in Women," in *Toward an Anthropology of Women*, ed. Rayna R. Reiter (New York, 1975); and "Thinking Sex: Notes for a Radical Theory of the Politics of Sexuality," in *Pleasure and Danger: Exploring Female Sexuality*, ed. Carole S. Vance (Boston, 1984). Following Michel Foucault, *History of Sexuality, Volume I: An Introduction* (New York, 1980), I assume the sexes to be mediated rather than natural. Although science relies on biology to define sex, biology itself does not provide any single all-inclusive and fixed demarcation between male and female persons. The exceptions and ambiguities in anatomical assignment become even more pervasive and disruptive when chromosome patterns, hormones, secondary sex characteristics, and behaviors are considered. The persistent concept of sex— that is, of two opposite and distinct sexes—is pressed upon ever-changing information about biology. Sex is thus a product of discourse rather than a natural condition. In this article, I use the word sex to refer to conventionally defined and discursively employed genital anatomy. Obviously, the construction of male and female sexes relies on gender operations as much as biology. Therefore, I am purposely playing with the slippery status of all the above terminology to expose its artificiality, unreliability, and manipulability. (Indeed, as much as sorting out these terms, my current project calls for moving with them.)

2 Richard Dyer, "Male Sexuality in the Media," in *The Sexuality of Men*, ed. Andy Metcalf and Martin Humphries (London, 1985), 28–43; and Peter Lehman, "*In the Realm of the Senses*: Desire, Power, and the Representation of the Male Body," *Genders* 2 (Summer 1988): 91–110.

3 See "Redressing the Natural: The Temporary Transvestite Film" (chap. 6 of my dissertation cited above). In this chapter, I identify and analyze a subgenre of temporary transvestite films in which male and female characters cross-dress for sexual disguise. (Examples of such films include *Some Like It Hot, Victor/Victoria, Tootsie,* and *Sylvia Scarlett.*) I note that male transvestism is portrayed in mainstream film as undesired, impractical, and laughable. At the same time that these films question gender construction, attempts to cross boundaries of sex "prove" futile.

4 Esther Newton, *Mother Camp: Female Impersonators in America* (Chicago, 1972),

97–111. For additional discussion of drag in relation to cross-dressing and transvestism, see chap. 6 of my dissertation.

5 My use of the term "Medusan" throughout this paper is inspired by Hélène Cixous's radical description of the mythological Medusa who aggressively exposes her genitals and laughs at the terror this causes to men. See "The Laugh of the Medusa," in *New French Feminisms*, ed. Elaine Marks and Isabelle de Courtivron (New York, 1981).

6 This indexical male bulge is becoming a more common sight in contemporary fashion where the male image is increasingly sexualized. However, it still is associated predominantly with motivated costume—as in exercise culture—and is *not* associated with a subsequent exposure of the penis itself. We shall find in the discussion that follows that, just as the drag queen's gender deconstruction depends on a contradictory display of sexual codes, female iconography in the bi-sexed She-man often instigates a display of the male sex as well.

7 Esther Newton, "The Mythic Mannish Lesbian: Radclyffe Hall and the New Woman," *Signs* 9 (Summer 1984): 560–61, 573.

8 Mary Ann Doane, "Film and the Masquerade: Theorising the Female Spectator," *Screen* 23.3–4 (September–October 1982): 81–82.

9 A photograph of this performance can be found in *The Amazing Decade: Women and Performance Art in America 1970–1980*, ed. Moira Roth (Los Angeles, 1983), 15.

10 See Laura Mulvey, "Visual Pleasure and Narrative Cinema," *Screen* 16.3 (1975): 6–18; and Claude Lévi-Strauss, *Structural Anthropology*, trans. Claire Jacobson and Brooke G. Schoepf (Garden City, 1967).

11 Woman writing her sexual body is a thematic concern throughout Hélène Cixous's work. See Marks and Courtivron, eds., *New French Feminisms*; and "Castration or Decapitation," trans. Annette Kuhn, *Signs* 7 (Autumn 1981): 41–55.

12 Luce Irigaray, *This Sex Which Is Not One*, trans. Catherine Porter and Carolyn Burke (Ithaca, 1985), 23–33.

13 Lisa Lewis, "Form and Female Authorship in Music Video," in *Media in Society: Readings in Mass Communication*, ed. Caren Deming and Samuel Becker (Glenview, Il., 1988), 140, 143.

14 Richard Goldstein, "Tube Rock: How Music Video Is Changing Music," in Deming and Becker, eds., *Media in Society*, 50–51.

15 Simon Frith, *Music for Pleasure* (Cambridge, 1988), 166–67.

16 Rosalind Krauss, "Video: The Aesthetics of Narcissism," in *New Artists Video*, ed. Gregory Battcock (New York, 1978), 43–64.

17 Douglas Davis, "Filmgoing/Videogoing: Making Distinctions," in *Artculture: Essays on the Post-Modern*, ed. Douglas Davis (New York, 1977), 79–84.

18 A good example of this is the Communards "Never Can Say Good-bye" in which constant sweeping camera movements "bring" viewers to the singers/stars, and swirling camera movements incorporate both stars and viewers into a large group of dancers. The stars are both center and part of the dynamic social group. This accomplishes a "live and let live" solidarity in which it no longer matters if one

is gay or straight as long as he/she can dance. (The Communards are openly gay; the diegetic audience is composed primarily of heterosexual couplings, though the rapid pace achieved by cinematography and editing fragments this coupling.)

19 Parker Tyler raises the interesting question of who is imitating whom between Mae West and the drag queen. "Miss West's reaction to comments that connected her with female impersonators . . . was reported as the boast that, of course, she 'knew that female impersonators imitated her.' It is often hard, as everyone knows, to establish primacy of claims to originality, whether actually asserted or only indicated statistically. Perhaps one ought simply to say that Miss West's style as a woman fully qualifies her—as it always did—to be a Mother Superior of the Faggots." See Tyler's *Screening the Sexes: Homosexuality in the Movies* (New York, 1972), 1. This question is relevant to my evaluation of the She-man as a new and separate entity that transcends/abandons any original male agency.

20 For further discussion of this, see Gaylyn Studlar, "Midnight Excess: Cult Configurations of 'Femininity' and the Perverse," *Journal of Popular Film and Television* 17 (Spring 1989): 2–13, esp. 6. Discussing Divine's film appearances, Studlar argues that "we believe Divine is a woman primarily because she is fat. As Noelle Caskey observes, fat is 'a direct consequence of her [woman's] sexuality. . . . Fat and femininity cannot be separated physiologically.'" Her Noelle Caskey quote is taken from "Interpreting Anorexia Nervosa," in *The Female Body in Western Culture,* ed. Susan Rubin Suleiman (Cambridge, Mass., 1986), 176, 178, 66–67.

21 See Jane Gallop, *The Daughter's Seduction: Feminism and Psychoanalysis* (Ithaca, 1982), for an elaboration of the concept of phallic mother.

22 Mary Ann Doane, *The Desire to Desire: The Woman's Film of the 1940s* (Bloomington, 1987).

23 See Doane, "Film and the Masquerade" and *Desire to Desire.*

24 John Berger, *Ways of Seeing* (London, 1972), 47.

25 Laurie Schulze, "On the Muscle" In *Fabrications: Costume and the Female Body,* ed. Jane Gaines and Charlotte Herzog (New York, 1990), 59, 68, 70.

26 C. Carr, "Unspeakable Practices, Unnatural Acts: The Taboo Art of Karen Finley," *Village Voice,* 24 June 1986, 17–20, 86.

Dead Ringer: Jacqueline Onassis

and the Look-Alike

Jane Gaines

★ ★ ★ ★ ★ ★ In *Ownership of the Image*, Bernard Edelman shows how nineteenth-century French law originally understood photography as machine-produced, not allowing it to be protected as the work of an author-creator, and later reversed its position, maintaining that the photographer *did* have an author's right in the photograph. But the author was admitted at this stage, Edelman says, on condition that he not merely "reproduce" the "real" before the camera but that he actually "produce" it.[1] He must become a creator of it. Much of Edelman's argument has to do with showing how the creative subject inserted between the world before the camera and the machine itself becomes that legal subject who has been historically constructed as holding rights. This notion of the subject endowed with rights in turn depends upon an earlier Hegelian sense of the free subject who possesses both himself and his attributes or characteristics.[2]

But what if the real (before the camera) is neither municipal building nor landscape scene which as public domain belong to everyone, but is instead the face and figure of another person who, by the same basic principle, already owns the real which the photographer appropriates? As Edelman theorizes this issue:

> The subject makes "his" a real which also belongs to the "other."
> In the very moment they invest the real with their personality,
> the photographer and the film-maker apprehend the property of
> the other—his image, his movement, and sometimes "his private
> life"—in their "object-glass," in their lens.[3]

It is, as it happens, this same apprehended subject who, by virtue of the possession of himself and his attributes, lays claim to the image of himself in the photograph. Thus it is that, as Edelman points out, two contradictory claims can be advanced over the same object before the camera, both with their basis in a culturally secured notion of personhood and personality.

I want to move from Edelman's point about the intervention of the photographer as creative subject in the act of picture-taking to concentrate on the construction of the legal real on the other side of the camera, so to speak, taking with me Edelman's concept of the insertion of the legal subject. For it seems to me that there is a kind of symmetry in the way the photographer subject stands in relation to the mechanical act and the way the photographed subject stands (on the other side, now) in relation to the natural body before the camera. (Natural bodies, we need to recall, are endowed by society with personhood and its attendant rights, not born with them.) What I want to consider next is how it is that the law deals with conflicting claims advanced by two different legal subjects who assert proprietorship over the same photographic likeness, on the basis that they are both entitled to "authorize" the use of their own images. The notion of "authorization" importantly emphasizes the symmetry of the photographer and the photographed, both of whom assert "something irreducibly" their own,[4] something so unique that no one else could possibly assert it in the identical way. The photographer and the photographed might also be seen as having a parallel material-mechanical connection with the photographic act, the one having clicked the shutter (and in French law thus having effected the "imprint of personality")[5] and the other having left an imprint on the chemically sensitive surface of the photographic film or plate effected by light reflected from her own bodily presence. It hardly needs repeating that in both cases the claim of the subject is based on the notion that even though this is the act of a machine, the contribution of the personality outweighs what might be considered purely mechanical functions.

The right of the photographer is also similar to the right of the photographed because of an underlying deference to "origin" in Anglo-American law. Authorship in copyright law, for instance, is understood as meaning "originating" as much as or more than "originality" in the sense of uniqueness. The human subject before the camera could, in some senses, be seen as the origin of the photographic image: that is, following the cause and effect version of how photography works, the subject's physical presence creates the image-impression. This version of the process might correspond with Charles Peirce's concept of the indexical relation between the sign (the photograph) and the referent (the subject before the camera), in which case the subject is a kind of originator. The subject as the originating source stands in relation to his photograph as, for instance, Christopher Wren stood in relation to the form of the death mask produced by his facial features.[6]

Where the subject behind the camera (the photographer) differs from the subject before the camera is in the advantage the latter enjoys by virtue of a one time appearance as "reality." However fleeting the fraction of a second before the camera, early attempts to theorize photography and motion pictures gave significant weight to this fraction of experience. Not only could the photograph testify to the existence of an empirical world, it was itself a kind of translucent "skin" of that real.[7] Although contemporary theories of film and photography have been dedicated to showing up the fallacy of the claims to truth status made by and for photographic signs, common sense persists in granting this special status to these images. And it is this commonsense assumption about the empirical real and its evidence (which tempts even the most sophisticated of theorists in their everyday lives) that is often, though not always, at work in the legal decisions that interest me here.

For instance, privacy doctrine and the publicity right which has evolved out of it, as they have pertained to issues regarding celebrity images, depend upon an unexamined assumption that the unauthorized use of a photograph is an appropriation of the identity of the person photographed.[8] The authority of the real is seen in the way the photographic image serves as the support for the reassertion of the rights of the subject photographed, assumed to be the same subject whose resemblance is, so to speak, "captured" in the image. In a 1972 California trial involving a dispute over the image of Bela Lugosi in the role of Dracula, the judge found that Lugosi's right of privacy did survive him, resulting in a decision in favor of the Lugosi family over the actor's former employers, Universal Pictures. According to the reasoning of the judge in this decision, although Lugosi was not alive to object to any invasion of his privacy caused by Universal's use of his photograph in the role of Dracula on T-shirts and cocktail stirring rods, the photographic "proof" of his existence in the past overwhelmed the portion of the image shared with the fictional character Dracula. Although the California Court of Appeals later reversed this decision and the state Supreme Court finally upheld the appellate reversal in 1979, the point is that *Lugosi v. Universal Pictures* suggests the threat posed to the law by the return of the referent. Bela Lugosi, a person no longer alive and thus not able to assert a right of privacy, still asserts a presence more potent, although with fewer legal teeth, than the character of the Count, still protected by the Universal Pictures copyright in the motion picture *Dracula* (1931). The presence of Bela Lugosi's body (before the camera) in the past, preserved intact in the image in the present, threatens to displace the right to Bela Lugosi as Dracula which Universal Pictures argued that they held in perpetuity.[9]

What, however, does the law do with a photographic likeness of a living celebrity which has not been created in the past by that celebrity's physical presence, but has its origins in the empirical body of a second person before the camera? According to the spirit of privacy doctrine which assumes an identity between the photographic sign and its referent, the person to whom the photographic image "belongs" is the person ultimately concerned with the use of the image. It would seem that the owner of the body before the camera is the legal subject whose publicity right is at stake and who is negotiating the right to have his or her privacy invaded. But the question becomes somewhat different when one legal subject is a celebrity and the other is an ordinary person who has an identity of her own. Whose identity is signified, the identity of the person to whom the body belongs or the identity of the celebrity? Can one body (without the aid of a masquerade) stand for two identities at once?

These are the issues raised on appeal in a 1984 right of privacy action heard by the Supreme Court of New York. In this action, Jacqueline Kennedy Onassis brought suit against Christian Dior for use of her image without consent in an advertisement for Dior sportswear. The image of Jacqueline Onassis appeared in a one-page color photograph portraying the mock wedding of the Diors, a fictional couple created in a series of advertisements photographed by Richard Avedon for J. Walter Thompson's Lansdowne Division (see Figure 1). The staged wedding advertisement appeared in the September or October 1983 issues of *Harper's Bazaar, Esquire, Time,* the *New Yorker,* and *New York* magazines, along with the caption: "The wedding of the Diors was everything a wedding should be: no tears, no rice, no in-laws, no smarmy toasts, for once no Mendelssohn. Just a legendary private affair."[10] To suggest the social prominence of the fictional Diors, actress Ruth Gordon, television film reviewer Gene Shalit, and familiar model Shari Belafonte are represented along with Jacqueline Onassis in the crowd watching the bride throw the customary bouquet.

Onassis brought suit against Dior on the basis of a violation of her right of privacy granted by sections 50 and 51 of the New York Civil Rights Law, which prohibit the commercial use of the portrait of a living person without consent.[11] To knowingly use for trade purposes the "name, portrait, or picture" of any living person without written consent gives rise to criminal and civil liability. The injured party is entitled to recovery of damages and the right to injunction. Onassis, who sought an injunction on the basis that she had suffered irreparable injury, maintained in an affidavit that she did not give consent for the use of her image in the Dior campaign and that she had never

Figure 1. Portion of Christian Dior advertisement appearing in various magazines, fall 1983.

allowed her name or her picture to be used in conjunction with advertisement for commercial products. Only in a very few instances had she given consent for the use of her name in connection with the arts, education, or civic causes with which she was affiliated.[12]

The defendant's argument, in this case, was that the New York law of privacy had not been violated. The woman in the photograph was not, after all, Jacqueline Kennedy Onassis, but Barbara Reynolds, a Washington secretary who was hired by Dior as a model for the advertisement. Dior's position was based on the fact that the person photographed was Barbara Reynolds and that it was her identity which had been used with her permission. The Dior lawyers argued that Onassis sought to prohibit Reynolds from using what was after all Reynolds's own image. Or, as Judge Edward J. Greenfield phrased this issue, ". . . can one person enjoin the use of someone else's face?"[13]

Barbara Reynolds was described in the case headnote as "masquerading" as Jacqueline Onassis, and the judge stated that she had "misappropriated" the other's identity. But what must be understood immediately is that Barbara Reynolds did not disguise herself with the aid of props, costumes, or special makeup, which would indicate that she had assumed a false identity. Neither was she an actress playing the role of the famous wife of the former president. If she was not disguised, and if she did not use an actor's skills of impersonation, how is it that she was seen as someone else? Barbara Reynolds was taken to be Jacqueline Onassis because, colloquially, she "looks like" her, so much like her, in fact, that she worked part-time for the Los Angeles firm Ron Smith Celebrity Look-Alikes, making appearances as "Jacqueline Kennedy Onassis."

In criminal cases the law tends to regard the camera as witness and the photograph as empirical proof of events in the real world. When it comes to cases of image appropriation, which are usually taken up in terms of the "likeness," the emphasis upon identification and recognizability suggests that legal practice has constructed the representational image as transparent. The question of recognition becomes, "Could one see the person in the likeness?" In its discussion of the Dracula image, the California Supreme Court made a distinction between the likeness of Lugosi in the portrayal of Dracula and his "natural" likeness, but the medium conveying this likeness would seem to have evaporated. Does "natural" likeness in this case refer to a drawing that resembles, to a photographic image of Lugosi himself, or to his real life physical features?

The point is that privacy law has tended to treat iconic likeness as straightforward and unproblematic: a likeness is that which someone recognizes as someone else. What makes the Onassis case significant is not only that the law is forced to take the conveyors or vehicles of likeness into consideration in its decision, but also, in deciding whether or not the image of Jacqueline Onassis had been appropriated by Dior, it had to construct the legal real. By "legal real" I do not mean a real that only operates within the closed system of Anglo-American law, since, because of the relation between law and society, this construction will have ramifications elsewhere. Suggesting the way this works, Paul Hirst and Elizabeth Kingdom say that "Law both 'imaginedly' fixes and sanctions social relations. It compels things to be as it recognizes they are."[14] What Onassis v. Dior shows is that the real we would have expected the law to recognize does not turn out to be the final real. If the law of privacy were interested in the empirical evidence offered by the photograph, there would be no doubt that the image in question belonged to Barbara Reynolds and therefore that Dior had a right to use it. But photographic realism and privacy doctrine want different guarantees. The one defers to a conviction that there is a final, verifiable, empirical real, and the other defers to a construction of personhood which does not require the existence of a real body (whether in the past or in the present) as its support.

Photographic realism with its empirical stance asks: "Who is the real referent?" But privacy law is finally not interested in this question. First of all, let's look at how the judge in Onassis v. Dior got around the issue of the empirical evidence of the photograph. In his ruling, Judge Greenfield aligned the case with precedents based on the problem of appropriation of the image without authorization in a wide range of media—from sound recording to literary fiction. The "truth" status of the photographic image was thus circumvented by the court's interpretation of the New York Civil Rights Code's "portrait or picture" in the widest possible way as "a representation which conveys the essence and likeness of an individual, not only actuality, but the close and purposeful resemblance to reality."[15] In other words, Dior may not have appropriated Jacqueline Onassis's *photograph*, but it has used her "portrait or picture" without permission. In arguing that it does not matter whether resemblance is created with recorded sound, photography, drawing, or word portrait, the law whisks away any privileged relation between the subject before the camera and the photograph. Essentially, then, what the Onassis decision did was to skip over the photographic medium and consider only the look-alike body as medium, the signifier whose signified is "Jacqueline Onassis."

The legal problem posed by the look-alike returns us to the epistemological issues raised by the iconic sign. We are again faced with Umberto Eco's "mysterious phenomenon of the image which 'resembles,'" and which is commonly thought to deliver the world to us in some way, whether by capturing some part of it or by reflecting it back.[16] And if we stop at the photographic sign, this is just what we have before us—an image of the wife of the former president. Except that the image in question is not the photographic image of Jacqueline Onassis. We are not dealing with an image which resembles but rather with an image of a person who resembles. And if the iconicity of the photographic sign has made it susceptible to transparency, then how do we consider the iconicity of the look-alike which is only transparent if we actually mistake her for the celebrity referent? And if we don't mistake her for the celebrity, but take the person to be herself, then the look-alike is in no sense a sign since something cannot stand in for or represent something with which it is identical.

The perversity of the look-alike phenomenon is that we *are* tempted to say, "But the woman in the photograph really *is* Barbara Reynolds," and for a moment we are returned to the stage in the theorization of iconic signs at which these illusive signifiers seemed to have successfully eluded systematic analysis. We rehearse the dilemma of the semiotician's approach to photography, cinema, and television, those mimetic technologies which mass-produce look-alike signs. We understand again the legacy of the false start in this field—Roland

Barthes's declaration that the photograph was a message without a code.[17] And we realize how very little theoretical help we have (as well as very little confirmation of what we see as astonishing similarity) in Eco's correction of Barthes: if the only thing that the iconic sign has in common with its referent is the perceptual habituation of the viewer who confronts two similar visual patterns, then why are we so impressed with and so susceptible to being convinced by look-alike signs?[18]

It might at this time be useful to say that the frustration with the iconic sign is entirely a poststructuralist condition. In a way, then, the Onassis case confirms the poststructuralist insight about the way signification works since we have in the legal dilemma an admission that the meaning of the figure in the Dior ad is indeterminable, or at least put off indefinitely. It even seems that we have nabbed the discourse of advertising in the very act of creating the postmodern aesthetic, in Baudrillard's words, "the virtual and irreversible confusion of images and the sphere of a reality, whose principle we can grasp less and less."[19] The admitted goal of the creators of the campaign featuring a semi-scandalous menage à trois in the style of *Design for Living*, was, after all, "to specify nothing but suggest everything."[20] But it would seem that it is the Onassis and not the Dior argument which is aligned with postmodernism and poststructuralism. While Dior's argument about the photograph is in essence, "It is what it *is*," the Onassis argument, "It is what it *says* it is," comes down on the side of the reader.[21] It appears, then, that since the law doesn't hold the photographic sign at its word that it is just as well that we no longer consider this sign as able to access the real world, and that therefore we cannot expect the sign to take any responsibility for what happens in the world.

Isn't this, after all, the conclusion that feminist film theory came to in regard to the cinematic representation of the female body? In its earliest formulations, commercial cinema used the female body decoratively, negating "woman" who as "woman" could never be grasped or signified by patriarchal discourses.[22] Later, the argument was advanced that not only was she not really present in representation, but that her femininity was itself a masquerade.[23] Even the documentary film which featured women's struggles in the workplace (showing her real relations to production) could not be said to deliver the "truth" of her oppressive circumstances or the analysis of the economic conditions which maintained them.[24] There were, after all, no real bodies or actual lives that we could hope to know about in any other way except via the photographic, linguistic, and electronic signs which delivered them to us. Is Barbara Reynolds, then, part of this long legacy of female body-signs fitted up as models and actresses in magazine advertising, television drama, and fiction film, drained of meaning and stripped of identity in order to serve as vehicles for the discourses of commerce?

But isn't there something slightly different about the Barbara Reynolds case? One could say that the law is on some level concerned about the commercial appropriation of bodies and that it was deployed as an objection on behalf of the society to the way Dior emptied Barbara Reynolds's body in order to fill it by the connotation "Jacqueline Onassis." The judge's concerns were stated in terms of the theft of the celebrity's identity, but he also asked what should be done with the identity claim of the noncelebrity as he returned to the issue, ". . . can one person enjoin the use of someone else's face?" From my point of view, the significance of the Onassis case *is* the stand it took against "theft" of identity as well as against the "confusion" of identities. However, at this point my argument will swerve away from the concerns of feminist film theory. Therefore, I will not be objecting to the commercial uses of the female body. I have a different interest in "theft" and "confusion," terms which open out onto legal issues that lead in another direction. In the end, protection of personhood, difficult to fault from a humanistic point of view, turns into something quite different as it contributes (incrementally and almost imperceptibly) to the creation of a new legal entity. This entity (which I have not yet identified) is one and the same as the legal real to which Judge Greenfield defers, and which wins out over the photographic real and its claim.

While the law in *Onassis v. Dior* appeared to be concerned only about personal injury and unauthorized appropriation, it was equally concerned about other principles signaled by the references to "theft" and "confusion." In order to show up the double development whereby it becomes possible to engage sympathy for prohibiting in-

jury to one's feelings in support of prohibiting injury to one's commercial value (a distinctly different kind of offense), I need to refer
back briefly to the origins of privacy law in New York. The issues
which are foregrounded in *Onassis* were first raised in *Roberson v.
Rochester Folding Box* (1902), in which Abigail Roberson objected
to the unauthorized use of her photographic image on a flour mill
company advertising poster placed in warehouses, saloons, and other
public places. Roberson was denied relief in this case, but the public outcry in response to the outcome encouraged the legislature to
enact a statute prohibiting the use of a person's name, portrait, or
picture for trade without their consent.[25] The original spirit of sections 50 and 51 of the 1903 New York Civil Rights Act was, as one
would expect, maintained in Judge Greenfield's language in *Onassis:*

> If we truly value the right of privacy in a world of exploitation,
> where every mark of distinctiveness becomes grist for the mills of
> publicity, then we must give it more than lip service and grudg-
> ing recognition. Let the word go forth—there is no free ride. The
> commercial hitchhiker seeking to travel on the fame of another
> will have to learn to pay the fare or stand on his own two feet.[26]

Privacy, the umbrella doctrine encoded in sections 50 and 51, and
at issue in *Roberson* and later *Onassis*, does not, however, have its
origins in protection against marketplace exploitation. Neither does
it derive from a concept of defamation, as one might expect. The
branch of United States law referred to as "privacy" has its historical
origins in a particular idea of a right to seclusion from the public
eye. Paradoxically, over the course of this century, the same doctrine
which promised to shelter private persons from the public circulation of their names and likenesses (an inevitability produced by the
development of mass information technologies), has come to allow
the reverse. Privacy law as it becomes publicity law makes it possible for celebrities to circulate their images in public without fear of
commercial piracy.[27]

There is an equally important question which suggests a historical parallel with the development of "privacy" into "publicity," and
it is worth a digression here to fill out this perspective. The question is this: why is it that the public circulation of a person's photo-

graphic likeness should be analogous to intrusion into one's private life, analogous even to the public exposure of inner thoughts and feelings? Social historians have shown that the notion of the body as somehow synonymous with selfhood is a modern concept. The contemporary sense we have of the body as expressive of the notion of a "personality," evidenced on it through gesture and expression, almost as an involuntary symptom, is as recent as the turn of the century.[28] But where one might think that the use of a mechanical instrument would interfere with the pure essence of the person before the camera (as it had negated the unique touch of the photographer-creator in French legal history), portrait photography was thought to investigate scientifically, to probe the "inner" character, more and more thought to be the "true" person.[29] Why is it that two layers of mediation (the face as medium in addition to the photograph), rather than distancing or distorting, are thought to render the "real" person more immediate?

Film theorists from Béla Balázs to Roland Barthes and Gilles Deleuze have considered the language of the motion picture close-up, which seems to have ratified the contemporary currency of and the recent fascination with the face. Although early critics argued that the close-up was a kind of disorienting dismemberment, Balázs would argue that it was not a part but had come to assume the proportions and the significance of a self-sufficient whole.[30] Deleuze would take Balázs a step further and suggest that the image of the face in close-up (the affection-image) is a "component of all images" and a quality ("faceicity") transferrable to representations of other parts of the body and even to other objects.[31] The question arises as to why the face would fuse so easily with the forms produced by new mechanical and electronic technologies. And why, further, in the face (so to speak) of the potential of mass replication, would the face in close-up still stand for the individual, one-of-a-kind personality? It is almost as though the romantic ideal of humanness, developed as a countervaluation against the institution of "the market," had persistently planted itself right where it had been permanently obliterated—in the reproducible image of the human face. If the face were unreadable and unfathomable, epitomized by the image of Garbo which, Barthes says, "plunged audiences into the deepest ecstasy,"[32] why would the image-visage still be a means of identification, based on its readability? At some point, Deleuze says, when the close-up is taken to the limit, as in Ingmar Bergman's modernist moments when the depths of the face engulf us in nothingness, individuation is "suspended."[33] Andy Warhol's postmodern postage-stamp portraits of Liz Taylor, Elvis Presley, and Marilyn Monroe make this clear: individuation is stamped-out, mass-produced. So why the insistence that the photographic portrait is one's identity when by now it should be clear that the image has undergone a thorough transformation and even devaluation in this regard?

Onassis v. Dior asserted the opposite; that is, that in the contemporary world the face has come to stand for the honor and integrity of the individual. Judge Greenfield advanced the position that the facial image had superseded the name which was once thought to be personhood's nugget of value. After citing Shakespeare on how for men and women the good name is "the immediate jewel of their souls,"[34] the judge went on:

> In those days, as the touchstone of recognition, name was all, conveyed in writing or by word of mouth. Today, the visual have superseded the verbal arts, and news photography, television, and motion pictures can accord instant world-wide recognition to a face. For some people, even without their American Express cards, the face is total identification, more than a signature or a coat of arms.[35]

The judge further asked why it was that, since the image is "total recognition," the unauthorized use of it was not treated as similar to the use of a person's signature:

> The unauthorized use of a person's signature would not pass muster under the statute because it was claimed merely to be a facsimile. Is a picture or a portrait intended to look like someone not that person's picture if it is similarly a facsimile or a simulation?[36]

The emphasis on facsimile is telling in another way. As we have seen, for privacy law the real is not the natural world. This law is finally not interested in what is commonly thought to be a natural bond between the body and the self, summarized in the idea of proper name, personal image, and the self-evidence of the identity between the body and the person which tautologically becomes "proof of identity." Privacy law is no longer, if it ever was, about personal offense and affrontery. In *Onassis v. Dior*, it is structured along lines of copyright law, which asks questions about authorial creativity in order to determine whether or not there has been theft of a work. Copyright law, having seen so much of similarity, is unimpressed with it, and thus returns some sanity to the iconic sign. In this regard, I like what W. T. J. Mitchell has said about the problem semiotics has had with systematizing analogical representation. Iconicity, it seems, is everywhere:

> One reason the icon has proved so difficult for semiotics to define is that similarity is such a capacious relationship that almost anything can be assimilated into it. Everything in the world is similar to everything else in some respects.[37]

Copyright law, then, cannot be based on the commonsense notion of absolute uniqueness or a one-of-a-kind ideal. It recognizes claims based on firstness in order to break ties when two objects of culture appear to be identical or, in legal terms, "substantially similar."[38] In order to dismiss Dior's claim that Barbara Reynolds had a right to use her image as she saw fit, the judge constructed the Dior ad as similar to an act of plagiarism, a substitution of a counterfeit for the real:

> The juxtaposition of the counterfeit figure just behind the real-life figures of a veteran actress, a television personality, and a well-known model lends to the whole ensemble an air of verisimilitude and accentuates the grievance, for it imparts an aura of authenticity to the trumped-up tableau.[39]

Further, the judge's remarks echoed the terms of the Romantics' disdain for imitation, now become the commonsense wisdom of the elementary school science lesson:

> While some imitators may employ artistry in the use of voice, gesture and facial expression, a mere similarity of features is no more artistry than the mimicry of the Monarch butterfly by its

look alike, the Viceroy butterfly. To paint a portrait of Jacqueline Kennedy Onassis is to create a work of art; to look like Jacqueline Kennedy Onassis is not.[40]

Theoretically, then, would copyright law defer to Barbara Reynolds's claim if she had impersonated Jacqueline Onassis or if she had painted her picture? (If Reynolds had created the role of Jacqueline Onassis as an actress, however, the law in this country would not necessarily have protected her dramatic interpretation.) Barbara Reynolds, in other words, cannot just be herself and advance any claim to the "portrait" of Jacqueline Onassis her face and body effortlessly make. She must produce this likeness. We come around again to Edelman, and although still on the other side of the camera, we note the remarkable symmetry in these two problems in the production of the real. Just as French law would not defer to the claim of the photographer without first seeing his human hand at work "producing" the real, so the look-alike cannot by nature and sheer existence be the image of a celebrity, but must "produce" that likeness as a fine artist. Neither the mechanical act nor the fluke of nature is protectable without the intervention of the authorial hand of the creative subject. The body of Barbara Reynolds is a mere copy of the body of Jacqueline Onassis produced by no one (and here it is clear that the divine hand has no legal subjecthood); a sketch, the judge called Barbara Reynolds's body—a sketch evidencing neither "creativity" nor "originality." According to this interpretation, although one can "authorize" the use of one's image, one cannot "author" one's physiognomy.[41] An actor or actress may use the "raw material" of his or her own physical features and bodily endowments as ingredients in a star image,[42] but must create a public persona, and with that a secondary meaning (requiring public recognition), in order to have a fully protectable image-property.[43] This is yet another reminder that the "real" to which privacy law defers (and which it has itself created) is not the empirical real (as we would have thought). What, then, is this real, reconstituted, as Edelman says, as a legal object, "susceptible to appropriation, sale, and contracts?"[44]

I have argued thus far that the Onassis case shows that privacy law, contrary to our expectations, does not automatically defer to the authority of a real tangible presence backing up the photographic image and neither does it hold that the signifier is bound to its real world referent. The "real" that is signified, although intangible, is nevertheless constituted by the law as its "real." The law does not always match up rights with empirical bodies, as we know from the women's movement's struggles to assert the right to abortion as a woman's right to control her own body. Rather, the law respects rights in the "real" it constructs. It is a characteristic of law, says Edelman, to reciprocally recognize through legal mechanisms the very legal subject it has constituted.[45] And this is what it did in *Onassis v. Dior*. Dior came up against a "real" which was already the property of another subject, an intangible property (the image), but nonetheless a property, and nonetheless constituted as more "real" than the body before the camera. The question ". . . can one person enjoin the use of another person's face?" might then mean that the judge did not deny Barbara Reynolds's property right to her own face. In legal terms, two rights were asserted which matched up with two property-images. One way that the judge could then find for one property over another would be to argue that one of the two properties had been "stolen" on the analogy of infringement in copyright law. Thus the objection to the Dior ad was that using the natural body of the look-alike was copying the original, protected body-property. But the final concern, and, in my analysis, the unacknowledged issue upon which the outcome of the case rested, was not copying, but the "confusion" of the copy with the original. To quote Judge Greenfield: "No one has an inherent or constitutional right to pass himself off for what he is not."[46] "Passing off" and "likelihood of confusion," of course, are tests of trademark, not copyright, infringement.[47] Trademark, a branch of unfair competition law, regulates the marketplace by upholding clarity of delineation between products and consistency in the indication of sources behind consumer goods. This law stands against the attempt to confuse the consumer and the attempt to misrepresent or pass off the goods of one merchant as the goods of another. I have argued elsewhere that the shift from copyright to trademark as a legal remedy in the entertainment field indicates a move away from the humanist values associated with "originality" called up in the defense of rights to literary property.[48] The "passing off" argument in *Onassis v.*

Dior indicates a parallel development in privacy law. What we see in *Onassis* is that the image is, as it were, more protectable on the analogy with commercial property than it is on the analogy with the person who experiences injury to feelings, the older basis of privacy. This also means that if the judge was ultimately concerned about "passing off," then the decision in favor of Onassis was not a decision *for* the multiplicity of meaning, but against it. And therefore those who view postmodern culture with alarm should not be concerned. United States courts, as they resolve "passing off" disputes, are holding the line against massive slippage.

Dior, then, attempted to appropriate intangible private property—the image of Jacqueline Kennedy Onassis. And Dior lost the suit. The judge's assertion that the image of the wife of a former president was protectable private property has ramifications beyond the publication of one advertisement which ran in several upscale magazines in 1983. For the entire text of the advertising copy in question, since the outcome of *Onassis v. Dior*, is placed in a kind of authorial limbo. If, as the answer to my request for permission to reprint their ad copy suggests, Christian Dior-New York, Inc., is not at "at liberty" to authorize the reproduction of this text, the question remains whether Jacqueline Onassis is "at liberty" to authorize the use of Barbara Reynolds's face, as she could encounter, in reverse, the private property "real" of the other woman's image. This problem in the circulation of texts which are at once shared culture and private property lurks in every public use of such protected discourse. I am reminded of Judge Learned Hand's description of the ordinary sign which achieves secondary meaning and thus protected trademark status as wearing its protection as a "penumbra" or fringe.[49] And culture which is widely circulated yet tightly held as private property is similarly edged or bordered on all sides.

Does *Onassis v. Dior* have implications for other scholarly endeavors? I am thinking of the elementary semiotics lesson which features a comparison between two versions of Jacqueline Kennedy's 1967 trip to Cambodia based on a close analysis of two magazine covers. As the *Life* cover has coded her, Onassis is only vacationing, but on the cover of *Paris-Match*, she is part of the ritual afforded royalty. In Guy Gauthier's "The Semiology of the Image," these photographs are constituted as objects of study, examples of the codes of culture which students are led to analyze in terms of the dress and posture of the president's wife, her relation to other figures in the frame, the style of the photographs, and the linguistic text accompanying them.[50] Gauthier's "Initiation à la semiologie de l'image," translated and published by the British Film Institute in 1976 as a study unit complete with slides and still widely used in film studies courses in Britain and the United States, is an introduction to the politics of the image. And what is most political about the "publicity image," as John Berger dubbed the photographic product of consumer culture, is that which is seemingly absent from the image we perceive.[51] In our teaching we tease out the cultural knowledge backing up the taken-for-granted codes of the world which stood before the camera and stress the stages and conditions of the material production of glossy advertising images. But we do not ask about the conditions which determine whether such images as those of Jacqueline Kennedy, Adolf Hitler, George Wallace, and Mary Ann Vecchio (the runaway who became the national symbol of the Kent State tragedy) could be reproduced as covers of *Life*, *Paris-Match*, *Der Spiegel*, and *Newsweek*, and reproduced again as classroom texts. Each case is slightly different. The image of Adolf Hitler, for instance, is produced by an anonymous defacing of the image of George Wallace. One would think that this is a clear case of a caricature that belongs to the world, except that it appears on the cover of a German magazine and would be protected by its copyright. The right of the publisher is also asserted in the boldface *Newsweek* logo crowning the famous Pieta-like pose of Mary Ann Vecchio, now rephotographed from the original, retouched and reprocessed until it emerges as the emblem of the Kent State deaths.

But the subject of my inquiry is as much the more problematic commercial use of the celebrity image, a use which United States courts do not exempt as either cultural heritage or as news even when the life of the person photographed is newsworthy. These are the images in which the emergent publicity right of the person photographed can displace the right of photographer, publisher, and employer. The marks of labor are effaced in these images by the deep impression of ownership which often involves no labor whatsoever. This impression is the stamp of the face itself. Both residue of real person and effective mark of trade, the face fully determines the proprietary status of the image while leaving neither trace nor clue of this, the epitome of self-effacement. In the classic cases of commercial image appropriation involving Cary Grant, Cher Bono, and Clint Eastwood, not to mention Bela Lugosi, we have an inkling of what Deleuze means when he says that it is the face that is the vampire.[52] Since the ideology of private property (the assumption that everything in the world is privately owned by someone) diverts us from the question of protection and reproducibility, we are not inclined to think of the meaning of the image as in any way related to the proprietary attachments on it. If the question comes up at all, we generally take it up with reference to the polite concept "permission." Why? Do we in fact also take for granted that if an image is mechanically produced it is therefore meant to be unproblematically "seen"? This question has to do with private as opposed to public looking—a whole new problem that invites consideration.

And what would seem to be more unproblematically public than the events surrounding the Kent State tragedy and the presidential visit to Cambodia? Aren't these events newsworthy and historically significant? United States copyright law, of course, provides for the public interest in the doctrine of "fair use" which expresses a commitment to free dissemination of ideas as an exception to private right restrictions on the circulation of reproducible culture. Furthermore, it is customary for the law to exempt celebrity images constructed as "political speech" from such protection as would curtail free circulation of such expression.[53] In cases early in the century, it was established that news could not be copyrighted.[54] Likewise, it is generally held that history cannot be copyrighted.[55] But a closer examination of the common law relevant to intellectual property suggests that the proprietary status of information is a matter of constant contestation and that the private claims on what we thought was our cultural heritage are often asserted with success. As we have seen in *Onassis v. Dior*, private claims do effectively attach themselves to discourses which have cultural and historical significance.

For if we can agree on nothing else, we can agree that information about a former first lady is newsworthy. The fact that the every-day life of Jacqueline Onassis is news has been legally confirmed in *Onassis v. Galella* in which the self-admitted paparazzo was not denied the right to photograph the widow of the former president, but was required to remain at a specified distance from Onassis and her children, stipulated in number of feet.[56] But why isn't Dior's visual reference to Onassis excluded from private protection on the basis of its status as news or even political enunciation? If her image is news why isn't it also a part of our shared culture? I will put it bluntly. The issue is no longer whether or not one person can enjoin the use of another's face or whether another person can use her own body to usurp the identity of another. The question is: "Who owns our cultural heritage?" In order to underscore how the logic of United States intellectual property law structures the ambiguity which invites the question of the ownership of our common heritage, I turn to *Six Seconds in Dallas*.

First we need to consider the relationship between the Super 8-mm color motion picture footage shot with a telephoto lens at normal speed by the Dallas dress manufacturer Abraham Zapruder, and the assassination of John F. Kennedy on 22 November 1963. The 480 frames of the Zapruder film, 40 of which show some details of the shooting, are the fullest existing visual record of the events in Dallas. As such, the Warren Commission employed the footage as evidence in their investigation. But of more significance to us, three days after the shooting, Time, Inc., began to negotiate the purchase of the footage. The original and the three existing copies of the footage were eventually purchased from Zapruder for $150,000. *Life* magazine reproduced 30 of the frames a week after the assassination, and in the December issue, 9 frames were featured, enlarged and in color. A third issue the following October reproduced 5 color frames on the cover, and another 8 inside accompanied reprinted portions of the Warren Commission report. All of the issues of the magazine were copyrighted, and, in addition, in May 1967, *Life* registered the motion picture footage with the United States copyright office.[57]

The status of the motion picture record of the historical events of

22 November 1963 becomes a question because Bernard Geis, Associates, publishers of Joshua Thompson's *Six Seconds in Dallas* (1967), approached *Life* with a request to reprint some of the Zapruder frames in Thompson's book, a journalistic history and analysis of the assassination. Denied permission to copy the frames, Geis employed an artist to sketch in charcoal parts of 22 of the frames; these sketches were then reproduced in Thompson's book.[58] Time, Inc., sought a judgment against Geis for infringement of copyright, and although the United States District Court of New York ruled in favor of Geis and Thompson on the basis of "fair use," what concerns me is not the outcome of the case but the possibility the court entertains that history might be protectable private property. For what the court maintains on *this* issue is that although history itself is not subject to copyright, the "form of expression" of the events of the past is, and thus *Life* can claim to own the motion picture "expression" of the assassination.[59]

There is no doubt that this theory flies in the face of the most basic lessons of poststructuralism.[60] How else is history conveyed to us if not via some form of expression?[61] *Life* has argued, and the court has upheld their claim, that they have no copyright in the actual events of November 1963: "They can be freely set forth in speech, in books, in pictures, in music, and in every other form of expression."[62] These, of course, are also forms subject to copyright, and one wonders how we are ever to reproduce and make available the scenes of the past without recourse to forms. How do we disseminate "the facts" regarding the past without first converting them into some reproducible medium of expression?

Lest we get too alarmed over this aspect of *Time, Inc., v. Geis* (as Bernard Edelman seems to have done),[63] let me say that the emphasis on "forms of expression" is nothing more than a restatement of the expression/ideas dichotomy basic to United States intellectual property doctrine—in essence, an attempt to free up underlying ideas so that they may become available to the public. Expression, the materiality which conveys these ideas, or the form they take upon publication, can enjoy copyright's limited monopoly. It seems likely that the expression/ideas duality can expect a showdown in the near future because the protection of the computer program, a system which cannot be used without copying, renders the division more and more untenable. Some have already argued that the merger of ideas and expression in the iconic sign makes the arbitrariness of the distinction all too evident.[64] We see this in the case of the image of Jacqueline Onassis. If we consider, as Norman Mailer has, that the woman is no longer a celebrity but has become a "historic archetype,"[65] then she is analogous to the character typage which the courts have understood as comparable to "underlying ideas."[66] And if Jacqueline Onassis is an underlying type, she is an idea which cannot be reserved, a type which informs and fills out the trend-setting socialite character stereotype constructed in the Dior wedding tableau; as such an idea she is part of the materials of culture which intellectual property law holds should be available to all artists. *Onassis v. Dior* has shown us the inseparability of expression and ideas. But in the end, for the judge, it did not matter what form the expression took, whether "Jacqueline Onassis" was signified by an image produced by her own body or by the body of another person. "Jacqueline Kennedy Onassis" in any form is potentially protected private property.

But privacy law has its other side which mirrors the principle behind the ideas/expression distinction which leaves underlying ideas as a cultural preserve. As the Onassis judge stated, Ron Smith Celebrity Look-Alikes can "market its clients for fun and profit," and Barbara Reynolds can "capitalize" on her resemblance at parties and even on television.[67] We are free to wear our hair as Onassis does, to dress up, and to try our hand at impersonation. Even Australian Leigh Raymond, whose hobby is crashing parties by rushing into a room wearing a pill box hat and covered with red dye, is completely free to entertain his friends.

Notes

1   Bernard Edelman, *Ownership of the Image*, trans. Elizabeth Kingdom (London, 1979), 42–43.
2   See *Hegel's Philosophy of Right*, trans. T. M. Knox (Oxford, 1965).
3   Edelman, *Ownership*, 39.
4   I refer here to one of the important theorizations of authorship in United States

law by Justice Oliver Wendell Holmes, in Bleistein v. Donaldson Lithographing Co., 188 U.S. 239 (1903).

5   Edelman, *Ownership*, 51.

6   This is a reference to André Bazin, "The Ontology of the Photographic Image," in *What is Cinema?* trans. Hugh Gray (Berkeley, 1967), 1: 12; Victor Burgin, "Photographic Practice and Art Theory," in *Thinking Photography*, ed. Victor Burgin (London, 1982), discusses the degree to which the photograph is "caused" by the referent (61). For an account of the correspondence between Bazin's theory of photography and Charles Sanders Peirce's notion of the indexical sign, see Philip Rosen, "History of Image, Image of History: Subject and Ontology in Bazin," *Wide Angle* 9.4 (1987): 11–13.

7   Oliver Wendell Holmes, "The Stereoscope and the Stereograph," in *Classic Essays on Photography*, ed. Alan Trachtenberg (New Haven, 1980), 81.

8   See J. Thomas McCarthy, *The Rights of Publicity and Privacy* (New York, 1988), chap. 1; Melville Nimmer, *Cases and Materials in Copyright and Other Aspects of Entertainment Litigation* (St. Paul, 1985), chap. 16; Jane Gaines, "Dracula and the Right of Publicity," unpublished paper.

9   Lugosi v. Universal Pictures, 25 Cal. 3d 813 (1979).

10 Onassis v. Dior, 122 Misc. 2d 603 (1984), 605.

11 Ibid., 603.

12 Ibid., 605.

13 Ibid., 603.

14 Paul Hirst and Elizabeth Kingdom, "On Edelman's 'Ownership of the Image,'" *Screen* 20.3, 4 (Winter 1979–80): 139.

15 Ibid., 611.

16 Umberto Eco, "Articulations of the Cinematic Code," in *Movies and Methods*, ed. Bill Nichols (Berkeley, 1976), 595.

17 I refer to Roland Barthes, "The Photographic Message" and "Rhetoric of the Image," in *Image, Music, Text*, trans. Stephen Heath (New York, 1977), 15–51.

18 Eco goes on to say, ". . . it may be enough for the moment to have recognized processes of codification concealed in the mechanisms of perception themselves" ("Articulations," 595). It is generally accepted that Eco's argument here for seeing the image as coded at the level of perception successfully unseated the notion of photography as uncoded. I am drawing attention to the tentativeness he has expressed about his own conclusions. For further background, see Burgin, ed., *Thinking Photography*, 60–63.

19 Jean Baudrillard, "Beyond Right and Wrong or the Mischievous Genius of Image," in *Resolution: A Critique of Video Art*, ed. Patti Podesta, trans. Laurent Charreyron and Amy Gerstler (Los Angeles, 1986), 8.

20 Onassis v. Dior, 605.

21 Thanks to William Price for this idea about readership as well as invaluable legal research assistance and advice.

22 I allude to the "impasse" in feminist film criticism, effected by the theorization

of "woman" as absence. For an overview, see "Feminist Film Criticism: An Introduction," in *Re-vision*, ed. Mary Ann Doane, Patricia Mellencamp, and Linda Williams (Frederick, Md., 1984), 1–17.

23 Mary Ann Doane, "Film and the Masquerade—Theorising the Female Spectator," *Screen* 23.3, 4 (1982): 74–87.

24 See E. Ann Kaplan, *Women and Film: Both Sides of the Camera* (New York, 1983), chap. 10, for a good overview of this position.

25 For a succinct discussion of *Roberson v. Rochester Folding Box Co.* and its relationship to the 1903 New York statute enacted as the result of its outcome, see McCarthy, *Rights of Publicity and Privacy*, 1.14–16, 6.56–65.

26 *Onassis v. Dior*, 612.

27 The irony of my introduction of "publicity" into a discussion of *Onassis* will not escape legal commentators who will know that New York has notoriously resisted the evolution of a concept of "Right of Publicity" within state courts and consistently backed off enacting the kind of legislation that exists in other states.

28 Richard Sennett, *The Fall of Public Man* (New York, 1974), chap. 8; Warren Susman, *Culture as History* (New York, 1984), chap. 14.

29 See Alan Sekula, "The Traffic in Photographs," in *Modernism and Modernity*, ed. Benjamin H. D. Buchloh et al. (Nova Scotia, 1983), 133, for a discussion of the "scientific" portraiture of August Sandler.

30 Béla Balázs, *Theory of the Film*, trans. Edith Bone (New York, 1970), 51–52, 60–61.

31 Gilles Deleuze, *Cinema 1: The Movement-Image*, trans. Hugh Tomlinson and Barbara Habberjam (Minneapolis, 1986), 87–88.

32 Roland Barthes, *Mythologies*, trans. Annette Lavers (New York, 1972), 56.

33 Deleuze, *Cinema 1*, 100.

34 *Onassis v. Dior*, 610.

35 Ibid., 611.

36 Ibid.

37 W. J. Mitchell, *Iconology* (Chicago, 1985), 29.

38 See Arthur R. Miller and Michael H. Davis, *Intellectual Property* (St. Paul, 1983), 255–68, for a discussion of similarity as it applies to both copyright and trademark.

39 *Onassis v. Dior*, 613.

40 Ibid.

41 McCarthy, in a different vein, says, "One is not the 'author' of one's face, no matter how much cosmetic surgery has been performed. Either God, fate, or our parents' genes 'authored' this 'work'" (*Rights of Publicity and Privacy*, 44).

42 Edgar Morin, *Stars*, trans. Richard Howard (New York, 1961), 140.

43 J. Thomas McCarthy, *Trademarks and Unfair Competition* (Rochester, 1984), 1: 656–717.

44 Edelman, *Ownership*, 38.

45 Ibid., 101.

46 *Onassis v. Dior*, 614.

47 McCarthy, *Trademarks*, 54–55, 666–68.

48 See Jane Gaines, "SUPERMAN, Television, and the Protective Strength of the Trademark" (Paper delivered at the International Television Studies Conference, University of London, July 1988).

49 McCarthy, *Trademarks*, 663.

50 Guy Gauthier, "The Semiology of the Image," trans. British Film Institute (London, 1976), 9. For more on the methodology see Manuel Alvarado, "Photographs and Narrativity," *Screen Education* 32, 33 (Autumn–Winter, 1979–80): 5–17.

51 John Berger, *Ways of Seeing* (London, 1972), chap. 7.

52 Deleuze, *Cinema 1*, 99.

53 Paulsen v. Personality Posters, Inc., 59 Misc. 2d 444 (1969).

54 International News Service v. Associated Press, 248 U.S. 215 (1918); National Tel. News Co. v. Western Union, 119 Fed. 294 (7th Cir. 1902).

55 See Hoehling v. Universal City Studios, 618 F.2d 972 (2d Cir. 1980) for a discussion of this.

56 Onassis v. Galella (1973), 43–44.

57 Time, Inc., v. Bernard Geis, 293 F. Supp. 130 (1967).

58 Ibid., 138.

59 Ibid., 143.

60 See, for instance, Roland Barthes, "The Discourse of History," in *The Rustle of Language*, trans. Richard Howard (New York, 1986), 131–32, for a critique of the "chastity of History," untouched by historians and their forms.

61 See Michel de Certeau, *The Writing of History*, trans. Tom Conley (New York, 1988), 21, for a discussion of the peculiarity of the discipline which uses the same term (history) to refer to both the object of study and the discourse on it. In my argument I am taking advantage of the ambiguity.

62 Onassis v. Dior, 143.

63 Edelman, *Ownership*, 66–67, reading *Time v. Geis* with fresh eyes from the point of view of French law, is astounded to find Judge Wyatt had stated that the "form" of history was copyrightable, but not the "foundation," or underlying ideas. Vincent Porter, "Film Copyright and Edelman's Theory of Law," *Screen* 20.3, 4 (1979–80): 144–45, quite rightly points out that Edelman had not read enough United States law to know that the distinction was basic to intellectual property doctrine.

64 John Frow, "Repetition and Limitation: Computer Software and Copyright Law," *Screen* 29.1 (1988): 8.

65 Onassis v. Dior, 613.

66 See Warner Brothers, Inc. v. American Broadcasting Co., 720 F.2d 231 (2d. Cir. 1983), 242–43, for a discussion of Superman as a generic type that cannot be reserved.

67 Onassis v. Dior, 613.

Nostalgia for the Present

Fredric Jameson

★ ★ ★ ★ ★ ★ There's a novel by Philip K. Dick called *Time Out of Joint* which, published in 1959, evokes the fifties: President Eisenhower's stroke, Main Street USA, Marilyn Monroe, a world of neighbors and PTAs, small retail chain stores (the produce trucked in from the outside), favorite television programs, mild flirtations with the housewife next door, game shows and contests, sputniks distantly revolving overhead, mere blinking lights in the firmament, hard to distinguish from airliners or flying saucers. If you were interested in constructing a time capsule, or an "only yesterday" compendium or documentary-nostalgia video-film of the fifties, this might serve as a beginning: to which you could add short haircuts, early rock-n-roll, short skirts. The list is not a list of facts or historical realities (although its items are not invented and are in some sense "authentic"), but rather a list of stereotypes, of ideas of facts and historical realities.

Did the "period" see itself this way? Did the literature of the period deal with this kind of small-town American life as its central preoccupation and if not, why not? What other kinds of preoccupations seemed more important? To be sure, in retrospect, the fifties have been summed up culturally as so many forms of protest against the fifties "themselves," against the Eisenhower era and its complacency, against the sealed self-contentment of the American small (white middle-class) town, against the conformism and the family-centered ethnocentrism of a prosperous United States learning to consume in the first big boom after the shortages and privations of the War, whose immediacy has by now largely lost its edge. The first beat poets, an occasional anti-hero with "existentialist" overtones, a few daring Hollywood impulses, nascent rock-n-roll, the compensatory importation of European books, movements, and art films, a lonely and premature political rebel or theorist like C. Wright Mills: such, in retrospect, seem to make up the balance sheet of fifties culture. All the rest is Peyton Place, best-sellers, and TV series: and it is indeed just those series—living-room comedies, single-family homes menaced by *The Twilight Zone* on the one hand, and gangsters and escaped convicts from the outside world on the other—that give us the content of our positive image of the fifties in the first place. If there is "realism" in the fifties, in other words, it is presumably to be found there, in mass cultural representation, the only kind of art to be willing (and able) to deal with the stifling Eisenhower realities of the happy family in the small town, of normalcy and nondeviant everyday life. High art can apparently not deal with this kind of subject matter except by way of the oppositional, the satire of Wyndham Lewis, the pathos and solitude of Edward Hopper or of Sherwood Anderson. Of naturalism, long after the fact, the Germans used to say that "it stank of cabbage": that is, it exudes the misery and boredom of its subject matter, poverty. Here too, with the fifties, the content seems somehow to contaminate the form, only the misery is the misery of happiness, or at least contentment which is in reality complacency, the misery of Marcuse's "false" happiness, the gratifications of the new car, the TV dinner, and your favorite program on the sofa—which are now themselves secretly a misery, an unhappiness that doesn't know its name, that has no way of telling itself apart from genuine satisfaction and fulfillment since it has presumably never encountered such fulfillment.

When the notion of the oppositional is contested, however, in the mid-eighties, we will know a fifties revival in which much of this "degraded mass culture" returns for possible reevaluation. At the time, however, it was high culture in the fifties that was authorized (as it still is) to pass judgment on reality, to say what real life is and what is mere appearance: and it is by leaving out, by ignoring, by passing over in silence and with the repugnance one may feel for the dreary stereotypes of television series that high art palpably issues its judgments. Faulkner and Hemingway, the Southerners and the New Yorkers, pass this small-town North American raw material by in a detour considerably greater than the proverbial ten-foot pole; indeed, of the great writers of the period, only Philip Dick comes to mind as the virtual poet laureate of this material, of squabbling couples and marital dramas, of petty bourgeois shopkeepers, neighborhoods, and afternoons in front of television, and all the rest. But of course he does something to it, and it was already California already.

This small-town content was not, in the postwar period, really "provincial" any longer (as in Lewis or John O'Hara, let alone Dreiser): you may want to leave, you may still long for the big city, but something has happened—perhaps something as simple as television and the media—to remove the pain and sting of absence from the center, from the metropolis. Little of it exists any longer, even though we still have small towns (whose downtowns are now in decay—but so are the big cities); what has happened is that the autonomy of the small town (in the provincial period a source of claustrophobia and anxiety; in the fifties the ground for a certain comfort and even a certain reassurance) has vanished. What was once a separate point on the map has become a mere imperceptible thickening in a continuum of identical products and standardized spaces from coast to coast. One has the feeling that the autonomy of the small town, its complacent independence, also functioned as an allegorical expression for the situation of Eisenhower's America in the outside world as a whole—contented with itself, secure in the sense of its radical difference from other populations and cultures, insulated from their vicissitudes and from the flaws in human nature so palpably acted out in *their* violent and alien histories.

This is clearly, however, to shift from the realities of the 1950s to the representation of that rather different thing, the "fifties," a shift which obligates us in addition to underscore the cultural sources of all the attributes with which we have endowed the period, many of which seem very precisely to derive from its own television programs: in other words, its own representation of itself. However, although one does not confuse a person with what he or she thinks of himself or herself, such self-images are surely very relevant indeed and constitute an essential part of the more objective description or definition that one seeks. Nonetheless, it seems possible that the deeper realities of the period—read, for example, against the very different scale of, say, diachronic and secular economic rhythms, or of synchronic and systemic global interrelationships—have little to do with either our cultural stereotypes of years thus labeled and defined in terms of generational decades. The concept of "classicism," for example, has a precise and functional meaning in German cultural and literary history, which vanishes when we move to a European perspective in which those few key years disappear without a trace into the vaster opposition between Enlightenment and Romanticism. It is a speculation which presupposes the possibility that at an outer limit the sense people have of themselves and their own moment of history may ultimately have *nothing* whatsoever to do with its reality: that the existential may be absolutely distinct, as some ultimate "false consciousness," from the structural and social significance of a collective phenomenon; and this is surely a possibility rendered more plausible by the fact of global imperialism, in terms of which the meaning of a given nation-state—for everyone else on the globe—may be wildly at odds from their own inner experiences and their own interior daily life. Eisenhower wore a well-known smile for us, and an equally well-known scowl for foreigners beyond our borders, as dramatically attested by the state portraits in any United States consulate during those years.

There is an even more radical possibility: namely, that period concepts finally correspond to no realities whatsoever, and that whether they are formulated in terms of generational logic, or by the names of reigning monarchs, or according to some other category or typological and classificatory system, the collective reality of the multitudinous lives encompassed by such terms is nonthinkable (or nontotalizable, to use a current expression) and can never be described, characterized, labeled, or conceptualized. This is, I suppose, what one could call the Nietzschean position, for which there are no such things as "periods," nor have there ever been. In that case, of course, there is no such thing as "history" either, which was probably the basic philosophical point such arguments sought to make in the first place.

This is the moment to return to Dick's novel and to record the twist that turns it into Science Fiction: for it transpires, from an increasing accumulation of tiny but aberrant details, that the environment of the novel, in which we watch the characters act and move, is not really the fifties after all (I do not know that Dick ever uses this particular word). It is a Potemkin village of a historical kind: a reproduction of the fifties—including induced and introjected memories and character structures in its human population—constructed in 1997, in the midst of an interstellar atomic civil war, for reasons that need not detain us here. I will only note that a twofold determination plays across the main character, Ragle Gumm, who must thus be read according to a negative and a positive hermeneutic simultaneously. The village has been constructed in order to trick him, against his will, into performing an essential wartime task for the government: in that sense, he is the victim of a manipulation which awakens all our fantasies of mind control and unconscious exploitation, of anti-Cartesian predestination and determinism. On this reading, then, Dick's novel is a nightmare and the expression of deep unconscious collective fears about our social life and its tendencies.

Yet Dick also takes pains to make clear that the fifties village is also very specifically the result of infantile regression on the part of the protagonist, who has also in a sense unconsciously chosen his own delusion and has fled the anxieties of the Civil War for the domestic and reassuring comforts of his own childhood during the period in question. From this perspective, then, the novel is a collective wish fulfillment and the expression of a deep unconscious yearning for a simpler and more human social system, a small–town Utopia very much in the North American frontier tradition.

I should also note that the very structure of the novel articulates the position of Eisenhower's America in the world itself, and is thereby to be read as a kind of distorted form of cognitive mapping, an unconscious and figurative projection of some more "realistic" account of our situation, as it has been described earlier: the hometown reality of the United States surrounded by the implacable menace of world communism (and, in this period, to a much lesser degree, the menace of third world poverty). This is also, of course, the period of the classic Science Fiction films, with their more overtly ideological representations of external threats and impending alien invasions (also generally set in small towns). Dick's novel can be read in that way—the grimmer "reality" disclosed behind the benign and deceptive appearance—or it can be taken as a certain approach to self-consciousness about the representations themselves.

What is more significant from the present perspective is the paradigmatic value of Dick's novel for questions of history, representation, and historicity in general. One of the ways of thinking about the subgenre to which this novel belongs—that "category" called Science Fiction, which can be expanded and dignified by the addition of all the classical satiric and Utopian literature from Lucian on, or restricted and degraded to the pulp-and-adventure tradition—is as a historically new and original form which offers analogies with the emergence of the historical novel in the early nineteenth century. Lukács has interpreted this last as a formal innovation (by Sir Walter Scott) which provided figuration for the new and equally emergent sense of the history of the triumphant middle classes (or bourgeoisie) as that class sought to project its own vision of its past and its future, and to articulate its social and collective project in a temporal narrative distinct in form from those of earlier "subjects of history," such as the feudal nobility. In that form, the historical novel—and its related emanations, such as the costume film—has fallen into disrepute and infrequency, not merely because, in the postmodern age, we no longer tell ourselves our history in that fashion, but also because we no longer experience it that way, and, indeed, perhaps no longer experience it at all.

One would want, in short, to stress the conditions of possibility of such a form—and of its emergence and eclipse—less in the existential experience of history of people at this or that historical moment, than in the structure of their socioeconomic system, in its relative opacity or transparency, and the access its mechanisms provide to some greater cognitive as well as existential contact with the thing itself. This is the context in which it seems interesting to explore the hypothesis that Science Fiction as a genre entertains a dialectical and structural relationship with the historical novel, a relationship of kinship and inversion, all at once, of opposition and homology (just as comedy and tragedy have often been supposed to do, or lyric and epic, or satire and Utopia, as Robert C. Elliott analyzed them). And time plays a crucial role in this generic opposition, which is also something of an evolutionary compensation. For if the historical novel "corresponded" to the emergence of historicity, of a sense of history in its strong modern post-eighteenth-century sense, Science Fiction equally corresponds to the waning or the blockage of that historicity, and, particularly in our own time, in the postmodern era, to its crisis and paralysis, its enfeeblement and repression. Only by means of a violent formal and narrative dislocation could a narrative apparatus come into being capable of restoring life and feeling to this only intermittently functioning organ which is our capacity to organize and live time historically. Nor should it be thought that the two forms are symmetrical, insofar as the historical novel stages the past and Science Fiction the future.

Historicity is neither a representation of the past nor a representation of the future (although its various forms use such representations): it can first and foremost be defined as a perception of the present as history: that is, as a relationship to the present which somehow defamiliarizes it and allows us that distance from immediacy which we call historical. It is appropriate, in other words, to insist on the historicality of the process of representation, which is our way of conceiving of historicity in this particular society with its particular modes of production; appropriate also to observe that what is at stake is essentially a process of reification, whereby we draw back from our immersion in the here-and-now (not yet identified as a "present") and grasp it as a kind of thing—not merely a "present" but a present that can be dated and called the eighties or the fifties. My presupposition has been that today this is more difficult to achieve, that it is a more complicated operation than at the time of Sir Walter Scott, when a contemplation of the past seemed able to renew one's sense of one's present.

Time Out of Joint offers a very different machine for producing historicity than Sir Walter Scott's apparatus: what one might in the strong sense call a trope of the future anterior—the estrangement and renewal of our own reading present: the fifties as history by way of the apprehension of that present as the past of a specific future. The future, Dick's 1997, is not centrally significant as a representation or an anticipation; it is the narrative means to a very different end: namely, the brutal transformation of a realistic representation of the present, of Eisenhower America and the fifties small town, into a memory and a reconstruction. Reification is indeed built into the novel itself and, as it were, defused and recuperated as a form of praxis: the fifties is a thing, but a thing that we can build—just as the Science Fiction writer builds his own small-scale model. At that point, then, reification ceases to be a baleful and alienating process, a noxious side effect of our mode of production—if not, indeed, its fundamental dynamic—and is transferred to the side of human energies and human possibilities. (The reappropriation has, of course, a good deal to do with the specificity of Dick's own themes and ideology—in particular, the nostalgia about the past and the "petty bourgeois" valorization of small craftsmanship, as well as small business and collecting.)

This novel has, however, necessarily become a historical one: for its present—the fifties—has become our past in a rather different sense than that proposed by the text itself. The latter still "works": we can still feel and appreciate the transformation and reification of its readers' present into a historical period; we can even, by analogy, extrapolate something similar for our own moment in time. Whether such a process today can be realized concretely, in a cultural artifact, is a rather different question. The accumulation, indeed, of books like *Future Shock*, the incorporation of habits of "futurology" into our everyday lives, the modification of our perception of things to include their "tendency," and our reading of time to approximate a scanning of complex probabilities: this new relationship to our present includes elements formerly incorporated in the experience of the "future" even as it blocks or forestalls any global vision of the latter as a radically transformed and different system. If catastrophic "near future" visions of, say, overpopulation, famine, or anarchic violence are no longer as effective as they were a few years ago, the weakening of those effects and of the narrative forms that were designed to produce them is not necessarily due only to overfamiliarity and overexposure: it is perhaps also to be seen as a modification in our relationship to those imaginary near futures, which no longer strike us with the horror of otherness and of radical difference. Here a certain Nietzscheanism operates to defuse anxiety and even fear: the conviction—however gradually learned and acquired—that there is only the present and that it is always "ours" is a kind of wisdom that cuts both ways. For it was always clear that the terror of such near futures —like the analogous terror of an older naturalism—was class-based and deeply rooted in class comfort and privilege. The older naturalism let us briefly experience the life and the life-world of the various underclasses, only to return with relief to our own living rooms and armchairs: the good resolutions it may have encouraged were always, then, a form of philanthropy. In the same way, yesterday's terror of the overcrowded conurbations of the immediate future could just as easily be read as a pretext for complacency within our historical present, in which "we" do not yet have to live like that. In both cases, at any rate, the fear is that of proletarianization, of slipping down the ladder, of losing a comfort and a set of privileges which we tend increasingly to think of in spatial terms: privacy, empty rooms, silence, walling other people out, protection against crowds and other bodies. Nietzschean wisdom, then, tells us to let go of that kind of fear and reminds us that whatever social and spatial form our future misery may take, it will not be alien because it will by definition be ours: *Dasein ist je mein eigenes*. Defamiliarization, the shock of otherness, is a mere aesthetic effect and a lie.

Perhaps what is implied is simply an ultimate historicist breakdown, and that we can no longer imagine the future at all, under any form, Utopian as well as catastrophic. Under those circumstances, a formerly futurological Science Fiction (such as "cyberpunk" today) turns into mere "realism" and an outright representation of the present; the possibility Dick offered us of an experience of our present

as past and as history is slowly excluded. Yet everything in our culture suggests that we have not, for all that, ceased to be preoccupied
by history; indeed, at the very moment in which we complain of
the eclipse of historicity, we also universally diagnose contemporary
culture as irredeemably historicist, in the bad sense of an omnipresent and indiscriminate appetite for dead styles and fashions, indeed
for all the styles and fashions of a dead past. Meanwhile, a certain
caricature of historical thinking—which we may not even call *generational* any longer, so rapid is its momentum—has also become
universal, and includes at least the will and intent to return upon
our present circumstances in order to think them generationally (as
the "eighties") and to draw the appropriate marketing and forecast-
ing conclusions. Why is this not historicity with a vengeance? And
what is the difference between this now generalized approach to the
present and Dick's rather cumbersome and primitive laboratory approach to a "concept" of his own fifties?

The structure of the two operations is instructively different: the
one mobilizing a vision of the future in order to determine its return to a now historical present; the other mobilizing, but in some
new allegorical way, a vision of the past, or of a certain moment of
the past. Several recent films encourage us to see the newer process
in terms of an allegorical encounter; yet even this formal possibility
will not be properly grasped unless we set in place its preconditions
in the development of nostalgia film generally. For it is by way of
the so-called nostalgia film that some properly allegorical processing
of the past becomes possible, and it is because the formal apparatus of nostalgia films has trained us to consume the past in the form
of glossy images that new and more complex "post-nostalgia" state-
ments and forms become possible. I have elsewhere tried to identify
the privileged raw material or historical content of this operation of
reification, particularly the transformation into the filmic image of
the crucial antithesis between the twenties and the thirties, and the
historicist revival of the stylized expression of that antithesis in "art
deco."[1] The symbolic working out of that tension—between aristocracy and worker, as it were—evidently involves something like the
symbolic reinvention or production of a new bourgeoisie, a new form
of identity. Yet like photorealism, the products are as bland as they

are visually elegant, while the plot structures of such films suffer from a schematization (or typification) which seems to be inherent in the project. While we anticipate more of these films, since the taste for them corresponds to durable features and needs in our present economic-psychic constitution (image-fixation *cum* historicist cravings), it was perhaps only to be expected that some more complicated and interesting formal sequel would rapidly develop.

What was more unexpected—but very "dialectical" indeed, in a virtually orthodox textbook way—was the emergence of this new form from a kind of cross, if not synthesis, between the two filmic modes we had been imagining as antithetical: that is, the high elegance of nostalgia films on the one hand, and the grade-B simulations of iconoclastic punk film on the other. For one thing, both are significantly mortgaged to music, though the musical signifiers are rather different in the two cases—from sequences of high-class dance music to the contemporary proliferation of rock groups. Meanwhile, any "dialectical" textbook of the type of film already referred to might have alerted us to the probability that an ideologeme of "elegance" depends in some measure on an opposite of some kind, an opposite and a negation which seems in our time to have shed its class content (still feebly alive when the "beats" were felt to entertain a twin opposition to bourgeois respectability and high modernist aestheticism), and to have gradually migrated into that new complex of meanings that bears the name "punk."

Thus the new films, such as *Something Wild* or *Blue Velvet*, will first and foremost be allegories of their own coming into being as a synthesis of nostalgia-deco and punk: they will in one way or another tell their stories as the need and search for this "marriage" (the wonderful thing about aesthetics—unlike politics, alas—being that the "search" automatically becomes the thing itself: to set it up is by definition to realize it). Yet this resolution of an aesthetic contradiction is not gratuitous, since the formal contradiction itself has its socially and historically symbolic significance.

In *Something Wild* a young "organization man" is abducted by a crazy girl, who initiates him into cutting corners and skipping out without paying your bills, until her husband, an ex-convict, shows up and pursues the couple, bent on vengeance. In *Blue Velvet* a young high-school graduate discovers a severed ear, which puts him on the trail of a torch singer mysteriously victimized by a local drug dealer, from whom he is able to save her. Such films invite us to return somehow to history: the central scene of *Something Wild*—or at least the one on which the plot structure pivots decisively—is a class reunion, the kind of event which specifically demands historical judgments of its participants: narratives of historical trajectories, as well as evaluations of moments of the past nostalgically re-evoked but necessarily rejected or reaffirmed. This is the wedge or opening through which a hitherto aimless but lively filmic narrative suddenly falls into the deeper past (or that deeper past into it), for the ten-year reunion takes us back twenty more, when the "villain" unexpectedly emerges, over your shoulder, marked as "familiar" in all his unfamiliarity to the spectator (he is the heroine's husband, and worse). Ray represents, in part, yet another reworking of that boring and exhausted paradigm, the Gothic romance, in which—on the individualized level— a sheltered woman of some kind is terrorized and victimized by an "evil" male. But I think it would be a great mistake to read such literature as a kind of protofeminist denunciation of patriarchy and in particular a protopolitical protest against rape.

Certainly the Gothic mobilizes anxieties about rape, but its structure gives us the clue to a more central feature of its content which I have tried to underscore by means of the word "sheltered." The Gothic romance is ultimately a class fantasy (or nightmare) in which the dialectic of privilege and shelter is rehearsed: your privileges seal you off from other people, but by the same token constitute a protective wall through which you cannot see, and behind which, therefore, all kinds of envious forces may be imagined in the process of assembling, plotting, preparing to give assault. It is, if you like, the shower-curtain syndrome (from Hitchcock's *Psycho*), whose classic form turns on the privileged content of the situation of middle-class women—the isolation, but also the domestic idleness imposed on them by newer forms of middle-class marriage—and adds such texts, as symptoms, to the history of women's situations, but does not lend them any particular political significance (unless the significance consists merely in a coming to self-consciousness of the disadvantages of privilege in the first place). But the form can also, under certain circumstances, be reorganized around young men to whom some similarly protective distance is imputed: intellectuals, for example, or "sheltered" young briefcase-carrying bureaucrats, as in *Something Wild*. (That this gender substitution risks awakening all kinds of supplementary sexual overtones is here self-consciously dramatized in the extraordinary tableau moment in which the stabbing, seen from behind—and from the woman's visual perspective—looks like a passionate embrace between the two men.) The more substantive and formal leap comes when the individual "victim"—male or female—is replaced by the collectivity, the American public, which now lives out the anxieties of its economic privileges and its sheltered "exceptionalism" in a seemingly political version of the Gothic, under the threats of stereotypical madmen and "terrorists" (mostly Arabs or Palestinians for some reason). These collective fantasies are less to be explained by some increasing "feminization" of the American public self than by its guilt and the dynamics of comfort; like the private version of the traditional Gothic romance, they depend for their effects on the revitalization of *ethics* as a set of mental categories, and on the pumping up again and artificial reinvigoration of that tired and antiquated binary opposition between virtue and vice, which the eighteenth century cleansed of its theological remnants and thoroughly sexualized before passing it on down to us.

The modern Gothic, in other words—whether in its rape-victim or its political-paranoid forms—depends absolutely in its central operation on the construction of *evil* (forms of the good are notoriously more difficult to construct, and generally draw their light from the darker concept, as though the sun drew its reflected radiance from the moon). Evil is here, however, the emptiest form of sheer otherness (into which any type of social content can be poured at will). I have so often been taken to task for my arguments against ethics (in politics as well as in aesthetics) that it seems worth observing in passing that otherness is a very dangerous category, which we are well off without but fortunately, in literature and culture, it has also become a very tedious one (but then all of Stanislaw Lem's work—in particular the recent *Fiasco*—can be read as an argument against the use of such a category). Ridley Scott's *Alien* may still get away with it, but surely the Ray of *Something Wild* and the Frank Booth of *Blue*

Velvet don't scare anybody any longer; nor ought we really to require our flesh to creep before reaching a sober and political decision as to the people and forces who are really "evil" in our contemporary world.

On the other hand, it is only fair to say that Ray is not given us as a representation of evil as such, but rather as the representation of someone *playing at being evil*, which is a rather different matter. Nothing about Ray, indeed, is particularly authentic. His malevolence is as false as his smile. And his clothes and hairstyle give a further clue, point us in a different direction from the ethical one. For not only does Ray offer a simulation of evil, he also offers a simulation of the *fifties*, and that seems to me a far more significant matter: a simulation of the oppositional fifties, to be sure, the fifties of Elvis rather than the fifties of Ike—but can we really tell the difference anymore, given our historical gap and our nostalgia-tinted spectacles? In any event, it becomes clear, as the Gothic trappings of *Something Wild* fall away, that we have to do here with an essentially allegorical narrative in which the eighties meet the fifties. What kind of accounts actuality has to settle with this particular historical ghost (and whether it manages to do so) is for the moment less crucial than how the encounter was arranged in the first place: by the intermediary and of course, inadvertant good offices of the sixties.

Everything turns, therefore, on this distinction between the sixties and the fifties: the first desirable (like a fascinating woman), the second fearful, ominous, and untrustworthy (like the leader of a motorcycle gang). As the title suggests, it is the nature of "something wild" which is at stake, the inquiry into it focused by Audrey's first glimpse of Charley's nonconformist character (he skips out on his lunch bill). Indeed, the nonpaying of bills seems to function as the principal index for Charley's "hipness" or "squareness"—it being understood that neither of these categories (nor those of conformity/ nonconformity) corresponds to the logic of this film, which can be seen as an attempt very precisely to construct new categories in this area, to replace those older, historically dated and period-bound (uncontemporary, unpostmodern) ones. We may describe this particular "test" as involving white-collar crime (as opposed to "real" or lower-class crime, the grand theft and mayhem practiced by Ray), but it is petty-bourgeois white-collar crime (even Charley's illicit use of company credit cards is scarcely commensurable with the genuine criminality which the existence of his corporation can be expected, virtually by definition, to imply). But such class-markers are not explicitly present in the film, which can in another sense be seen very precisely as an effort to repress the language and categories of class and class differentiation and to substitute for them other kinds of semic oppositions that emerge in the framework of the Lulu (Audrey) character, within the sixties allegory (which is something like the "black box" of this particular semic transformation). If the fifties stands for genuine rebellion, with genuine violence and genuine consequences, it also stands for the *romantic representations* of such rebellion, in the films of Brando and James Dean. Ray thus functions as a kind of Gothic villain within this particular narrative, but also, on the allegorical level, as the sheer *idea* of the romantic hero, the tragic protagonist of another kind of film that can no longer be made. And unlike the heroine of *Desperately Seeking Susan*, Lulu is not an alternate possibility, an embodiment of rebellion and difference; the framework here remains exclusively male, as the lamentable ending—her chastening or taming—testifies, along with the significance of clothing, which we will look at in a moment. Everything depends on the new kind of *hero* Lulu somehow allows or enables Charley to become, by virtue of her own semic composition (since she is a good deal more than a mere woman's body or fetish).

What is interesting about that composition is that it first of all gives us the sixties seen through the fifties (or the eighties?): Lulu "does" alcohol rather than drugs. The schizophrenic, drug-cultural side of the sixties is systematically excluded along with its politics: what is dangerous, in other words, is not Lulu at her most frenzied, but Ray: not the sixties and its countercultures and "life-styles," but the fifties and its revolts. Yet the continuity between the fifties and the sixties lay in what was being revolted *against*, in what "life-style" the new "life-styles" were alternatives *to*. It is, however, difficult to find any content in Lulu's stimulating behavior, which seems organized around sheer caprice—that is to say, around the supreme value of remaining unpredictable and immune to reification and categorization: shades of André Gide (as in *Lafcadio's Adventures*), or of all

those Sartrean characters desperately attempting to evade that ultimate objectification by another's Look (it is impossible, and they end
up simply being labeled "capricious"). Lulu's costume changes lend
this otherwise purely formal unpredictability a certain visual content; they translate it into the language of image-culture and afford
a purely specular pleasure in Lulu's metamorphoses (which are not
really psychic).

Yet viewers as well as protagonists still have to feel they are on
their way somewhere (at least until the appearance of Ray gives the
film a different kind of direction): as thrilling and improvised as it
seems, therefore, Lulu's abduction of Charley from New York has at
least an empty form which will be instructive, for it is the archetypal descent into middle America, into the "real" USA—either of
lynching and bigotry, or of true wholesome family life and American
ideals, one doesn't quite know which. Nonetheless, like those Russian populist intellectuals in the nineteenth century setting forth on
foot to discover "the people," Lulu and Charley embark on a journey
that is or was the *scène à faire* for any American allegory worthy of
its vocation: what this one reveals, however, is that there is no longer
anything to discover at the end of the line. For Lulu/Audrey's family
—reduced in this case to a mother—is no longer the bourgeoisie of
sinister memory: there is neither the sexual repression and "respectability" of the fifties, nor the Johnsonian authoritarianism of the sixties. This mother plays the harpsichord, "understands" her daughter,
and is fully as much an oddball as everybody else. No oedipal revolts
are possible any longer in this American small town, and with them
the social and cultural dynamics of the periods in question. Yet if
there are no longer any "middle classes" to be found in the heartland,
there is something else which may serve as a substitute for them, at
least in the dynamic of narrative structure: for what we find at Lulu's
class reunion (besides Ray and her own past) is Charley's business
colleague, a yuppie bureaucrat, along with his pregnant wife. These
are then no doubt the baleful "parents," but of some distant and not
quite imaginable future, not of the older traditional American past:
they occupy the semic slot of the "squares," but no longer with any
social basis or content (they can scarcely be read as embodiments
of the Protestant ethic, for example, or of puritanism, or of white

racism, or of patriarchy). But they at least help us to identify the deeper ideological purpose of this film: to differentiate Charley from his fellow yuppies by making him over into a hero or protagonist of a different generic type than Ray. If unpredictability is a matter of *fashion* (clothing, hairstyle, and general body language), then Charley must pass through this particular matrix, and his metamorphosis is concretely realized, appropriately enough, when he sheds his suit for a more relaxed and tourist-type disguise (T-shirt, shorts, dark glasses, etc.). At the end of the film, of course, he also sheds his corporate job but it would probably be asking too much to wonder what he does or can become instead, except within the "relationship" with Lulu, where he moves from a passive, handcuffed position to that of the master and the senior partner. The semic organization of all this, therefore, might be laid out as follows (and symmetry preserved by seeing the pregnant and disapproving yuppie wife as the concrete manifestation of the neutral term):

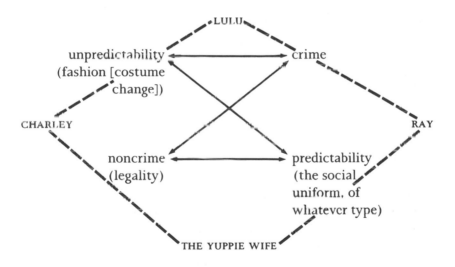

The mention of handcuffs brings me to *Blue Velvet*, another narrative allegory whose combinations and atmosphere are, however, very different from those in *Something Wild*. *Blue Velvet* tries to place sadomasochism squarely on the mass-cultural map with an earnestness altogether lacking in the Demme movie (whose handcuff love scene is as sexy as it is frivolous). Indeed, sadomasochism has become the latest and the last in a long line of taboo forms of content which, beginning with Nabokov's nymphets in the fifties, rise one after the other to the surface of public art in that successive and even progressive widening of transgressions which we once called the counterculture, or the sixties. In *Blue Velvet*, however, it is explicitly related to drugs, and therefore to crime—although not exactly to organized crime, but to a collectivity of misfits and oddballs; and the transgressive nature of this complex of "rebellions" is rather tediously reinforced by repetitive obscenity on the part of the Dennis Hopper character, Frank.

If history is discreetly evoked and invoked in *Something Wild*, it is its opposite—nature—which is given us as the overall frame and inhuman, transhuman perspective in which to contemplate the events of *Blue Velvet*: for the father's stroke, which opens the film—an incomprehensible catastrophe, an act of God which is peculiarly an act of scandalous violence within this peaceful American small town— is positioned by David Lynch (also director of *Eraserhead*) within the more Science Fictional horizon of the Darwinian violence of all nature. From the shot of the father lying paralyzed, the camera withdraws into the bushes surrounding the house, enlarging its microscopic focus as it does so, until we confront a horrible churning, which we take first and generically in good horror-film format to indicate the hidden presence of the maniac, but which proves to be the mandibles of an insatiable insect. The later insistence on robins with worms twisting desperately in their beaks also reinforces this cosmic sense of the dizzying and nauseating violence of all nature —as though within this ferocity without boundaries, this ceaseless bloodshed of the universe as far as the eye can see or thought can reach, a single peaceful oasis had been conquered by the progress of humanity and whatever divine providence guided it. Unique in the animal kingdom as well as in the horrors of human history is the North American small town. Into this precious and fragile conquest of civilized decorum wrenched from a menacing outside world, then, comes violence: in the form of a severed ear, in the form of an underground drug culture, and of a sadomasochism about which it is finally not yet really clear whether it is a pleasure or a duty, a matter of sexual gratification or just another expression of violence.

History therefore enters *Blue Velvet* in the form of ideology if not of myth: the garden and the fall, American exceptionalism, a small town far more lovingly preserved in its details (like a simulacrum of Disneyland under glass somewhere) than anything the protagonists of *Something Wild* were able to locate on their travels. *Blue Velvet* is complete with high-school leads on the order of the most authentic fifties movies; even a fifties-style pop psychoanalysis can be invoked around this fairy tale, since besides a mythic and sociobiological perspective on the violence of nature, the film's events are framed by the crisis in the paternal function—the stroke that suspends paternal power and authority in the opening sequence, the recovery of the father and his return from the hospital in the idyllic final scene. That the other father is the police detective lends a certain plausibility to this kind of interpretation, which is strengthened by the abduction and torture of the third, absent father, of whom we only see the ear. Nonetheless the message is not especially patriarchal-authoritarian, particularly since the teenage boy manages to assume the paternal function very handily: rather, this call for a return to the fifties coats the pill by insistence on the unobtrusive benevolence of all these fathers, and on the unalloyed nastiness of their opposite number.

For this particular Gothic subverts itself fully as much as *Something Wild*, but in a rather different way In *Something Wild* the simulated nature of Ray's evil which was underscored for us even while he remained a real threat—revolt, statutory illegality, physical violence, ex-convicts—these are genuine and serious matters. What *Blue Velvet* gives us to understand about the sixties, in contrast, is that despite the grotesque and horrendous tableaux of maimed bodies, this kind of evil is more distasteful than it is fearful, more disgusting than threatening: here evil has finally become an image, and the simulated replay of the fifties has generalized itself into a whole simulacrum in its own right. Now the boy without fear of the fairy tale can set out to undo this world of baleful enchantment, free its princess (while marrying another), and kill the magician. The lesson implied by all this—which is rather different from the lesson transmitted by it— is that it is better to fight drugs by portraying them as vicious and silly than by awakening the full tonal range of ethical judgments and indignations and thereby endowing them with the otherwise glamorous prestige of genuine evil, of the transgressive in its most august religious majesty. Indeed, this particular parable of the end of the fifties is also, on another metacritical level, a parable of the end of theories of transgression, which so fascinated that whole period and its intellectuals. The sadomasochistic materials, then—even though contemporary with a new postmodern punk scene—are finally called on to undo themselves, and to abolish the very logic on which their attraction/repulsion was based in the first place.

These films, therefore, can be read as dual symptoms: they show a collective unconscious in the process of trying to identify its own present at the same time that they illuminate the failure of this attempt, which seems to reduce itself to the recombination of various stereotypes of the past. Perhaps, indeed, what follows upon a strongly generational self-consciousness, such as what the "people of the sixties" felt, is often a peculiar aimlessness. What if the crucial identifying feature of the next "decade" is, for example, a lack of just such strong self-consciousness, which is to say a constitutive lack of identity in the first place? This is what many of us felt about the seventies, whose specificity seemed most of the time to consist in having no specificity, particularly after the uniqueness of the preceding period. Things began to pick up again in the eighties, no doubt, and in a variety of ways: but the identity process is not a cyclical one, and this is essentially the dilemma. Of the eighties, as against the seventies, one could say that there were new political straws in the wind, that things were moving again, that some impossible "return of the sixties" seemed to be in the air and in the ground. But the eighties, politically and otherwise, have not really resembled the sixties, especially if one defines them as a return or a reversion. Even that enabling costume-party self-deception of which Marx spoke, the wearing of the costumes of the great moments of the past, is no longer on the cards in an ahistorical period of history. The generational *combinatoire* thus seems to have broken down at the moment it confronted serious historicity, and the rather different self-concept of "postmodernism" has taken its place.

Dick used Science Fiction to see his present as (past) history; the classical nostalgia film, while evading its present altogether, registered its historicist deficiency by losing itself in mesmerized fascination with lavish images of specific generational pasts. The two current hits, while scarcely pioneering a wholly new form (or mode of historicity), nonetheless seem, in their allegorical complexity, to mark the end of that and the now open space for something else.

Notes

1 For more on this hypothesis, see my forthcoming *Messages of the Visible* (Routledge and Chapman, Hall, 1989).

Reading Dynasty: Television

and Reception Theory

Jane Feuer

★ ★ ★ ★ ★ ★ By the time literary studies had rediscovered the reader, the field of mass communication—conceived as a form of empirical social science—was just beginning to admit that texts existed apart from immediate behavioral effects on audiences.[1] Thus there had never been a formalist moment in television studies; mass communication researchers were only too happy to consider audiences as their primary focus. I mention this history because I am about to belabor two points regarding the television text that make it very different from literary and even filmic texts: first, the problem of defining the work itself, and second, the problem of defining the text as activated by the reader. This emphasis on the process of constructing a text from a work (or in this case, a text from a program) is central to any kind of reader-response criticism. In the case of television studies, it also provides an antidote to the prevailing view that the text could easily be subsumed into the behavior or the individualistic psychology of empirical audiences. For television, then, the question

Joan Collins, John Forsythe, and Linda Evans in *Dynasty*. © 1991 Capital Cities/ABC, Inc. Reproduced by permission.

of the very constitution of the text becomes an issue in a way it does not even for popular literature and film.

In their work on the James Bond phenomenon, Tony Bennett and Janet Woollacott have had to adapt reception theory to the exigencies of popular literature and film.[2] Bennett's concepts are based on the example of the James Bond novels and hero, and his concern is a diachronic one: he is interested in the shifting relations of reading over time, and the longevity of the Bond phenomenon allows him to pursue that interest. But other texts extend Bennett's sort of analysis. For a moment in the mid-1980s the television serial *Dynasty* ceased being merely a program and took on the proportions of a major mass-cultural cult. *Dynasty*'s moment of notoriety was intense but brief; indeed in the time between my first version of this paper and the present one, that moment has already passed. In the case of *Dynasty*, then, at least today, the synchronic dimension is the more compelling, and the question becomes how the text is "activated" across different contemporary "reading formations."[3]

How, in other words, do we separate the text from its contemporary "incrustations": the fan magazines, the ads, the product tie-ins, the books, the myriad publicity articles, the fashions, etc.? Indeed, is it even possible to separate the text from its own commercials, many of which reproduce the mise-en-scène of the program and two of which make direct intertextual references to the program? What should be included in defining *Dynasty* as a work, a program? How many episodes need one view to say that one has "seen *Dynasty*"? How are we to constitute the "text of *Dynasty*" that forms the ostensible subject of this paper? According to traditional notions which assume that a text has a determinate meaning, these questions would be easy to answer. We would say that the text *Dynasty* refers to a weekly prime-time serial drama which is empirically present by virtue of broadcasting. Yet even this conventional literary definition would create some problems when used to refer to television. For instance, does the term *Dynasty* refer to a particular broadcast, to a season of the continuing drama, or to the entirety of its televisual existence? Does it include all those "interruptions" of the diegesis in the form of commercials, promos, newsbreaks? If so, are we to interpret the interruptions as crucial to the meaning of the text or as independent of that meaning but important to the formal operation of the multiple-plot structure? Is the text *Dynasty* the same text when broadcast as when videotaped?

These difficulties could presumably be resolved without questioning the status of the text. It would simply be a matter of defining the prime-time serial as a particular kind of text which differs in significant ways from literary or filmic texts. (In fact there has already been a great deal of work in this area.) This text would be said to exist independently of the reading subject, although we could allow for different interpretations of it. Even so, some of those interpretations would be seen as more accurate than others, as validated by their ability to recover the text's meaning. This meaning, in turn, would be posited as either the author's intention or the text's signification or some other form of meaning seen to adhere to the text's signification. Thus, some readings of the text would be viewed as "inaccurate" or as "misreadings" even for those theorists of determinacy who allow for multiple readings. And in the case of a television program that became a mass-culture cult, these issues become even more complex.

Let me begin with a text, bracketing for now its relationship to a presumed "text of *Dynasty*":

> *Dynasty* Night parties have started to spring up all over the country in night clubs and supper houses. When I was in Hawaii in April, I found a club which built its entire Wednesday night around the show, even though *Dynasty* is seen a week behind the mainland's showing. And in Los Angeles, one such club shows first the previous week's episode, and then the current episode. The marked difference is the fact that the audience is very vocal about the proceedings. Every time ALI MACGRAW (Ashley) came on the screen she would be hissed like a villain, which she is, of course, not. JOAN COLLINS (Alexis) is received with cheers, not only when she appears in the opening credits, but every time she appears in a new NOLAN MILLER creation. LINDA EVANS (Krystle) is mildly received, but her dark-haired character, friend of Sammy

Jo (HEATHER LOCKLEAR) is literally laughed at. The clientele is mostly male and at times the dialogue is difficult to hear because of remarks, often very funny, made about what is happening on the two giant screens.[4]

From a traditional literary standpoint, our text at hand (from *Soap Opera Digest*) does not belong to the text of *Dynasty*, but instead represents a metatext, a critical commentary—at however vulgar a level —on the text of *Dynasty*. According to Tony Bennett, the traditional critic would attempt to study a popular fiction such as a James Bond novel by means of textual analysis and then regard other texts—reviews, interviews, "fan mags," fashion systems, commodity designs —as "supplementary evidence to be cited in support of the analysis of the 'primary' texts."[5] In this way the fan mag item might be viewed as an example of a particular type of misreading of the text of *Dynasty*. Bennett, on the other hand, refers to texts such as fan mags as "hermeneutic activators," popular readings of popular texts located within critical apparatuses such as the star system or interviews. These are "hermeneutic systems that pin down the meaning of popular texts in particular ways, thus fixing the ideological coordinates within which they are to be read."[6] This would seem to indicate that the quoted item was offered as a commentary on the text. However, Bennett also says that taking account of what Pierre Macherey has called the "incrustations" that build up around a text involves the recognition that "except as a methodological fiction, the text does not have any existence that is separable from such incrustations; as a consequence, to study the connection between literary phenomena and social processes requires that everything that has been said or written about a text, every context in which it has been inscribed, should, in principle, be regarded as relevant to and assigned methodological parity within such a study."[7] Although by "incrustations" Bennett is referring to those contexts in which the text has been inscribed, the uses to which it has been put and the interpretations to which it has been subject, in the case of *Dynasty* it is arguable that the "hermeneutic activators" themselves constitute part of the text of *Dynasty*.[8]

The text from *Soap Opera Digest* thus possesses an overdetermined relationship to the text of *Dynasty*: it represents a report on *Dynasty* as an event while at the same time belonging to the *Dynasty* event. It also represents an interpretation of *Dynasty* from within a popular critical apparatus. Our critic (the esteemed Tony Rizzo) appears to be a disciple of E. D. Hirsch in his slavish adherence to the idea of textual determinacy. Therefore he is not a very astute analyst of the fascinating and complex phenomenon of reading on which he reports in *Soap Opera Digest*. His reading assumes a morally stable reading formation implied by traditional conceptions of melodrama. It also assumes that the critic's own reading of the program (that is, his attribution of good and evil labels to the characters) is a correct reading of the text, against which the reading by a very different interpretive community (that is, as his subtext implies, the gay male community) is seen as aberrant, or, at the very least, a distortion of the true meaning of the text. Rizzo appears puzzled that two of the "good" characters are greeted with laughter, while the villainess of the melodrama (and her wardrobe) is greeted with cheers. But of course this reading disregards the nature of a "camp" decoding which is usually an oppositional one if only because it is made from a social position outside of dominant social values. Here the criteria being applied are not moral but aesthetic. Lady Ashley is not an evil character; Ali MacGraw is a terrible actress. And not just a regular "bad actress"—for everyone on *Dynasty* is that—but a bad *camp* actress. By looking at the entire reading formation, rather than centering on a reading of a text, this becomes obvious. Yet even to say that we need to look at a camp decoding on the part of the gay community is to assume that there is a preferred reading for which this one would be oppositional. *Dynasty* teaches us that this is not true. For the camp decoding is also a preferred reading of the text. According to one critic, "*Dynasty* represents something extraordinary: the incursion of so-called gay taste into the mainstream of American Culture."[9] Camp is not a property of a text, but exists in the nature of the activations; however, not just any text can be camped, and *Dynasty* certainly facilitates the process. If there were ever a moment prior to the camp activations by the mainstream, that moment preceded *Dynasty*'s popularity. Very early on, its producers were aware of camp decodings and intended to encode them in the text by devising "outrageous plots" and "walk[ing] a fine line, just this side of camp."[10] So the concept of a preferred reading is called into question by a text for which the model reader is also already an "aberrant" decoder, since the camp decoding may be said to be one that is also "preferred" by the text.

It is perhaps a logical consequence of reception theory that I am discussing a text from *Soap Opera Digest* rather than *Dynasty* "itself," whatever that may be. In fact, in practice it is often very difficult to distinguish between text and metatext, particularly in those cases where textuality is "fully penetrated by capital." Historians of advertising and of the soap opera have emphasized the idea of the "interwoven commercial." According to Roland Marchand, the advertising community initially believed that the radio audience would not accept direct advertising, since it would represent an intrusion into the family circle. It was felt that advertising which was interwoven into the very fabric of the program would appear more subtle and thus less jarring to the sensibilities of the listener.[11] Robert Allen has shown the extent to which radio soap operas diegetically interwove advertising and programming.[12] Although for many years the United States networks moved away from these practices, they are now returning to them because advertisers fear the dreaded postmodern practice of "zapping"—rapidly changing channels whenever an ad appears. Thus on MTV the commercials are often virtually indistinguishable from the videos.

Dynasty, as a fully commodified text, also returns us to these practices. Many of the ads, particularly those directly following a program segment, are for perfume and other cosmetic products; they reproduce the opulent mise-en-scène of the Carrington mansion and Alexis's postmodern penthouse. But two ads in particular relate directly to the program "text." These are usually shown between the end of the episode and the previews, and they feature Krystle Carrington herself—or is it Linda Evans? We're not sure. The ads for Ultress and Forever Krystle are so closely linked to the mise-en-scène and narrative of the parent program that only a knowledge of the conventions of television flow permit us to distinguish them. And indeed the placement of these ads relies upon the continuity provided by flow in order to erase the boundaries of the different program segments. According to the different conceptions of "text" and "metatext" I have suggested, we can read these ads either as diegetic continuity or as hermeneutic activators (metacommentaries). As part of the text of *Dynasty*, the ads for Ultress and Forever Krystle are easily read diegetically. The perfume ad merely continues the development of the perfect relationship between Blake and Krystle, the "love that lasts forever." Although there is no discontinuity in the mise-en-scène or characters, on some weeks when the ad concludes the program, viewers particularly intent on constructing an Aristotelian narrative out of *Dynasty* might be disturbed at the quick reconciliation between the two (when, say, they have been about to get divorced in the program). However, for the regular viewer such narrative discontinuity is normative. We know that the vissicitudes of the Carringtons' marriage do not correspond to the real-world logic of the progressive deterioration of a relationship, and that abrupt changes from eternal devotion to divorce are typical of *Dynasty*'s plot construction. The producers' barometer registers viewer dissatisfaction immediately; for example, when *Dynasty*'s rating dropped from the top of the charts to number fifteen in December 1985, two of the offending plot lines were immediately truncated. According to *TV Guide*, "ABC officials reportedly asked Esther Shapiro . . . to go on the air with a public apology for inflicting on America the Moldavia plot and the two Krystles." [13]

In this way the narrative of *Dynasty* responds not to the moral imperatives of the outside world nor to the plausibility of the plot, but rather to fluctuations in the creator's readings of a presumably fickle audience. It does not seem unusual, then, that Blake and Krystle should abruptly reconcile and then reward each other by having fragrances created especially for each other. The Ultress commercials (we now have three versions) are a little harder to incorporate. But a diegetic reading of the earliest one might go as follows: To be sure, there is Krystle, walking down the sweeping staircase of a somewhat bourgeoisified version of the Carrington mansion (perhaps she is visiting), talking to us about her hair, and caressing the hair of various other women at the gathering. But who is the strange gentleman whose arm Krystle takes at the end of her stroll? And where is Blake? Even these questions may accommodate themselves to the typical discontinuities of the text. Perhaps another Daniel Reese has appeared on the scene? Will Krystle finally cheat on her husband? Does this account for the bounce in her walk and the shine in her hair?

The sober-minded among us might intervene here to make the point that of course no one actually activates this type of cross-diegetic reading, even though reader response criticism would say that it's a possible reading. We all know the difference between the program and the ads, between narrative and the rhetoric of commodification. Perhaps, at least, at a literal level. But these boundaries are by no means discrete when it comes to activating *Dynasty* as a mass cultural event. Indeed one may want to argue that the Ultress ads are the text for which the program segments become a prop.

Contemporary literary interpretive communities differ greatly from those for mass-mediated culture in the sense that their raison d'être is reading. They are, that is to say, groups of professional interpreters, whereas television reception theorists have always assumed that popular audiences are always already socially constituted. As Bennett and Woollacott put it, the "inter-textually" constituted reader meets the "inter-textually" constituted text.[14] This formulation has very different consequences than does the literary notion of the interpretive community popularized by Stanley Fish. Fish has been criticized from within literary studies for failing to recognize that "interpretive communities are bound to be communities on other grounds as well, bound to have common interests besides the production of interpretations, bound to correspond to other social differentiations."[15] This critique is even more valid when discussing interpretive communities for television programs.

In literary reception theory, the notion of the reader activating the text has to do with cognitive processes rather than any kind of motor activity. But when the reader activates *Dynasty*, the text becomes an event and even, in some cases, a way of life. As we have seen in the interwoven commercials, the Carrington life-style is offered as something to be achieved rather than merely something to be interpreted. Although I cannot think of a single instance in which I was encouraged to *smell* a literary text, advertising for Forever Krystle and Carrington offer up the odor of great romance in a quite literal way by including "scent strips" with the ad. When the product insert exhorts me "to experience the love that lives forever. . . . Rub center-fold along your pulse points," the gap between fantasy and fulfillment appears narrow indeed. *Dynasty*-as-event provides the perfect example of the pleasure to be obtained from being commodified.

Dynasty's becoming an event was not entirely imposed from above; there is a great deal of evidence to consider it a type of subcultural appropriation of a text, the difference being that in this case the subcultural group *was* the so-called mass audience. In fact, a study of the various activations of *Dynasty* makes clear the idea that the process of commodification is an interactive one, neither entirely spontaneously generated from below nor imposed from above, but a dialectical interplay of each. The passage from *Soap Opera Digest* describes an actual subcultural activation in its portrayal of camp decodings.[16] It is important to stress that the camp attitude toward *Dynasty* in both gay and mainstream culture does not preclude emotional identification; rather, it embraces both identification and parody—attitudes normally viewed as mutually exclusive—at the same time and as part of the same sensibility. As Richard Dyer has written, the gay sensibility "holds together qualities that are elsewhere felt as antithetical: theatricality and authenticity . . . intensity and irony, a fierce assertion of extreme feeling with a deprecating sense of its absurdity."[17]

On the evening of the fall 1985 season premiere that would reveal the outcome of the previous season's cliff-hanger (the Moldavian massacre), the lead story on the ABC-affiliate evening news in my local market concerned the way in which local citizens had gathered to celebrate this event. Nothing illustrates the camp sensibility toward *Dynasty* better than the news clip reporting on these "*Dynasty* parties." The camp attitude is apparent both in the style of the report and in its content. On the one hand, the *Dynasty* craze is taken seriously enough to justify its being the lead story on the eleven o'clock news; on the other hand, the station has to indicate that they do not really take the phenomenon seriously. In this way both the fans and the reporter are camping: the reporter through a tongue-in-cheek tone; the fans through their energetic but inevitably failed attempts to provide a simulacrum of the Carrington's life-style.

Over shots of fans arriving at the Hyatt Hotel in evening clothes, the *Dynasty* theme is playing. But something is not quite right. The evening clothes are makeshift and one young man is sipping champagne in a crew neck sweater. The narration is ironic: "They came looking as dashing as Blake Carrington, as daring as Alexis and everyone seemed to enjoy playing their chosen roles." When the reporter switches to another *Dynasty* party—this time at a singles bar—the revelers seem to be camping for the cameras: a young woman with a rhinestone tiara and long white gloves toasts us self-consciously. Perhaps the most ironic costume is that of another young woman masquerading in camouflage as a Moldavian terrorist and bearing plastic arms. These fans are willing to go to extremes, yet they are unwilling to admit to the cameras that they are intensely emotionally involved—whether in the program itself or in the camp event. And their attitude is remarkably similar to that of the audience in Hawaii. All are especially scornful toward Ali MacGraw (Lady Ashley). As one fan tells the reporter, "the big news is that Lady Ashley is dead, Ali MacGraw no more." And an older woman reports that "every kid in the office chose Lady Ashley to die." When, at the end of the report the reporter does a sarcastic yet detailed stand-up on the outcome of the Moldavian massacre, the circuit of camp simulation is completed.

The desire to simulate the world of the Carringtons is both a product of and an influence upon the show's producers. As a 1985 *Cosmopolitan* article explains, "appearances are important because if there is any single component that separates *Dynasty* from the rest of television, it is what everyone associated with the show—from executive producer Aaron Spelling on down—refers to as the look." [18] The article goes on to describe—as do so many other reports in the popular press during this period—the extreme care the producers of *Dynasty* take with its "look": they worry about the jewelry matching, the colors of the clothes matching the mood, even the manner in which the dinner table settings are photographed (in detail, with close-ups). As the article points out, "a huge cult following has developed around [Alexis's] gustatory habits. Interest is so great that several newspapers have been running contests for fans to guess what she'll put in her mouth next." Every detail is authentic: when Blake presented Krystle with a Rolls-Royce Corniche, the scene had to be reshot because the keys he handed her weren't standard Rolls keys.

Not only was *Dynasty* the only television program to have a resident fashion designer, it was the only program which thrust its costume designer into stardom. It is no accident that in the Tony Rizzo *Soap Opera Digest* column quoted earlier, the name of designer Nolan Miller figures as prominently as that of the show's major stars. In 1984 *Dynasty* had a costume budget of $25,000 per episode with $100,000 allocated for the royal wedding that closed the season. According to the *Wall Street Journal*, Nolan Miller received over one hundred fan letters weekly in 1984. No star could have a more devoted following, as evidenced by the following testimonial: "your designs and styles overwhelm me, sometimes they actually take my breath away. . . . I usually miss each scene's first lines because I'm too busy studying each outfit." [19]

When Nolan Miller appeared on the *Phil Donahue Show* with his collection of ready-to-wear garments based on the show, each outfit was greeted by near-delirious applause. He played the role of *auteur* to the hilt: "I'm responsible for *everything*." Since, as many commentators have pointed out, the program served as an hour-long commercial for the clothes, it was only a matter of time before a desire to possess the material objects of the Carrington life-style would emerge in the audience. Whereas the homemade simulacra exhibited at *Dynasty* parties could not profit the show's producers directly, the potential for mass-produced products based upon the show might satisfy both voracious fans and the needs of capital. Hence was born the *Dynasty* collection whose products include lingerie, hosiery, shoes, blouses, suits, linens, sheets, china, glassware, perfume, tuxedos, and even Alexis and Krystle porcelain dolls in Nolan Miller fashions (real mink stoles, real diamond necklaces) retailing for $10,000 apiece.[20] Previous programs had licensed commercial products tied in to their narratives, but the *Dynasty* collection would be the first upscale product licensing geared to an adult public. *Dynasty*'s producers and their equivalents at 20th Century-Fox Licensing Corporation made endless claims that the *Dynasty* collection emerged in response to spontaneous audience requests for copies of the Carringtons' goods. *Dynasty* co-creator Esther Shapiro says, "People seem fascinated with the trappings. After one episode . . . we got 4,500 requests from women who wanted to know where to buy Joan Collins's suit."[21]

According to Chuck Ashman, president of 20th Century-Fox Licensing Corporation, "The idea for tie-ins came from those fanatical fans. The mail that comes in is as often directed to a dress as much as it is to a star." Esther Shapiro says that she realized "people want to be part of it all, so it just seemed logical that we extend to merchandising."[22] The licensing corporation had reason to believe that *Dynasty* would be the perfect vehicle. Its demographics were superb—the number-one rated show among women of all ages. "In one informal survey 29 of 30 women stopped on Seventh Avenue admitted an addiction to the show—and confessed that they watched it largely for the clothes."[23] Not surprisingly, when the *Dynasty* collection premiered at Bloomingdale's, over twenty thousand fans packed the store in order to view not just the collection but also some of the show's stars who were there for the event. "We have not had such excitement in Bloomingdale's since the Queen of England visited in 1976," remarked Chairman Marvin Traub. The *New York Times* goes on to describe one of the fans present: "She was wearing a blue T-shirt with '*Dynasty* addict' spelled out in rhinestones."[24]

According to hypodermic or effects theories, the *Dynasty* merchandising campaign could not fail. And yet, although some of the less expensive products such as the perfumes were financial successes, it would appear that most of the collection did indeed fail to attract the fans. In 1986, the big-ticket items were taken off the market.[25] Apparently, *Dynasty*'s mass audience had the power to desire the items but not to purchase them. The ultimate financial failure of the *Dynasty* collection raises interesting questions for a reception aesthetics which acknowledges the commodified nature of mass cultural decodings but which does not construct a binary opposition between commodification and subcultural activation.

Given all of this, in what sense do we want to call these activations of *Dynasty* "readings" in the literary sense? When we speak of a reading or interpretation of a literary text, we usually assume that we are referring to an attribution of meaning at a somewhat high level of abstraction—telling what the text means. Reader-response theorists have taught us that there exists a far more basic sense of reading consisting of the attribution of meaning to the actual words on the page. But does even this basic level of meaning attribution occur when, in the "Nolan Miller" reading of *Dynasty*, viewers watch to see the clothes? And what kind of interpretive act is signified by attempts to replicate the material signifiers of the Carringtons in the lives of the audience? Indeed the audience activation of *Dynasty* through ritualized events may represent a refusal of meaning attribution as a positive act and thus could be labeled "postmodern" in Baudrillard's sense. When Baudrillard speaks of the masses in relationship to meaning, he could be describing what the masses do with *Dynasty* (in a postmodern sense as opposed to one derived from subcultural theory):

> Thus, in the case of the media, traditional resistance consists of reinterpreting messages according to the group's own code and for its own ends. The masses, on the contrary, accept everything and redirect everything *en bloc* into the spectacular, without requiring any other code, without requiring any meaning, ultimately without resistance, but making everything slide into an indeterminate sphere which is not even that of non-sense, but that of overall manipulation/fascination.[26]

The activations of *Dynasty* could also be called postmodern in another sense, having to do with the relationship between the program and its simulators. The homemade Nolan Miller gowns, like the commodified ones, might be considered a form of pastiche, what Fredric Jameson considers to be the postmodern form of parody. According to Jameson, pastiche is "blank parody" in an age when personal style is no longer there to be imitated; hence it lacks the satirical or critical edge of modernist parody. It simply mimics the preexisting form.[27] In its use of pastiche, then, the *Dynasty* reading formation is working within the postmodern era and in a postmodern style.

But ultimately neither of these senses of the postmodern captures the double-edged quality of Dyer's definition of the camp sensibility in which blank mimicry and a critical edge may coexist. That is to say, we are observing both subcultural appropriation and post-modern pastiche at the same time and from within the same sensi-bility. It is this double-edged quality, according to Linda Hutcheon, that distinguishes postmodern parody.[28] Arguing against Jameson, she proposes that postmodern architecture is a contradictory enterprise when viewed from the perspective of its actual praxis. And parody, she believes, is one of its primary weapons if we define parody as "repetition with critical distance that allows ironic signaling of dif-ference at the very heart of similarity." In postmodern architecture, parody occurs from an inside position, and it is combined with a kind of historical reverence. Hutcheon quotes Charles Jencks's com-ment that the Venturis's desire to learn from Las Vegas expresses "a mixed appreciation for the American Way of Life. Grudging respect, not total acceptance. They don't share all the values of a consumer society, but they want to speak to this society, even if partially in dissent." Hutcheon's description of postmodern parody as setting up "a dialectical relationship between identification and distance" pre-figures my discussion of the camp sensibility toward *Dynasty*.[29]

In the case of *Dynasty*, however, the parodic attitude is found *in* the mass culture; it does not require an avant-garde sensibility to make a postmodern parody of *Dynasty*. The mini-series *Fresno* exem-plifies such a mass-cultural parody—only our knowledge that *Fresno* was supposed to be a satire distinguishes it from its models, *Dallas*, *Dynasty*, and *Falcon Crest*. The double-edged attitudes toward *Dy-nasty* cited here make avant-garde activations of the text almost su-perfluous, as in the example of Joan Braderman's *Joan Does Dynasty* (1986), a clever work of video art that reproduces what the mass audience already "did" with *Dynasty*. Braderman quite literally in-serts her body into scenes from the program, all the while delivering a running ironic commentary expressing her ambivalence toward *Dy-nasty*. Her camp activation is certainly postmodern, but no more so than wearing a blue T-shirt with "*Dynasty* addict" spelled out in rhinestones.

Of course we can also locate more traditional interpretations of *Dy-nasty* both in popular critical apparatuses and in more academic publications. These I call "ideological readings" because although they do attempt to spell out what *Dynasty* means, it's always in terms of the political zeitgeist of the era, and never in terms of any kind of immanent meaning. Several writers have remarked upon the similarities between the Carringtons and the Reagans, noting that *Dynasty* began broadcasting during the first Reagan inaugural in 1981. Historian Debora Silverman is interested in *Dynasty* because the show seems to support her claim that Diana Vreeland's exhibits at both the Metropolitan Museum and Bloomingdale's typify the aristocratic ideology of the 1980s. She notes "a mutually reinforcing connection between popular opulent fashion and the dual roles of White House Nancy Reagan on the one hand and the television fantasy of *Dynasty*'s Krystle Carrington on the other." She concludes that Reagan's remarkable success is dependent upon tapping "*Dynasty* themes in ordinary Americans' imaginations."[30] And in "The Season of the Reagan Rich," Michael Pollan takes this argument further by arguing that TV shows about rich people have thrived in the Reagan era precisely because the imagery of the Reagans and their TV analogues are mutually reinforcing ideologically:

> Like the millionaires who propelled Ronald Reagan into politics—Charles Z. Wick, Justin Dart, the late Alfred Bloomingdale—the rich of prime time are all self-made men who accumulated vast fortunes in the West. As Washington society noted sourly on its arrival, the Reagan crowd is hopelessly *nouveau riche*, deficient in the graces and decorum that distinguishes the older families of the East. . . . Television's rich and the Reagan rich also share something more insidious—their nostalgic fantasy of wealth in America. . . . [B]oth imply that the American dream of self-made success is alive and might be made well by releasing the frontier instincts of the wealthy from the twin shackles of taxes and regulation.[31]

Arguably, there is a link between the postmodern readings and the ideological ones, since the ideological readings are presumably *interpreting* the postmodern activations. Silverman's agenda appears to be to "read" the reading formation of Reaganite cultural politics which in turn have produced the shallow, aristocratic postmodern activations in the mass culture. This is not what she achieves, however, because she does not understand the subcultural aspects of the post-modern readings. The danger of an ideological reading is that it will proceed directly from thin description to condemnation. As Janice Radway has shown, it is only by seeing from the perspective of those inside a reading formation that the true complexity of popular reading can be understood.[32] The ideological critics are attempting to fix *Dynasty*'s meaning since any interpretation stabilizes the meaning of a text. However, these ideological readings tend to miss the camp activations, attributing to prime-time serials a parallelism between the represented attitudes or symbols and Reaganomics. From this type of traditional ideological reading, it is easy to read effects—always negative—upon the viewer. Watching *Dynasty* must be bad for us, mustn't it? Reaganism proves the dangerousness of *Dynasty*, while *Dynasty* proves the dangerousness of Reaganism. Looking at *Dynasty* from a modernist/Marxist cultural perspective can produce only this type of ideological reading. But from the perspective of a postmodern concept of ideology, the activations of *Dynasty* may be understood in all of their multivalence and ambivalence.

For in the case of *Dynasty*, the reading formation *is* the text. Thus *Dynasty*'s interpretive communities never merely interpret—they enact, they are counted as demographics, they consume not just a fictional text but a whole range of products as well. Not only would I posit that the interpretive community *is* the text, it also *produces* the text and in addition is produced *by* the text. Postmodern reading formations produce a "dominant reading" of the program insofar as many different contemporary interpretive communities approach the program from the postmodern perspective. But studying the camp sensibility that surrounds *Dynasty* within both gay and mainstream culture, and placing the program's reception within the entire circuit of commodity tie-ins calls into question the whole notion of a "dominant reading" as it is usually conceptualized by ideological criticism. Interpretive communities for *Dynasty* are not producing the same kind of interpretations as are interpretive communities for *Ulysses*. Seen in terms of reading formations, the activation of *Dynasty* is easily the more complex: what is produced is not exactly a reading and it is not exactly dominant either. Nor is the kind of ironic activation described—typical of the gay sensibility—exactly part of a "dominant ideology" that pervades American culture. It is something slippery and not easily transcodable into direct political and cultural effects. For all of these reasons, one must conclude that literary reception theory does not exactly work for media texts, and that the more hermeneutically oriented varieties of reception theory do not work at all for any type of reception in our postmodern culture. But such a massive critique might be too great a weight to place upon Nolan Miller's (padded) shoulders.

Notes

I would like to thank Jim Collins for his generous contribution to my revision of this paper.
1   See the issue entitled "Ferment in the Field," *Journal of Communication* 33 (Summer 1983).
2   Tony Bennett and Janet Woollacott, *Bond and Beyond* (New York, 1987).
3   These terms are from Tony Bennett. Although their meaning is more easily grasped in context, he does offer the following definition of a "reading formation": "a set of intersecting discourses that productively activate a given body of texts and the relations between them in a specific way" ("Texts, Readers, Reading Formations," *Bulletin of the Midwest Modern Language Association* 16 [Spring 1983]: 5). In the same article, Bennett proposes the term "activation" as a means of "displacing . . . the concept of interpretation and the particular construction of relations between texts and readers that it implies" (3).
4   Tony Rizzo, "West Coast Reporting," *Soap Opera Digest*, 16 July 1985, 94.
5   Tony Bennett, "The Bond Phenomenon: Theorizing a Popular Hero," *Southern Review* 16 (July 1983): 220.
6   Bennett, "Texts, Readers, Reading Formations," 16. Elsewhere Bennett uses the terms "hermeneutic operators" and "textual shifters" to refer to this phenomenon.
7   Tony Bennett, "Texts and Social Processes: The Case of James Bond," *Screen Education* (Winter/Spring 1982): 9.
8   Ibid., 7.
9   Stephen Schiff, "What *Dynasty* Says about America," *Vanity Fair*, December 1984, 64.
10 Joe Klein, "The Real Star of *Dynasty*," *New York*, 2 September 1985, 34.
11 Roland Marchand, *Advertising the American Dream* (Berkeley, 1985), 89–110.
12 Robert C. Allen, *Speaking of Soap Operas* (Chapel Hill, 1985), 151ff.
13 Mary Murphy, "Behind *Dynasty*'s Breakdown—And Recovery," *TV Guide*, 17 May 1986, 18.
14 Bennett and Woollacott in *Bond and Beyond* define "inter-textuality" as follows:

"Whereas Kristeva's concept of *intertextuality* refers to the system of references to other texts which can be discerned within the internal composition of a specific individual text, we intend the concept of *inter-textuality* to refer to the social organisation of the relations between texts within specific conditions of reading" (44–45).

15 Mary Louise Pratt, "Interpretive Strategies/Strategic Interpretations: On Anglo-American Reader-Response Criticism," in *Postmodernism and Politics*, ed. Jonathan Arac (Minneapolis, 1986), 52.

16 For other examples of gay male subcultural activations see Schiff, "What *Dynasty* Says about America," and Mark Finch, "Sex and Address in 'Dynasty,' " *Screen* 27 (November/December 1986): 37.

17 Richard Dyer, *Heavenly Bodies: Film Stars and Society* (New York, 1986), 154.

18 Elaine Warren, "Backstage with Dynasty," *Cosmopolitan*, August 1985, 182–85.

19 *Wall Street Journal*, 23 March 1984, 1.

20 *Los Angeles Times*, 10 February 1985, 6.

21 *New York Times*, 15 March 1984, sec. 3, p. 29.

22 *People*, 17 December 1984, 69.

23 *New York Magazine*, 6 August 1984, 15.

24 *New York Times*, 20 November 1984, sec. 3, p. 15.

25 *Wall Street Journal*, 23 January 1986, 31.

26 Jean Baudrillard, *In the Shadow of the Silent Majorities and Other Essays*, trans. Paul Foss, Paul Patton, and John Johnston (New York, 1983), 43–44.

27 Fredric Jameson, "Postmodernism, or the Cultural Logic of Late Capitalism," *New Left Review* 146 (July–August 1984): 64–66.

28 Linda Hutcheon, "The Politics of Postmodernism: Parody and History," *Cultural Critique* 5 (Winter 1986–87): 179–208.

29 Ibid., 185, 194, 206.

30 Debora Silverman, *Selling Culture: Bloomingdale's, Diana Vreeland, and the New Aristocracy of Taste in Reagan's America* (New York, 1986), 152–55.

31 Michael Pollan, "The Season of the Reagan Rich," in *Fast Forward*, ed. Les Brown (Kansas City, 1983), 163.

32 Janice Radway, *Reading the Romance* (Chapel Hill, 1984).

Dialogues of the Living Dead

John O. Thompson

I have endeavour'd . . . to imitate you in the End you proposed. As all your Dialogues include their Moral, so all my Dead moralize; 'twou'd not else have been worth while to make 'em speak, for the Living might have suffic'd to say Things of no Use. —Fontenelle

★ ★ ★ ★ ★ ★ The slouch toward celebrity is the everyday matter of sitting up straight and talking on a talk show. The distinctiveness of talk shows, as a cultural *achievement* of ours, is best brought out by contrast: Why are talk shows so patently *ours*, rather than products of some other culture? Generally, I feel, media studies suffer from restricting generic comparisons to what is, in terms of species culture overall, a very compressed time frame. Both our television achievements and our disappointments with them might come into clearer focus if set against a less restricted background of forms.

So I intend to contrast our television to an imaginary television, one which might have carried a different kind of Celebrity Slot characterizable as "Dialogues of the Dead." Script by, for example, in

Greece in the second century A.D., Lucian; in early eighteenth-century France, Fénelon or Fontenelle; in mid-eighteenth-century England, Lord Lyttelton; in nineteenth-century England, Walter Savage Landor. But before settling into this exercise in anachronism, I need to develop the phrase I used a moment ago: "Our achievements and our disappointments with them."

We are well accustomed by now to the to-ing and fro-ing within television studies between broadly positive and broadly negative evaluative assessments of the phenomena under scrutiny. The arguments can be conducted with lesser or greater sophistication. Take, for instance, two of the obvious complaints that can be made about most television: its forms and its contents are very repetitious, and they are terribly constrained in a number of ways. (The repetition thematic opens onto the whole question of stereotyping, while the constraint thematic encourages studies of commercial and ideological pressures upon the medium.) With regard to both these reproaches a sophisticated defense of the medium can be mounted. On repetition: repetitious behavior is *rule-governed*; we know from the experience of linguistics, of ethnomethodology, of anthropology in general, that, were we to sit down and try to formalize the rules that are being followed in producing Standard Television, we would emerge amazed by the intricacy of the rule system and the combination of skilled behaviors involved. On constraint: having to work within limits produces *formal* solutions with their own elegance and beauty. Wouldn't it be a bit philistine to point to the constraints of the sonnet as making it unlikely that the poet could produce satisfying work, having to keep to fourteen lines and a rhyme scheme? In media studies the outstanding example of formalist rehabilitation of elaborately constrained work has been our discovery of how very, very beautiful, whatever else they may be, the products of the classic Hollywood studio system were.

The trouble with the sophisticated defenses is that something still seems to be wrong: television, and perhaps especially American television, seem *badly* repetitious and constrained somehow, even once we refuse to consider repetition and constraint to be automatically bad things. The negative task then becomes the more careful description of just what there is to object to. Of the considerable body of interesting writing which tries to do this, I've been especially impressed recently by Mark Crispin Miller's essay "Deride and Conquer."[1] This witty—and, one must say, wittily *derisive*—polemic against a broad range of current American television concludes with a fine expression of the something-is-wrong sentiment: "And it certainly is despised. Everybody watches it, but no one really likes it."[2]

Miller's full argument is intricate and tightly bound to his analysis of particular examples, but for my purposes I will encapsulate some of it thus: television becomes increasingly self-referential by closing itself off from anything that might disturb the enclosure of (repetitive-constrained) "normal" television; it is happy to mock itself, along with whatever is not-itself, in the interests of that enclosure. So irony, or more brutally derision, becomes the pervading *mood* of the medium; correlative to this is the denial of something that Miller calls "transcendence." In this argument, "transcendence" stands for all value systems that stand outside of, hence potentially "against," the market ethos, the world of consumption as involved in television as an advertisers' medium.[3]

What I want to sketch is how Miller's attack on a television dedicated to the suppression of transcendence might interact with an attempt to define the rule system that governs the talk show as a television genre. In order to do this, I present contrastively the Dialogue of the Dead, in ideal form, as standing in a different relation to transcendence.

In a Dialogue of the Dead, a conversation is constructed among two or more famous or representative figures from the past, represented either in an afterlife or (as in Landor) in their own time. So Lucian represents Alexander the Great talking to his father, Philip of Macedon, or Diogenes the cynic philosopher talking to Hercules the hero; Fénelon represents Alexander and Julius Caesar, or Horace and Virgil; and so on. For present purposes, the genre can be imagined with potential film studies examples. Consider an Imaginary Conver-

298 : John O. Thompson

sation between André Bazin and Sergei Eisenstein, for example; or between Lumière and Méliès; or between Orson Welles and William Randolph Hearst; or between Mae West and Carl Dreyer.

Such a form clearly differs from any sort of recording of an actual debate: between David Bordwell and Robin Wood, say, or between Pauline Kael and Andrew Sarris. You *could* write an Imaginary Conversation between Bordwell and Wood, of course, but it might feel eerie just because you would be treating them thereby *as* dead.

The dead person is *known for* something; he (overwhelmingly it is "he") is put in juxtaposition to another person, and out of their respective completed essences can be written a dialogue with a *point*. The speakers are complete because they are dead. The dialogue itself is complete because it is a literary composition, set up to instruct through pleasing. Its method of pleasing can certainly be satiric, with either contemporary foibles or the dead person's hubris as the target. But the genre points outside of itself constantly (to the extent, indeed, of being a rather unstable, self-destructive one): notable extradialogic "appeals" are to history, to ethical values and heroic accomplishments, and—at the genre's more nihilist core—to death itself, as putting into a different judgmental frame the accomplishments on which the speakers' celebrity is based.

But of course what makes the Dialogues of the Dead so *un*satisfactory is that the dead become puppets, simulacra speaking to the *writer's* point. What we really want, what we can now technologically demand, is the equivalent of fly-on-the-wall, Bazinian *documentation* of Caesar talking to Pompey, or of Shakespeare and Ben Jonson in a pub together, or of Douglas Sirk interrogating Senator McCarthy. Or do we? Part of the older genre's charm lies in setting up spatiotemporally impossible juxtapositions (Douglas Sirk meets Euripides?); but even in cases where meetings would have been possible, we know from experience that in actual conversation nothing essential need be said, nothing that really illuminates why the famous people interest us, why what they stand for is pertinent to us.

Television talk show formats operate in terms of a rule system that combines Bazinian-"realist" elements with Dialogues of the Dead elements. On the "realist" side: we are given mechanically reproduced and transmitted images of real (live!) people, who really are spatio-temporally copresent (even if this involves electronic linkages); and because they are alive they can surprise, they are not merely their own essences or meanings personified. Furthermore—to introduce a new element into the discussion—they can enlighten us about how they have accomplished what they are famous for doing.

And yet the rules of the format bring back essence, meaning, closure and nondisclosure with a vengeance. If a space and time are found for the conversation, time itself is kept strictly limited: in y minutes there will be x number of guests. The possibility of flat, unrevealing, pointless documentation is averted by setting up the dialogue, between televisual host and guest, in the form of (polite, good-humored, jokey) interrogation. The host is supposed to operate as a stand-in for us, the audience, asking the questions that are "ours" (simulations of whatever questions we as individuals may or may not want to pose to Joan Collins or Stephen King or Dan Quayle). And the art of interviewing is to give "point" to, to bring to some sort of "meaningful" completion, the brief spell of talk.

This is a collaborative achievement between host and guest, of course. And it is here that the guest, in presenting his or her own celebrity, his or her "known-ness," tends to stick to the known. Essence appears and reappears show by show: in answer to the same questions, we get roughly the same answers, the same anecdotes, the same jokes. The living celebrity thus achieves, in the real, in front of the Bazinian camera, a stability of identity, within the well-wrought interview format (art concealing art), an identity which is—to justify my title—more than a bit deathlike in its "finish."

So the talk show is more like a Dialogue of the Dead than one might think. And yet it has also, unlike the older genre, managed to drain "transcendence," in Miller's sense, from itself. How?

There seem to be at least two reasons why the talk show fits in so well to a television closed in upon itself in the manner that Miller describes. One has to do with the pragmatics of self-presentation, which explains the resort to the same answers, the same anecdotes,

300: John O. Thompson

the same jokes, on the part of the guest. This is especially true of performers (who thereby, not coincidentally, become the prototype guests).

I have mentioned that we seek from contact with celebrities an account of *how they do it*—whatever "it" is that has made them worthy of appearing on television. This is a divided move in terms of hierarchy: to ask it is egalitarian ("all skills are communicable"), as befits market capitalism's ethic; but to need to ask it, and to accept the more complacent of the answers given, is to acquiesce in hierarchical assumptions about genius, luck, and the "otherness" of the celebrity, as befits market capitalism's stratified fallout.

I myself have wanted, as someone interested in analyzing screen acting, to make use of interviews with actors. Actors are central to talk shows. I have learned to feel that I need not collect these interviews: few are enlightening about the interviewees' craft. But this is not wholly the fault of the talk show format.

It is difficult for practitioners, of any sort, to speak illuminatingly about their craft. So much of it involves tacit knowledge; so much of it is incommunicable to a listener without any shared technical background. It is difficult for actors in particular to speak illuminatingly about their craft. In addition to the considerations just mentioned, we have at least two other problems to deal with. The actor may justifiably feel that his or her craft depends to some extent upon its mystery: to analyze the mystery might dispel the effect. Equally, acting quite exceptionally exposes its practitioners to the risk of contempt. Actors who are felt to have failed but who allow us to hear why they prepared and performed as they did risk redoubling the contempt.[4]

Under these circumstances, it is surely rational of actors within a talk show format to talk about anything *but* their craft. At the same time, it is rational of talk show hosts to avoid asking the questions that might lead their guests into humiliating, or pretentious-seeming, or baffling answers. So we get anecdotes about the circumstances surrounding performances, each with its own little "point" or twist; we get general "views" on the world (usually fairly anodyne); we get "me-versus-my-role" explorations (where both poles of the comparison can be drained of any threat by predictably shrewd handling of the contrast).

Much more could be said about the pragmatics of "being the guest." I'm inclined to think that this is a case for invoking the sophisticated pro-television position, even if ruefully (it really would be nice to hear more about how acting is done!); no sensible person, in the position of the actor, would be *more* forthcoming. Yet this means that one potential vector of transcendence, the one pointing outward to the work of the guest, is blocked: that work is reduced to its anecdotal periphery, and to the chummy, irony-suffused "we're in the business together (and so are our fans)" line of auto-referential television.

Pseudoegalitarianism—the other reason television so readily accommodates the talk show—seems to me less inevitable and more damaging. What I have in mind is the talk show genre's relentless determination (very much embodied in the figure of the host) to have "us" talk to the guest as an equal. The guest really isn't allowed to teach us anything; nor can he or she appeal easily to an "outside" wherein network styles are not definitive of value. Since almost all of us live in an outside wherein television doesn't define value, this means that the people who are "inside television" are separated from us, or at least from the "us" television doesn't define, almost as radically as the dead are from the living.

This is supposed to be part of a situation in which, cheerily, outside hierarchies are by the magic of the medium abolished. They aren't. More viciously, they are not admitted. Thereby we find closed off both a vector moving outside television in the direction of the ethical (except for the ethical-as-currently-televisually-defined, a rule system no doubt of great intrinsic interest, etc.), and a vector which we might anachronistically call the heroic, by means of which the suspect concept of celebrity might find itself underpinned by a serious consideration of *exceptional achievement* (which need not, indeed had better not, be a category explored in grovelingly celebratory mode). Pseudoegalitarianism is comforting, and even proto-utopian, but it operates in Miller's terms as a foreclosing of transcendence. Brecht might say: We *learn* nothing. And this brings me to a final speculation.

The Dialogues of the Dead genre is ruled, even if ironically, by the notion of instruction, of the dead as instructive figures. In this it shows itself to be linked to the ethos of the premodern, traditional cultures, of cultures wherein "everything solid *doesn't* melt into air," to recall Marx's phrase. In such cultures, as anthropology richly demonstrates, the dead, via myth and ritual, are made to play key instructive roles.[5] I wonder whether, in our nontraditional culture, facing our technological-scientific, markets-plus-regulation future with, for now, no foreseeable alternative, we have fully thought through why the dead can no longer be our teachers in the older way.

Or can we say who "our" dead *are*? Are we imposing on particular living people the (paid) duty of being our dead? And then—which would be the waste—systematically deadening the very stretches of time we give them to tell us anything?

To give my readership a taste of the Dialogues of the Dead genre (for how many of us ever have occasion to encounter it?), I want to quote from one at length. It seems a good idea to reproduce one of the dialogues that inaugurate the genre, written in the second century A.D. by Lucian of Samosata. This is number 13, between Diogenes and Alexander, beginning thus:

> DIOGENES: Dear me, Alexander, *you* dead like the rest of us?
>
> ALEXANDER: As you see, sir; is there anything extraordinary in a mortal's dying?
>
> DIOGENES: So Ammon lied when he said you were his son; you were Philip's after all.
>
> ALEXANDER: Apparently; if I had been Ammon's, I should not have died.
>
> DIOGENES: Strange! there were tales of the same order about Olympias too. A serpent visited her, and was seen in her bed; we were given to understand that that was how you came into the world, and Philip made a mistake when he took you for his.
>
> ALEXANDER: Yes, I was told all that myself; however, I know now that my mother's and the Ammon stories were all moonshine.
>
> DIOGENES: Their lies were of some practical value to you, though; your divinity brought a good many people to their knees. . . .

As the (brief) dialogue unfolds, Diogenes speaks as the voice of sardonic experience to the hero-despot who discovers not only that he is not superior to death but that his "wise" teacher Aristotle has failed to prepare him to a properly stoical degree for the renunciatory aspect of death:

> DIOGENES: . . . What, crying? silly fellow! did not your wise Aristotle include in his instructions any hint of the insecurity of fortune's favours?
>
> ALEXANDER: Wise? call him the craftiest of all flatterers. Allow me to know a little more than other people about Aristotle; his requests and his letters came to *my* address; *I* know how he profited by my passion for culture; how he would toady and compliment me, to be sure! now it was my beauty—that too is included under The Good; now it was my deeds and my money; for money too he called a Good—he meant that he was not going to be ashamed of taking it. Ah, Diogenes, an imposter; and a past master at it too. For me, the result of his wisdom is that I am distressed for the things you catalogued just now, as if I had lost in them the chief Goods.
>
> DIOGENES: Wouldst know thy course? I will prescribe for your distress. Our flora, unfortunately, does not include hellebore; but you take plenty of Lethe-water— good, deep, repeated draughts; that will relieve your distress over the Aristotelian Goods. Quick; here are Clitus, Callisthenes, and a lot of others making for you; they mean to tear you in pieces and pay you out. Here, go the opposite way; and remember, repeated draughts.[6]

This is actually quite savage (though in character for Diogenes) in both its treatment of Alexander as a dramatic character and of Aristotle as intellectual-turned-flatterer. There is at the same time a vein of cordiality running through it (partly constituted by how the speakers cooperate conversationally so quickly: Alexander is *already* prepared to speak from what is basically Diogenes' position), and even of nurturance on Diogenes' part. Note the "transcendent" (and death-based) distrust of any merging of the Good with the Goods of commerce, power, beauty.

I want to hold onto Diogenes as a character by quoting next a stretch from a Dialogue by George, Lord Lyttelton, written in the mid-eighteenth century. I would characterize it as exemplifying "the graver, more ponderous tone possible" within the genre; rereading the passage, though, I am struck again by the violence of it, as Lyttelton allows Diogenes to express powerfully an Enlightenment hatred of hierarchical social bonds and the myths that legitimate them.

DIOGENES: Don't tell me of the Music of Orpheus, and of his taming wild Beasts. A wild Beast brought to *crouch* and *lick the Hand of a Master*, is a much viler Animal than he was in his natural State of Ferocity. You seem to think, that the Business of Philosophy is *to polish Men into Slaves;* but I say, it is to teach them to assert, with an untamed and generous Spirit, their Independence and Freedom. You profess to instruct those who want to *ride* their Fellow-creatures, how to do it with an easy and gentle Rein; but I would have them thrown off, and trampled under the feet of all their deluded or insulted Equals, on whose backs they have mounted. Which of us two is the truest Friend to Mankind?

PLATO: According to your Notions all Government is destructive to Liberty; but I think that no Liberty can subsist without Government. A State of Society is the *natural* state of Mankind. They are impelled to it by their Wants, their Infirmities, their Affections. The Laws of Society are Rules of Life and Action necessary to secure their Happiness in that State. Government is the due enforcing of those Laws. That Government is the best which does this most effectually, and most equally; and that People is the freest, which is most submissively obedient to such a Government.

DIOGENES: Show me the Government which makes no other Use of its Power than duly to enforce the Laws of Society, and I will own it is intitled to the most absolute Submission from all its Subjects.

PLATO: I cannot show you Perfection in Human Institutions. It is far more easy to blame them than it is to amend them: Much may be wrong in the best: but a good Man respects the Laws and the Magistrates of his Country.

DIOGENES: As for the Laws of my Country, I did so far respect

---

them, as not to philosophise to the prejudice of the first and greatest Principles of Nature and of Wisdom, Self-Preservation. Though I loved to prate about High Matters as well as Socrates, I did not chuse to drink Hemlock after his Example. But you might as well have bid me to *love* an ugly Woman, because she was drest up in the Gown of Lais, as *respect* a Fool or a Knave, because he was attired in the Robe of a Magistrate.

PLATO: All I desired of you was, not to amuse yourself and the Populace by throwing Dirt upon the Robe of a Magistrate, merely because he wore that Robe, and you did not.

DIOGENES: A Philosopher cannot better display his Wisdom than by throwing Contempt on that Pageantry, which the ignorant Multitude gazes at with a senseless Veneration.

PLATO: He who tries to make the Multitude *venerate Nothing* is more senseless than they. Wise Men have endeavoured to excite an awful Reverence in the Minds of the Vulgar for external Ceremonies and Forms, in order to secure their Obedience to Religion and Government, of which these are the Symbols. Can *a Philosopher* desire to defeat that good Purpose?

DIOGENES: Yes, if he sees it abused to support the evil Purposes of Superstition and Tyranny. . . .[7]

Lyttelton, forgotten though he now is, is the subject of the final (and perhaps deliberately anticlimactic) life in Samuel Johnson's *Lives of the Poets*; there, Johnson criticizes the Dialogues thus: "The names of his persons too often enable the reader to anticipate their conversation; and when they have met, they too often part without any conclusion."[8] The first half of this objection is surely generic; the second half suggests a Bazinian quality to the Dialogues which might, if anything, commend them to us.

Next I want to move backward in time slightly, to John Hughes's 1708 translation of Fontenelle's *Dialogues of the Dead*. The Fontenelle/Hughes tone is more on the deflating, Lucianic side, as the following excerpt from dialogue 4, between Adrian the Emperor and Margaret of Austria, demonstrates.

MARGARET OF AUSTRIA: What's the Matter, I beseech you? I see you're in a Heat.

ADRIAN: I have just now been engag'd in a fierce Dispute with *Cato* of *Utica*, concerning the manner of our Deaths; and I maintain'd that in this last Scene I shew'd more of a Philosopher than he.

MARGARET OF AUSTRIA: How! you had a World of Assurance, upon my Word, that you durst encounter a Death so famous as his. Cou'd any thing be more glorious than to order Affairs with that Wisdom in *Utica*, to make his Friends secure, and then kill himself that he might expire with the Liberty of his Country, and avoid falling into the Hands of a Conqueror, from whom he was yet certain to have receiv'd a Pardon?

ADRIAN: Oh! if you examine strictly, you'll find there's enough to be objected to this Death. In the first Place he was so long preparing for it, and with Efforts so visible, that there was not a Man in *Utica* but knew that *Cato* was about to kill himself. Secondly, before he durst venture upon the Stroke, he was forc'd to read several times over *Plato*'s Dialogue concerning the Immortality of the Soul. Thirdly, this Design had put him so out of Humour, that being in Bed, and missing his Sword from under his Pillow (for in Suspicion of what he was about to do, his Friends had remov'd it) he call'd one of his Slaves to ask him for it, and gave the poor Fellow such a Blow on the Face with his Fist, that he broke his Teeth, and brought back his Hand all bloody.

MARGARET OF AUSTRIA: 'Twas an unlucky Blow I must own, and quite spoils this Philosophical Death.[9]

By this point, the "logic of the supplement" seems to be corroding my argument in the familiar Derridean way. Isn't this much more like than unlike Miller's "derision"?

Two moments from Hughes's introduction seem worth bringing forward here. Hughes characterizes the readerly pleasure given by Fontenelle's style in terms which do indeed anticipate popular television's stylistic weightlessness:

In all his Writings he chooses the Style and Air of Conversation, and no where appears with the formality of an Author; which makes him particularly Entertaining, and is no small part of his Excellence, since few are so reasonable as to content themselves with being instructed, if they are not pleas'd.'Tis a Secret almost wholly his own, to say the most extraordinary things so carelessly, as if he were scarce sensible he had said any thing uncommon.[10]

But note how firmly this achievement remains tethered to an instruction model, and how what is to be said "as if" carelessly still needs to be something extraordinary. As for the derisive mode: Hughes is concerned to defend Fontenelle against a contemporary criticism, "a Piece call'd *Jugement de Pluton*."

> But there is another Question more material, *Where is the Respect due to Antiquity, and why must its Hero's be degraded?* This hangs much in [the critic's] Head, and he often repeats it afterwards; therefore, once for all, what signifies Respect to Antiquity, when we wou'd discover Truth? Is *Cato's* Death the more commendable in it self, because it has had the Applause of the Majority for seventeen hundred Years, and is it impossible that the Majority shou'd be (as they often are) in the wrong?
> . . . [T]his degrading the Hero's of Antiquity is, it seems, a Crime which runs thro' our Author's whole Book, and where's the Wonder? since the very End of Writing it was to unmasque Characters, to disrobe counterfeit Virtue, and attack common Opinion and Prepossessions.[11]

The transcendent role of Truth here is clear enough: Fontenelle is presented almost as an early Barthesian demythologizer, breathing the bracing air of a classicism whose logical outcome can only be a no-holds-barred Enlightenment.[12]

I want to conclude with a sequence of dialogues which appear in Steve Benson's *Blue Book*.[13] Benson, a poet/performer associated with the "language poetry" school within current American writing (and what an exciting body of work the school has produced!), seems worth presenting as representative of another possible way out of the talk show ethos.[14]

Dialogue itself here is problematized, "made strange" (while at the same time represented in terms of its naturalistic indecision and waywardness); in particular, the "meaning" of the Name of the Dead

Celebrity seems to dissolve in the nameless speakers' hands. As Barrett Watten's blurb on the back of *Blue Book* puts it, "A point of departure in Steve Benson's work is the uneasiness of the speaker."

> I want to say Bela Lugosi but I don't particularly want to mean what the words Bela Lugosi mean.
> I could say two things. (A.) It *sounds* like you've been rehearsing that for a long time, saying it over and over in different ways and gradually perfecting it, or saying not what you actually want to say but more, rather, to present the statement in the way that you think would make the best possible impression, that would be somehow typical of what it is you're trying to express, of the sort of thing you want to say, without actually knowing, all the same, rationally, with what intensity and on what parameters you want particularly to put that impression across.
> Or who I want you to be—who I consider you to be.
> Or, (B.) Let's start back at the beginning. What might have led up to your saying that about Bela Lugosi? You *said* it as though it stood there as a statement by itself, possibly prepared to incite response or criticism, but not as though you had anything on your mind before you said it, or any particular further conversation—
> You mean like, what's behind those words Bela Lugosi? What other words might they mean?
> And not as though we had actually been talking particularly beforehand. So did you have the feeling you were starting something or continuing something?
> Continuing *something*, but I can't say what, or from where— It was in my head, I was thinking, and then I wanted—to talk to you, and this Bela Lugosi phrase—came up, as though—
> You didn't know what else to say to me! You didn't know *what* to say to me. You didn't have, what they might say, what you might call a reason to speak to me, but you—you had something to *say*!
> Yes, and it turned out to be Bela Lugosi, just because that was the closest I could think to get to anything I wanted to say to you.

Who do you think I am? I hear myself saying that but I'm not really offended, actually I'm interested, I'm not interested in who I am—or rather, I am, but not right now so much as, not really even who you think I am, as in how I am, become taken up in the dynamic of the demands of this conversation—[15]

The dialogue moves away from Bela Lugosi for a while, but circles back by the end, as the first speaker finishes with a long, halting "aria":

What is "potent" language?

Well I don't know if I'd want to impose the opposition "potent" to that—but—what was I going to say?—I think there's language that's going to confirm an impression and there's language that's designed to challenge or alter it, the idea, the myth, or mirage, or a stable impression, that we all can share. I don't think there's a stable impression that we all can share, but you can reinforce the sense that there is one, using a language, and it's inevitable, it's necessary, to communicate, to get some sense of stability, since we're so social, but to *undermine* assumptions, you can also only use the language of these recognitions, there isn't any other. . . . So if we're going to call it "potent"—it's language that does *both* those things, that has that dynamic and tension between them, whereas "sterile" doesn't do *anything*, but just indifferently *seems*—. . . . So that Bela Lugosi, even if it's de-contextualized so that it's used for something that has nothing to do with—whatever it usually goes with, something that you might think might be totally arbitrary, to *it*, still the meanings associated with it, the *kinds* of recognition, the particular ways that works, has some *use*—[16]

Benson is careful not to let his speaker conclude; but even in the dialogue's inconclusion, a potent-sterile opposition *is*—transcendently?—posited which addresses, to my ear, the "disappointment" I've been trying to talk about. I too would rather not conclude: better to send the reader now to another page of this volume where, in "Dead Ringer," Jane Gaines also has occasion to invoke the name of

Bela Lugosi in speaking of the rights of the dead and living "recognized ones."

Notes

1 Mark Crispin Miller, "Deride and Conquer," in *Watching Television*, ed. Todd Gitlin (New York, 1987), 183–228.

2 Ibid., 228.

3 Ibid., 215: "In short, the point of TV comedy is that *there can be no transcendence*. Such is the meaning of Dad's long humiliation [in the sit-coms] since the fifties, and the meaning of every gratuitous and all-inclusive moment of derision. Because he would have stood out as an archaic model of resistance to the regime of advertising, Dad was, through the sixties and the seventies, reduced from a complicated lie to a simple joke."

4 For a stimulating, if rather gloomy, proposal for a framework for a nonpositivistic social psychology within which, in the "expressive order," the gaining of respect and the avoidance of contempt is seen as central to human social action, see Rom Harré, *Social Being* (Oxford, 1979).

5 *Death and the Regeneration of Life*, ed. Maurice Bloch and Jonathan Parry (Cambridge, 1982), provides an excellent collection of articles on the anthropology of death and the "meanings" of the ancestors.

6 *The Works of Lucian of Samosata*, trans. H. W. Fowler and F. G. Fowler (Oxford, 1905), 1:129–30.

7 George Lyttelton, *Dialogues of the Dead* (London, 1768), 377–80.

8 Samuel Johnson, *The Lives of the English Poets* (London, 1906), 2:468.

9 *Fontenelle's Dialogues of the Dead, in Three Parts*, trans. John Hughes (London, 1708), 78–79.

10 Ibid., xii.

11 Ibid., xii, xviii–xix.

12 Miller tips his hat to an American tradition of "spectatorial subversion of the powerful" involving "our most celebrated humorists: Artemus Ward, Josh Billings, Mr. Dooley, 'Honest Abe,' Mark Twain, Will Rogers," which clearly has this sort of Enlightenment commitment. But, he argues, "the history of this subversive irony has reached its terminus, for now the irony consists in nothing but an easy jeering gaze that TV uses not to question the exalted, but to perpetuate its own hegemony." Today's TV irony is both conformist ("promot[ing] consumption as a way of life") and corrosive ("discredit[ing] any sign of an incipient selfhood") ("Deride and Conquer," 222–23). Miller's argument can be interestingly compared with that of one of George Eliot's essays, "Debasing the Moral Currency," collected in *Impressions of Theophrastus Such* (Edinburgh and London, n.d.). The Eliot attack is directed against "the burlesquing spirit," which she sees as something that devalues the spiritual, the noble, the elevated, the generous, the charming. While

the Eliot essay is in detail curious and in broad outline repressive in its confidence that any burlesque must involve not only derision but desecration, rereading after Miller leaves one feeling that it has considerable prophetic force.

13 Steve Benson, *Blue Book* (New York, 1988), 131–46.

14 An attractive point of entry into this body of writing is *Writing/Talks*, ed. Bob Perelmen (Carbondale, 1985).

15 Benson, *Blue Book*, 140.

16 Ibid., 141.

Image/Machine/Image: On the Use and Abuse of Marx and Metaphor in Television Theory

Richard Dienst

I, from the orient to the drooping west
(Making the wind my post-horse), still unfold
The acts commenced on this ball of earth.
— 2 *Henry IV*, Induction, 3–5

★ ★ ★ ★ ★ ★ Of all the economies television is supposed to operate,
the most basic one, the one we will have to go on calling "political
economy," remains the hardest to see. Although television has never
been mistaken for a purely aesthetic realm untouched by commerce,
the all-too-visible kinds of economic traffic scarcely begin to exhaust
the scope of the televisual morphologies of value. A political economy
of television has to account for a variety of situations in which long
chains of force—money, state power, cultural interests—intersect
and change form. If television works both at the most global levels
of exchange and at the most everyday levels of ordinary existence,
any adequate theory of this system will have to find a set of mobile
abstractions capable of recognizing links between the most disparate

situations. In this essay, a map of television's possible economies is organized between two conceptual poles called—in highly compressed shorthand—"machine" and "image." My contention is that any specific analysis of television must encounter irreducible dimensions of machine and image, even when one is allowed to eclipse the other; further, our immediate decisions about the status of these terms will determine the definition of that *other* inescapable term always in play and at stake here: capitalism.

I begin with a simple assertion: *Television is part of the machinery of global capitalism*. The weight of each term and the balance of the sentence depend on the sense of the phrase "part of": if this relation is taken at face value, the proposition can be reduced to the simple idea that television is a product of, portrays, and plays some role in capitalist relations. True enough, but nothing has been advanced; although we know that televisual technology was achieved entirely according to capitalist imperatives, it has never been simply a tool of accumulation or just one commodity among others. If, on the other hand, the chiasmus between television and capital works in some extensive metaphoric and metonymic (that is to say, *figural*) way, then both television and contemporary capitalism have to be reconfigured as a complex system in which political economy and culture circulate through each other instantly and endlessly.

But it is crucial that these figural readings (television as machine, capital as image) do not turn into one of those superstable theoretical stacks so common in television studies, where the critic piles up discursive or symbolic or affective economies without interrogating the status of the economic model itself. Behind the attraction of economic metaphorics is a systemic impulse, an attempt to link phenomena in terms of an absent or invisible logic of value. But the model must always make a fatal choice about its units or its ultimate term: no sooner has "labor power" been rejected in favor of "the signifier" or "desire" than the whole problematic must turn around to confront the truth claims of systemic thinking and reason itself. (A major strain of 1970s theory followed this trajectory; Lyotard is a case in point.) If we want to say that television operates several economies at once, we have to ask not only how that is possible but how we could say it.

The radical possibility of metaphor opens the model of "economy" to a scattered diffusion of images (or, to use another code, representations). But that is not all; metaphor can also be a productive and propulsive device, a built thing, a veritable machine serving the ends of sense. Whenever the relations between knowledge, sense, and representation are at stake, "economy" is not just one metaphoric out of many: it carries along in its very figure the axioms of value and structure that are supposed to guarantee the truth claims of discourse itself. By the same token, "machinery" is not simply one figure out of many that describe the economic process. It is the figure of the implacably objective, referring to everything automatic, inhuman, and deathly about social life. There are a couple of ways to deal with all these images and machines, all these metaphors and economies running through each other. On one hand, the (disciplinary) discourse on political economy can be read as a shifting composition of concepts and metaphors already caught in the process of making its knowledge *visible*, while, on the other hand, the stream of visible images on television can be read as moments of economic circulation decomposed into abstract markers of value-in-process. It goes both ways: any account of "the political economy of television" hinges not only on the *value of images* but on the *images of value*.

Little wonder that "machinery" (along with "mechanism," "device," "motor," etc.) appears as one of the constitutive figures in interpretive language, most prominently in those descended from psychoanalysis and Marxism. For its part, film theory has invested heavily in such apparatuses, fusing cameras and projectors to cognitive switchboards: interpretation becomes the normative prediction of sensory and symbolic output given a certain input. Machinery operates as the guaranteed connector, transmitter, mediator, and communicator between forces, an object that stands in for a process without subjective agency or contingent variation. Little wonder, again, that "machinery" appears so prominently in the critiques of interpretive method carried out by de Man, or by Foucault, Deleuze, and Guattari, in which metaphoric distance is collapsed and "machinery" (as *dispositif* and *assemblage*) becomes the literal blueprint for immanent accounts of power. "Machinic" irresistibly enters our critical vocabulary to account for the constructions of power in an ordered environment. As a result, writing and theory no longer operate in some poetic, metamachinic space of truth; they become tools and machines in their own right.

Many more examples are available. I need mention only one red-letter instance: in the midst of doling out "aesthetic worth" to various occupations in the *Critique of Judgement*, Kant castigates rhetoric by calling it the "machinery of persuasion"—no doubt a raw, noisy, and nasty image in its time, but nevertheless still a ripe one.[1] As Derrida points out in "Economimesis," this joint dismissal of rhetoric and the machine remains classical: it is the denunciation of a speech without animating intention, of a language running on its own, un-motivated by an internal *intention*.[2] It is, indeed, the definition of "representation" itself as mechanical; that is, as repetitive, superficial, and disconnected from consciousness. Like rhetoric the machine is empty, vacant, a pure function; it adds nothing, presents nothing of its own. In its senseless duplications it reproduces and banalizes what might once have been original, creative, or full in the original act of speaking or working. As the apparent conventionality of Kant's phrase shows, machinery acquired its metaphoric senses at the negative pole in a general schema assigning proper and improper value in commerce and speech. Although related to a certain philosophical attitude toward technics, this sense of "machinery" does not derive from a science (natural or applied). Instead, "machinery" here signifies *interest*—not only an economic interest that depends on machines instead of craft, but any interest that operates the apparatus of representation as a means of economy rather than expression. Thus, at a certain point—dated conveniently by Kant as the end of the eighteenth century[3]—"machinery" emerges as a worldly, public figure. It is more than a metaphor for the (mundane) economic world; it is literally a metaphor of (ordinary) metaphors. In fact, it can be the most ordinary and inconspicuous of figures, one that labors in language without a hitch: it toils in the background, at the level of "it goes without saying," among everyday things. "Machinery" always designates something real, not just because it must be objectlike but because it serves the world of interests and economy.

"Machinery" has become a voracious figure precisely because it knows no limiting scale or exterior contrary: it tends to absorb and retool its conceptual determinations in each place, displacing parts and wholes, causes and effects. The figure of the machine has reversible sides: one side faces economy and conceptuality and the other faces the play of metaphoricity, representation, and appearances. In a given text it *mediates* (as a mechanical relation) the distance between whatever is structurally absent about the economy in question and whatever is immediately, automatically visible about its products, its images. That is why machines have crowded into all kinds of discourse over the past few centuries, regulating the spaces of expression and action. At this moment, when economy and image are undergoing a thorough revaluation at every level, the semantic tangle of the machine—which had distilled the essence of modernity—has been assumed by the screen spaces of television and computers (which are inseparably linked, as we shall see).

And so the question does not have to be, Where does television fit into the economic machine? or, How do televisual images form an economy or a representational machine? Instead, we must ask, Where does the problem of television (visibility, information, and the symbolic) intersect a system of political economy? To pose this question we will first go—not by accident—back to Marx, who knew something about all of this long ago. After examining the function of machinery in Marx, we can turn to the various positionings of television in contemporary accounts of capitalism.

Marx's writings, of course, are suffused with metaphor: spatial, visual, organic, and machinic. But the reading of Marx that concerns us here is not a literary or even a literal one—rather it is the contemporary reading of Marx that begins with his concept of circulation as the key to economy, or, to be more exact, the reading in which the old conceptual stability of "production" is turned toward its most dynamic possibilities, crossing through "distribution" and "consumption," leaving no single point of origin or creation of value. Marx explains how capital flows in fits and starts; it will turn out, I suspect, that this description has more than passing resemblance to a formal description of television as the transmission of images. Indeed the resemblance is intimate: a reading of Marx can show why machinery, far from being inert matter, has always been involved in matters of representation and how the historical expansion of the machine system grants television, at a certain moment in history, new zones of value and new circuits of power.

"Value as such is always an effect, never a cause," Marx explains in the *Grundrisse*;[4] there he is constantly struggling with his key notion, labor power, trying to find a way to prevent it from becoming a pure origin of value. He proposes the concept of "value-in-process" to indicate the continuity and restless transformations of capital; with this notion Marx points to the historically specific way in which capital achieves its circumnavigation of the whole social sphere.[5] (I should note that the emphasis on process allows us to speak of capital in an active tense without casting it as a single character—it is the Fantômas of value.) Each point of capital's itinerary—labor power, money, commodity, machinery, capital—is linked to and formed by the others through specific operations and sets of conditions; each movement between terms is a refiguration and reprojection of value, both an abstract movement of representation and a concrete point of contestation.[6] The formal lesson of the notion of value-in-process should be familiar from contemporary theory: the only possible referent for one term in an economy is another term in that economy; that is, that reference is (in) motion.

Since capital loves movement, it takes on fantastic and bizarre shapes whenever it has been stopped for very long—when it becomes "fixed." Machinery is Marx's most consistent example and metaphor of fixed capital, to the point where it becomes the internal perfection of capital's representational movement: "*Machinery* appears, then, as the most adequate form of *fixed capital*, and fixed capital, in so far as capital's relations with itself are concerned, appears as *the most adequate form of capital* as such."[7] In a moment he goes on to say, however, that money is the most adequate form of capital for "external relations," which is why he spends so much time elsewhere explaining how money conceals the inner workings of capital. The comparison of machines and money is taken further when Marx refers to money as "a machine which saves circulating time."[8] Both money and machines hold time as value, but in forms suited to quite different speeds of metamorphosis. Indeed, capital has rebuilt the world as a landscape of jagged time lapses.[9] Today, in the globally mobile sphere of late capital, driven by a jet stream of interest, credit, and speculation, each individual capital can withdraw from one location and move to another almost instantaneously, facilitated by the mechanisms of the electronic financial system. The existence of such a transmission mechanism—information and telecommunication machinery—can be explained in terms of capital's imperative to circulate, its capacity to change form as quickly as possible. Marx saw these possibilities when he pointed out that the "tendency of capital is *circulation without circulation time*; hence also the positing of the instruments which merely serve to abbreviate circulation time as mere formal aspects posited by it."[10] Capital, in other words, seeks to make each moment of its circulation ideal, irreducibly symbolic but abstract, in order to generalize its space of operation. Accordingly, capital spreads along several routes and at different speeds; where the expansion of exchange relations heralds the incorporation of previously distant economies, the emplacement of machinery establishes the *socialization of all labor* and points toward the *planetary entrenchment of capitalist relations.*[11]

What is so symbolic or abstract about machinery as fixed capital? Here is a power loom, there a factory building; certainly the capitalist bought these things for no other reason than to produce surplus value. But since fixed capital consists of commodities which nevertheless remain in the production sphere, they are not immune to a kind of fetishism. Marx struggles to define it: "*Fixed capital*, actually fixated capital, [is] fixated in one of the different particular aspects, phases, through which it must move."[12] Fixed capital is not entirely itself, not all there, "never completely occupied."[13] Distracted or dormant, maybe, but not dead. In Marx's persistent contrast between "living" labor and fixed capital, a complex and technical distinction about the movement of value is drawn. The place of machinery in the labor process has a twofold character.

First, machinery functions as a component in the continuing circulation of value. It transfers its value (we shall leave aside the question of its price) by increments slowly back into the products it helps to make, until it has no more value to dispense (obsolescence and final depreciation). We can call this its capital-value loop: it stores and dispenses some previously produced quantity of value. (Spivak would call this a "continuist" loop, since there is an assumption that the machine is a zero-sum stage.) In volume 2 of *Capital*, Marx analyzes at some length the cost structure of fixed capital in terms of its gradual dissemination of its "fixed" value.[14] The contingent "fixedness" of fixed capital relates to three factors: the durability of the physical thing (its "use form"), its convertibility into circulating capital, and the changing level of available technology. These criteria, which cover both the value of the machine's construction and its situational utility, determine when a machine can be employed productively. Only when a machine can transfer its value to a commodity does it remain part of capital; upon this rule rests Marx's theory of economic cycles, attached to the periodic replacement of worn-out fixed capital (as I will discuss below).[15] From capital's point of view, machinery follows a fatally entropic course, slowed only by repairs and hastened by the advent of new and better machines.

Second, and most crucially, the machine exerts a social force over the labor process which cannot be simply quantified. As a powerfully new kind of object, the machine takes on a kind of sovereign power, even to the point where it appears to function "for nothing," "like a natural force," becoming a "mighty organism" that overwhelms labor.[16] Here, the key analogy Marx draws is not between machines and money but between machines and the laborer; yet both analogies concern a mediation. In brief, the worker and the machine enter into henceforth irreversible relations of reciprocal constitution. Both become "effects" of capital, existing on the same plane as "value as such" but (unlike value) positioned as "causes," or rather, "use values," within the production process. In sorting out lines of causality between machine and worker, the metaphorics of machinery come up against the metaphorics of the body. Since the production of surplus value can take place only through "living" labor, something about the expenditure of work time seems to remain irreducibly organic, as opposed to machinic. But the line of difference is more analogical than oppositional, so that the powers proper to the laboring body are transposed onto the body of capital (and vice versa): "[in] the human body, as with capital, the different elements are not exchanged at the same rate of reproduction, blood renews itself more rapidly than muscle, muscle than bone, which in this respect may be regarded as the fixed capital of the human body."[17]

From capital's point of view, this residue of living matter known as the human body can be managed easily enough. Its first weapon, of course, is the machine itself. Marx clearly lays out in chapter 15 of *Capital*, volume 1, the material aspects of *a historically original subjection to machinery*, in which the modern body is submitted to a new technology of power (i.e., the Foucauldian "discipline"). It should be emphasized that the role machinery plays in social reproduction is profoundly ideological (in Althusser's sense). The machinic form of value accomplishes what the exchange of commodities cannot: it constitutes bodies as conscious (self)-representations through the technical knowledge of economy. Marx tells the story this way: "once adopted into the production process of capital, the means of labor passes through different metamorphoses, whose culmination is the *machine*, or rather, an *automatic system of machinery* . . . this automaton consisting of numerous mechanical and intellectual organs, so that the workers themselves are cast *merely as its conscious linkages*."[18] The worker works as a relay in the transmission of value along the same twofold lines as the machine: first as a calculable labor power which receives a wage and buys commodities to reproduce itself, and second as a "watchman" or "conductor" of capital's machinic timetable of acceleration, a more or less efficient switch point, "absorbed into the body of capital," for the turnover of fixed and circulating value.[19] This abstraction and absorption of socialized labor power lends machinery further human accoutrements: "It is the machine which possesses skill and strength in place of the worker, is itself the virtuoso, with *a soul of its own* in the mechanical laws acting through it."[20] As in so much of the science fiction written since *Frankenstein*, the machine's soul stirs with rapture as it receives its human ingredient, "*as though its body were by love possessed*" (Marx quotes a drinking song from *Faust*—"als hätt' es Lieb im Leibe"— to evoke the moment).[21] While collective bodies are transmuted and transfigured, the so-called general intellect—in the form of institutions of science and knowledge—becomes the index and "organs" of the new social machinery. (Note that Marx's use of the word "organ" appears as another figural crossover from the body to the machine.) Beyond all these acts of submission and service, the final but deferred result of capitalist production is society itself, a set of relations played out between moving bodies, appearing to and vanishing from each other at differing speeds, in which the sole task left to human beings is to "renew themselves as they renew the world of wealth they create."[22]

The self-reproducing machinic skeleton of capital reappears, stronger than ever, in Sartre's late work, the *Critique of Dialectical Reason*. In detailing the situation of the worker at work, he notes first that the machine and the factory exist as the "dead" labor (the "practico-inert") of previous generations (existentially, not economically, dead). Social being is "crystallized" in material objects and built space, which then exert a collective force of Otherness over those who follow. Dead labor consumes the praxis of the living. Taking as one of his examples a working woman, Sartre identifies a "contradiction which opposes the productive forces to the relations of production," here taken as the confrontation between the practico-inert object and the worker herself. Sartre draws the most extreme conclusions: this encounter "forces the working woman to live a prefabricated destiny as *her reality*," a destiny which arrives from elsewhere as the imposition of an absent human unity. Neither she nor the capitalist "intends" it. He cites a study in which it is discovered that women have fragmentary sexual fantasies as they work at semiautomatic machines: "But it was the machine in them which was dreaming of love."[23] Because the machine requires a certain kind of half-conscious attention, the rhythms of thought are passively molded by machine time. Women's fantasies become the clipped and disjointed injections of an objective ensemble of body, brain, and machine. Men, by contrast, do not abandon themselves this way (Sartre says); presumably they are always active, undistracted, and undistanced, in work as in sex. In either case, however, the machine sets the limits of what can be thought and done at the same time, marking out a more or less empty temporal frame which leaves intervals for imaginary work inserted into machinic work. Though Sartre stops short of saying that the machine "produces" the images flashing through the workers' heads, there seems little doubt that the activities of consciousness are fully captured by the machinery. The mental images are a kind of by-product of the object being produced for commodity exchange. But this is not to say that capital has a sure-fire way of valorizing all the fantasies, daydreams, and self-images spun out in the wake of production. That there are loose subjective elements powering economy is recognized by Marx on the first page of *Capital*, where they are called "needs." Here Sartre indicates that these elements are caught and recycled in a dialectic of recognition, representation, and domination.

Sartre's image of the working woman as a mixing vessel for collective fantasy and machinic labor time raises the specter of total domination reaching into every corner of subjectivity. We do not have to take it at face value. But the image usefully recalls a key point made by Marx in *Capital*: that women's and children's labor is "the first result of the capitalist application of machinery."[24] In the first stages of industrialization, the machine baptises the entire proletarian family in the wage circuit. It breaches the already existing gendered division of labor and makes all subsequent divisions issues of direct economic exploitation (struggles over whose work counts as value) both in the factory and in the home.[25] At least since the appearance of capitalism, women's work in the home has always been the essential if not "exchanged" component in the reproduction of labor power, from day to day and from generation to generation. At the same time, women enter and leave the wage relation under obvious constraints, on the basis of both socially available life trajectories and the kinds of work required by capital at a given moment. As the material site of the division of labor, machinery has been gendered from the beginning. It may require certain skills that are socially apportioned, or alternatively may require a lack of skill socially imposed. It may in fact be built to exhaust its workers as quickly as a raw material, using up a particular physical capacity (such as eyesight) before releasing the worker from wage labor (i.e., to run a family). This is presently the dominant pattern in the Pacific Rim microelectronics industries.

A structural continuity can be traced through the machines women have operated, from the power looms of early industrialism to the typewriters of the metropolitan-imperial-era offices, to the data-processing and household appliances of our own age. This continuity is reinforced if we include television. The work of Tania Modleski, Gillian Dyer, and others has already shown how television "distracts" the labor and thought of the household worker in ways broadly similar to Sartre's scene: in each situation, the woman finds a way to choose what she cannot avoid, and thereby to exercise her margin of subjectivity through images.[26]

As the variability and flexibility of women's labor shows, the attachment of bodies to machines is not absolute, either for an instant or for a life span. The heroically mechanized male worker, familiar from so much early twentieth-century art and politics, was never the ideal for capital. On the contrary, the machine marks and maintains a distance and difference between two forces, one structural and the other subjective. The analytic of machinery remains bound, in the furthest reach of the Marxian text, to the labor theory of value and a subjective theory of consciousness, as it is expressed in the unclosed gap or fissure between machinic and organic metaphors in the text of economy.[27]

Through this fissure the Marxian metaphorics can lend their theoretical focus to the study of television: the conception of machinery as the body of capital introduces the bodies of humans into the pathways of value and allows us to question how "experiential" dimensions of the world—such as vision and time—can be produced within the circulation of capital.

A cultural analysis that begins with Marx's account of the capitalist's (as-yet-unrealized) machinic world will diverge sharply from the line of discussion that sees capitalist culture only in terms of its commodities (with its themes of reification, alienation, spectacle, etc.). It is clear, at any rate, that Marx's own broad characterizations of culture focused more on the state of productive technology than on its products, and more on the differentiated movements of economy than on some dead-end fascination with objects. After the mildly apocalyptic strains of "consumer society" and "information society" theory died down, several strands of the postmodernism debate renewed the analysis of capital as a formidable and complex ensemble of productive branches. For example, some of the recent accounts of the geography of capital begin from the definitions of fixed capital as built space (Manuel Castells, David Harvey, Edward Soja). So-called post-Marxist descriptions of articulated power networks retain the structural aspects of Marx's analysis of economy but discard the thesis (not necessarily Marx's) that economic lines of determination cross through every cell of a social space. Any emphasis on the material apparatus of capitalism must raise the difficult question of relations of *force* (domination, discipline, resistance) deployed wherever the relations of production are reproduced, which immediately transforms the economic scene into a political and cultural one.[28]

If television is regarded as nothing more than a commodity plaything or a propaganda megaphone—if, in other words, its place in contemporary capital can be isolated in some sphere of consumption (where anything is possible, even pleasure)—then it hardly deserves to be called a machine, and it hardly deserves to be promoted to the status of iconic object and bearer of the zeitgeist. But since we are now in a better position to recognize that capitalism's machinery includes any transfer point where value can be reconfigured, it should be easier to recognize that television images are themselves always value-in-process rather than some extraneous pretty picture at second hand, and that this absolute proximity to other forms of capital suggests that television's particular forms of value are centrally necessary in the current juncture.

The suspicion that television is more than window dressing for late capital has been expressed before. We can begin with Fredric Jameson's tantalizing formulation, which sets video in the historical frame of machinery:

> If we are willing to entertain the hypothesis that capitalism can be periodized by the quantum leaps or technological mutations by which it responds to its deepest systemic crises, then it may become a little clearer why video—so closely related to the dominant computer and information technology of the late or third stage of capitalism—has a powerful claim for being the art form of late capitalism *par excellence*.[29]

To rephrase the question: What is the nature of the intimacy between television and late capital, and what forms can it take? I will sketch four answers.

First, it has already been pointed out that the depreciating value loop of fixed capital sets the pattern for economic cycles. Marx saw that periodic replacement of machinery required a large reinvestment in the means of production (Department I). The rate of commodity production (Department II) may undergo variation, but it does not explain the cyclical crises capitalism has undergone since its first full bloom. The technical and economic relation between these departments is known as the "organic composition of capital." (That telling concept-metaphor is Marx's.)

Much of Ernest Mandel's *Late Capitalism* is concerned with this "structure of production" as the relation between branches, since it provides the material basis for his historical schema: an updated version of Kondratiev cycles—long waves of capitalist development and decline, running in roughly sixty-year intervals. The literature on Kondratiev waves is voluminous and need not detain us here. It can be pictured as a kind of kinetic or potential energy model for capitalism's long-term profit rates and investments. Mandel attaches great significance to technological turnover: "The characteristic element in the capitalist mode of production . . . is the fact that each new cycle of extended reproduction begins with different machines than the previous one."[30] Each of these changes came about through a dual accelerated growth in the institutions of scientific knowledge and the capacity of capital as a whole to incorporate new discoveries.[31] Mandel extends Marx's historical account into several additional stages:[32] from the tool to the (handmade) machine is the first step; from the machine to machines powered by machines is the second, fully capitalist, step, which then takes three major shifts: (1) steam (the moment of Marx); (2) electric and combustion (when the engines themselves become machine made); and (3) electronic and nuclear.[33]

Thus each stage of capital has its emblematic or privileged *power-source* technology, which leads the way to an epochal transformation in all the other branches of production, including commodity and agricultural production. The capacities and limits of this power source give shape and duration to the epoch, making possible new zones of profitable production and consumption. In this nuclear and electronic age, Mandel's examples are "jet transport planes, television, telex, radar and satellite communication networks, and atom-powered container freighters."[34] Later, he sums it up another way: "This new period [1940–65] was characterized, among other things, by the fact that alongside machine-made industrial consumer goods (as from the early 19th century) and machine-made machines (as from the mid-19th century), we now find machine-produced raw materials and foodstuffs. *Late capitalism . . . thus appears as the period in which all branches of the economy are fully industrialized for the first time.*"[35]

Television is thus situated—but not singled out—as one of the consequential products and the typical consumer good of the third stage. Apart from the fact that it shares with the other examples a global reach, television seems to bear no particular internal necessity to this late capitalist system. It does not express some change in patterns of consumption or in the establishment of a world market for a series of new products (i.e., information and culture). Its proper antecedents are simply all the other consumer goods churned out by capital for the previous 150 years. Furthermore, television appears to play no role in the spread of the dominant "instrumental ideology" that Mandel describes in his chapter "Ideology in the Age of Late Capitalism," or in the potentially revolutionary crisis in relations of production that he evokes at the end of the book.

Mandel does cite television during an economic explanation, however, in his introduction to the second volume of Marx's *Capital*:

> The production of television sets or *films* (including copies of such films) is obviously a form of commodity production, and wage-labour engaged in it is productive labour. But the hiring-out of completed films or the renting of a single television set to successive customers does not have the characteristics of productive labour. Similarly, wage-labour employed in making advertising films is productive, whereas the cajoling of potential clients to purchase such films is as unproductive as the labour of commercial representatives in general.[36]

In a discussion that attempts to demarcate between what adds to "social value" and what does not, Mandel opts for the most orthodox line: the "use" of television is "unproductive" in every form, whether as reproduction of the relations of production (as Althusser puts it),

as "cajoling" of consumer desire, or as the essential conduit for the
establishment of a global market. The exception made for advertising, however, indicates that Mandel grants a certain limited function
to those products and services (like consumer credit) that extend
the sphere of consumption and hence help alleviate "difficulties of
realization" (selling off commodities).[37]

Is this line so easy to draw? Only if we ignore the possibility that
television (and not just television but the whole culture industry)
does not distinguish, in a way decidable to anybody but perhaps
semioticians, between its advertisements for specific products and its
large-scale representations of entire social milieux entirely composed
of capitalism's signatures. If, on the other hand, the work of culture is
in this sense productive for capital and indispensable to it, television
would have to be counted (like the housewife) as an "unofficial"
conduit of value.

Second, in a liberal defense of long-wave theory, Peter Hall and
Paschal Preston have argued the connection between particular technologies and successive economic long waves.[38] Their research centers
on the increasingly central relationship of information technologies
to economic patterns, culminating in the current fourth Kondratiev
wave, "carried" specifically by electronics, computing, and telecommunication.[39] Information technologies, defined as all technologies,
of whatever power source, that "record, transmit, process and distrib-
ute information,"[40] had been secondary industries before the 1940s;
it was only after the immense corporate investment in laboratory research that they could be launched on the global scale necessary to
make them profitable. Both a deep involvement of capital in scientific
work (beyond the stage of the heroic inventor or entrepreneur) and
the establishment of a new stage of the world division of labor were
the preconditions for this emergence.

As a "consumer good" element of this onslaught, television supported the wave strongly at first (1950s–1960s), only to yield its key
components in the long run to the "producer good" or fixed capital applications (satellites, surveillance, computer screens, military
hardware, etc.). As opposed to Mandel, Hall and Preston accord television absolute proximity to the decisive economic circuits of the
era, which are simultaneously intrinsic to, and a product of, the

surge of capital. No further comparison or distinction is drawn between the "information" carried by, say, computer networks and that
carried by television: having abandoned a labor theory of value, there
would be no way for Hall and Preston to distinguish between these
transmissions, or to decide whether the modes of transmission and
valorization across the range of information technologies might have
quite different economic or political applications for capital. Still,
television is here placed in a different technological continuum from
Mandel's: it appears as the profitable culmination of different strands
of innovation which are resolved at a certain juncture—information
can at last become a global commodity when gathered and propelled
by sufficient voltage.

Third, a kind of intermediate point for television—between machinery and commodity—can be found in David Harvey's compendium of Marxist categories, *The Limits of Capital*. There he places
television in a most logical, if vague, economic slot: the "consumption fund," defined as "commodities [that] perform in the realm of
consumption a somewhat analogous role to that played by fixed capital in the production process."[41] The phrase "consumption fund" occurs most prominently in *Capital*, volume 2, where it designates
"means of consumption" that ensure turnover of consumable commodities in the lengthy reproduction equations. So television takes
its place alongside forks and spoons, sidewalks, washing machines,
even houses: all of these things somehow make consumption possible. (It makes a certain obvious sense: without a "consumption
fund" popcorn maker, you won't buy popcorn.) But this is a solution
that solves nothing: the term is hardly useful if it can be so easily
extended to cover all public and private space, as well as all those
commodities that we don't happen to eat, drink, or destroy right
away. Nor does it offer any clue about the crucial questions: How
is consumption "produced" by the instruments of consumption? Do
different items in the consumption fund (say, a refrigerator and a
television set) "produce" different kinds of consumption and different circuits of spending? Harvey's more recent book, *The Condition of
Postmodernity*, gives a straightforward answer: yes, "television use"
contributes to a necessary increase in demand, promoting a culture
of consumerism. But he explicitly leaves aside the analysis of what

new cultural and aesthetic techniques have enabled television to perform such a task; after correctly dismissing an easy equation between
television and postmodernism itself, he lets the problem fade into the
background.[42]

Fourth, in their summary of post-Fordist and French poststructural
theory, Eric Alliez and Michel Feher suggest that the mobilization of
information by capital provides an "economic definition of postmodernism": rather than having an ideological use, information is now
calculated in strict exchange-value terms according to "the cost of
the information, measured in the time necessary for its formulation
and comprehension, [which] must be minimized while its exchange
value is increased by the multiplication of references, allowing it
to reach a broad public."[43] This new economy can be characterized
by its own machine-subject ensembles: the television viewer is now
totally assimilated to the "permanent spectacle."[44] The mental operations of "formulation and comprehension" correspond to simple production, the labor of viewing, measured in time; on the other hand,
consumption or reception is assumed to be automatic, a function of
"referring" to, or addressing, the consumers. "Multiplying the references" is the key phrase for Alliez and Feher; it describes a formal,
internal transformation of information into commodity. Information
itself changes shape: it is clear they assume that "reference" is something built into the unit of information rather than a function of the
apparatus of circulation (as I have been suggesting).

Perhaps this is the place to lodge a complaint against a certain use
of the word "consumption" in media criticism, especially as in the
phrase "to consume images." This is at best an imperfect way to describe an action which cannot even be assumed to occur. It disguises,
as the final term in an economic sequence, the uncertainty of a reception, an interpretation, or a production of sense. For Marx, of course,
consumption always led to the production of a new force. This turn-
around—which is precisely where all questions of agency in the face
of machinery reside, and where social reproduction in the broadest
sense occurs—requires the most careful analysis, the most cautious
modulation between terms, rather than a hasty metaphorical escape.

Instead of supplying a formal definition for the new postmodern
commodity, then, Alliez and Feher in fact rehearse the "lowest common denominator" theory of television programming and informa-

tion distribution, in which the mass media are blamed for the loss of stable and singular meanings. (At this point they seem to lean much more heavily on Baudrillard than on theories of post-Fordism.) As a result, a machine called "television" and a population called an "audience" are equally totalized as "spectacle," an absolute space within which televisual images are supposed to circulate and arrive with cybernetic efficiency and transparency. It is a production in which nothing is transformed: information and mental labor fuse into a single commodity expended in the white noise combustion of the spectacle. Like others in the Debord-Baudrillard tendency, they tell a story in which the image form of capital achieves a final washout: capital has become image. But it can be seen as the opposite—that images have become capital, expanding its repertoire and range of forms. But while Alliez and Feher find no escape *through* television, they hold out hope that there can be an escape *from* television. At the conclusion of this portrait of a fully instrumental capitalism, Alliez and Feher hold back a little, suggesting that capital's subsumption of "the totality of time" nevertheless leaves some open spaces at the margins, overlooked but not created by it, waiting to be filled with insurrection. Whatever these forces are, it is clear that they have nothing to do with the televisual circulation of images and value.

We can therefore outline two poles in the debate about television's work for capital. If Mandel is insufficiently alert to television's figural relation to capitalist economy, Alliez and Feher are oversensitive to it, collapsing all productions of time and value to a single smooth spectacular process, without allowing for the persistence of interruptions and flickering metaphysical leaps in the circuit, which are, after all, what makes culture still *valuable*. While television is integral to the distinctive movements of value under late capital, at the same time it drags economy back from the brink of abstraction to the messy realm of collective imagination. Indeed, television can be distinguished from the other machines of its age (such as the computer) by the fact that it must pass through the variable times of visibility; that is, it can only perform its tasks for capital in the old, stubbornly slow time of human subjects. Though television may be part of the new information flow, converging with the others all the time, its analysis as economy has to face the trauma of having to have a content, the fact that while its diffusion may be instantaneous (like the monetary particle signs coursing through the lines of finance), its reception as images must be lived moment by moment.

What are television's tasks? What does it produce? Now it is necessary to join the two hypotheses proposed so far: first, that television works as a machine according to the basic Marxian account, serving as a transfer point between quantities of time (value), translating between the time of images and the time of viewing (always imperfectly), thereby motivating further productions and circulations. Second, that television appeared at a certain moment to incorporate culture as images into the body of capital. Neither of these yet takes account of site-specific operations. Certainly, it must be assumed that every machine will be placed in a particular location ("context"), and that the system's output will therefore hinge on a number of local factors. At the same time, however, as we have seen, the machine operates as an outpost—the representing representative—of the global system, integrating local subjective and reproductive flows with overall productive ones.

How does this global machinery make itself visible through televisual images (all of them, each and every one)?

As Jameson suggests, television produces images within a new space and time. The televisual image is not produced "after" or "inside" its temporal and spatial frames; rather, these are effects of the apparatus. The volatility of the televisual image's frame distinguishes it from photography and cinema, the two image commodity forms corresponding to previous epochal structures of production. Still, since its appearance television has changed its mode of imaging. For example, "direct" transmission or broadcasting of "live" events proved incompletely profitable without greater technical manipulation and arrangement of the event.[45] Television's real vocation lies in the transformation of material images through the production of new frameworks.

Television's work on the image follows two directions at once, corresponding to its machinic attributes.

The first, corresponding to the prefix "tele-," involves space: by sending images, the machine gives them a new form and a new value. Marx had in fact made this observation when he included the act of bringing the product to market as part of its production.[46] At any geographic scale, from a single-channel backwater to a multi-input honeycomb, television engineers a specular "market" of images. (This applies to state-run systems as well, where the televisual market can be controlled like all the others.) Everywhere television captures distance by grounding itself as a set of material objects: it exists as a vast number of scattered machines connected by the diffusion of a production occurring elsewhere. Most of the means of production and transmission (broadcasting facilities, cables, and satellites) remain in the hands of economic and state institutions; but through an arrangement that bespeaks its capitalist essence, everybody else is permitted to pay for their share of the machine. In this sense, television can be seen as a continuous extension—through "economic democracy"—of previous technologies of distribution, although an extension that nevertheless alters the composition and strategy of the world market. It would be a mistake to expect television to saturate everyone's lives equally: it can expand only when a reflux of value justifies its efforts.

The second direction of the televisual image concerns a transformation in the capacities of capitalism itself, through a new production of time. The most obvious—though limited—aspect of this change is advertising itself. Several arguments have been made about advertising's relation of time to value on television; let us review two of the most pertinent. Nick Browne's seminal essay on the "television super-text" takes the position that televisual time is arranged on two registers: "codes of realistic representation" and the various durations of the working day, week, year, and so on.[47] For Browne, the relation between these two registers follows a clear logic: the first order of time, belonging to the content of televisual flow, is the calculated bait in the capture of the second order of human (free) time. A familiar dualism arises: the "discursive" or "textual" economy receives its temporal logic from a "general" economy controlled by advertisers and programmers. As he presents it, the units of analysis are the visible segments of the schedule; these must be put together by the critic to reconstruct the program, which is the logical sum of the advertiser's and broadcaster's interests. The program translates between the general economy and the textual one, directed by market research on the habits and tastes of the populace. Advertising images—because they participate directly in the production of consumption—are assumed to function one way, with direct and statistically available results, while all the other images are somehow there to keep up the flow and to prop up the attention of viewers, vaguely reinforcing the sales pitch. Sut Jhally carries this hierarchy further, aligning programming as the "necessary" time the broadcaster is forced (by some mysterious social imperative) to give up, while advertising is the payoff, the "surplus value" extracted from viewers.[48]

Though both accounts make the connection between the different forms of televisual image and the competition of different capitals, each continues to accept advertising as the primary economic mechanism of television when it is only one possibility. In other words, these accounts stay close to the advertiser's own version of the story, which is part of every commercial's ideological protocol: the companies insist that they just want to buy slots of time that will be witnessed by a certain demographic slice. We, the audience, are supposed to understand, sympathize, play along. But with the multiplication of channels and the new attachment of VCRs, this arrangement, this pact of complicity, has become even more fragile. Witness the frantic attempts by the networks to shore up their crude model of television viewing through more sophisticated statistical methods. (New devices built into televisions look out at the viewers, measuring their presence in the room and their facial orientation to the screen.) Like currency exchange and interest rates, advertising-based explanations are based on a faith that certain transactions will always come off, that the general equivalent (ratings) really does represent something else (attention, perception, reception, and consumption), that cause-and-effect lines can be traced from one order to another—in this instance, from the scheduling of images straight to desires and deferred gratifications.

If, on the other hand, television can take or leave that kind of advertising, if television can survive and expand after all guarantees about the viewer's behavior are gone, other forces must be at work, and must have always been at work. Certainly advertisers buy time, but it is *socialized time*. Just as the capitalist buys labor power rather than an individual's labor, so the advertiser buys a unit of social time power—the fusion of "free" time and "free" images calibrated in value according to estimates and averages of productivity and potential return. Television, in its fundamental commercial function, socializes time in the sending of visible images of quantifiable duration, range, and cultural value.

Rather than the "official" time of programming, the unit of analysis must be the volatile time of the image—not only the sequences ordered by narrative or direct address but the fleeting images of channel zapping and quick cuts, approaching an impossible synchrony. Every image takes up a certain amount of positive time, preceded and succeeded by other images. In the jostling for recognition, images can disengage from and obliterate a sequence or syntax. Televisual images are not assembled as a uniform semiotic substance or flow; they are always subject to interruption, decomposition, and disappearance. A molecular aesthetics develops, with new kinds of abstraction, new means of spinning out or freezing up their duration. The program—a prodigious projection of structured time—has always been an ideal construct foiled by its diffusion.

What the VCR makes possible, in fact, is the further ramification of televisual time by altering its speed, and in this sense it retools the televisual apparatus for a new economic cycle. Television's new speeds, however, should be seen not simply as a matter of expanded individual choice but as a new zone of fixed capital and image valorization. The potential to change the time scheme of broadcasting by inserting other sets of images makes televisual time more flexible, more capable of capturing and redistributing culture in televisual form. One such form—the capacity to record television transmissions ("time shifting")—is not at all a matter of "storing" or "writing" what was, before the VCR, a self-sufficient and full event.[49] The VCR, like television itself, does not *make* something textual; on the contrary, it seizes on all kinds of textual events and submits them to a reframing and a retransmission. In this lies its usefulness to capital, especially on a global scale, which can profit only if all culture (high, low, and homemade) makes itself visible through televisual circuits.

The resources of television's abstraction of images have hardly been exhausted; in each new reconfiguration of time and image are possibilities for a transduction of value—that is, for a different machinic function. It follows from my earlier discussion of capital's circuitry that each instant is both a sign of value and a movement toward another form—since television as a whole is coextensive with the space of capitalist production, each of its moments can occupy multiple positions in the overall movement of production and reproduction. Television, in other words, becomes "part of" the way in which value is constructed, distributed, and attached to bodies formed in the general circulation of labor, commodities, and money. It has expanded the zones of value by changing (mediating, that is, mechanizing) lived relations. Television therefore cannot be an analogy of the old factory machines or the model for an entirely new mode of labor. It is a machine working on its own scale, with its own product—time—and its own raw materials (electricity, videotape, light, the metaphysics of writing, etc.). At the point when televisual forms no longer follow a single representational logic, it should be clear that a plateau of totalization has been reached: televisual images can adhere to every body in motion; they exist in a time placed in reserve, waiting for the chance to reenter the machinery, whether as need or as work. Televisual images do not represent something so much as they take up time, and to live through this time is the most pervasive way that subjects suffer through, participate in, and perhaps even glimpse the absent global unity of late capital.

Of the political economy of television, one thing is clear: it is simply neither here nor there, neither this nor that, but finally its contours as an object of thought or perception have disappeared, much like capital itself.

At the end of his introduction to the *Grundrisse*, Marx scribbled a little list of things "not to be forgotten." The sixth heading reads: "*The uneven development of material production relative to e.g. artistic development.*"[50] Famously, he did not get around to elaborating this point, nor did he imagine what an art form or cultural practice fully adequate to and coextensive with capitalism would look like, or whether it might be possible for cultural development to be no longer a part of, expression of, or metaphor for economy, but its very mode of visibility.

The next item reads: "(7) *This conception appears as necessary development*. But legitimation of chance. How. (Of freedom also, among other things.) (Influence of means of communication. World history has not always existed; history as world history a result.)"[51] This point, too—the necessity of relating production and circulation to forms of consciousness and power—remained largely untouched. For us, the path must be skipped backward: back from the production of a world history by capital, past the legitimation of chance as necessity in our histories and theories of technology and communication (toward a freedom still to be rescued from the other things that obscure it).

Notes

1   Immanuel Kant, *Critique of Judgement*, trans. J. H. Bernard (New York, 1951), 171–72.
2   Jacques Derrida, "Economimesis," trans. R. Klein, *Diacritics* 11 (1981): 3–25.
3   Raymond Williams, *Keywords* (New York, 1983), 201–2.
4   Karl Marx, *Grundrisse*, trans. Martin Nicolaus (New York, 1973), 673.
5   Ibid., 536; see also Antonio Negri, *Marx Beyond Marx*, trans. Harry Cleaver, Michael Ryan, and Maurizio Viano (South Hadley, Mass., 1984), 114–15.
6   The indispensable text on Marx's "economic text" remains Gayatri Chakravorty Spivak's "Scattered Speculations on the Question of Value," in *In Other Worlds: Essays in Cultural Politics* (New York, 1987), 154–75.
7   Marx, *Grundrisse*, 694.
8   Ibid., 671.
9   It should not be forgotten that time is in fact the "substance" processed by capital into a new and quantifiable stratum; or better, it is that which is "captured" in the moment of exchange, when a potential force is rendered actual: "having acquired labor capacity in exchange as an equivalent, capital has acquired labor time . . . in exchange without equivalent" (*Grundrisse*, 674).
10 Ibid., 671.
11 Ibid., 712.
12 Ibid., 620–21.
13 Ibid., 623.
14 Karl Marx, *Capital*, vol. 2, trans. David Fernbach (Harmondsworth, 1978), 237–43.
15 Karl Marx, *Capital*, vol. 3, trans. David Fernbach (Harmondsworth, 1983), 370–71.
16 Karl Marx, *Capital*, vol. 1, trans. Ben Fowkes (New York, 1977), 512; *Grundrisse*, 693.
17 Marx, *Grundrisse*, 670; see also *Grundrisse*, 701, and *Capital*, 1:286.
18 Ibid., 692; emphasis added to latter phrase.

19 Ibid., 674. See also *Grundrisse*, 705, and *Capital*, 1:285.

20 Ibid., 693; emphasis added.

21 Ibid., 704.

22 Ibid., 712.

23 Jean-Paul Sartre, *Critique of Dialectical Reason*, trans. Alan Sheridan-Smith (London, 1976), 233.

24 Marx, *Capital*, 1:517.

25 See, for example, Christine Delphy, "The Main Enemy," *Feminist Issues* (Summer 1980).

26 The work along these lines is already extensive and rich: see Tania Modleski, *Loving with a Vengeance* (Hamden, 1982), and the articles collected by Helen Baehr and Gillian Dyer, eds., *Boxed In: Women and Television* (London, 1987).

27 For a rather different account of this fissure, see Donna Haraway, "A Manifesto for Cyborgs: Science, Technology and Socialist Feminism in the 1980s," *Socialist Review* 80 (1985). I would stress that this metaphoric pair can be mobilized within capital's own techniques of labor organization and ideology; it can hardly point the way back to some lost authenticity.

28 See R. Panzieri, "The Capitalist Use of Machinery: Marx versus the 'Objectivists,' " in *Outlines of a Critique of Technology*, ed. Phil Slater (London, 1980).

29 Fredric Jameson, "Surrealism without the Unconscious," in *Postmodernism, or, The Cultural Logic of Late Capitalism* (Durham, 1990).

30 Ernest Mandel, *Late Capitalism* (London, 1975), 110.

31 Ibid., 249–50.

32 Marx, *Capital*, 3:173–74.

33 Mandel, *Late Capitalism*, 118.

34 Ibid., 119.

35 Ibid., 190–91; his emphasis.

36 In Marx, *Capital*, 2:45; his emphasis.

37 Mandel, *Late Capitalism*, 390–98.

38 Peter Hall and Paschal Preston, *The Carrier Wave: New Information Technology and the Geography of Innovation 1846–2003* (London, 1988).

39 Ibid., 164.

40 Ibid., 5.

41 David Harvey, *The Limits of Capital* (Chicago, 1982), 229.

42 David Harvey, *The Condition of Postmodernity* (Oxford, 1989), 61.

43 Eric Alliez and Michel Feher, "The Luster of Capital," *Zone* 1–2 (1987): 331.

44 Ibid., 348.

45 See Jane Feuer, "The Ontology of Live Television," in *Regarding Television*, ed. E. Ann Kaplan (Frederick, Md., 1983).

46 Marx, *Grundrisse*, 635.

47 Nick Browne, "The Political Economy of the TV (Super) Text," in *Television: The Critical View*, ed. Horace Newcomb (New York, 1987), 588.

48 Sut Jhally, *The Codes of Advertising: Fetishism and the Political Economy of Meaning in Consumer Society* (New York, 1987).

49 This is a central thesis in Sean Cubitt, *Timeshift: On Video Culture* (London, 1991), based on a strong misreading of Derrida's critique of Lévi-Strauss in *De la Grammatologie*.

50 Marx, *Grundrisse*, 109.

51 Ibid.

Notes on Contributors

Rick Altman, Professor of French and Communication Studies at the University of Iowa, is the editor of *Genre: The Musical and Cinema/Sound*. His 1987 book, *The American Film Musical*, has recently appeared in a paperback version and will shortly be published in French translation. He received his B.A. and M.A. degrees from Duke University in 1966.

Richard Dienst, Assistant Professor of English at Purdue University, has written *Still Time in Real Life: Theory after Television*, forthcoming from Duke University Press.

Jane Feuer, Associate Professor of English, teaches film and popular culture at the University of Pittsburgh. She is currently working on a book about television in the Reagan era, and used to be a *Dynasty* fan.

Jane Gaines is Associate Professor of Literature and English at Duke University, where she teaches film and television studies. "Dead

Ringer" is part of *Contested Culture: The Image, the Voice, and the Law* (University of North Carolina Press, 1991).

Christine Gledhill, formerly with the British Film Institute Education Department, now teaches at Staffordshire Polytechnic. She edited *Home Is Where the Heart Is: Studies in Melodrama and the Woman's Film* (British Film Institute, 1987) and is one of the organizers of "Melodrama: Stage/Picture/Screen," a conference held in London in the summer of 1992.

Miriam Hansen is Professor of English at the University of Chicago and an editor of *New German Critique*. She has written numerous articles on American silent film, new German cinema, and critical theory. This essay is from her book *Babel and Babylon: Spectatorship in American Silent Film* published by Harvard University Press. She is currently working on a study of the film theory of the Frankfurt School.

Norman N. Holland is Milbauer Eminent Scholar at the University of Florida, where he founded the Institute for Psychological Study of the Arts. A leading writer on literature and psychology, he recently published *The Brain of Robert Frost* (1988).

Fredric Jameson is the Director of Duke University's Graduate Program in Literature and the Duke Center for Critical Theory. "Nostalgia for the Present" is part of his *Signatures of the Visible* (Routledge and Chapman, Hall, 1989).

Bill Nichols has edited two volumes of *Movies and Methods* and written *Ideology and the Image*. He recently finished a study of documentary entitled *Representing Reality* (Indiana University Press, 1992). He graduated from Duke University in 1964 as a premed chemistry major.

Janet Staiger teaches critical and cultural studies and is Professor of Film in the Department of Radio-Television-Film at the University of Texas at Austin. She has recently published *Interpreting Films* (Princeton University Press, 1992).

Chris Straayer is Assistant Professor in the Cinema Studies Department at New York University. She has written widely on feminist film theory, the postmodern body, and avant-garde video. A book incorporating a gay and lesbian perspective on the avant-garde and the popular is forthcoming from Columbia University Press.

John O. Thompson, formerly of Liverpool University, is currently Education Officer/M.A. Course Director at the British Film Institute in London. The author of the seminal "Screen Acting and the Commutation Test," he also coedited *The Media Reader* with Manuel Alvarado (British Film Institute, 1990).

Library of Congress Cataloging-in-Publication Data

Classical Hollywood narrative : the paradigm wars / edited by Jane Gaines.

Originally published as vol. 88, no. 2 (spring 1989), of South Atlantic quarterly.

With additional chapters and index.

Includes bibliographical references.

ISBN 0-8223-1276-X (cloth). — ISBN 0-8223-1299-9 (pbk.)

1. Motion pictures—Philosophy.   2. Motion pictures—Social aspects.

I. Gaines, Jane, 1943–

PN1995.C537   1992

791.43'01—dc20   92-16657 CIP